Praise for *E:* ... *lation*

"If I were writing ... The material is very ... Also, I love how ... me to get a really ... design and buil... ... *llect.com)*

"Explicit support ... ajor contribution. Many ... authors, such as ... g activities (think weeks ... adopting a workflow a ... nt the workflow techno... ... cflow foundation in the ... achable and yet authorit... ...

... *rporation*

"The Windows W... ... ming and state machin... ... und to have a profound ... ears. In the style of the classic *Essential COM* by Don Box, Dharma and Bob have done a great job making this technology accessible to any developer already versed in C#, VB, and the .NET Framework, and who wants to achieve declarative enlightenment. Don't miss out."

—*Joe Duffy, program manager, Common Language Runtime (CLR) team, Microsoft Corporation*

"I think WF should and will be used as the main application model for web service applications. Developers working on web services will want to learn about this technology from this book; it comes straight from the source and explains the technology well and in depth."

—*Krzysztof Cwalina, program manager, Microsoft Corporation*

"This book provides an enlightening exploration of Windows Workflow Foundation for both the novice and the veteran alike."

—*Nate Talbert, software design engineer, Microsoft Corporation*

Essential Windows Workflow Foundation

Essential Windows Workflow Foundation

■ Dharma Shukla
Bob Schmidt

✦✦Addison-Wesley

Upper Saddle River, NJ • Boston • Indianapolis • San Francisco
New York • Toronto • Montreal • London • Munich • Paris • Madrid
Cape Town • Sydney • Tokyo • Singapore • Mexico City

...ers and sellers to distinguish their products are claimed as trade-
...his book, and the publisher was aware of a trademark claim, the
...pital letters or in all capitals.

...the preparation of this book, but make no expressed or implied
...bility for errors or omissions. No liability is assumed for inciden-
...ial or consequential damages in connection with or arising out of the use of the information or programs contained herein.

The publisher offers excellent discounts on this book when ordered in quantity for bulk purchases or special sales, which may include electronic versions and/or custom covers and content particular to your business, training goals, marketing focus, and branding interests. For more information, please contact:

U.S. Corporate and Government Sales (800) 382-3419
corpsales@pearsontechgroup.com

For sales outside the United States please contact:

International Sales
international@pearsoned.com

This Book Is Safari Enabled

The Safari, Enabled icon on the cover of your favorite technology book means the book is available through Safari Bookshelf. When you buy this book, you get free access to the online edition
for 45 days.

Safari Bookshelf is an electronic reference library that lets you easily search thousands of technical books, find code samples, download chapters, and access technical information whenever and wherever you need it.

To gain 45-day Safari Enabled access to this book:

- Go to http://www.awprofessional.com/safarienabled

- Complete the brief registration form

- Enter the coupon code 7CDH-VDBE-DLQH-KJDK-8EEU

If you have difficulty registering on Safari Bookshelf or accessing the online edition, please e-mail
customer-service@safaribooksonline.com.

Visit us on the Web: www.awprofessional.com

Library of Congress Cataloging-in-Publication Data

Shukla, Dharma.
  Essential Windows workflow foundation / Dharma Shukla, Robert B. Schmidt. — 1st ed.
     p. cm.
  ISBN 0-321-39983-8 (pbk. : alk. paper) 1. Internet programming. 2. World Wide Web. I. Schmidt,
Robert B. II. Title.

  QA76.625.S53 2006
  006.7'6—dc22

                     2006021593

ISBN 0-321-39983-8
Text printed in the United States on recycled paper at R. R. Donnelley in Crawfordsville, Indiana.
Second printing, December 2006

To Bina   —Dharma
To my parents   —Bob

Contents

About the Authors

Dharma Shukla is an architect at Microsoft working on next-generation programming models. A founding member of the Windows Workflow Foundation (WF) team, Dharma played a key role in defining the architecture of WF. Dharma holds a bachelor's degree in electronics engineering.

Bob Schmidt is a senior program manager at Microsoft working on next-generation programming models. Since 2003, his primary focus has been on the design of Windows Workflow Foundation. Bob earned bachelor's and master's degrees in computer science at Stanford University.

Foreword

A S I WRITE THIS FOREWORD in July 2006, I know something big is about to happen.

Developers are discovering the power of having machine-readable representations of their programs that match their intention. This idea is sometimes referred to using the shorthand phrase *code as data*.

More importantly, developers are realizing that no runtime architect or language designer is all that qualified to define the schema for that data— a domain expert is the only one who has the right expertise. This idea is sometimes referred to as *domain-specific languages*.

Systems like Smalltalk, the Java Virtual Machine (JVM), and the Common Language Runtime (CLR) have proven that there is value in having machine-readable representations of type definitions for things such as reflection, serialization, and generative programming. However, the basic representation of a type (e.g., fields, methods, classes) is largely a closed world, which doesn't allow users to model (as data) things such as control flow, concurrency, logic constructs, or domain-specific ideas such as discount policy or dotted whole note except as largely opaque instructions strewn across multiple method bodies.

People are now asking themselves, "If my type definition is available as data, why aren't other design-time constructs as well?"

Fortunately, one of the people asking those questions back in 2003 was my good friend Dharma Shukla, who was then working on the Biztalk Server team.

When the Biztalkers set out to generalize their XLANG orchestration engine as an embeddable platform component, they could have simply taken the language constructs from XLANG and put yet another XML syntax around them (that proposal was certainly on the table). This is the most obvious approach and would have satisfied their charter for building the Windows Orchestration Engine (WinOE) perfectly well.

Fortunately, Dharma had the foresight to know that he wasn't the right guy to define "the one true schema" for all programs and instead decided to "go meta" and steer the project toward building an extensible runtime that allows users to define their own opcodes that match the domain they're working in. Add to this the decision to support defining and composing these opcodes in an XML dialect and you have a system that lets anyone decide what the vocabulary and sentence structure is for describing applications in a given domain.

As Dharma Shukla and Bob Schmidt so aptly show with this book, Windows Workflow Foundation (WF) is an excellent example of a meta-runtime that puts developers in control of how programs are written and how programs execute. The developer defines the schema for a program and then provides an interpretation over that schema to allow it to be deployed and run. It is a simple idea that has huge ramifications.

Like I said, something big is about to happen.

Don Box
July 2006, Yarrow Point, WA

Preface

WINDOWS WORKFLOW FOUNDATION (WF) is a general-purpose programming framework for creating reactive programs that act in response to stimulus from external entities. The basic characteristic of reactive programs is that they pause during their execution, for unknown amounts of time, awaiting input.

Reactive programs are, of course, not a new phenomenon. Ever since computers have been organized into networks, it has been useful for programs on one machine to communicate with programs on other machines. Techniques for exchanging data are also applicable to programs running on a single computer. A variety of technologies ranging from sockets to web services has been used over the years to get programs to communicate. Although the interoperability, scalability, and approachability of the programming models at hand have improved greatly over the years, relatively scant attention has been paid to the manner in which developers put reactive programs together. For example, popular web programming models put the burden of enforcing appropriate control flow among operations squarely on the developer. WF attempts to change this.

The focal point of the WF programming model is the concept of an activity—a program statement in a WF program. An activity's execution is inherently resumable and unfolds in an episodic manner, pausing and resuming according to the activity's interactions with external entities. Just as you can stick a bookmark in a page of this book when you are finished reading for the night, it is natural for an activity to bookmark its execution

■ Essential Windows Workflow Foundation

(when it is awaiting input) and then continue right where it left off at a later time (when the relevant input arrives).

WF is a framework, not a fixed set of programming constructs defined by a language grammar. WF's notion of an activity is extensible, which allows the expressiveness and control flow in WF programs to be richer than what is provided by a language like C# or Visual Basic. You can represent WF programs using domain-specific activities and specialized control flow constructs, and thereby capture complex interactions among people and software with a high degree of fidelity to the particulars of the problem being solved.

The WF runtime is a meta-runtime that builds upon the Common Language Runtime (CLR) and manages the execution of WF programs. WF programs naturally pause and resume, and can execute over arbitrarily long periods of time within a distributed (multi-machine) execution environment without any extra work on the part of the programmer. A WF program will neither fail nor cause undue strain on system resources if it sits idle for weeks. The CLR's job, in the context of WF, is to manage objects that transiently represent WF programs while they are in memory. The WF runtime's job is to manage the full lifecycle of WF programs, which can span CLR threads and application domains, operating system processes, and even machines.

In sum, WF provides a programming model for writing and executing reactive programs. WF programs are constructed using domain-specific program statements called **activities**, which allow domain experts to express their programming intent in the parlance of their domain.

About the Book

There is a simple reason why this book was written. Both of us believe there is a novel synthesis of noteworthy ideas at the heart of WF. These ideas are seeing the light of day for the first time in a mainstream platform. Because WF's activity-oriented programming approach rests on a different set of principles than do today's popular programming paradigms, the best way to learn WF is to focus first on the fundamental ideas around which the WF programming model is built. There is more to becoming an effective WF developer than just familiarizing yourself with the types that reside in the new `System.Workflow` namespace of the .NET Framework.

To that end, this book does not aim to exhaustively discuss the 350+ types present in the three assemblies that constitute WF. We deliberately disregard some outer layers of WF so as to focus on the essence—the core programming model and runtime feature set. Experience has taught us that learning the capabilities of the framework from first principles is the surest way to becoming a proficient WF developer.

The writing of this book has led us to examine and debate our beliefs and assumptions about the nature of reactive programs and how such programs can be developed. If this book, and WF, provides someone with a fresh idea upon which to build further, we will consider our efforts a success.

The organization of this book is as follows. Chapter 1, "Deconstructing WF," examines the key ideas that underpin the WF programming model: bookmarks, continuations, thread and process agility, passivation, resumable program statements, and a runtime for resumable programs. These ideas are discussed in their barest form, outside the context of WF, to maximize the clarity of the discussions.

Chapter 2, "WF Programs," maps the concepts introduced in the first chapter onto the richer programming surface of WF, and therefore acts as a bridge to the rest of the book. Here we begin developing activities, composing them into simple WF programs, and running those programs.

Chapters 3, "Activity Execution," and 4, "Advanced Activity Execution," discuss detailed aspects of how activities execute including bookmarking, fault handling, cancellation, and compensation. The unifying theme is the activity automaton that describes the lifecycle of all activities. Chapter 5, "Applications," explores how to build applications that host the WF runtime and leverage its points of extensibility. Chapter 6, "Transactions," discusses the critical role of transactions in the execution of WF programs. Chapter 7, "Advanced Authoring," covers a number of advanced topics related to activity and WF program authoring, including validation and compilation, and Chapter 8, "Miscellanea," introduces several feature areas of WF that are built around the previously discussed core concepts.

Appendix A, "Activity Automaton," is a reference for the activity automaton. Appendix B, "Control Flow Patterns," presents the code for several composite activities that are more complex than those developed in the main text. These examples highlight extensibility points of the WF programming model, and demonstrate the capability of composite activities to capture complex control flow patterns.

Our focus in this book is exclusively on Windows Workflow Foundation. We assume prior understanding of C# 2.0 and the basics of the CLR; see *The C# Programming Language, Second Edition* by Anders Hejlsberg, et al. (Addison-Wesley, ISBN: 0321334434) and *Essential .NET, Volume I: The Common Language Runtime* by Don Box and Chris Sells (Addison-Wesley, ISBN: 0201734117) for definitive discussion of these subjects. Examples we present in this book are simple—purposefully stripped of scenario noise—so as to minimize distractions from the concepts being discussed. After you learn the ropes, we expect you'll try applying the ideas and techniques explained here to the domain of your choosing.

Acknowledgments

THE WF PROJECT BEGAN IN EARNEST about three years ago. A small team of engineers felt strongly that there was substantial promise in a few novel ideas about how to change the way programs are built. Our first trial by fire was proving to the Microsoft Office team that our brand-new technology was the right foundation for their planned workflow features. Things accelerated with that success, and we are proud that the first public release of WF will be a part of the .NET Framework 3.0 released with Microsoft Windows Vista (WF also underlies the workflow features in Microsoft Office 2007). Many people helped improve the design of WF as it underwent revision and refinement along the way to its public release. It is impossible to thank everyone who contributed, but we are grateful to them all for their efforts.

Our reviewers did a great job telling us what made sense and what did not, and pointing out errors and omissions in drafts of the various chapters. Angel Azcarraga, Don Box, Krzysztof Cwalina, Joe Duffy, Omri Gazitt, Ian Griffiths, Mark Michaelis, Dennis Pilarinos, Jeffrey Richter, Andrei Romanenko, Akash Sagar, Chris Sells, Clemens Szyperski, Nate Talbert, and Eric Zinda deserve credit for making this book better, through their feedback and advice, than it otherwise would have been. Ian provided especially pointed and insightful comments. Aditya Bhandarkar provided exceptional help on the design-time sections. Don not only provided constructive suggestions, but was also generous enough to write the Foreword.

Writing this book in those precious hours outside of our day jobs has been a challenge. We would like to thank Karen Gettman and

Curt Johnson at Addison-Wesley, and all the publishing professionals there who patiently assisted us along the way, and who in the end realized our words as actual printed pages and helped bring those pages to you.

Mistakes that remain are ours.

I consider myself fortunate to have been deeply involved with WF since its birth. WF was by far the most intense and fun project I have worked on at Microsoft. Writing this book, for me, was indeed a *continuation* of building the technology. Now that the book is done, I can finally rest.

Over the years, Don Box has been a constant source of inspiration for me. I will always remain indebted to Don for encouraging me to write this book. Don was kind enough to spend time with me and help me discover and shape the story I wanted to tell. Thanks, Don.

Bob Schmidt and I shared a common vision for the type of book we wanted to write. It has been a great pleasure to work with Bob—first while building the technology, and later during the writing of this book. Thanks, Bob, for making the journey enjoyable.

Thanks go out to the Code Ninjas for making the impossible, possible.

I will always be grateful to Abhay Parasnis for creating a unique environment that not only fostered deep technical innovation, but enabled shipping brand-new technology in an incredibly short period of time. Being wired to do my best work in startup environments, I will always carry fond memories of the WinOE days.

I am immensely grateful to my parents for their unreasonable sacrifices, and to Pushpa for her unwavering support.

I would like to thank my wife, Bina, for always being there for me, and our daughter, Anya, for being wonderful—you both make everything worthwhile.

Dharma Shukla
July 2006

I joined the WF team as its first program manager, convinced there was an opportunity to change the way programs are built. I have since had the good fortune of contributing my ideas and energy to the development of this new technology. The opportunity to also write a book about WF, and the ideas that sparked and sustained my enthusiasm, has been especially rewarding.

I will always be grateful to Dharma Shukla for asking me to co-author this book with him. His insights, his passion, and his relentless pursuit of clarity always make our discussions invigorating. His vision gave this book its élan.

I am thankful that Don Box lent us his support, his guidance, and his sharp editing eye. His knack for zeroing in on the essence of incipient ideas helped focus my efforts.

Abhay Parasnis deserves kudos not only as the driving force behind the WF project, but also as an exemplary role model whose leadership inspired me in ways he could not know.

I give heartfelt thanks to my wife, Elaine, for her steadfast support and quiet sacrifices. I pledge summers full of ice cream and baseball to our boys, Thomas and Andrew, for patiently respecting my frequent book-writing sessions and also for knowing when to barge into my office for some fun. As they always have, my parents provided me with invaluable support, not least their example of how a devoted team can do great things.

Bob Schmidt
July 2006

1

Deconstructing WF

NTRODUCTORY PROGRAMMING TEXTS often begin with a "Hello, World" program that prints a simple message to the standard output device. Here's that program in C#:

```
using System;

class Program
{
  static void Main()
  {
    Console.WriteLine("hello, world");
  }
}
```

Hello, World is a popular starting point because it avoids a number of hard problems that most real-world programs need to address. Practitioners know that it doesn't take much work to expand even Hello, World to induce thorny problems rather quickly. For example, consider a simple variation—let's call it "Open, Sesame"—that requires the user to enter a key before the traditional greeting is printed:

```
using System;

class Program
{
  static void Main()
  {
    // Print the key
    string key = DateTime.Now.Millisecond.ToString();
```

```
    Console.WriteLine("here is your key: " + key);

    string s = Console.ReadLine();

    // Print the greeting if the key is provided
    if (key.Equals(s))
      Console.WriteLine("hello, world");
  }
}
```

The Open, Sesame console program is unremarkable in all aspects but one: Because it is dependent upon the user entering a line of text at the console, it takes an arbitrarily long period of time to complete its execution. You can compile and run the program, let it sit there for a few weeks, and then enter the key that causes it to print the expected greeting. This is by design.

Open, Sesame is an example of a **reactive program**. A reactive program is responsive to, or indeed dependent upon, stimulus from an external entity during the course of its execution. Sometimes that external entity is a person. Sometimes that external entity is another program. Either way, reactive programs spend most of their time stuck waiting for input and therefore present challenges that are not part of the equation when writing programs like Hello, World.

Most computer programs are reactive. Software is used everywhere you look within real-world processes of all kinds: collaborative editing of documents, management of customer orders, raw materials procurement, preparation of tax returns, provisioning, administration of product development efforts, online shopping, management of customer relationships, and coordination of plant and warehouse operations. The list goes on and on. Programs in the midst of these processes need to react to input provided both by people and other programs.

Some reactive programs are developed using frameworks such as ASP.NET and Java Servlets. Others are homegrown solutions that are built directly upon execution environments such as the Common Language Runtime (CLR) and Java Virtual Machine (JVM). Still others are written in languages like C or (unmanaged) C++.

However, if we look at *how* these reactive programs are written, we find that most are not at all like our simple Open, Sesame console program. Let's see how we can write a web service (a web application would be an equally illuminating choice) that does the same thing as our Open, Sesame console program.

Here is a translation of Open, Sesame into an ASP.NET web service:

```
using System;
using System.Web.Services;

[WebService]
public class Service : WebService
{
  [WebMethod(EnableSession = true)]
  public string PrintKey()
  {
    string key = DateTime.Now.Millisecond.ToString();
    Session["key"] = key;
    return "here is your key: " + key;
  }

  [WebMethod(EnableSession = true)]
  public string PrintGreeting(string s)
  {
    if (Session["key"].Equals(s))
      return "hello, world";

    return null;
  }
}
```

This web service has two operations, and is not very complicated. However, we have entirely lost the control flow of Open, Sesame—the cold hard fact that `PrintKey` must occur before `PrintGreeting`, and that each of these steps must run exactly once in order for the program to be considered complete. To establish constraints on the ordering of its operations, we can modify the web service by adding the following code shown in boldface:

```
using System;
using System.Web.Services;

[WebService]
public class Service : WebService
{
  [WebMethod(EnableSession = true)]
  public string PrintKey()
  {
    bool alreadyDidStep1 = (Session["key"] != null);
    if (alreadyDidStep1)
      throw new InvalidOperationException();
```

```
    string key = DateTime.Now.Millisecond.ToString();
    Session["key"] = key;
    return "here is your key: " + key;
}

[WebMethod(EnableSession = true)]
public string PrintGreeting(string s)
{
    bool didNotDoStep1Yet = (Session["key"] == null);
    if (didNotDoStep1Yet)
        throw new InvalidOperationException();

    bool alreadyDidStep2 = (Session["programDone"] != null);
    if (alreadyDidStep2)
        throw new InvalidOperationException();

    Session["programDone"] = true;

    if (Session["key"].Equals(s))
        return "hello, world";

    return null;
    }
}
```

We are now using a set of runtime checks to guarantee the correct control flow for our web service, but that logic is diffuse, implicit, and error prone. The straightforward sequencing of program statements in our Open, Sesame console program has dissolved into opaque logic that is spread throughout our web service operations. Imagine being asked to work out the control flow (not to mention the flow of data) if you are given only the web service source code. It can be done with a few seconds of code inspection for this simple example since there are only two operations, but think about doing it for a web service ten times this size, where the control flow involves branching and looping.

Why can't we use natural C# control flow constructs (we are programming in C#, after all) to specify the relationships between web service operations, and constrain what can happen when? The Open, Sesame console program has *exactly* the control flow and manipulation of local variables that we need for this simple program. Why is it impossible to write our web service, or a similar web application—or just about any real-world program—in this way?

Here are two good reasons:

- In the Open, Sesame console program, `Console.ReadLine` blocks the caller's thread of execution. As written, the program might spend days stuck waiting for input. If many programs like this one were run simultaneously, and all were awaiting input, the system would grind to a halt. Dedicating threads in this way is not an option for real-world programs, especially those deployed in multiuser environments.

- Real-world processes take a long time—days, weeks, or even months. It is wishful thinking to assume that the operating system process (or CLR application domain) in which the program begins execution will survive for the required duration.

For a console program that is used for pedagogical purposes, these issues rarely worry us. As a consequence, we are able to write Open, Sesame—just like Hello, World—in a very natural way. Reading the program code tells us exactly what the program does. But precisely the opposite is true for our web service. Scalability and robustness are usually of paramount concern when developing web services and web applications.

The ASP.NET runtime is designed to efficiently manage multiple services and applications, and can robustly maintain state for individual sessions (with the right configuration, a session can fail over from one machine to another). However, the code does not lie. The scalability and robustness benefits come at a price. In the preceding web service, the `key` variable that is shared by a pair of operations is manipulated as a weakly typed name-value pair. Moreover, the logic that enforces appropriate ordering of operations is clumsily expressed by testing, at the beginning of each operation, whether variables such as `key` have been previously assigned.

It appears that scalability and robustness concerns are at odds with the desire to have a natural way of expressing the state and control flow of reactive programs. The fact that there are millions of web applications and web services in the world confirms that developers are willing to work within the limitations of today's programming models to get their jobs done. Even so, web paradigms are appropriate choices for only a subset of solutions requiring reactive programs. The challenge at hand is to find a better, and general-purpose, approach to developing reactive programs, web-based or otherwise. Such an approach must provide the following:

1. A way to **write reactive programs** that does not sacrifice, and in fact enriches, the natural imperative style of control flow.
2. A way to **run reactive programs** in a scalable and robust manner.

Thread and Process Agility

Our ASP.NET web service solution for Open, Sesame is scalable and robust. Our console program is not. Let's take a closer look at the program statement within the Open, Sesame console program that seems to be the source of the problem:

```
string s = Console.ReadLin e();
```

The fundamental issue is that when the Open, Sesame console program calls `Console.ReadLine`, it will remain stuck there (ignoring failure scenarios) until the relevant stimulus arrives. Dedicating a thread—a fairly expensive resource—to every instance of this program will make it very hard to build a scalable solution in which multiple instances of Open, Sesame (or similar programs) are allowed to run simultaneously.

One common approach for getting around this problem is to fork the thread of execution by making asynchronous method calls. For example, the `ReadLine` method can be offered asynchronously as a pair of methods, using a standard .NET Framework pattern:

```
public static System.IAsyncResult BeginReadLine(
  System.AsyncCallback asyncCallback,
  object state
);

public static string EndReadLine(System.IAsyncResult ar);
```

Inside the `BeginReadLine` method, a work request can be created and enqueued in the CLR's work queue. This request will be serviced asynchronously by a thread drawn from the CLR thread pool, but in the meantime the `BeginReadLine` method will have returned to its caller.

The thread that calls `BeginReadLine` can poll the `System.IAsyncResult` object's `IsCompleted` property until the result is available, or can use the `AsyncWaitHandle` property to wait (as shown here), which is more efficient:

```
using System;

class Program
{
  static void Main()
  {
    // Print the key
    string key = DateTime.Now.Millisecond.ToString();
    Console.WriteLine("here is your key: " + key);

    IAsyncResult result = BeginReadLine(null, null);
    result.AsyncWaitHandle.WaitOne();
    string s = EndReadLine(result);

    // Print the greeting if the key is provided
    if (key.Equals(s))
      Console.WriteLine("hello, world");
  }
}
```

Although this program uses asynchronous invocation, it still consumes a thread by calling WaitOne on the IAsyncResult object.

We can start to see a way out of this dilemma by looking at the last two parameters of BeginReadLine. Asynchronous methods in the .NET Framework allow the caller of the Begin method to provide a delegate of type System.AsyncCallback (along with an object that holds any state[1] shared by the callback and the code invoking the Begin method; in our examples, this is null) with the expectation that the callee will signal the completion of the asynchronous operation by invoking this delegate.

Here's Open, Sesame written using the AsyncCallback mechanism:

```
using System;
using System.Threading;

class Program
{
  static string key;
  static void Main()
  {
    // Print the key
    key = DateTime.Now.Millisecond.ToString();
```

---

[1] In a manner not unlike the weakly typed session state variable we used in the web service.

```
    Console.WriteLine("here is your key: " + key);

    BeginReadLine(ContinueAt, null);
    Thread.Sleep(Timeout.Infinite);
  }

  static void ContinueAt(IAsyncResult ar)
  {
    string s = EndReadLine(ar);

    // Print the greeting if the key is provided
    if (key.Equals(s))
      Console.WriteLine("hello, world");

    Environment.Exit(0);
  }
}
```

Although this program still ties up the initial thread (this time by doing an infinite sleep), the use of an asynchronous callback allows some of our program logic to run on arbitrary threads. The ContinueAt method will run on a different thread than Main.

This version of Open, Sesame achieves a measure of thread agility in a very simple way. We use an asynchronous callback to separate, but link together, chunks of the program's execution logic. As important, we have changed the way we implement the variable key that is used across stages of the program's execution. Rather than using a stack-based local variable as in our original program, key is now a static field that is visible across methods. This stackless approach is the key to reducing our program's dependence on a given thread, while maintaining strongly typed data declarations.

Bookmarks

We've now seen that we can make (some of) our Open, Sesame program "thread agile" by using asynchronous method calls and AsyncCallback. We've done nothing, however, to make our program "process agile" which we know is a requirement for scalability and robustness.

The approach outlined previously (using AsyncCallback) does show promise. The delegate specifying the ContinueAt method acts like a **bookmark**—a logical location in the program's execution at which the execution can be resumed when appropriate stimulus arrives. This provides us with some leverage:

1. We can give bookmarks names, and also provide a manager of bookmarks.
2. We can make bookmarks serializable, which will allow them to be saved to, and loaded from, durable storage.
3. We can write a listener program that acts as a single point of entry for data that needs to be delivered to any of the bookmarks in our system.

Let's begin by defining a class called `Bookmark` that is essentially a named wrapper for a delegate of a custom type, `BookmarkLocation`:

```
[Serializable]
public class Bookmark
{
   public Bookmark(string name, BookmarkLocation continueAt);

   public string Name { get; }
   public BookmarkLocation ContinueAt { get; }
   public object Payload { get; }

   public BookmarkManager BookmarkManager { get; }
}

public delegate void BookmarkLocation(Bookmark resumed);
```

Bookmarks are managed by the `BookmarkManager`:

```
public class BookmarkManager
{
   public void Add(Bookmark bookmark);
   public void Remove(Bookmark bookmark);

   public void Resume(string bookmarkName, object payload);
}
```

A bookmark is a **continuation**—an object representing a program frozen in action. The *physical continuation point* of the program is specified by the bookmark's `ContinueAt` property. The bookmark is *named* so that it can be referred to and manipulated independent of the physical continuation point (which may be shared by multiple bookmarks). `BookmarkManager` simply maintains a set of bookmarks. When the `BookmarkManager.Resume` method is called, the appropriate program is resumed at the location indicated by the bookmark. The input (stimulus) that accompanies the resumption is made available to the program via the Payload property of the resumed bookmark.

We marked the Bookmark class as [Serializable] so that the bookmark manager can save all pending bookmarks to durable storage such as a database. In this way, wherever and whenever the BookmarkManager is instantiated—so long as it has access to the durable storage device (for example, by being provided with a database connection string)—it can reliably obtain its set of bookmarks. When a reactive program is stuck, awaiting stimulus, we can **passivate** it—save it to durable storage—as a set of bookmarks.

To enable entire programs to participate in bookmarking, we need to eliminate—not just reduce—our dependence on the stack. This means we cannot have a Main method that calls Thread.Sleep as our most recent implementation of Open, Sesame does. Instead, we will write an OpenSesame class that has instance methods and heap-allocated state.

Here is our new implementation of Open, Sesame:

```
[Serializable]
public class OpenSesame
{
   string key;
   public void Start(BookmarkManager mgr)
   {
     // Print the key
     key = DateTime.Now.Millisecond.ToString();
     Console.WriteLine("here is your key: " + key);
     mgr.Add(new Bookmark("read", ContinueAt));
   }

   void ContinueAt(Bookmark resumed)
   {
     string s = (string) resumed.Payload;

     BookmarkManager mgr = resumed.BookmarkManager;
     mgr.Remove(resumed);

     // Print the greeting if the key is provided
     if (key.Equals(s))
       Console.WriteLine("hello, world");
   }
}
```

The Open, Sesame program is now embodied by an *object* of type `OpenSesame`. It is easy to create such an object and "run" it (the `Start` method stands in for `Main`) within the context of a listener[2] that waits for input to arrive:

```
BookmarkManager mgr = new BookmarkManager();
OpenSesame openSesameProgram = new OpenSesame();
openSesameProgram.Start(mgr);

...

string str = // obtain input
mgr.Resume("read", str);

...
```

Resumable Program Statements

Although the preceding code is workable for a single instance of a single program, we would be much better served by a runtime—an execution environment for programs like our `OpenSesame` class—that can help us manage multiple instances of a variety of such programs.

We shall call this execution environment the mythical runtime:

```
public class MythicalRuntime
{
  // Starts a new program
  public ProgramHandle RunProgram(ProgramStatement program);

  // Returns a handle to a previously started program
  public ProgramHandle GetProgramHandle(Guid programId);

  // Passivates all in-memory programs
  public void Shutdown();
}

public class ProgramHandle
{
```

---

[2] The listener can obtain input from anywhere—a database, a data source like an MSMQ queue, a web service or web application, or even the trusty console. This logic is now decoupled from the Open, Sesame program.

```
  // Unique identifier for this program
  public Guid ProgramId { get; }

  // Passivate the program
  public void Passivate();

  // Resume a bookmarked program
  public void Resume(string bookmarkName, object payload);
}
```

The mythical runtime allows us to run a `ProgramStatement` object.

It's time to formalize the notion that the `OpenSesame` class is indeed a new kind of program. Given the sensible requirement that `OpenSesame` should be usable (as a single statement) within more complex programs (comprised of multiple statements), we will call the `OpenSesame` class a **resumable program statement**.

The `ProgramStatement` type standardizes an entry point for execution, and serves as the base class for all resumable program statements:

```
[Serializable]
public abstract class ProgramStatement
{
  public abstract void Run(BookmarkManager mgr);
}
```

Given the definition of `ProgramStatement`, the `OpenSesame` class is revised like this:

```
[Serializable]
public class OpenSesame : ProgramStatement
{
  string key;
  public override void Run(BookmarkManager mgr)
  {
    // Print the key
    key = DateTime.Now.Millisecond.ToString();
    Console.WriteLine("here is your key: " + key);
    mgr.Add(new Bookmark("read", ContinueAt));
  }

  // ContinueAt same as earlier, elided for clarity
  ...
}
```

A `ProgramStatement` object that is provided to the `RunProgram` method of the mythical runtime is a **resumable program**. When we give such an object to the mythical runtime, it becomes something more than just an ordinary CLR object. The object is now a *transient, in-memory representation* of a resumable program. Because the resumable program can be passivated, it has a logical lifetime that is potentially longer than that of the initial `ProgramStatement` object and the CLR application domain in which this object is created.

Every program managed by the mythical runtime has a globally unique identifier that can be obtained from the `ProgramHandle` object returned by the `Mythical-Runtime.RunProgram` method. The identifier can be passed between machines so that a passivated program can be brought back into memory via `MythicalRuntime.GetProgramHandle`, anywhere that the durable storage medium in which passivated programs are stored is available.

Because the execution logic of our resumable program uses bookmarking, it awaits stimulus without blocking a thread when it reaches a point at which an external entity must provide input. When this happens, the mythical runtime can passivate the program. When relevant data arrives, the program is brought back into memory and resumed (via `ProgramHandle.Resume`). The resumption of the passivated program might happen 47 weeks later on a different machine.

We can now sketch out generic listener code that listens for input, determines the program to which that input is addressed,[3] and resumes that program at the appropriate bookmark:

```
MythicalRuntime runtime = new MythicalRuntime();

...

while (true)
{
  // receive some input
  object input = ...

  // determine from the input which program to use
  ProgramHandle handle = runtime.GetProgram(...)
```

---

[3] In practice, the listener can also decide that a given input should trigger the creation of a new program. In this case, `MythicalRuntime.RunProgram` is invoked instead of `Program Handle.Resume`.

```
    // determine from the input which bookmark to resume
    string bookmarkName = ...

    handle.Resume(bookmarkName, input);
}
```

A given listener implementation obviously has latitude for deciding how to map inputs to appropriate bookmarks within programs. But that's a good thing—our goal is to support different conceptual models[4] on top of the general-purpose bookmarking substrate we are building; the mythical runtime is not coupled to any particular implementation of a listener.

We have succeeded in establishing a flexible bookmarking capability and a runtime for resumable programs. This is a general-purpose framework with two important characteristics:

- Bookmarked programs do not block threads while they await stimulus.
- Bookmarked programs can reside in durable storage, as continuations, while they await stimulus.

To summarize our progress so far, we have leveraged the idea of bookmarks to enable the writing of resumable programs that can be passivated. Because these programs maintain their state in serializable fields, they can be passivated and represented faithfully in durable storage as continuations. These programs now have both thread agility and process agility. Furthermore, the general nature of the bookmarking model means that we can employ it in the development of a variety of reactive programs, web-based and otherwise.

Composition

Our work is not done. The resumable OpenSesame program definitely does not have the control flow we are seeking. If we revisit our original Open, Sesame console program, we are reminded that it is a sequence of program statements:

---

[4] For example, web-based programming models such as ASP.NET map incoming requests to programs using logic that relies upon session identifiers (similar to `ProgramHandle.ProgramId`) and a static model for describing program resumption points (web service operation names are like bookmark names).

```
static void Main()
{
  // Print the key
  string key = DateTime.Now.Millisecond.ToString();
  Console.WriteLine("here is your key: " + key);

  string s = Console.ReadLine();

  // Print the greeting if the key is provided
  if (key.Equals(s))
    Console.WriteLine("hello, world");
}
```

We can use the standard technique of modularity here and decompose the resumable OpenSesame program into smaller units that each have the same basic structure as OpenSesame. This factoring will allow programs other than OpenSesame to make use of these building blocks.

The Read class shown here is a bookmark-savvy replacement for the Console.ReadLine statement in the original Open, Sesame console program:

```
[Serializable]
public class Read : ProgramStatement
{
  private string text;
  public string Text
  {
    get { return text; }
  }

  public override void Run(BookmarkManager mgr)
  {
    mgr.Add(new Bookmark("read", ContinueAt));
  }

  void ContinueAt(Bookmark resumed)
  {
    text = (string) resumed.Payload;

    BookmarkManager mgr = resumed.BookmarkManager;
    mgr.Remove(resumed);
  }
}
```

The Read class has a property, Read.Text, so that the caller of Read.Run can access the string that is provided as the payload of the resumed bookmark. But how does the caller know when the value of the Read.Text property is available? *We can use a bookmark to notify the caller of* Read.Run *when the* Read.ContinueAt *method completes.*

In our implementation of Read, we rely on a bookmark in order to allow execution to pause without blocking a thread and later resume when relevant input is provided by an external entity. By using exactly the same bookmarking approach for *internal* notification, the caller of the Read.Run method can acquire the same ability to pause, and then resume when Read has completed its execution!

Here is a slightly modified Read class (the implementation of the Text property remains exactly the same, and is elided for clarity):

```
[Serializable]
public class Read : ProgramStatement
{
  // Text property elided for clarity...

  private string outerBookmarkName;
  public Read(string outerBookmarkName)
  {
    this.outerBookmarkName = outerBookmarkName;
  }

  public void Run(BookmarkManager mgr)
  {
    mgr.Add(new Bookmark("read", ContinueAt));
  }

  public void ContinueAt(Bookmark resumed)
  {
    text = (string) resumed.Payload;

    BookmarkManager mgr = resumed.BookmarkManager;
    mgr.Remove(resumed);
    mgr.Resume(outerBookmarkName, this);
  }
}
```

Read accepts the name of an "outer" bookmark as a parameter to its constructor. Read holds on to this bookmark name and, after the text field is set (in the ContinueAt method), the BookmarkManager is asked to resume the "outer" bookmark. The `Read` has logically completed its execution, and its caller is being notified of this fact.

Program Statement Lifecycle

The technique for internal notifications shown previously works fine but there is no reason why `BookmarkManager` cannot nicely support this simple asynchronous notification pattern with an *internally managed bookmark*. We will explain the mechanics of this internal bookmark in a minute, but first let's look at a simplified `Read` class:

```
[Serializable]
public class Read : ProgramStatement
{
  // Text property elided for clarity...

  public override void Run(BookmarkManager mgr)
  {
    mgr.Add(new Bookmark("read", ContinueAt));
  }

  public void ContinueAt(Bookmark resumed)
  {
    text = (string) resumed.Payload;

    BookmarkManager mgr = resumed.BookmarkManager;
    mgr.Remove(resumed);
    mgr.Done();
  }
}
```

Instead of worrying about an "outer" bookmark, the `Read` program statement simply informs the bookmark manager when its execution is complete. The other half of this pattern surfaces in the caller of `Read`; in our case, this is the `OpenSesame` program:

```
[Serializable]
public class OpenSesame : ProgramStatement
{
  string key;
  public override void Run(BookmarkManager mgr)
  {
    // Print the key
```

```
      key = DateTime.Now.Millisecond.ToString();
      Console.WriteLine("here is your key: " + key);

      mgr.RunProgramStatement(new Read(), ContinueAt);
    }

  public void ContinueAt(Bookmark resumed)
  {
    Read read = (Read) resumed.Payload;
    string s = read.Text;

    // Print the greeting if the key is provided
    if (key.Equals(s))
      Console.WriteLine("hello, world");

    mgr.Done();
  }
}
```

We have decomposed the logic of OpenSesame by using a Read object to obtain the required string. Instead of calling the Read.Run method directly, OpenSesame now calls BookmarkManager.RunProgramStatement and provides the resumption point for a bookmark that will be managed internally by BookmarkManager. The bookmark manager invokes Read.Run on behalf of OpenSesame. The internal bookmark is never surfaced to Read, which reports its completion by calling BookmarkManager.Done. When its Done method is called, BookmarkManager resumes the (internally created) bookmark that was established during the prior invocation of BookmarkManager.RunProgramStatement. At this point, OpenSesame can access the Read.Text property (the Read object is passed, for convenience, as the payload of the resumed bookmark).

The BookmarkManager class now looks like this:

```
public class BookmarkManager
{
  public void Add(Bookmark bookmark);
  public void Remove(Bookmark bookmark);

  // Request execution of a program statement, using an
  // implicit bookmark that will be resumed when that
  // program statement completes its execution
  public void RunProgramStatement(ProgramStatement statement,
    BookmarkLocation continueAt)
```

```
   // Indicate that the current program statement is done,
   // so that internally managed bookmarks can be resumed
   public void Done();
}
```

Now that we have established a well-defined beginning (`ProgramStatement.Run`) and ending (`BookmarkManager.Done`) for the execution of any resumable program statement, we can express program statement *lifecycle* in terms of the automaton (also known as a **finite state machine**) shown in Figure 1.1.

Figure 1.1   Program statement automaton

When a program statement is created, it is in a "Latent" state, waiting to be run. When its `Run` method is invoked, the program statement moves to the "Running" state. The program statement remains in the "Running" state for an indeterminate amount of time until it asynchronously reports its completion.

As we will see in the next section, the introduction of an automaton that describes the lifecycle of any program statement sets the stage for general-purpose control flow.

Control Flow

In C#, a { } statement block is a container for a set of program statements. When the statement block executes, the contained program statements execute sequentially until all are complete.

We can further decompose the logic of the `OpenSesame` class into `PrintKey` and `PrintGreeting` program statements that correspond to the other C# program statements in the original Open, Sesame console program. Doing this allows us to order these resumable program statements, along with `Read`, within a *general-purpose program statement block* that functions like a resumable version of a C# statement block.

Here are the `PrintKey` and `PrintGreeting` program statements:

```
[Serializable]
public class PrintKey : ProgramStatement
```

```
{
  private string key;
  public string Key
  {
    get { return key; }
  }

  public override void Run(BookmarkManager mgr)
  {
    // Print the key
    key = DateTime.Now.Millisecond.ToString();
    Console.WriteLine("here is your key: " + key);

    mgr.Done();
  }
}

[Serializable]
public class PrintGreeting : ProgramStatement
{
  private string key;
  public string Key
  {
    get { return key; }
    set { key = value; }
  }

  private string s;
  public string Input
  {
    get { return s; }
    set { s = value; }
  }

  public override void Run(BookmarkManager mgr)
  {
    // Print the greeting if the key is provided
    if (key.Equals(s))
      Console.WriteLine("hello, world");

    mgr.Done();
  }
}
```

After each statement is captured as a `ProgramStatement`, we are ready to implement our resumable `ProgramStatementBlock`, which simply executes a set of contained program statements one by one, in sequence:

```
[Serializable]
public class ProgramStatementBlock : ProgramStatement
{
  int currentIndex;
  List<ProgramStatement> statements = new List<ProgramStatement>();
  public IList<ProgramStatement> Statements
  {
    get { return statements; }
  }

  public override void Run(BookmarkManager mgr)
  {
    currentIndex = 0;

    // Empty statement block
    if (statements.Count == 0)
      mgr.Done();
    else
      mgr.RunProgramStatement(statements[0], ContinueAt);
  }

  public void ContinueAt(Bookmark resumed)
  {
    BookmarkManager mgr = resumed.BookmarkManager;

    // If we've run all the statements, we're done
    if (++currentIndex == statements.Count)
      mgr.Done();
    else // Else, run the next statement
      mgr.RunProgramStatement(statements[currentIndex], ContinueAt);
  }
}
```

We can provide *any* list of `ProgramStatement` objects to `ProgramStatementBlock` and, just like in a C# statement block, those statements will be executed one by one, sequentially. The only difference, of course, is that `ProgramStatementBlock` uses bookmarks, which means that we now have a resumable program statement block with thread and process agility.

A program executed by the mythical runtime is just a `ProgramStatement` object. This means we can now build Open, Sesame like this:[5]

---

[5] Expressions and property databinding are outside the scope of Chapter 1.

```
ProgramStatementBlock openSesameProgram =
  new ProgramStatementBlock();

PrintKey printKey = new PrintKey();
Read read = new Read();
PrintGreeting printGreeting = new PrintGreeting();
printGreeting.Key = ... // bind to printKey.Key
printGreeting.Input = ... // bind to read.Text

openSesameProgram.Statements.Add(printKey);
openSesameProgram.Statements.Add(read);
openSesameProgram.Statements.Add(printGreeting);

MythicalRuntime runtime = new MythicalRuntime();
ProgramHandle handle = runtime.RunProgram(openSesameProgram);

...
```

That's it! The Open, Sesame program, as presented to the mythical runtime, is a now a hierarchy of program statements—a `ProgramStatementBlock` object that is configured with an appropriate list of contained program statements.

Composite Program Statements

`ProgramStatementBlock` is a general-purpose program statement used for control flow within a resumable program. Languages like C# include other control flow constructs (such as `if`, `switch`, `for`, `while`, and `foreach`) that are indispensable if we want to write programs that are more complicated than Open, Sesame.

Let's see how easy it is to implement other control flow constructs as resumable program statements. As a first step, we can quickly establish a base class for these **composite program statements** (program statements that contain other program statements):

```
public abstract class CompositeProgramStatement : ProgramStatement
{
  public IList<ProgramStatement> Statements { ... }
}
```

After we have the base class, we change `ProgramStatementBlock` to derive from it:

```
public class ProgramStatementBlock : CompositeProgramStatement
{
```

```
  // Same as earlier except that the Statements property
  // is now inherited from CompositeProgramStatement
}
```

The `CompositeProgramStatement` class derives from `ProgramStatement` and defines an `IList<ProgramStatement>` property that holds the set of program statements contained by the composite program statement. The set of contained program statements will have their execution managed by the `Composite ProgramStatement`.

We can now easily develop familiar control flow constructs. Here is a composite program statement that provides branching (we are assuming the existence of a `Boolean-Expression` type that defines an `Evaluate` method returning a Boolean value):

```
public class IfElse : CompositeProgramStatement
{
  // Property that represents a boolean expression
  BooleanExpression Expression { ... }

  // Run either the first or second contained program
  // statement (more than two should be disallowed)
  public override void Run(BookmarkManager mgr)
  {
    if (Expression.Evaluate())
       mgr.RunProgramStatement(Statements[0], ContinueAt);
    else if (Statements[1] != null)
       mgr.RunProgramStatement(Statements[1], ContinueAt);
  }

  public void ContinueAt(Bookmark resumed)
  {
    resumed.BookmarkManager.Done();
  }
}
```

Here is another composite program statement that provides looping:

```
public class While : CompositeProgramStatement
{
  // Property that represents a boolean expression
  BooleanExpression Expression { ... }

  // Run the contained program statement (more than one
  // should be disallowed) as long as the expression
  // evaluates to true
```

```
public override void Run(BookmarkManager mgr)
{
  if (Expression.Evaluate())
     mgr.RunProgramStatement(Statements[0], ContinueAt);
  else
     mgr.Done();
}

public void ContinueAt(Bookmark resumed)
{
  BookmarkManager mgr = resumed.BookmarkManager;

  // Evaluate boolean expression
  if (Expression.Evaluate())
     mgr.RunProgramStatement(Statements[0], ContinueAt);
  else
     mgr.Done();
}
}
```

Just like that, we have resumable branching and looping constructs that we can use in the resumable programs we build.

Control Flow Robustness

Our `ProgramStatementBlock` and other composite program statements that provide control flow do work, but we are playing a bit fast and loose with our implementation guarantees.

To really make `ProgramStatementBlock` correct, we need an assurance that its contained statements execute in the proper order. To be fair, the code of `ProgramStatementBlock` is doing nothing wrong. But what is stopping some other code that might get a reference to a `Read` (contained by `ProgramStatementBlock`) from calling its `Run` method? And what is stopping a `Read` (or any other program statement contained by a `ProgramStatementBlock`) from continuing to do work even after signaling that it is done?

We need the following guarantees:

- A program statement is run only by the (parent) composite program statement that contains it (in its `CompositeProgramStatement.Statements` collection).

- A program statement cannot do more work (has no pending bookmarks) after it signals that it is done.

Another way of stating these requirements is in terms of the automaton introduced earlier to describe the lifecycle of reactive program statements:

- Only the parent of a program statement can move that program statement from the Latent state into the Running state.

- The parent of a program statement needs to know when that program statement moves from the Running state into the Done state.

- After a program statement moves into the Done state, it cannot do any more work (it cannot have pending bookmarks).

As we now see, the automaton applies not only to the reactive program as a whole, but to all individual program statements within that program. Furthermore, the automaton is the basis for establishing a set of constraints on program statement execution, upon which the semantics of composite program statements are built.

The bookmark manager can satisfy the requirements listed previously by throwing exceptions when the rules are violated, as shown in the following code snippets:

```
BookmarkManager mgr = resumed.BookmarkManager;

// obtain a reference to a program statement that is not
// a member of the this.Statements collection
ProgramStatement statement = ...

// will throw an exception
mgr.RunProgramStatement(statement, ContinueAt);

...

// will throw an exception if there are pending bookmarks
mgr.Done();

...

// will throw an exception if Done has already been called
mgr.Add(new Bookmark(...))
```

To further enforce the desired restrictions, the accessibility of the `Run` method defined by `ProgramStatement` can be changed from `public` to `protected` `internal`. In this way, only the bookmark manager will be able to invoke the `Run` method (when requested to do so via `BookmarkManager.RunProgramStatement`).

These changes give our `ProgramStatementBlock`, and our other composite program statements, the robustness we expect from resumable versions of the tried and true C# { }, `if`, and `while` constructs.

Real-World Control Flow

Given the programming model for bookmarks, it is easy to go beyond the familiar control flow constructs of C#. This will allow us to develop composite program statements that help solve complex modeling problems.

The `Interleave` class is a composite program statement that runs its contained program statements simultaneously:

```
[Serializable]
public class Interleave : CompositeProgramStatement
{
  int numChildStatementsCompleted;

  public override void Run(BookmarkManager mgr)
  {
    numChildStatementsCompleted = 0;

    // empty
    if (Statements.Count == 0)
      mgr.Done();
    else
    {
      foreach (ProgramStatement ps in Statements)
        mgr.RunProgramStatement(ps, ContinueAt);
    }
  }

  public void ContinueAt(Bookmark resumed)
  {
    numChildStatementsCompleted++;
    BookmarkManager mgr = resumed.BookmarkManager;

    if (Statements.Count == numChildStatementsCompleted)
      mgr.Done();
  }
}
```

A program that contains an `Interleave` program statement can easily have multiple simultaneous pending bookmarks. Each program statement contained by the `Interleave` can, during its execution, pause—awaiting input—and then resume. This bookmarking can happen any number of times within each program statement contained by the `Interleave`. Because the required inputs can arrive in any order (the program statements contained by the `Interleave` are in this sense independent), the execution unfolds in an interleaved fashion.

One can imagine more elaborate models of execution as evolutions of the one just described. For example, we can associate a Boolean expression with `Interleave` (much as we did for `IfElse` and `While`), and have `Interleave` report its completion as soon as the expression evaluates to `true`. This lets us model situations such as the assignment of work items to multiple parties, where only a subset of the work items are required to complete in order to consider the goal of the overall program met (perhaps there are two redundant processes for determining a loan applicant's credit rating; as soon as one completes successfully, the other can be abandoned).

We can go further and attach Boolean expressions to *each* of the program statements contained by `Interleave`. Evaluation of these expressions determines the order in which the contained program statements run (perhaps Joe does not need to review the document until Don and Chris have completed their reviews, unless there are fewer than 24 hours until the deadline).

The important observation here is that each of these elaborations builds on a common model and mechanism for managing the execution of a set of contained program statements.

Declarative Programs

So far, we have shown code that programmatically creates resumable programs. Those resumable programs are hierarchical arrangements of resumable program statements. Those statements (and their arrangements) can be thought of as an explicit representation of the programmer's intention. That representation ultimately is just data.

Our programs are just data.

Because our mythical runtime only cares about being handed a `ProgramState-ment` object, we can represent the data that constitutes that program however we want.

For instance, the arrangement of statements that constitute the Open, Sesame program can be expressed as data in database tables. One table, shown in Figure 1.2, holds declarations of program statements, now named so that they may be referred to easily.

Statement: Qu...d.StatementDb)	ParentStatem....StatementDb)	StatementPro....StatementDb)
StatementType	**StatementName**	
ProgramStatementBlock	OpenSesame	
PrintKey	pk1	
Read	r1	
PrintGreeting	pg1	
NULL	NULL	

Figure 1.2   Table of program statements

The data in the second table, shown in Figure 1.3, defines the `Statements` collection of each composite program statement.

Statement: Qu...d.StatementDb)	**ParentStatem....StatementDb)**		StatementPro....StatementDb)
StatementName	**ParentStatementName**	**Position**	
pk1	OpenSesame	0	
r1	OpenSesame	1	
pg1	OpenSesame	2	
NULL	NULL	NULL	

Figure 1.3   Table of program statement composition

The third table, shown in Figure 1.4, holds expressions that can be evaluated when a program statement executes, in order to yield values for that statement's properties.

Statement: Qu...d.StatementDb)	ParentStatem....StatementDb)	StatementPro....StatementDb)

	StatementName	PropertyName	PropertyValue
▶	pg1	Key	pk1.Key
	pg1	Input	r1.Text
✱	*NULL*	*NULL*	*NULL*

Figure 1.4 Table of program statement properties

We are *declaring* the Open, Sesame program, not coding it. Our program clearly does not need to be compiled in order to be run by the mythical runtime. It is simply loaded from the database into a set of `ProgamStatement` objects and executed.

Alternatively, we could choose a textual representation for Open, Sesame, like this:

```
begin
  printkey pk1
  read r1
  printgreeting Key=pk1.Key Input=r1.Text
end
```

Here too, we only need to write a parser that accepts this text file as input and materializes a `ProgramStatementBlock` object with the specified collection of contained program statements. This approach of expressing our program in terms of a custom (and constrained) syntax is often called a **domain-specific language (DSL)**. The domain-specific aspect comes from the fact that the DSL grammar contains terms that are specific to a given problem domain. Our program statements are defined as CLR types, so we can simply map the terms in a DSL to these types—thereby turning the parse step into a straightforward deserialization step (initialization of objects).

The .NET Framework 3.0 includes a powerful general-purpose object initialization language (plus associated parsers and serializers) called XAML (eXtensible Application Markup Language).We can use XAML to define Open, Sesame like this:[6]

```
<ProgramStatementBlock ... >
  <PrintKey ... />
  <Read ... />
```

---

[6] XAML supports property databinding, but we are leaving these details for later chapters.

```
    <PrintGreeting ... />
</ProgramStatementBlock>
```

The XAML representation, the custom representation in our invented DSL, and the data in the database tables (and also the `ProgramStatementBlock` object that is materialized from any of these formats) are *isomorphic representations* of the same program logic.

Because the mythical runtime is format agnostic, it does not know or care whether we use XAML, database tables, a DSL, or any other means of representing Open, Sesame—even a Tablet PC ink drawing, as shown in Figure 1.5.

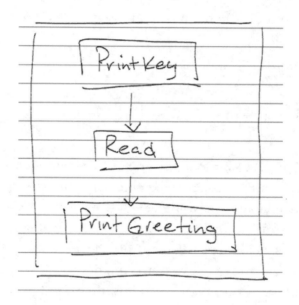

Figure 1.5   Tablet PC ink drawing of Open, Sesame program

At last, *the control flow of our program is expressed naturally*, and now mirrors[7] the original Open, Sesame console program.

---

[7] If we so choose, we can mirror the console program at a more granular level by replacing `PrintGreeting` with an `IfElse` composite program statement that contains a (to-be-implemented) `Write` program statement.

Where Are We?

This chapter began with a simple reactive program and the issues related to making that kind of program scalable and robust. Leveraging the ideas of bookmarks and continuations, we first decoupled the logic of our program from a given thread; the elimination of stack reliance, and the factoring of our program logic into distinct chunks of code, made our program resumable. We also made bookmarks available for serialization, which allowed us to passivate them; with this step, our program achieved process agility. We outlined the design of a listener, and a general-purpose runtime environment for resumable programs, that can be used to efficiently manage the execution of many instances of many different resumable programs within a distributed architecture.

But a programming model for bookmarks was not enough to buy us the control flow we were seeking. So we decomposed our program into a set of smaller building blocks, and standardized the notion of a resumable program as a composition of these resumable program statements. We built a set of composite program statements that map to familiar control flow constructs in C#. We also showed how to build composite program statements that capture more complex control flow patterns. Finally, we took advantage of the fact that resumable programs are data. We declared our program using formats other than C#, including data in a database table, a domain-specific language, XAML, and also a graphical notation, which allowed us to recover a natural style of control flow.

In short, we have engineered Windows Workflow Foundation.

2

WF Programs

I N CHAPTER 1, "DECONSTRUCTING WF," we introduced a new way of writing reactive programs. The basis of this approach is a bookmarking substrate upon which we developed a CLR type representing a reusable program statement. We also established the need for a small but specialized runtime environment that manages the execution of programs that are composed of these resumable program statements.

In WF, a resumable program statement is called an **activity**. A resumable program is a composition of activities. In WF, such a program is often called a workflow, but we favor the precision of the term **WF program** in this book because "workflow" is used colloquially. The execution environment for WF programs is called the **WF runtime**.

The ideas presented in Chapter 1 are the heart and soul of the WF programming model. But to actually write and run a WF program, we need to roll up our sleeves and start to use the types in the `System.Workflow` namespace that bring the ideas of bookmarking and continuations—presented in Chapter 1 in raw form—to fruition within a fully developed programming model. The goal of this chapter is to cover the basics: We will write several activities and then run WF programs that use those activities. Later chapters will explore, in great detail, the rich set of features that surround WF's core bookmarking capabilities, which constitute the foundation of the WF programming model.

The WF Programming Model

Activities are the building blocks of WF programs. An activity in a WF program represents a resumable program statement. The lifecycle of an activity—explored in full in Chapters 3, "Activity Execution," and 4, "Advanced Activity Execution"—centers around the fact that activity execution logic can exploit bookmarks. Bookmarks allow the execution of an activity (and, by extension, an entire WF program) to pause while awaiting stimulus, without holding a thread.

Activities

Listing 2.1 defines our first activity, Empty, which functions like an empty C# program statement (a lone semicolon).

Listing 2.1   Empty **Activity**

```
using System;
using System.Workflow.ComponentModel;

namespace EssentialWF.Activities
{
  public class Empty : Activity
  {
    protected override ActivityExecutionStatus Execute(
      ActivityExecutionContext context)
    {
      return ActivityExecutionStatus.Closed;
    }
  }
}
```

All activities inherit from System.Workflow.ComponentModel.Activity. The Execute method is overridden to define an activity's execution logic. In the case of Empty, the purpose of which is to act like a nop MSIL instruction, the Execute method returns immediately with a value indicating that the execution of the activity is complete.

Listing 2.2 shows the Activity type, the base class for all activities. This listing does not show all of the members of Activity, only those that will be discussed in the current chapter; this is a practice we will generally follow throughout the book.

Listing 2.2 `Activity` **Type**

```
namespace System.Workflow.ComponentModel
{
  public class Activity : DependencyObject
  {
    protected internal virtual ActivityExecutionStatus Execute(
      ActivityExecutionContext context);

    public event EventHandler<
      ActivityExecutionStatusChangedEventArgs> Closed;

    public bool Enabled { get; set; }
    public string Name { get; set; }

    public CompositeActivity Parent { get; }

    /* *** other members *** */
  }
}
```

Listing 2.3 defines a more interesting activity, `PrintKey`, which represents the first program statement in the WF version of the Open, Sesame program that we introduced in Chapter 1.

Listing 2.3 `PrintKey` **Activity**

```
using System;
using System.Workflow.ComponentModel;

namespace EssentialWF.Activities
{
  public class PrintKey : Activity
  {
    private string key;
    public string Key
    {
      get { return key; }
    }

    protected override ActivityExecutionStatus Execute(
      ActivityExecutionContext context)
    {
      key = DateTime.Now.Millisecond.ToString();
      Console.WriteLine("here is your key: " + key);

      return ActivityExecutionStatus.Closed;
    }
  }
}
```

The `PrintKey` activity generates a key, saves the value of the key in its `key` field, writes the key to the console, and then indicates that its execution is complete. The `Empty` and `PrintKey` activities don't create bookmarks because their execution logic is not dependent upon stimulus from an external entity.

Listing 2.4 defines our first activity that does need to use a bookmark. We have called this activity `ReadLine`, though in fact this activity is not at all dependent upon the console.

Listing 2.4   ReadLine **Activity**

```
using System;
using System.Workflow.ComponentModel;
using System.Workflow.Runtime;

namespace EssentialWF.Activities
{
  public class ReadLine : Activity
  {
    private string text;
    public string Text
    {
      get { return text; }
    }

    protected override ActivityExecutionStatus Execute(
      ActivityExecutionContext context)
    {
      WorkflowQueuingService qService =
        context.GetService<WorkflowQueuingService>();

      WorkflowQueue queue =
        qService.CreateWorkflowQueue(this.Name, true);
      queue.QueueItemAvailable += this.ContinueAt;

      return ActivityExecutionStatus.Executing;
    }

    void ContinueAt(object sender, QueueEventArgs e)
    {
      ActivityExecutionContext context =
        sender as ActivityExecutionContext;

      WorkflowQueuingService qService =
        context.GetService<WorkflowQueuingService>();

      WorkflowQueue queue = qService.GetWorkflowQueue(this.Name);
      text = (string) queue.Dequeue();
      qService.DeleteWorkflowQueue(this.Name);
```

```
            context.CloseActivity();
        }
    }
}
```

The execution logic of `ReadLine` uses a bookmark to wait for stimulus from an external entity. In WF, the data structure chosen to represent a bookmark's capacity to hold data is a queue. This queue, which we shall call a **WF program queue**, is created by `ReadLine` using the `WorkflowQueuingService`. The `WorkflowQueuingService`, shown in Listing 2.5, is obtained from the `ActivityExecutionContext`, which acts as a provider of services.

Listing 2.5 `WorkflowQueuingService`

```
namespace System.Workflow.Runtime
{
  public class WorkflowQueuingService
    {
      //  queueName is the bookmark name

      public WorkflowQueue CreateWorkflowQueue(
        IComparable queueName, bool transactional);
      public bool Exists(IComparable queueName);
      public WorkflowQueue GetWorkflowQueue(IComparable queueName);
      public void DeleteWorkflowQueue(IComparable queueName);

      /* *** other members *** */
    }
}
```

The `WorkflowQueue` object that is returned by the `CreateWorkflowQueue` method offers an event, `QueueItemAvailable`. Despite the syntactic sugar of the C# event, this event represents the asynchronous delivery of stimulus from an external entity to an activity, and is exactly the same pattern of bookmark resumption presented in Chapter 1. The more refined WF version of the programming model for bookmarks allows a bookmark's payload (a WF program queue) to hold an ordered list of inputs that await processing (instead of a single object as did the bookmark in Chapter 1). The physical resumption point of the bookmark is still just a delegate (`ContinueAt`, in Listing 2.4) even though in the WF programming model the delegate is indicated using the += event subscription syntax of C#.

The `WorkflowQueue` type is shown in Listing 2.6.

Listing 2.6 WorkflowQueue

```
namespace System.Workflow.Runtime
{
  public class WorkflowQueue
  {
    public event EventHandler<QueueEventArgs> QueueItemAvailable;

    public object Dequeue();

    public int Count { get; }
    public IComparable QueueName { get; }

    /* *** other members *** */
  }
}
```

As seen in Listing 2.4, the return value of the ReadLine activity's Execute method indicates that, at that point in time, the ReadLine has pending bookmarks; its execution is not complete. When an item is enqueued in its WF program queue, perhaps days after the ReadLine began its execution, the bookmark is resumed and, as a result, the ContinueAt method is invoked. After obtaining the item from its queue and setting the value of its text field, the ReadLine activity reports its completion.

The signature of ContinueAt in Listing 2.4 has a return type of void because this method is a System.EventHandler. Therefore, in contrast to the Execute method of PrintKey, an explicit call to the ActivityExecutionContext.CloseActivity method must be made by ReadLine in order to tell the WF runtime that its execution is complete.

Composite Activities

An activity that contains other activities is called a **composite activity**.

System.Workflow.ComponentModel.CompositeActivity is the base class for all composite activities, and is shown in Listing 2.7.

Listing 2.7 CompositeActivity

```
namespace System.Workflow.ComponentModel
{
  public class CompositeActivity : Activity
  {
    public ActivityCollection Activities { get; }
```

```
    public ReadOnlyCollection<Activity> EnabledActivities { get; }

    /* *** other members *** */
  }
}
```

`CompositeActivity` defines a property called `Activities` that holds the list of activities contained by the composite activity. The items in this list are called the composite activity's **child activities**. The `Activities` property is of type `ActivityCollection`, which is just a specialized `IList<Activity>` that is defined in the `System.Workflow.ComponentModel` namespace.

As shown in Listing 2.2, `Activity` defines a property called `Enabled`. If the value of this property is `false` (the default value is `true`), then the activity is disabled and is considered commented out of the WF program in which it has been declared, much like a program statement can be commented out of a C# program like this:

```
    // Console.WriteLine("hello, world");
```

If the activity that is disabled is a composite activity, then it and all of its child activities (no matter the values of their `Enabled` properties) are also disabled.

`CompositeActivity` defines a property called `EnabledActivities` that is a read-only list of those activities in its `Activities` collection that are enabled.

It is not possible in a WF program for an activity to be a child activity of more than one composite activity. `Activity` defines a readonly property called `Parent` that is a reference to its **parent activity**—the composite activity that contains it.

The `Parent` property will be `null` for exactly one activity in a WF program. Thus, a WF program has the shape of a tree (it is a hierarchical arrangement of activities) and the activity whose `Parent` property is `null` is called the **root activity** of the tree.

The root activity is the entry point of the WF program; its `Execute` method is akin to the `Main` method of a C# program.

The purpose of a composite activity is to provide *control flow* for WF programs. Composite activities manage the execution of their child activities, and rely upon bookmarks to be informed when child activities complete their execution.

Listing 2.8 defines our first composite activity, `Sequence`, which executes its child activities one by one sequentially (just like `ProgramStatementBlock` in Chapter 1).

Listing 2.8   Sequence **Activity**

```
using System;
using System.Workflow.ComponentModel;

namespace EssentialWF.Activities
{
  public class Sequence : CompositeActivity
  {
    protected override ActivityExecutionStatus Execute(
      ActivityExecutionContext context)
    {
      if (this.EnabledActivities.Count == 0)
        return ActivityExecutionStatus.Closed;

      Activity child = this.EnabledActivities[0];
      child.Closed += this.ContinueAt;
      context.ExecuteActivity(child);

      return ActivityExecutionStatus.Executing;
    }

    void ContinueAt(object sender,
      ActivityExecutionStatusChangedEventArgs e)
    {
      ActivityExecutionContext context =
        sender as ActivityExecutionContext;

      e.Activity.Closed -= this.ContinueAt;
      int index = this.EnabledActivities.IndexOf(e.Activity);

      if ((index + 1) == this.EnabledActivities.Count)
        context.CloseActivity();

      else
      {
        Activity child = this.EnabledActivities[index + 1];
        child.Closed += this.ContinueAt;
        context.ExecuteActivity(child);
      }
    }
  }
}
```

The Sequence activity executes its list of enabled child activities in a linear order, and therefore provides the same linear control flow as a { } statement block that demarcates a list of program statements within a C# program.

Sequence cannot directly execute its child activities since the Activity.Execute method (see Listing 2.2) has accessibility of protected internal. Instead,

Sequence requests the execution of a child activity via `ActivityExecution Context`.

Sequence subscribes to the `Activity.Closed` event (defined in Listing 2.2) before it requests the execution of a child activity. When the child activity completes its execution, the execution of the `Sequence` is resumed at the `ContinueAt` method. The `Sequence` activity's subscription to the `Closed` event of a child activity is syntactic sugar for the creation of a bookmark that is managed internally, on behalf of `Sequence`, by the WF runtime.

The `ActivityExecutionContext` type is effectively an activity-facing abstraction on top of the WF runtime, and is shown in Listing 2.9.

Listing 2.9   `ActivityExecutionContext`

```
namespace System.Workflow.ComponentModel
{
  public class ActivityExecutionContext : System.IServiceProvider
  {
    public void ExecuteActivity(Activity activity);
    public void CloseActivity();

    public T GetService<T>();
    public object GetService(Type serviceType);

    /* *** other members *** */
  }
}
```

`ActivityExecutionContext` will be discussed in great detail in Chapters 3 and 4 because it plays a substantial role in the realization of the automaton that governs the lifecycle of all activities.

WF Programs

A WF program is a hierarchy of activities. To be precise, a WF program—as managed by the WF runtime—is actually just an *object* whose type is a derivative of `Activity` and whose `Parent` property is null (the object is a root activity). If this object is a composite activity, as is typically the case, then it may contain other activities.

Before going further, we need to clarify some terminology. When we use the term **activity** we usually mean **activity declaration**—the declaration of a program statement within a WF program. Listing 2.10 shows a WF program that has one declaration of a Sequence and two PrintKey declarations.

Listing 2.10   A Simple WF Program Represented as XAML

```
<Sequence xmlns="http://EssentialWF/Activities">
  <PrintKey />
  <PrintKey />
</Sequence>
```

It is natural to describe the program in Listing 2.10 as a Sequence activity that contains two PrintKey activities (instead of as a Sequence activity declaration containing two PrintKey activity declarations), and we will follow this convention. As a consequence, we will refer to a *type* that derives from Activity (for example, the PrintKey class) as an **activity type**.

It is possible to write and run a WF program that consists of a single activity declaration, like this:

```
<PrintKey xmlns="http://EssentialWF/Activities">
```

The program in Listing 2.10, and the single-activity PrintKey program, are represented using XAML. The choice of XAML is just that—one option among many for representing our WF programs. When it comes time to run a WF program, we can hand it over to the WF runtime as XAML or in any other format, provided that a hierarchy of Activity objects can be materialized from that format. XAML is a pragmatic choice for the format of our program because the WF runtime supports loading from XAML by default. In Chapter 5, "Applications," we will see how custom formats are accommodated by the WF runtime.

The XAML in Listing 2.10 contains an XML namespace definition that helps locate the Sequence and PrintKey types. This is similar to a using statement in C#.

To map the XML namespace "http://EssentialWF/Activities" to a CLR namespace, the assembly containing the Sequence and PrintKey types must carry a special attribute:

```
using System.Workflow.ComponentModel.Serialization;

[assembly: XmlnsDefinition("http://EssentialWF/Activities",
"EssentialWF.Activities")]
```

The use of XmlnsDefinition is not required, but without it we must employ a different way of mapping element names in XAML to CLR type names; this approach is discussed in Chapter 7, "Advanced Authoring." Throughout this book, we assume that all example activities are defined in the EssentialWF.Activities CLR namespace and reside in an assembly, EssentialWF.dll, that is decorated with the XmlnsDefinition attribute as shown previously.

XAML is a language for specifying the initialization of objects. You can think of the XAML in Listing 2.10 as the equivalent of the following C# code (the using statement required to identify the CLR namespace for the Sequence and PrintKey types is omitted):

```
Sequence s = new Sequence();
s.Activities.Add(new PrintKey());
s.Activities.Add(new PrintKey());
```

The WF program in Listing 2.10 just prints a couple of keys to the console. Listing 2.11 shows a WF program that is more interesting—it is the familiar Open, Sesame program.

Listing 2.11   XAML-Based Open, Sesame Program

```
<Sequence x:Name="OpenSesame" xmlns="http://EssentialWF/Activities"
xmlns:x="http://schemas.microsoft.com/winfx/2006/xaml"
xmlns:wf="http://schemas.microsoft.com/winfx/2006/xaml/workflow">
  <PrintKey x:Name="pk1" />
  <ReadLine x:Name="r1" />
  <PrintGreeting x:Name="pg1" Key="{wf:ActivityBind pk1,Path=Key}"
Input="{wf:ActivityBind r1,Path=Text}" />
</Sequence>
```

The Key property of PrintGreeting is bound to the Key property of PrintKey, and the Input property of PrintGreeting is bound to the Text property of ReadLine. In order to make this work, we must implement a PrintGreeting activity type that supports **activity databinding**—the declarative flow of data from one activity to another.

The PrintGreeting activity type is shown in Listing 2.12.

Listing 2.12 `PrintGreeting` **Activity That Supports Databinding**

```
using System;
using System.Workflow.ComponentModel;

namespace EssentialWF.Activities
{
  public class PrintGreeting : Activity
  {
    public static readonly DependencyProperty KeyProperty
      = DependencyProperty.Register("Key",
          typeof(string), typeof(PrintGreeting));

    public static readonly DependencyProperty InputProperty
      = DependencyProperty.Register("Input",
          typeof(string), typeof(PrintGreeting));

    public string Key
    {
      get { return (string) GetValue(KeyProperty); }
      set { SetValue(KeyProperty, value); }
    }

    public string Input
    {
      get { return (string) GetValue(InputProperty); }
      set { SetValue(InputProperty, value); }
    }

    protected override ActivityExecutionStatus Execute(
      ActivityExecutionContext context)
    {
      if (Key.Equals(Input))
        Console.WriteLine("hello, world");

      return ActivityExecutionStatus.Closed;
    }
  }
}
```

The `GetValue` and `SetValue` methods called in the implementations of the `Key` and `Input` properties are inherited from `DependencyObject`, which is the type from which `Activity` derives (see Listing 2.2). The details of activity databinding—including complete discussion of the `DependencyObject`, `DependencyProperty`, and `ActivityBind` types upon which this feature rests—are covered in Chapter 7.

As you can see in Listing 2.12, activity databinding relies upon the fact that activities in a WF program are named: `Activity` defines a property of type `string` called `Name` (see Listing 2.2). `Activity.Name` is a **metadata property**, which means that its value is immutable at runtime. `Activity.Enabled` and `CompositeActivity.Activities` are also metadata properties; they are given values by the developer of a WF program but cannot be changed during the execution of instances of that program. The management of WF program metadata (the values of all metadata properties of all activities in a program) by the WF runtime is discussed in Chapter 5; the implementation of metadata properties by activities is discussed in Chapter 7.

XAML defines a special XML namespace for its core constructs. This namespace is "http://schemas.microsoft.com/winfx/2006/xaml" and by convention the prefix "x" is employed in its XML namespace definition. You will typically find the following namespace definition in the root element of a XAML document (such as in Listing 2.12) that describes a WF program:

```
xmlns:x="http://schemas.microsoft.com/winfx/2006/xaml"
```

The WF programming model also defines a special XML namespace. This namespace is "http://schemas.microsoft.com/winfx/2006/xaml/workflow" and it is mapped to CLR types that are defined in the `System.Workflow` namespaces. This namespace is by convention either specified as the default XML namespace in a XAML document containing a WF program, or using the prefix "wf" as shown here:

```
xmlns:wf="http://schemas.microsoft.com/winfx/2006/xaml/workflow"
```

In this book, we favor the use of the "wf" prefix because it allows us to use the default XML namespace for our custom activity types. All activity types defined as examples in this book reside in the "EssentialWF.Activities" CLR namespace that is mapped to the XML namespace "http://EssentialWF/Activities" using the `XmlnsDefinition` attribute.

The WF Runtime

The WF runtime is the execution environment for WF programs. In order to use the WF runtime, it must be hosted in a CLR application domain. This amounts to nothing more than instantiation of a `System.Workflow.Runtime.WorkflowRuntime` object. We refer to the application that instantiates the WF runtime as the **host application**.

The `WorkflowRuntime` type is shown in Listing 2.13.

Listing 2.13 `WorkflowRuntime`

```
namespace System.Workflow.Runtime
{
  public class WorkflowRuntime
  {
    public WorkflowRuntime();

    public void AddService(object service);
    public void RemoveService(object service);

    public void StartRuntime();
    public void StopRuntime();

    public WorkflowInstance CreateWorkflow(XmlReader reader);
    public WorkflowInstance GetWorkflow(Guid instanceId);

    /* *** other members *** */
  }
}
```

We can run a WF program by invoking the `WorkflowRuntime.CreateWorkflow` method with a `System.Xml.XmlReader` that provides access to XAML. `CreateWorkflow` returns an object of type `System.Workflow.Runtime.Workflow Instance`. A `WorkflowInstance` is a handle to a WF program instance.

The `WorkflowInstance` type is shown in Listing 2.14.

Listing 2.14 `WorkflowInstance`

```
namespace System.Workflow.Runtime
{
  public sealed class WorkflowInstance
  {
    public Guid InstanceId { get; }

    public void Start();
    public void Load();
    public void Unload();

    public void EnqueueItem(IComparable queueName,
      object item, IPendingWork pendingWork, object workItem);

    /* *** other members *** */
  }
}
```

Listing 2.15 is a console application that hosts the WF runtime. The console application uses the WF runtime to run one instance of the Open, Sesame program defined in Listing 2.11.

Listing 2.15 Hosting the WF Runtime and Running a WF Program

```
using System;
using System.Workflow.ComponentModel.Compiler;
using System.Workflow.Runtime;
using System.Xml;

namespace EssentialWF.Host.Chapter2
{
  class Program
  {
    static void Main()
    {
      using(WorkflowRuntime runtime = new WorkflowRuntime())
      {
        TypeProvider typeProvider = new TypeProvider(runtime);
        typeProvider.AddAssemblyReference("EssentialWF.dll");
        runtime.AddService(typeProvider);
        runtime.StartRuntime();

        WorkflowInstance instance = null;
        using (XmlTextReader reader =
          new XmlTextReader("OpenSesame.xoml"))
        {
          instance = runtime.CreateWorkflow(reader);
          instance.Start();
        }

        string s = Console.ReadLine();
        instance.EnqueueItem("r1", s, null, null);

        // Prevent Main from exiting before
        // the WF program instance completes
        Console.ReadLine();

        runtime.StopRuntime();
      }
    }
  }
}
```

The WF runtime must be told where to find the activity types that are used in the Open, Sesame XAML, and that is the job of the TypeProvider.

When the `Start` method is called on the `WorkflowInstance`, the WF runtime runs the WF program instance asynchronously (on a different thread than the one on which `Main` is running). Other threading models are supported by the WF runtime, and are discussed in Chapter 5.

When a `ReadLine` activity executes, it creates a WF program queue. When our console application (which is playing the role of a listener) reads a string from the console, it resumes the execution of the bookmark established by the `ReadLine` by enqueuing the string. The name of the WF program queue is the same name, "r1", that we gave to the `ReadLine` activity (per the execution logic of `ReadLine`).

Passivation

A reactive program like Open, Sesame is characterized by **episodic execution**—it performs small bursts, or episodes, of work that are punctuated by relatively long idle periods spent waiting for stimulus from an external entity. During these idle periods, the WF program instance is inactive because it cannot make forward progress and the WF runtime can **passivate** it—move it from memory to persistent storage such as a database. The instance will be resumed, possibly in a different process on a different machine, when relevant stimulus arrives. This is illustrated in Figure 2.1.

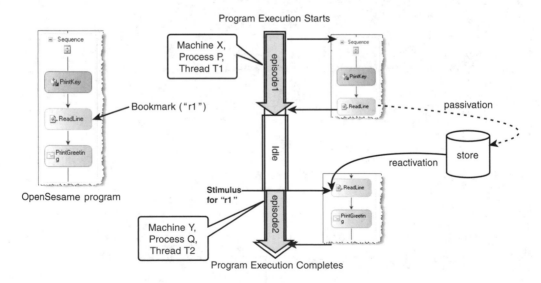

Figure 2.1   WF program execution is episodic and distributed.

In order to support the passivation of WF program instances, the WF runtime must be configured to use a **persistence service**. WF includes a default persistence service, named `SqlWorkflowPersistenceService`, that uses SQL Server as the durable storage medium for WF program instances. As we will see in Chapter 5, it is possible to plug in a custom persistence service that uses whatever storage medium is appropriate for your solution.

In order to use the `SqlWorkflowPersistenceService` in our solution, we of course must install SQL Server and create a database table that will be used to store passivated WF program instances.[1] To enable passivation, we can modify the console application logic to instantiate the `SqlWorkflowPersistenceService` and add it to the WF runtime:

```
using(WorkflowRuntime runtime = new WorkflowRuntime())
{
  SqlWorkflowPersistenceService persistenceService =
    new SqlWorkflowPersistenceService(...);
  runtime.AddService(persistenceService);
  ...
}
```

In order to illustrate the mechanics of passivation, we can write two different console applications. The first one, shown in Listing 2.16, begins the execution of an instance of the Open, Sesame program.

Listing 2.16   Passivating a WF Program Instance

```
using System;
using System.Workflow.ComponentModel.Compiler;
using System.Workflow.Runtime;
using System.Workflow.Runtime.Hosting;
using System.Xml;

namespace EssentialWF.Host.Chapter2
{
  class FirstProgram
  {
    static string ConnectionString =
      "Initial Catalog=SqlPersistenceService;Data
      Source=localhost;Integrated Security=SSPI;";
```

[1] The Windows Workflow Foundation SDK contains instructions and SQL scripts for setting up the SQL Server database tables used by the `SqlWorkflowPersistenceService`.

```
static void Main()
{
  using (WorkflowRuntime runtime = new WorkflowRuntime())
  {
    SqlWorkflowPersistenceService persistenceService =
      new SqlWorkflowPersistenceService(ConnectionString);
    runtime.AddService(persistenceService);

    TypeProvider typeProvider = new TypeProvider(runtime);
    typeProvider.AddAssemblyReference("EssentialWF.dll");
    runtime.AddService(typeProvider);

    runtime.StartRuntime();

    WorkflowInstance instance = null;
    using (XmlTextReader reader =
      new XmlTextReader("OpenSesame.xoml"))
    {
      instance = runtime.CreateWorkflow(reader);
      instance.Start();
    }

    Guid durableHandle = instance.InstanceId;
    // save the Guid...

    instance.Unload();

    runtime.StopRuntime();
  }
}
```

The WF program instance never completes because it is expecting to receive a string after it prints the key, and we do not provide it with any input. When the `WorkflowInstance.Unload` method is called,[2] the instance is passivated. Inspection of the SQL Server database table that holds passivated WF program instances will show us a row representing the idle Open, Sesame program instance.

In order to resume the passivated instance in another CLR application domain, we need to have some way of identifying the instance. That is precisely the purpose of the `InstanceId` property of `WorkflowInstance`. This globally unique identifier

---

[2] The call to `Unload` is not strictly necessary in this case since `WorkflowRuntime.StopRuntime` unloads all instances, but invocation of `Unload` makes our intention clearer.

can be saved and then later passed as a parameter to the `WorkflowRuntime`. `GetWorkflow` method in order to obtain a fresh `WorkflowInstance` for the WF program instance carrying that identifier.

This is exactly what we will do in a second console application, shown in Listing 2.17.

Listing 2.17   Resuming a Passivated WF Program Instance

```
using System;
using System.Workflow.ComponentModel.Compiler;
using System.Workflow.Runtime;
using System.Workflow.Runtime.Hosting;
using System.Xml;

namespace EssentialWF.Host.Chapter2
{
  class SecondProgram
  {
    static string ConnectionString =
      "Initial Catalog=SqlPersistenceService;Data
      Source=localhost;Integrated Security=SSPI;";

    static void Main()
    {
      using (WorkflowRuntime runtime = new WorkflowRuntime())
      {
        SqlWorkflowPersistenceService persistenceService =
          new SqlWorkflowPersistenceService(ConnectionString);
        runtime.AddService(persistenceService);

        TypeProvider typeProvider = new TypeProvider(runtime);
        typeProvider.AddAssemblyReference("EssentialWF.dll");
        runtime.AddService(typeProvider);

        runtime.StartRuntime();

        // get the identifier we had saved
        Guid id = ...
        WorkflowInstance instance = runtime.GetWorkflow(id);

        // user must enter the key that was printed
        // during the execution of the first part of
        // the Open, Sesame program
        string s = Console.ReadLine();
        instance.EnqueueItem("r1", s, null, null);

        // Prevent Main from exiting before
        // the WF program instance completes
        Console.ReadLine();
```

```
      runtime.StopRuntime();
    }
  }
 }
}
```

The passivated (bookmarked) WF program instance picks up where it left off, and writes its result to the console after we provide the second string.

Where Are We?

With a few C# classes and a little XAML, we have illustrated the central aspects of the WF programming model. It is easy to develop activities, such as `PrintKey` and `ReadLine`, that function as domain-specific program statements in WF programs. Activities like `ReadLine` use bookmarks (WF program queues) to wait for external stimulus. Composite activities like `Sequence` provide control flow for WF programs and also rely upon (internally managed) bookmarks. A WF program can be expressed declaratively in XAML, and the structure of the markup conveys the control flow of the program. The execution of a WF program instance is episodic and can span machine boundaries. The WF runtime, which is responsible for managing WF program instances, can be loaded in any CLR application domain by creating an object of type `WorkflowRuntime`. The addition of a persistence service allows the WF runtime to passivate idle WF program instances.

We've taken a quick tour of the WF programming model, so you should now be getting a feel for the kinds of solutions you can build with Windows Workflow Foundation. In the remainder of the book, we will take a much closer look at specific aspects of activities, WF programs, and the WF runtime. We'll begin in the next chapter by returning to and elaborating upon the idea—introduced in Chapter 1—of an automaton that describes the lifecycle of an activity.

3

Activity Execution

B ECAUSE A WF PROGRAM IS JUST an activity (that typically is the root of a tree of activities), the best way to understand how large WF programs execute is to first understand what happens at the level of a single activity.

The WF programming model codifies the lifecycle of an activity in terms of a finite state machine that we will call the **activity automaton**. Chapter 1, "Deconstructing WF," introduced a simple three-state version of this automaton for resumable program statements. The lifecycle of activities also follows this basic pattern but adds several additional states that will be discussed in this chapter and the next.

The execution model for activities is fundamentally asynchronous because it is designed to accommodate activities that perform **episodic execution**—short bursts of execution punctuated by relatively long periods of time spent waiting for external stimulus.

For efficiency reasons, it does not make sense to keep WF program instances in memory while they are idle waiting for data to arrive. When a WF program instance becomes idle, the WF runtime is capable of storing it in a (pluggable) durable storage medium and disposing the program instance. The process of storing the instance state and disposing the instance from memory is called **passivation**. When relevant stimulus arrives from an external entity, perhaps after days spent waiting, the WF runtime automatically **reactivates** the program, bringing it out of durable storage (where it had been passivated) into memory, and resuming its execution. Relative to its logical lifetime, a typical WF program instance lives for a short duration in memory.

Supporting passivation requires serialization of not only the program state but also the execution state (managed by the WF runtime). When WF program instances are passivated, they are captured by the WF runtime as continuations. A passivated program instance may be resumed in a different process or even on a different machine than the one on which it ran prior to passivation. This means that WF programs are thread-agile and process-agile. WF programs do indeed run on CLR threads, but the execution model for activities across resumption points is stackless because it does not rely on the stack associated with a CLR thread. The lifecycle of a WF program instance may, in a physical sense, span processes and machines and is distinctly different from the lifetimes of CLR objects (of type `Activity`) that transiently represent such a program instance while it is in memory.

Scheduling

In general, when an activity executes, it quickly performs some work and then either reports its completion or (having established one or more bookmarks) yields and waits for stimulus. This pattern maps nicely to a conceptual model in which work items are queued and then dispatched, one at a time, each to a target activity.

This pattern, depicted in Figure 3.1, is generally known as **scheduling**, so the component of the WF runtime that encompasses this functionality is known as the **scheduler**. The scheduler dispatches work items one at a time (from a queue), in a first-in-first-out (FIFO) fashion. Additionally, because the WF runtime never intervenes in the processing of a work item that has been dispatched, the scheduler behavior is strictly nonpreemptive.

To distinguish the scheduler's internal queue of work items from WF program queues (which are explicitly created by activity execution logic), we will call the queue that holds scheduler work items the **scheduler work queue**. When its scheduler work queue is empty, a WF program instance is considered idle.

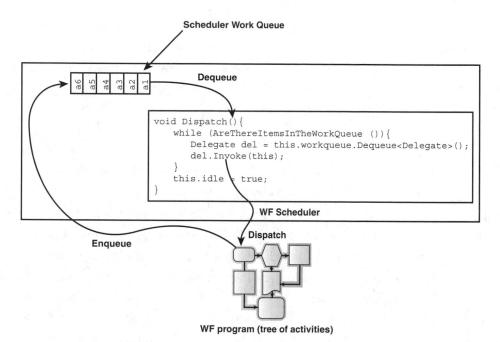

Figure 3.1   WF scheduler

Scheduler Work Items

The work items in the scheduler work queue are delegates. Each work item (delegate) corresponds to a method on an activity in the WF program instance. The activity method that is indicated by a work item (delegate) in the scheduler work queue is known as the **execution handler** of that work item.

Although there is no API to directly manipulate (or view) the scheduler work queue, certain actions taken by activities will cause work items to be enqueued. Delivery of input to a WF program queue can also cause work items to be enqueued.

A given activity's execution may include the invocation of any number of execution handlers. The state on which execution handlers operate is preserved across invocations of execution handlers of the same activity. This state is heap-allocated and is managed independently of the stack that is associated with the currently running CLR thread. The execution of activities across resumption points is stackless.

Scheduling of work items (delegates) is the mechanism by which methods on activities are invoked. This simple machinery drives activity, and WF program, execution. But in order to understand the rules about how and when work items are enqueued, we must understand the lifecycle of an activity, and that is our next topic.

Activity Automaton

The CLR virtualizes the instruction set of machine processors by describing its execution capabilities in terms of a hardware-agnostic instruction set, Microsoft Intermediate Language (MSIL). Programs compiled to MSIL are ultimately translated to machine-specific instructions, but virtualization allows language compilers to target only MSIL and not worry about various processor architectures.

In the WF programming model, the program statements used to build WF programs are classes that derive from `Activity` and `CompositeActivity`. Therefore, unlike MSIL, the "instruction set" supported by WF is not fixed. It is expected that many kinds of activities will be built and used in WF programs, while the WF runtime only relies upon the base classes. An activity developer can choose to implement anything—domain-specific or general-purpose—within the very general boundaries set by the WF runtime. Consequently, the WF runtime is freed from the actual semantics of specific activities.

The WF programming model does codify aspects of the interactions between the WF runtime and activities (such as the dispatch of execution handlers) in terms of an **activity automaton** (a finite state machine), which we will now explore in depth, with examples.

This chapter focuses solely on the normal execution of an activity. An activity that executes normally begins in the *Initialized* state, moves to the *Executing* state when its work begins, and moves to the *Closed* state when its work is completed. This is shown in Figure 3.2. The full activity automaton, shown in Figure 3.3, includes other states that will be discussed in Chapter 4, "Advanced Activity Execution."

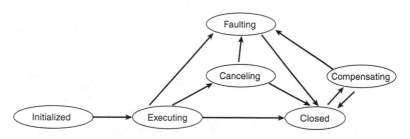

Figure 3.2   Basic activity automaton

Figure 3.3   Complete activity automaton

The lifecycle of any activity in an executing WF program is captured by the states of the activity automaton and the transitions that exist between these states. Transitions from one state to another are brokered by the WF runtime to ensure the correctness of WF program execution.

Another way to view the activity automaton is as an abstract execution contract that exists between the WF runtime and any activity. It is the responsibility of the WF runtime to enforce that the execution of an activity strictly follows the transitions of the activity automaton. It is the responsibility of the activity to decide when certain transitions should occur. Figure 3.4 depicts the participation of both the WF scheduler and an activity in driving the automaton.

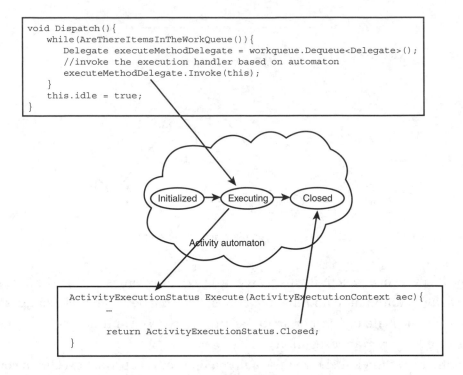

Figure 3.4   The dispatch of execution handlers is governed by the activity automaton.

Activity Execution Status and Result

The `WriteLine` activity shown in Listing 3.1 prints the value of its `Text` property to the console and then reports its completion.

Listing 3.1   `WriteLine` **Activity**

```
using System;
using System.Workflow.ComponentModel;

namespace EssentialWF.Activities
{
  public class WriteLine : Activity
  {
    public static readonly DependencyProperty TextProperty
      = DependencyProperty.Register("Text",
        typeof(string), typeof(WriteLine));
```

```
    public string Text
    {
      get { return (string) GetValue(TextProperty); }
      set { SetValue(TextProperty, value); }
    }

    protected override ActivityExecutionStatus Execute(
      ActivityExecutionContext context)
    {
      Console.WriteLine(Text);
      return ActivityExecutionStatus.Closed;
    }
  }
}
```

The execution logic of WriteLine is found in its override of the Execute method, which is inherited from Activity. The Execute method is the most important in a set of virtual methods defined on Activity that collectively constitute an activity's participation in the transitions of the activity automaton. All activities implement the Execute method; the other methods are more selectively overridden.

Listing 3.2 shows members defined by the Activity type that we will cover in this chapter and the next.

Listing 3.2 Activity **Revisited**

```
namespace System.Workflow.ComponentModel
{
  public class Activity : DependencyObject
  {
    protected virtual ActivityExecutionStatus Cancel(
      ActivityExecutionContext context);

    protected virtual ActivityExecutionStatus Execute(
      ActivityExecutionContext context);

    protected virtual ActivityExecutionStatus HandleFault(
      ActivityExecutionContext context, Exception fault);

    protected virtual void Initialize(
      IServiceProvider provider);

    protected virtual void Uninitialize(
      IServiceProvider provider);
```

```
    protected virtual void OnExecutionContextLoad(
      IServiceProvider provider);

    protected virtual void OnExecutionContextUnload(
      IServiceProvider provider);

    protected virtual void OnClosed(
      IServiceProvider provider);

    public ActivityExecutionResult ExecutionResult { get; }
    public ActivityExecutionStatus ExecutionStatus { get; }

    /* *** other members *** */
  }
}
```

By returning a value of `ActivityExecutionStatus.Closed` from its `Execute` method, the `WriteLine` activity indicates to the WF runtime that its work is done; as a result, the activity moves to the *Closed* state.

`Activity` defines a property called `ExecutionStatus`, whose value indicates the current state (in the activity automaton) of the activity. The type of `Activity.ExecutionStatus` is `ActivityExecutionStatus`, which is shown in Listing 3.3.

Listing 3.3   `ActivityExecutionStatus`

```
namespace System.Workflow.ComponentModel
{
  public enum ActivityExecutionStatus
  {
    Initialized,
    Executing,
    Canceling,
    Closed,
    Compensating,
    Faulting
  }
}
```

`Activity` also defines a property called `ExecutionResult`, whose value qualifies an execution status of `ExecutionStatus.Closed`, because that state can be entered from any of five other states. The type of `Activity.ExecutionResult` is `ActivityExecutionResult`, which is shown in Listing 3.4. An activity with an execution status other than *Closed* will always have an execution result of *None*.

Listing 3.4 `ActivityExecutionResult`

```
namespace System.Workflow.ComponentModel
{
  public enum ActivityExecutionResult
  {
    None,
    Succeeded,
    Canceled,
    Compensated,
    Faulted,
    Uninitialized,
  }
}
```

The values of the `ExecutionStatus` and `ExecutionResult` properties are settable only by the WF runtime, which manages the lifecyle transitions of all activities.

You can determine the current execution status and execution result of an activity by getting the values of its `ExecutionStatus` and `ExecutionResult` properties:

```
using System;
using System.Workflow.ComponentModel;

public class MyActivity : Activity
{
  protected override ActivityExecutionStatus Execute(
    ActivityExecutionContext context)
  {
    System.Diagnostics.Debug.Assert(
      ActivityExecutionStatus.Executing == ExecutionStatus);

    System.Diagnostics.Debug.Assert(
      ActivityExecutionResult.None == ExecutionResult);

    ...
  }
}
```

The `ExecutionStatus` and `ExecutionResult` properties only have meaning at runtime for activities within a WF program instance.

Activity Execution Context

The `Execute` method has one parameter of type `ActivityExecutionContext`. This object represents the execution context for the currently executing activity.

The `ActivityExecutionContext` type (abbreviated AEC) is shown in Listing 3.5.

Listing 3.5   `ActivityExecutionContext`

```
namespace System.Workflow.ComponentModel
{
  public sealed class ActivityExecutionContext: IDisposable,
    IServiceProvider
  {
    public T GetService<T>();
    public object GetService(Type serviceType);

    public void CloseActivity();

    /* *** other members *** */
  }
}
```

AEC has several roles in the WF programming model. The simplest view is that AEC makes certain WF runtime functionality available to executing activities. A comprehensive treatment of AEC will be given in Chapter 4.

The WF runtime manages `ActivityExecutionContext` objects carefully. AEC has only internal constructors, so only the WF runtime creates objects of this type. Moreover, AEC implements `System.IDisposable`. An AEC object is disposed immediately after the return of the method call (such as `Activity.Execute`) in which it is a parameter; if you try to cache an AEC object, you will encounter an `ObjectDisposedException` exception when you access its properties and methods. Allowing AEC objects to be cached could easily lead to violation of the activity automaton:

```
public class MyActivity : Activity
{
  private ActivityExecutionContext cachedContext = null;

  protected override ActivityExecutionStatus Execute(
    ActivityExecutionContext context)
  {
    this.cachedContext = context;
    return ActivityExecutionStatus.Executing;
```

```
  }

  public void UseCachedContext()
  {
    // Next line will throw an ObjectDisposedException
    this.cachedContext.CloseActivity();
  }
}
```

Activity Services

`ActivityExecutionContext` has a role as a provider of services; these services are an activity's gateway to functionality that exists outside of the running WF program instance. AEC implements `System.IServiceProvider` and offers the required `GetService` method plus (for the sake of convenience) a typed `GetService<T>` wrapper over `GetService`. Using these methods, an activity can obtain services that are needed in order to complete its work.

In fact, AEC chains its service provider implementation to that of the WF runtime. This means that an activity can obtain custom services proffered by the application hosting the WF runtime, as shown in Figure 3.5.

Consider a `WriterService` that defines a `Write` method:

```
using System;

namespace EssentialWF.Activities
{
  public abstract class WriterService
  {
    public abstract void Write(string s);
  }
}
```

By defining the writer service abstractly (we could also have used an interface), activities that use the service are shielded from details of how the service is implemented. We can change our implementation of the service over time without affecting activity code.

Here is a simple derivative of `WriterService` that uses the console to print the string that is provided to the `Write` method:

```
using System;
using EssentialWF.Activities;
```

```
namespace EssentialWF.Services
{
  public class SimpleWriterService : WriterService
  {
    public override void Write(string s)
    {
      Console.WriteLine(s);
    }
  }
}
```

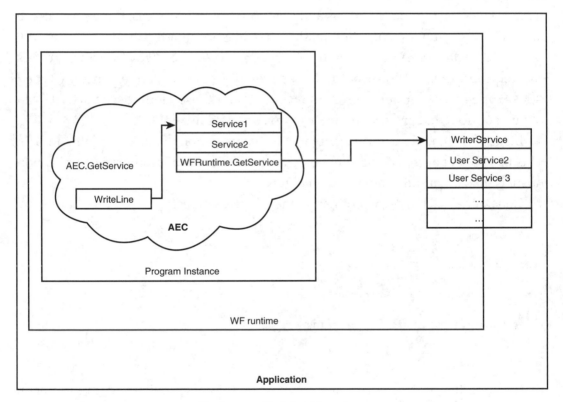

Figure 3.5   Chaining of services

A `SimpleWriterService` object can be added to the WF runtime, which acts as a container of services:

```
using (WorkflowRuntime runtime = new WorkflowRuntime())
{
  runtime.AddService(new SimpleWriterService());
```

```
    ...
  }
```

We can now change the execution logic of `WriteLine` to obtain a `WriterService` and call its `Write` method:

```
public class WriteLine : Activity
{
  // Text property elided for clarity...

  protected override ActivityExecutionStatus Execute(
    ActivityExecutionContext context)
  {
    WriterService writer = context.GetService<WriterService>();
    writer.Write(Text);

    return ActivityExecutionStatus.Closed;
  }
}
```

This change may seem like a small matter, but if `WriterService` is defined as an abstract class (or an interface), it can have multiple implementations. In this way, the application hosting the WF runtime can choose the appropriate writer service without affecting WF program instances that contain `WriteLine` activities (that rely only upon the definition of that service).

In Chapter 6, "Transactions," we will bring transactions into the picture and explore how services used by activities (and activities themselves) can partipate in the transactions that attend the execution of WF program instances.

Bookmarks Revisited

The simplest activities (in terms of execution logic) are like the `WriteLine` activity; they complete their work entirely within their `Execute` method. If all activities did this, you would not be able to build very interesting WF programs. Don't get us wrong; simple activities are useful, and indeed are essential to the definition of most WF programs. Typical duties for such activities include obtaining services and exchanging data with those services, and manipulating the state of the WF program instance.

Most real-world processes, however, reach points in time at which further computational progress cannot be made without stimulus (input) from an external entity. It may be that a WF program waits for a person to make a decision about which branch of execution logic should be taken. Or it may be that an activity delegates some computation to an external entity and then waits for the result of that computation to be returned asynchronously.

In order to understand the mechanics of how this kind of activity executes, we will begin by looking at a contrived example: an activity that delegates work to…itself. Consider the version of WriteLine that is shown in Listing 3.6.

Listing 3.6 WriteLine **Activity That Uses a Bookmark**

```
using System;
using System.Workflow.ComponentModel;

namespace EssentialWF.Activities
{
  public class WriteLine : Activity
  {
    // Text property elided for clarity...

    protected override ActivityExecutionStatus Execute(
      ActivityExecutionContext context)
    {
      base.Invoke(this.ContinueAt, EventArgs.Empty);
      return ActivityExecutionStatus.Executing;
    }

    void ContinueAt(object sender, EventArgs e)
    {
      ActivityExecutionContext context =
        sender as ActivityExecutionContext;

      WriterService writer = context.GetService<WriterService>();
      writer.Write(Text);

      context.CloseActivity();
    }
  }
}
```

Although the example is contrived, there are several things worth looking at here.

By calling `Invoke<T>` (a protected method defined by `Activity`), the `WriteLine` activity creates a bookmark and immediately resumes that bookmark. The bookmark's resumption point is the `WriteLine.ContinueAt` method, and the payload for the resumed bookmark is `EventArgs.Empty`.

The bookmark created by the call to `Invoke<T>` is managed internally by the WF runtime, and because the `Invoke<T>` method also resumes this bookmark, an item is enqueued in the scheduler work queue (corresponding to the `ContinueAt` method).

Because it creates a bookmark (and is awaiting resumption of that bookmark), the `WriteLine` activity can no longer report its completion at the end of the `Execute` method. Instead it returns a value of `ActivityExecutionStatus.Executing`, indicating that although `WriteLine` is yielding the CLR thread by returning from `Execute`, its work is not complete since there is a pending bookmark. The `WriteLine` activity remains in the *Executing* state and does not transition (yet) to *Closed*.

When the scheduler dispatches the work item corresponding to the `ContinueAt` method, it passes an `ActivityExecutionContext` as the `sender` parameter. This allows the `WriteLine` to have access to its current execution context.

The `ContinueAt` method conforms to a standard .NET Framework event handler signature and therefore has a return type of `void`. Because of this, the WF runtime cannot use the return value of `ContinueAt` as the way of determining whether or not the activity should remain in the *Executing* state or transition to the *Closed* state. The `CloseActivity` method provided by `ActivityExecutionContext` can be used instead. If this method is called, the currently executing activity moves to the *Closed* state; if the method is not called, there is no change in the state of the activity. Because `ContinueAt` calls `CloseActivity`, the `WriteLine` activity moves to the *Closed* state.

The version of the `WriteLine` activity that uses `Invoke<T>`, though contrived, is still illustrative of the general pattern that you will need to use in many of the activities you develop. Although it is possible for an activity to complete its work within the `Execute` method (as with the version of `WriteLine` that returns `ActivityExecutionStatus.Closed` from its `Execute` method), this is a special case. Just as subroutines are a special, simple case accommodated by the richer concept of a coroutine, activities whose execution logic is embodied in a single `Execute` method are a special, simple form of episodic computation, in which there is always exactly one episode.

WF Program Execution

Now that we understand the basics of how to write activity execution logic, we can take a closer look at the execution mechanics of a WF program. We will start with a WF program that contains just one activity:

```
<WriteLine Text="hello, world" xmlns="http://EssentialWF/Activities" />
```

Running this program results in the expected output:

```
hello, world
```

In Chapter 2, "WF Programs," we briefly looked at the code that is required to host the WF runtime and run WF programs. We will return to the host-facing side of the WF runtime in Chapter 5, "Applications." For now, it is enough to know the basics: First, the `WorkflowRuntime.CreateWorkflow` method returns a `WorkflowInstance` representing a newly created instance of a WF program; second, the `WorkflowInstance.Start` method tells the WF runtime to begin the execution of that WF program instance.

The call to `WorkflowRuntime.CreateWorkflow` prepares a scheduler (and the accompanying scheduler work queue) for the new WF program instance. When this method returns, all activities in the WF program are in the *Initialized* state.

The call to `WorkflowInstance.Start` enqueues one item in the the scheduler work queue—a delegate corresponding to the `Execute` method of the root activity of the WF program. The root activity—in our example, the `WriteLine`—is now in the *Executing* state, even though the `Execute` method has not actually been called (the work item has not yet been dispatched). The scheduler work queue is shown in Figure 3.6.

Figure 3.6   Scheduler work queue after WorkflowInstance.Start

Let's assume that we are using the version of `WriteLine` that doesn't call `Invoke<T>`.

When the `Execute` method returns a value of `ActivityExecutionStatus.Closed`, the `WriteLine` activity moves to the *Closed* state. In this case, the WF runtime recognizes that the program instance is complete since the root activity in the program instance is complete.

The asynchronous version of `WriteLine` is only slightly more complex. The call to `Invoke<T>` within `Execute` will enqueue a work item in the scheduler work queue (corresponding to the resumption of the internally created bookmark).

Thus, when the `Execute` method (of the version of `WriteLine` that does call `Invoke<T>`) returns, the activity remains in the *Executing* state and the scheduler work queue looks as it is shown in Figure 3.7.

Figure 3.7   Scheduler work queue after WriteLine.Execute

When the `WriteLine.ContinueAt` method returns, the `WriteLine` activity moves to the *Closed* state and the program instance completes.

WF Program Queues

Any activity that requires input from an external entity must figure out a way to (a) let that external entity know that it requires input, and (b) receive notification when the input is available. This simple pattern is at the heart of episodic computation, and it is supported in a first-class way by the WF runtime. The plain requirement is that an activity must be able to receive input even if the WF program instance in which it exists is idle and sitting in persistent storage like a SQL Server database table. When the input arrives, the WF program instance must be reactivated and its execution resumed (at the appropriate bookmark).

In Chapter 2, we developed an activity called `ReadLine` (shown again in Listing 3.7), which waits for a string to arrive from an external entity. If you understand how this activity is built and how it executes, you will have the right basis for

understanding and creating higher level communication patterns that are used in
WF programs. All such patterns are built on top of the same notion of bookmarks.[1]

Listing 3.7   ReadLine **Activity**

```csharp
using System;
using System.Workflow.ComponentModel;
using System.Workflow.Runtime;

namespace EssentialWF.Activities
{
  public class ReadLine : Activity
  {
    private string text;
    public string Text
    {
      get { return text; }
    }

    protected override ActivityExecutionStatus Execute(
      ActivityExecutionContext context)
    {
      WorkflowQueuingService qService =
        context.GetService<WorkflowQueuingService>();

      WorkflowQueue queue =
        qService.CreateWorkflowQueue(this.Name, true);
      queue.QueueItemAvailable += this.ContinueAt;

      return ActivityExecutionStatus.Executing;
    }

    void ContinueAt(object sender, QueueEventArgs e)
    {
      ActivityExecutionContext context =
        sender as ActivityExecutionContext;

      WorkflowQueuingService qService =
        context.GetService<WorkflowQueuingService>();

      WorkflowQueue queue = qService.GetWorkflowQueue(this.Name);
      text = (string) queue.Dequeue();
      qService.DeleteWorkflowQueue(this.Name);
```

---

[1] Although various communication technologies (such as WCF or ASMX) can be layered upon
WF, they all must use the WorkflowQueuingService to robustly deliver data to passivated
WF program instances.

```
      context.CloseActivity();
    }
  }
}
```

The execution logic of the `ReadLine` activity uses a **WF program queue**. A WF program queue is essentially a named location (a bookmark) where an activity can receive data, even if the WF program instance in which the activity exists is not in memory. A WF program queue is not the same as the WF program instance's scheduler queue, which is managed by the WF runtime. Think of a WF program queue as the data structure in which an explicitly created bookmark holds its payload (to be delivered upon the resumption of the bookmark). It is an addressable location where external entities can deliver data.

The `Execute` method of `ReadLine` obtains the `WorkflowQueuingService` from its `ActivityExecutionContext`. The `WorkflowQueuingService` is asked to create a WF program queue with a name that is the same as that of the activity (`this.Name`). The name of a WF program queue can be any `IComparable` object; usually a `string` will suffice. We are choosing a simple queue naming convention here, but other schemes are possible. Regardless, the external code that provides input to a WF program instance must know the name of the appropriate WF program queue.

The `WorkflowQueuingService` type is shown in Listing 3.8.

Listing 3.8   `WorkflowQueuingService`

```
namespace System.Workflow.Runtime
{
  public class WorkflowQueuingService
  {
    public WorkflowQueue CreateWorkflowQueue(IComparable queueName,
      bool transactional);
    public bool Exists(IComparable queueName);
    public WorkflowQueue GetWorkflowQueue(IComparable queueName);
    public void DeleteWorkflowQueue(IComparable queueName);

    /* *** other members *** */
  }
}
```

The same WF program queue name may be used in more than one WF program instance. This just means that if we write a WF program containing a `ReadLine` activity named "r1", we can execute any number of instances of this WF program without any problems. Each instance will create a separate WF program queue with the name "r1". Because data is always enqueued to a specific WF program instance (via `WorkflowInstance.EnqueueItem`), there is no conflict or ambiguity. Another way of stating this is that WF program queues are not shared across WF program instances. This allows us to think of the logical address of a WF program queue as the `WorkflowInstance.InstanceId` identifying the WF program instance that owns the WF program queue, plus the WF program queue name.

A WF program queue acts as a conduit for communication between external entities and an activity in a WF program instance. Code outside of the WF program instance can deposit data into a WF program queue using the `EnqueueItem` method defined on the `WorkflowInstance` class. An activity (and, by extension, a WF program) can create as many distinct WF program queues as it requires.

The `CreateWorkflowQueue` method returns a `WorkflowQueue` object that represents the WF program queue. The `WorkflowQueue` type is shown in Listing 3.9.

Listing 3.9   `WorkflowQueue`

```
namespace System.Workflow.Runtime
{
  public class WorkflowQueue
  {
    public IComparable QueueName { get; }
    public int Count { get; }

    public object Dequeue();
    public object Peek();

    public event EventHandler<QueueEventArgs>
      QueueItemAvailable;

    /* *** other members *** */
  }
}
```

The `QueueItemAvailable` event is raised when an item is enqueued into the WF program queue. Under the covers, this is just a bookmark (disguised using C# event syntax).

The `QueueItemAvailable` event is also raised if, when an activity subscribes to this event, there are already (previously enqueued) items present in the WF program queue. This permits a decoupling of the delivery of data to a bookmark and the resumption of that bookmark.

Here is a simple WF program that contains only a single `ReadLine` activity:

```
<ReadLine x:Name="r1" xmlns="http://EssentialWF/Activities"
xmlns:x="http://schemas.microsoft.com/winfx/2006/xaml" />
```

If we save this WF program as a file called "Read.xoml", we can execute it using the console application of Listing 3.10, which hosts the WF runtime and delivers data to the `ReadLine` activity via the WF program queue.

Listing 3.10   A Console Application That Delivers Data to a `ReadLine` Activity

```csharp
using System;
using System.Workflow.ComponentModel.Compiler;
using System.Workflow.Runtime;
using System.Xml;

class Program
{
  static void Main()
  {
    using (WorkflowRuntime runtime = new WorkflowRuntime())
    {
      TypeProvider tp = new TypeProvider(null);
      tp.AddAssemblyReference("EssentialWF.dll");
      runtime.AddService(tp);

      runtime.StartRuntime();

      runtime.WorkflowIdled += delegate(object sender,
        WorkflowEventArgs e)
      {
        Console.WriteLine("WF program instance " +
          e.WorkflowInstance.InstanceId + " is idle");
      };

      runtime.WorkflowCompleted += delegate(object sender,
        WorkflowCompletedEventArgs e)
      {
        Console.WriteLine("WF program instance " +
          e.WorkflowInstance.InstanceId + " completed");
      };
```

```
    WorkflowInstance instance = null;
    using (XmlTextReader reader = new XmlTextReader("Read.xoml"))
    {
      instance = runtime.CreateWorkflow(reader);
      instance.Start();
    }

    string text = Console.ReadLine();
    instance.EnqueueItem("r1", text, null, null);

    // Prevent Main from exiting before
    // the WF program instance completes
    Console.ReadLine();

    runtime.StopRuntime();
    }
  }
}
```

The console application calls `WorkflowRuntime.CreateWorkflow`, which loads the WF program from XAML. It then calls `WorkflowInstance.Start`, which causes the `Execute` method of `ReadLine`—the root activity in the WF program—to be scheduled.

The console application then waits for the user to enter text at the console. Meanwhile, the WF runtime begins the execution of the WF program instance on a thread that is different than the thread on which `Main` is running. The `ReadLine` activity has its `Execute` method invoked. The `ReadLine` activity creates its WF program queue and then waits for data to arrive there. Because there are no other items in the scheduler work queue, the WF program instance is idle.

The console application subscribes for the `WorkflowRuntime.WorkflowIdled` event and, when this event is raised by the WF runtime, writes the `InstanceId` of the WF program instance to the console:

```
WF program instance 631855e5-1958-4ce7-a29a-dc6f8e2a9238 is idle
```

When a line of text is read, the console application calls `EnqueueItem`, passing the text it received from the console as payload associated with the resumption of the bookmark.

The implementation of `WorkflowInstance.EnqueueItem` enqueues (in the scheduler work queue) work items for all activities that are subscribed to this WF program queue's `QueueItemAvailable` event. This is depicted in Figure 3.8.

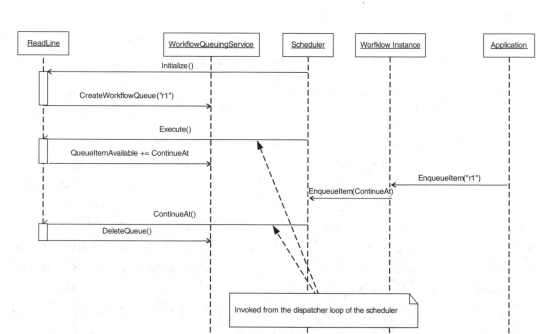

Figure 3.8   Enqueuing data to a WF program queue

In our example, the `ReadLine` activity's callback is called `ContinueAt`. This delegate will be scheduled as a work item and dispatched by the scheduler; if the idle WF program instance had been passivated (not shown in this example), the WF runtime would automatically bring it back into memory.

The `ReadLine` activity will set its `Text` property with the string obtained from the `Dequeue` operation on its WF program queue. In the example, we are doing no error checking to ensure that the object is indeed of type `string`. The `ContinueAt` method informs the WF runtime that it is complete by calling `CloseActivity`. The WF program instance, because it only contains the `ReadLine`, also completes. The console application, which subscribed to the `WorkflowRuntime.WorkflowCompleted` event, prints this fact to the console.

```
WF Program instance 631855e5-1958-4ce7-a29a-dc6f8e2a9238 completed
```

If the console application tries to enqueue data to a WF program queue that does not exist, the `EnqueueItem` method will throw an `InvalidOperationException` indicating that the WF program queue could not be found. In our implementation of `ReadLine`, the WF program queue is not created until the `ReadLine` activity begins executing. Thus, the following lines of code are problematic:

```
WorkflowInstance instance = runtime.CreateWorkflow(...);
instance.EnqueueItem("r1", "hello", null, null);
```

The preceding code omits the call to `WorkflowInstance.Start`, and because of this the WF program queue named "r1" does not yet exist. In other words, the implementation of `ReadLine` requires that the application doesn't enqueue the data until after the `ReadLine` activity starts to execute. Even the code in the console application of Listing 3.9 presents a race condition because the execution of the WF program instance occurs on a different thread than the execution of the console application. We may be able to work around this race condition quite easily in our contrived example where the WF program is just a single `ReadLine` activity. But in a larger WF program, with many activities managing WF program queues, and executing at different times, this is a lot trickier.

One of the ways to mitigate this problem is to allow activities to create WF program queues during the creation of a WF program instance. This will ensure that, after the call to `WorkflowRuntime.CreateWorkflow`, the WF program instance can immediately receive data (even if it cannot yet process it, which will only begin once `WorkflowInstance.Start` is called). In a later section, we will change `ReadLine` to do exactly this.

Timers

Another example of an activity that cannot complete its execution logic entirely within the `Execute` method is a `Wait` activity that simply waits for a specified amount of time to elapse before completing. The `Wait` activity is shown in Listing 3.11.

Listing 3.11   `Wait` *Activity*

```
using System;
using System.Workflow.ComponentModel;
using System.Workflow.Runtime;

namespace EssentialWF.Activities
{
  public class Wait : Activity
```

```
{
  private Guid timerId;

  public static readonly DependencyProperty DurationProperty
    = DependencyProperty.Register("Duration",
      typeof(TimeSpan), typeof(Wait));

  public TimeSpan Duration
  {
    get { return (TimeSpan) GetValue(DurationProperty); }
    set { SetValue(DurationProperty, value); }
  }

  protected override ActivityExecutionStatus Execute(
    ActivityExecutionContext context)
  {
    WorkflowQueuingService qService =
      context.GetService<WorkflowQueuingService>();

    timerId = Guid.NewGuid();

    WorkflowQueue queue = qService.CreateWorkflowQueue(
      timerId, true);
    queue.QueueItemAvailable += this.ContinueAt;

    TimerService timerService = context.GetService<TimerService>();
    timerService.SetTimer(timerId, Duration);

    return ActivityExecutionStatus.Executing;
  }

  void ContinueAt(object sender, QueueEventArgs e)
  {
    ActivityExecutionContext context =
      sender as ActivityExecutionContext;

    WorkflowQueuingService qService =
      context.GetService<WorkflowQueuingService>();

    WorkflowQueue queue = qService.GetWorkflowQueue(timerId);
    qService.DeleteWorkflowQueue(timerId);

    context.CloseActivity();
  }
}
}
```

Listing 3.11 shows the basic implementation of a `Wait` activity that depends upon an implementation of a `TimerService` (see Listing 3.12) for the actual management of the timer. The `Wait` activity, in its `Execute` method, creates a WF program queue providing the bookmark resumption point (`ContinueAt`) and calls `TimerService.SetTimer`, passing a unique identifier representing the timer. The `TimerService` is responsible for managing the actual timers. When the timer is triggered, the timer service resumes the bookmark by enqueuing data in the WF program queue created by the `Wait` activity. When the `ContinueAt` method is invoked by the scheduler (with the AEC as the `sender` argument), the `Wait` activity deletes the WF program queue and transitions to the Closed state.

The `TimerService` defines a `SetTimer` method that allows the activity to specify the duration of the timer as a `TimeSpan`, along with the name of the WF program queue that the `TimerService` will use to deliver a notification using `WorkflowInstance.EnqueueItem` (with a null payload) when the specified amount of time has elapsed.

Listing 3.12 `TimerService` **Used by the** `Wait` **Activity**

```
using System;
using System.Workflow.ComponentModel;
using System.Workflow.Runtime;

namespace EssentialWF.Activities
{
  public abstract class TimerService
  {
    public abstract void SetTimer(Guid timerId, TimeSpan duration);
    public abstract void CancelTimer(Guid timerId);
  }
}
```

A simple implementation of the timer service is shown in Listing 3.13.

Listing 3.13 *Implementation of a* `TimerService`

```
using System;
using System.Collections.Generic;
using System.Threading;
using System.Workflow.ComponentModel;
using System.Workflow.Runtime;
using EssentialWF.Activities;
```

```
namespace EssentialWF.Services
{
  public class SimpleTimerService : TimerService
  {
    WorkflowRuntime runtime;
    Dictionary<Guid, Timer> timers = new Dictionary<Guid, Timer>();

    public SimpleTimerService(WorkflowRuntime runtime)
    {
      this.runtime = runtime;
    }

    public override void SetTimer(Guid timerId, TimeSpan duration)
    {
      Guid instanceId = WorkflowEnvironment.WorkflowInstanceId;
      Timer timer = new Timer(delegate(object o)
        {
          WorkflowInstance instance = runtime.GetWorkflow(instanceId);
          instance.EnqueueItem(timerId, null, null, null);
        }, timerId, duration, new TimeSpan(Timeout.Infinite));

      timers.Add(timerId, timer);
    }

    public override void CancelTimer(Guid timerId)
    {
      ((IDisposable)timers[timerId]).Dispose();
      timers.Remove(timerId);
    }
  }
}
```

The `SimpleTimerService` mantains a set of `System.Threading.Timer` objects. The `timerId` that is passed as a parameter to the `SetTimer` method serves as the name of the WF program queue created by the `Wait` activity. When a timer fires, the callback (written as an anonymous method) enqueues a (null) item into the appropriate WF program queue, and the `Wait` activity resumes its execution.

In Chapter 6 we will discuss transactions, and we will see how transactional services (such as a durable timer service) can be implemented. Because we have followed the practice of making the `Wait` activity dependent only on the abstract definition of the timer service, we can change the implementation of the timer service without affecting our activities and WF programs.

As mentioned earlier, the WF runtime is a container of services. Custom services that are added to the WF runtime can be obtained by executing activities. An implementation of a `TimerService` can be added to the WF runtime like so:

```
using (WorkflowRuntime runtime = new WorkflowRuntime())
{
  runtime.AddService(new SimpleTimerService(runtime));
  ...
}
```

Executing the `Wait` activity within a simple WF program will cause the program to pause (and potentially passivate) and later, when the timeout occurs, resume the execution. The following program will start and then pause for 5 seconds, and finally resume its execution and complete:

```
<Wait Duration="00:00:05" xmlns="http://EssentialWF/Activities" />
```

Our reason for introducing the `Wait` activity is to illustrate a general pattern.

There is nothing at all special about timers. The `Wait` activity makes a request to a service on which it depends, and indicates to the service where (to which WF program queue) the result of the requested work should be delivered. The service takes some amount of time to complete the requested work. When the work is done, the service returns the result of the work to the activity via the WF program queue.

This bookmarking pattern is the basis for developing WF programs that are "coordinators of work" that is performed outside their boundaries.

Activity Initialization and Uninitialization

In the activity automaton, *Initialized* is the start state in which all activities begin their lifecycle. When the `WorkflowRuntime.CreateWorkflow` method returns, all activities in the newly created WF program instance are in the *Initialized* state.

Within the implementation of `CreateWorkflow`, the WF runtime calls the `Initialize` method of the root activity in the WF program. There are other interesting details related to the creation of new WF program instances, and they will be covered in Chapter 5; here we will focus only on activity initialization.

Activities can use the `Initialize` method to perform whatever initialization is necessary when a WF program instance is created. Custom services added to the WF runtime (and also the `WorkflowQueuingService`) can be obtained by the activity via the `IServiceProvider` that is passed as a parameter to `Initialize`. `ActivityExecutionContext` is not available because the activity (indeed, the WF program) has not yet begun its execution.

The `CompositeActivity` class overrides `Initialize` and in its implementation invokes the `Initialize` method of all enabled child activities. If you develop a composite activity, or indeed any activity that requires initialization logic, you should always call `base.Initialize` within your implementation of the `Initialize` method to ensure proper initialization of the WF program instance.

The WF runtime's scheduler machinery is not used during initialization to dispatch the calls to `Initialize`. It would be overkill to do so because the WF program instance is not yet running. Because invocation of `Initialize` is synchronous, the WF runtime can guarantee that when the `WorkflowRuntime.CreateWorkflow` method returns, the WF program instance is fully initialized and ready for execution.

If an exception is thrown from any activity's `Initialize` method, the initialization of the WF program instance fails, and the `WorkflowRuntime.CreateWorkflow` method will throw an exception indicating that this has occurred.

So, what can an activity do in its `Initialize` method? `Initialize` carries one parameter of type `System.IServiceProvider`. No execution context exists at this time for the activity, so it is not correct for the WF runtime to provide AEC. Still, the `IServiceProvider` of `Initialize` does the same service chaining that AEC does. Any custom services that you add to the `WorkflowRuntime` are proffered by this service provider so that an activity may do whatever resource initialization is required. The `WorkflowQueuingService` is available too, so that WF program queues may be created.

To summarize, the *Initialized* state is the start state of the activity automaton. Activities in this state have not started their execution, and can be said to be in a latent form, but do get a chance to perform initialization logic in their `Initialize` method.

Listing 3.14 updates the `ReadLine` activity so that it creates its WF program queue within its `Initialize` method.

Listing 3.14 **The** ReadLine **Activity with Initialization Logic**

```csharp
using System;
using System.Workflow.ComponentModel;
using System.Workflow.Runtime;

namespace EssentialWF.Activities
{
  public class ReadLine : Activity
  {
    private string text;
    public string Text
    {
      get { return this.text; }
    }

    protected override void Initialize(
      IServiceProvider provider)
    {
      WorkflowQueuingService qService =
        (WorkflowQueuingService) provider.GetService(
          typeof(WorkflowQueuingService));

      if (!qService.Exists(this.Name))
        qService.CreateWorkflowQueue(this.Name, true);
    }

    protected override ActivityExecutionStatus Execute(
      ActivityExecutionContext context) {

      WorkflowQueuingService qService =
        context.GetService<WorkflowQueuingService>();

      WorkflowQueue queue = qService.GetWorkflowQueue(Name);
      if (queue.Count > 0)
      {
        this.text = (string) queue.Dequeue();
        return ActivityExecutionStatus.Closed;
      }

      queue.QueueItemAvailable += this.ContinueAt;
      return ActivityExecutionStatus.Executing;
    }

    void ContinueAt(object sender, QueueEventArgs e)
    {
      ActivityExecutionContext context =
        sender as ActivityExecutionContext;
```

```
        WorkflowQueuingService qService =
          context.GetService<WorkflowQueuingService>();

        WorkflowQueue queue = qService.GetWorkflowQueue(Name);
        this.text = (string) queue.Dequeue();
        context.CloseActivity();
      }

      protected override void Uninitialize(IServiceProvider provider)
      {
        WorkflowQueuingService qService =
          (WorkflowQueuingService) provider.GetService(
            typeof(WorkflowQueuingService));

        if (qService.Exists(this.Name))
          qService.DeleteWorkflowQueue(this.Name);
      }
    }
  }
```

The implementation of Execute accounts for the fact that by the time the activity executes, there may already be an item in its WF program queue. If an item is indeed available, there is no need to subscribe to the QueueItemAvailable event. The ReadLine activity also contains an implementation of the Uninitialize method, in which the WF program queue is deleted.

The Uninitialize method is the logical counterpart of the Initialize method.

Uninitialize is called (synchronously, not via a work item in the scheduler work queue) as the final part of an activity's transition to the *Closed* state from the *Executing* state. It is called when it is determined by the WF runtime that an activity in the *Initialized* state will never be executed. The latter case occurs when the parent of an activity transitions to the *Closed* state without having requested the execution of that child activity.

Activities cannot assume that they will always be executed, just as the program statements in all but one branch of a C# if statement will be passed over. Any resources created in an activity's Initialize method should therefore be cleaned up in its Uninitialize method.

As part of an activity's transition to the *Closed* state (and just prior to the invocation of Uninitialize), the WF runtime synchronously invokes the OnClosed method that is defined by Activity. In this method, activities can clean up the resources they allocated during their execution (as opposed to during their initialization).

You might wonder why `OnClosed` exists when we also have `Uninitialize`. The simple answer is that `Uninitialize` should clean up resources allocated in `Initialize`, whereas the purpose of `OnClosed` is to clean up resources allocated during the execution of the activity. An executing activity can transition to the *Closed* state from several different states (which will be discussed more in the next chapter), and the `OnClosed` method will be called in each of these cases.

To summarize, when we execute a `ReadLine` activity, `ReadLine` has its methods invoked in the following order:

- `Initialize`
- `Execute`
- `ContinueAt`
- `OnClose`
- `Uninitialize`

If a `ReadLine` activity is present in a WF program, but never executes, it will only have its `Initialize` and `Uninitialize` methods called.

Activities as CLR Objects

Because `Activity` implements `System.ComponentModel.IComponent`, which extends `System.IDisposable`, activities are given yet another opportunity to perform cleanup of resources. The `IDisposable.Dispose` method, however (like an activity's constructor), is a practicality necessitated by the fact that a WF program instance is transiently realized as a set of CLR objects when that program instance is in memory. These objects, like any objects, are created and destroyed subject to the rules of the CLR. However, transitions in the CLR object lifecycle are logically unrelated to the execution lifecycle of the WF program instance (and the activities within it). In other words, the calling of the `Activity.Dispose` method reflects the passivation cycles of a WF program instance—every time a WF program instance is passivated, the activity objects that represent the program instance while it is in memory are disposed because they no longer represent the (passivated) program instance.

The WF runtime will call the `Dispose` method on the CLR object representing an activity every time the WF program instance containing the activity is passivated. In contrast, `Initialize` and `Uninitialize` are called exactly once during the logical lifetime of an activity, which can span any number of passivation cycles. In contrast, `Dispose` may be invoked multiple times for an activity during its lifetime.

It is recommended that activities not perform any resource management in their object constructors. CLR objects that transiently represent an activity may be constructed and disposed multiple times during the course of the activity's execution lifetime. The constructor of an activity may be called multiple times even during the creation of a single program instance (or reactivation of an instance). It is crucial to understand that because an activity is an intrinsically resumable entity, its logical lifespan is governed by the activity automaton and not by the lifetime of any CLR object.

In order to provide well-defined points for resource allocation and cleanup, `Activity` defines two additional methods, `OnExecutionContextLoad` and `OnExecutionContextUnload`, which bracket the lifetime of a CLR object representing an activity in a WF instance. You can rely upon the WF runtime to call `OnExecutionContextLoad` during the creation (or reactivation) and `OnExecutionContextUnload` during the passivation of a WF instance. `OnExecutionContextUnload` is essentially just like `Dispose` except that it accepts an `IServiceProvider` as a parameter and therefore has access to runtime services.

`Dispose`, `OnExecutionContextLoad`, and `OnExecutionContextUnload` are side effects of the fact that the WF runtime is layered on top of the CLR, and are related to the management of CLR objects which transiently represent a WF program instance. In contrast, `Initialize`, `Uninitialize`, and `OnClose` are related to the lifetime of the activity as described by the activity automaton. It is crucial to understand this difference between CLR programs and WF programs. From the perspective of the CLR, a CLR program instance is defined by its in-memory existence and lifetime. From the point of view of the WF runtime, a WF program instance is defined on an altogether different plane, and in fact can spend most of its lifetime in persistent storage. Because a WF program instance may passivate and reactivate many times (perhaps on different machines), objects that represent the activities in that instance in memory might need to be constructed and disposed of many times before the WF program instance completes (see Figure 3.9).

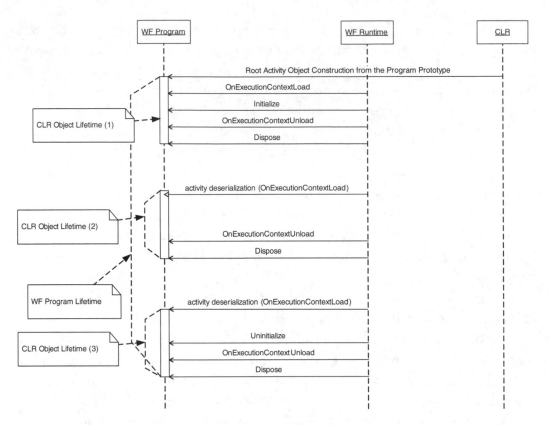

Figure 3.9   Lifecycle of a WF program instance

Many activities require only an empty constructor and `Dispose` method, but it is important nonetheless to know when and why they will be called.

Composite Activity Execution

Enough with WF programs that are only a single activity! It's time to develop some composite activities and then declare and run some more interesting WF programs.

We will begin with the `Sequence` activity of Chapter 2, shown again here:

```
public class Sequence : CompositeActivity
{
  protected override ActivityExecutionStatus Execute(
```

```
    ActivityExecutionContext context)
{
  if (this.EnabledActivities.Count == 0)
    return ActivityExecutionStatus.Closed;

  Activity child = this.EnabledActivities[0];
  child.Closed += this.ContinueAt;
  context.ExecuteActivity(child);

  return ActivityExecutionStatus.Executing;
}

void ContinueAt(object sender,
  ActivityExecutionStatusChangedEventArgs e)
{
  ActivityExecutionContext context =
    sender as ActivityExecutionContext;

  e.Activity.Closed -= this.ContinueAt;
  int index = this.EnabledActivities.IndexOf(e.Activity);

  if ((index + 1) == this.EnabledActivities.Count)
    context.CloseActivity();

  else
  {
    Activity child = this.EnabledActivities[index + 1];
    child.Closed += this.ContinueAt;
    context.ExecuteActivity(child);
  }
}
```

The job of the Sequence activity is to emulate a C# { } statement block, and execute its child activities one by one. Only when the final child activity of a Sequence finishes can the Sequence report that it is complete.

The Execute method of Sequence first checks to see if there are any child activities at all. If none are present, the method returns ActivityExecution Status.Closed. The Sequence is done because it has nothing to do. It is like an empty C# statement block. If one or more child activities are present, though, the first child activity needs to be scheduled for execution. In order to do this, two lines of code are necessary:

```
child.Closed += ContinueAt;
context.ExecuteActivity(child);
```

These two statements constitute a very simple bookmarking pattern that you will encounter repeatedly in composite activity implementations. The subscripton to the `Closed` event of the child activity sets up a bookmark that is managed internally by the WF runtime. The `Activity.Closed` event is merely syntactic sugar on top of the bookmark management infrastructure. The += results in the creation of a bookmark, and the dispatch of the `Closed` event (the resumption of the bookmark), is brokered via the scheduler.

The invocation of `ActivityExecutionContext.ExecuteActivity` requests that the indicated child activity be scheduled for execution. Specifically, the `Execute` method of the child activity is added as a work item in the scheduler work queue.

In order to enforce the activity automaton, the WF runtime will throw an exception from within `ExecuteActivity` if the child activity is not in the *Initialized* state. If the call to `ExecuteActivity` succeeds, an item is added to the scheduler work queue, representing the invocation of the child activity's `Execute` method. A successful call to `ExecuteActivity` also immediately places the child activity in the *Executing* state.

The `Sequence` activity's code that schedules the execution of its first child activity and subscribes for this child activity's `Closed` event is analogous to the `ReadLine` activity's logic that creates a WF program queue and subscribes to that queue's `QueueItemAvailable` event. In both cases, the activity is dependent upon some work, outside of its control, and can proceed no further until it is notified that this work has been completed. The code is somewhat different, but the bookmarking pattern is exactly the same.

Of course, for a composite activity like `Sequence`, the pattern must be repeated until all child activities have completed their execution. This is achieved in the `ContinueAt` method, which is scheduled for execution when the currently executing child activity moves to the *Closed* state. When it receives notification that a child activity has completed its execution, `Sequence` first removes its subscription for that child activity's `Closed` event. If the child activity that just completed is the last child activity in the `Sequence`, the `Sequence` reports its own completion. Otherwise, the bookmarking pattern is repeated for the next child activity.

There are a couple of crucial aspects to the WF runtime's role as the enforcer of state transitions. If the `Sequence` activity tries to report its completion while a child activity is in the *Executing* state, this transition will not be allowed. This fact is the cornerstone of the WF runtime's *composition-related enforcement* (and is not implied by the activity automaton).

The corollary to this rule is that only an activity's parent is allowed to request that activity's execution. A call to `ActivityExecutionContext.ExecuteActivity` by its parent is the *only* stimulus that will cause an activity to move to the *Executing* state.

These simple enforcements play a huge role in establishing the meaning and ensuring the integrity of composite activities and, by extension, WF programs.

Of course, there must be one exception to the rule that only the parent of an activity can schedule its execution, and that is for the root activity, whose `Parent` property is `null`. As we have already seen, it is the application hosting the WF runtime that makes a request to the WF runtime to schedule the execution of the root activity's `Execute` method.

Effectively, as part of the creation of a WF program instance, the WF runtime creates an implicit bookmark whose resumption point is the `Execute` method of the root activity. The invocation of `WorkflowInstance.Start` resumes this bookmark, and begins the execution of the program instance.

It will be instructive to trace the execution of a simple WF program that uses `Sequence`, noting the changes that occur at each step to the scheduler work queue. The XAML in Listing 3.15 is a `Sequence` with a set of `WriteLine` child activities.

Listing 3.15   A WF Program That Uses Sequence

```
<Sequence x:Name="s1" xmlns="http://EssentialWF/Activities"
xmlns:x="http://schemas.microsoft.com/winfx/2006/xaml">
  <WriteLine x:Name="w1" Text="One" />
  <WriteLine x:Name="w2" Text="Two" />
  <WriteLine x:Name="w3" Text="Three" />
  <WriteLine x:Name="w4" Text="Four" />
</Sequence>
```

Running an instance of this program will result in the expected output.

```
One
Two
Three
Four
```

When the application hosting the WF runtime calls `WorkflowInstance.Start`, it is telling the WF runtime to resume the initial, implicit bookmark. The result of the call to `Start` is that the scheduler work queue for this instance contains a single item—a work item for the `Execute` method of the root activity.

The root activity—in our example, the `Sequence`—is now in the *Executing* state, even though its `Execute` method has not actually been called. Figure 3.10 shows the scheduler work queue, along with the state of the WF program instance (with *Executing* activities shown in boldface).

Figure 3.10 WF program instance after `WorkflowInstance.Start`

At this point, the WF runtime's dispatcher logic enters the picture, and invokes the `Sequence` activity's `Execute` method, removing the corresponding item from the scheduler work queue. From this point forward, it is the activities in the WF program that drive the program forward; the WF runtime plays a passive role as the scheduler of work and the enforcer of activity state transitions.

The `Execute` method of `Sequence` will, as we know, schedule its first child activity for execution. When the `Execute` method returns, the scheduler work queue looks as it is shown in Figure 3.11. The first `WriteLine` activity is now in the *Executing* state (again, even though its `Execute` method has not been called). The `Sequence` too is in the *Executing* state.

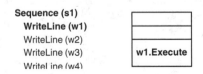

Figure 3.11 WF program instance after `Sequence.Execute`

As we know from the basic pattern used for child activity execution, `Sequence` has, at this point, also subscribed to the `Closed` event of its first child activity. Even though `Closed` (and the other events defined on the `Activity` class) looks like a normal event, under the covers it is an internally managed bookmark.

When the `Execute` method of `WriteLine` returns, the `WriteLine` activity moves to the *Closed* state. Because the `Sequence` has subscribed to the event corresponding to this transition, an appropriate work item will be placed in the scheduler work queue. The current state of the program instance is as shown in Figure 3.12; the first `WriteLine` is underlined to indicate that it has completed its execution and is in the *Closed* state.

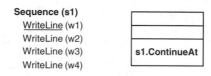

Sequence (s1)
WriteLine (w1)
WriteLine (w2)
WriteLine (w3)
WriteLine (w4)

s1.ContinueAt

Figure 3.12   WF program instance after first child activity completes

Now the work item for the `ContinueAt` method of `Sequence` is dispatched. As we know, `ContinueAt` will follow the standard pattern for requesting the execution of the second child activity. When `ContinueAt` method returns, the program state is as shown in Figure 3.13, with the second `WriteLine` activity now in the *Executing* state.

Sequence (s1)
WriteLine (w1)
WriteLine (w2)
WriteLine (w3)
WriteLine (w4)

w2.Execute

Figure 3.13   WF program instance after first callback to `Sequence.ContinueAt`

This pattern will continue as the `Sequence` marches through the list of its child activities. When the last child activity reports its completion, the `ContinueAt` method will report the completion of the `Sequence`. The WF runtime will observe this (you can think of the WF runtime as a subscriber to the root activity's `Closed` event), and will do the necessary bookkeeping to complete this WF program instance.

Figure 3.14 summarizes the execution of our WF program as an interaction diagram.

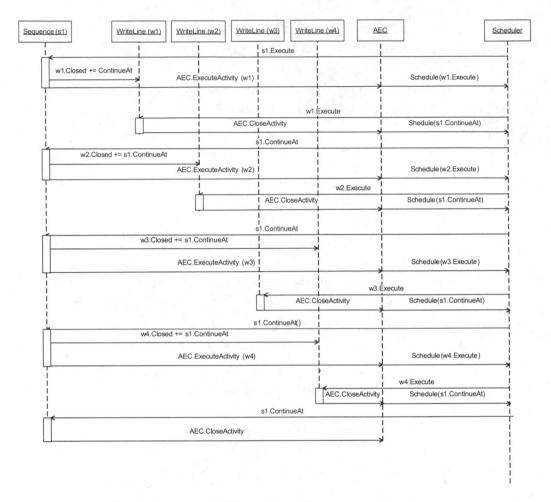

Figure 3.14 Interaction diagram of the execution of Listing 3.15

One crucial point about the `Sequence` activity is that it implemented sequential execution of its child activities using the general-purpose methods and events available on AEC and `Activity`. The WF runtime contains no knowledge of sequential activity execution; it only pays attention to the activity automaton and the containment relationships between activities in its role as enforcer of state transitions.

To see how easy it is to define other forms of control flow as composite activities, let's write a composite activity that executes its child activities in an interleaved manner.

The `Interleave` activity shown in Listing 3.16 implements an AND join by first scheduling the execution of all child activities in a single burst and waiting for them all to complete before reporting its own completion.

Listing 3.16   `Interleave` **Activity**

```
using System;
using System.Collections;
using System.Workflow.ComponentModel;

namespace EssentialWF.Activities
{
  public class Interleave : CompositeActivity
  {
    protected override ActivityExecutionStatus Execute(
      ActivityExecutionContext context)
    {
      if (this.EnabledActivities.Count == 0)
        return ActivityExecutionStatus.Closed;

      IList<Activity> shuffled = ShuffleList(EnabledActivities);

      foreach (Activity child in shuffled)
      {
        child.Closed += ContinueAt;
        context.ExecuteActivity(child);
      }

      return ActivityExecutionStatus.Executing;
    }

    void ContinueAt(object sender,
      ActivityExecutionStatusChangedEventArgs e)
    {
      e.Activity.Closed -= ContinueAt;

      ActivityExecutionContext context =
        sender as ActivityExecutionContext;

      foreach (Activity child in this.EnabledActivities)
      {
        if ((child.ExecutionStatus !=
             ActivityExecutionStatus.Initialized)
          && (child.ExecutionStatus !=
             ActivityExecutionStatus.Closed))
          return;
      }
```

```
      context.CloseActivity();
    }

    // ShuffleList method elided for clarity
  }
}
```

We will discuss the finer points of the `Interleave` activity's execution (which induces a form of pseudo-concurrency) a bit later in this chapter. First, though, let's look at the mechanics of how `Interleave` executes, just as we did for `Sequence`.

You can see right away that the code for `Interleave` is quite similar to that of `Sequence`. In the `Execute` method, all of the child activities are scheduled for execution, not merely the first one as with `Sequence`. In the implementation of `ContinueAt`, the `Interleave` reports itself as completed only if all child activities are in the `Closed` state.

There is one other interesting line of code:

```
IList<Activity> shuffled = ShuffleList(EnabledActivities);
```

`ShuffleList` is presumed to be a private helper method that simply shuffles the list of child activities into some random order. The `Interleave` activity will work just fine without `ShuffleList`, but we have added it so that users of `Interleave` cannot predict or rely upon the order in which child activities are scheduled for execution.

The XAML in Listing 3.17 is an `Interleave` activity that contains a set of `WriteLine` child activities.

Listing 3.17 Interleaved Execution of `WriteLine` Activities

```
<Interleave x:Name="i1" xmlns="http://EssentialWF/Activities"
xmlns:x="http://schemas.microsoft.com/winfx/2006/xaml">
  <WriteLine x:Name="w1" Text="One" />
  <WriteLine x:Name="w2" Text="Two" />
  <WriteLine x:Name="w3" Text="Three" />
  <WriteLine x:Name="w4" Text="Four" />
</Interleave>
```

Running the program in Listing 3.17 may result in the following output:

```
Four
Two
```

```
Three
One
```

Or the following:

```
Three
One
Four
Two
```

Or the following:

```
One
Two
Three
Four
```

Or any of the other possible orderings of the four strings printed by the four `WriteLine` activities.

Let's trace through the execution of an instance of this program, showing the scheduler work queue and program state. The program is started exactly like the one we developed earlier with `Sequence`; an item is placed in the scheduler work queue representing a call to the `Execute` method of the root activity, and the root activity is placed in the `Executing` state (see Figure 3.15).

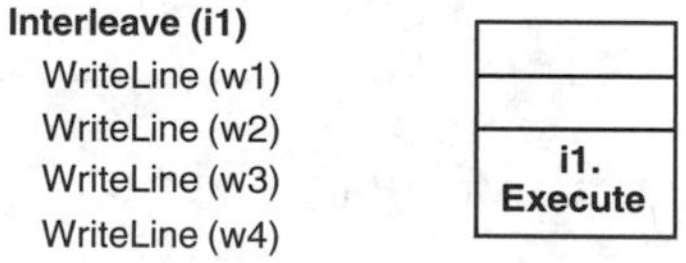

Figure 3.15   WF program instance in Listing 3.17 after `WorkflowInstance.Start`

Let's assume that the call to `ShuffleList` results in the following ordering of child activities: w2, w4, w1, w3. When the `Execute` method of `Interleave` returns, the program state is as shown in Figure 3.16.

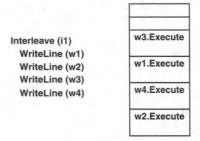

Figure 3.16 WF program instance in Listing 3.17 after `Interleave.Execute`

Now all four child activities are queued for execution and all four child activities of the `Interleave` are in the *Executing* state. The dispatcher will pick the item from the front of the queue (`Execute` "w2"). This will cause the `Execute` method of `WriteLine` named "w2" to be invoked. When this method returns, "Two" will have been printed to the console and the state of the program is as shown in Figure 3.17.

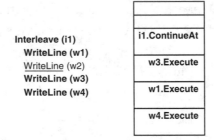

Figure 3.17 WF program instance in Listing 3.17 after `WriteLine` "w2" completes

As expected, because `Interleave` has subscribed to the `Closed` event of each child activity, there is a callback to the `ContinueAt` method present in the scheduler work queue. This item, however, sits behind three other items—the execution handlers for the `Execute` methods of w4, w1, and w3. The process outlined for w2 will therefore repeat three more times, resulting in the state shown in Figure 3.18.

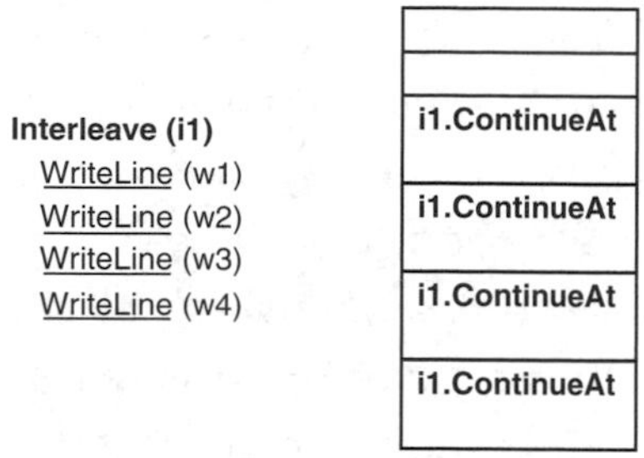

i1.ContinueAt
i1.ContinueAt
i1.ContinueAt
i1.ContinueAt

Interleave (i1)
　WriteLine (w1)
　WriteLine (w2)
　WriteLine (w3)
　WriteLine (w4)

Figure 3.18　WF program instance in Listing 3.17 after `WriteLine` "w4" completes

At this point, all four `WriteLine` activities have completed. The `Interleave` activity, though, has not actually received any notifications because its work items are still in the scheduler work queue. The four work items in the scheduler work queue are all resumptions of the same bookmark. The resumption point is the `ContinueAt` method of `Interleave`; the four work items differ only in the `EventArgs` data that is the payload of each resumed bookmark.

When the first work item is delivered to `Interleave`, the logic of the `ContinueAt` method will determine that all child activities are in the `Closed` state, so the `Interleave` itself is reported as complete. When the other three callbacks are subsequently dispatched, the WF runtime observes that the `Interleave` is already in the *Closed* state, so the callbacks are not delivered (they are simply discarded); delivery of these callbacks would violate the activity automaton because the `Interleave` cannot resume execution once it is in the *Closed* state.

Now, what we have seen in the execution of this WF program is quite a bit different than what we saw for the WF program that used `Sequence`. Things get even more interesting, though, if each child activity of the `Interleave` is not a simple activity like `WriteLine`, but a `Sequence` (which might contain other `Interleave` activities). Furthermore, it's clearly not very interesting or useful to simply execute `WriteLine` activities in an interleaved manner. It is much more realistic for each branch to be performing work that depends upon external input. In this way, the ordering of the execution of activities is determined, in part, by the timing of `EnqueueItem` operations performed by external code on WF program queues. By modeling these interactions in an `Interleave`, no branch is blocked by any other (because activities use bookmarks when their execution awaits external stimulus) and the execution of the activities within the branches can interleave.

As we know, the `Interleave` activity uses an explicit shuffling technique to decide the ordering in which its child activities are scheduled for execution. The influence of `Interleave`, however, ends there. If a `Sequence` activity is added as a child activity of an `Interleave`, the `Interleave` controls when the `Sequence` executes, but only the `Sequence` controls when its child activities are executed.

The XAML in Listing 3.18 is an `Interleave` with a set of `Sequence` child activities that contain child activities. The name of the WF program queue created by `ReadLine` in its `Initialize` method is the name of the activity. So, four WF program queues will be created during the initialization of a WF program instance, and these WF program queues are named r1, r2, r3, and r4.

Listing 3.18   Interleaved Execution of Sequence **Activities**

```
<Interleave x:Name="il" xmlns="http://EssentialWF/Activities"
xmlns:x="http://schemas.microsoft.com/winfx/2006/xaml"
xmlns:wf="http://schemas.microsoft.com/winfx/2006/xaml/workflow">
  <Sequence x:Name="s1">
    <ReadLine x:Name="r1" />
    <WriteLine x:Name="w1" Text="{wf:ActivityBind r1,Path=Text}" />
    <ReadLine x:Name="r2" />
    <WriteLine x:Name="w2" Text="{wf:ActivityBind r2,Path=Text}" />
  </Sequence>
  <Sequence x:Name="s2">
    <ReadLine x:Name="r3" />
    <WriteLine x:Name="w3" Text="{wf:ActivityBind r3,Path=Text}" />
    <ReadLine x:Name="r4" />
    <WriteLine x:Name="w4" Text="{wf:ActivityBind r4,Path=Text}" />
  </Sequence>
</Interleave>
```

We are not going to go through the execution of an instance of this program step by step—it would take a few pages of diagrams—but we know enough about the execution logic of the `Sequence` and `Interleave` activities to predict what will happen. Assuming that no items are enqueued into any of the WF program queues, the program will reach the state shown in Figure 3.19.

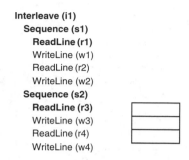

Interleave (i1)
  Sequence (s1)
    ReadLine (r1)
    WriteLine (w1)
    ReadLine (r2)
    WriteLine (w2)
  Sequence (s2)
    ReadLine (r3)
    WriteLine (w3)
    ReadLine (r4)
    WriteLine (w4)

Figure 3.19 WF program instance in Listing 3.18 after reaching ReadLine activities

At this point, the program is idle. Both Sequence activities have started executing, and each has, in turn, requested the execution of their first child activity (which happens to be a ReadLine activity in both cases). Each ReadLine activity is stuck waiting for an item to appear in its WF program queue. If the Interleave had a third child activity that was a Sequence of any number of WriteLine activities, then this Sequence would run to completion.

If we enqueue the string "hello" into WF program queue "r3", there will be an episode of action. The ContinueAt method of the ReadLine activity with name "r3" will be scheduled (the name of the WF program queue created by ReadLine is the same as its Name property). This will cause the ReadLine activity to complete, which will schedule notification of its Closed event to the enclosing Sequence "s2". That Sequence will schedule the execution of the WriteLine "w3" that follows the just-completed ReadLine. The WriteLine will get the string received by the ReadLine activity (via activity databinding) and write it to the console. The WriteLine will complete, again causing a notification to the enclosing Sequence. The Sequence will then move on to its third child activity, another ReadLine, which will now wait until an item is enqueued into its WF program queue.

The series of steps just described will result in the state of the program shown in Figure 3.20.

Interleave (i1)
  Sequence (s1)
    ReadLine (r1)
    WriteLine (w1)
    ReadLine (r2)
    WriteLine (w2)
  Sequence (s2)
    ReadLine (r3)
    WriteLine (w3)
    ReadLine(r4)
    WriteLine (w4)

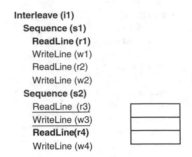

Figure 3.20   WF program instance in Listing 3.18 again in an idle state

This example is typical of the episodic execution we described at the outset of the chapter. As a result of stimulus from the external world, the WF program instance moves forward. And it is truly the composite activities that are driving the program's execution by providing the control flow; the WF runtime is passively dispatching whatever items appear in the scheduler work queue while enforcing adherence to the activity automaton.

Once you understand the activity automaton and the execution-related rules of activity composition, it is easy to model other control flow patterns beyond simple sequential and interleaved execution. This allows your programs to mirror more precisely whatever processes they are trying to coordinate. In the next chapter, we will look at several additional aspects of composite activity development that aid in building different kinds of control flow.

It may be helpful to pause here and consolidate what you've learned from this chapter so far. As an exercise, we suggest writing a custom composite activity. An appropriate choice on which to test your skills is `PrioritizedInterleave`. The `PrioritizedInterleave` activity executes its child activities in priority order. Each child activity has a property, named `Priority`, of type `int`.

When `PrioritizedInterleave` executes, first all child activities with a priority of 1 are executed in an interleaved manner; when those are completed, all child activities with a priority of 2 are executed (also in an interleaved manner). This continues until all child activities have been executed. As you might guess, the execution logic of `PrioritizedInterleave` is something of a combination of the logic we developed for `Sequence` and the logic we developed for `Interleave`.

Listing 3.19 shows an example WF program containing a `Prioritized-Interleave`. The seven child activities of the `PrioritizedInterleave` are grouped into three different sets according to the values of their `Priority` property. The best way to implement the `Priority` property is as an **attached property**, which supports the XAML syntax shown in Listing 3.19. Attached properties are covered in Chapter 7, "Advanced Authoring." You can take a simpler approach and add a `Priority` property to `WriteLine` and then test your `PrioritizedParallel` activity using the modified `WriteLine`.

Listing 3.19 WF Program that Is a `PrioritizedInterleave`

```
<PrioritizedInterleave xmlns="http://EssentialWF/Activities">
  <B PrioritizedInterleave.Priority="1" />
  <C PrioritizedInterleave.Priority="2" />
  <A PrioritizedInterleave.Priority="1" />
  <E PrioritizedInterleave.Priority="2" />
  <F PrioritizedInterleave.Priority="3" />
  <G PrioritizedInterleave.Priority="3" />
  <D PrioritizedInterleave.Priority="2" />
</PrioritizedInterleave>
```

This WF program is depicted in a more readable form in Figure 3.21, which conveys the interleaved execution that occurs within the groupings of child activities.

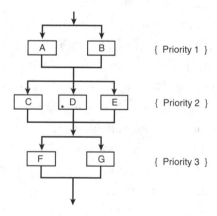

Figure 3.21 `PrioritizedInterleave` **activity containing three groupings**

You might conclude from Figure 3.21 that this WF program could just as easily be built using the `Sequence` and `Interleave` activities we developed previously. True, but there is another way of looking at things. Both `Sequence` and `Interleave` are nothing but degenerate cases of our `PrioritizedInterleave`, in which the priorities of the child activities are either all different or all the same, respectively. This is a simple but instructive example of the control flow flexibility afforded by the composition model of WF.

WF Threads

From the point of view of activities, the WF runtime makes no guarantee about which CLR thread is used to dispatch a work item in a scheduler work queue. It is possible for any two work items, even consecutively enqueued work items, to be dispatched using different threads.

It is the application hosting the WF runtime that decides how CLR threads are to be allocated to WF program instances (though the WF runtime does impose a limit of one thread at a time for a specific WF program instance). It is also solely the host application that determines when a WF program instance should be passivated. Typically, passivation occurs when a WF program instance becomes idle, but it is possible, as we will see in Chapter 5, for a WF program instance to be passivated even when its scheduler work queue is not empty. As a developer of activities, the safest assumption is that every work item is dispatched on a different thread. Although in practice the same CLR thread will be used to dispatch a set of work items, it is best to not make any assumption about the CLR thread on which activity methods are invoked. This means not storing data in the thread context or call context or, more generally, not relying on `Thread.CurrentThread` in any way.

The WF runtime does guarantee that the scheduler managing the work items for a single WF program instance utilizes *exactly one* CLR thread at a time, for a given episode of the WF program instance. In other words, the scheduler never performs concurrent dispatch of work items in its work queue. Dispatch always occurs one item at a time. Furthermore, the WF runtime never preempts the execution of a dispatched work item. Activities are counted upon to employ bookmarks when they are logically blocked, allowing them to yield the CLR thread while they await stimulus.

The fact that the WF runtime uses a single CLR thread at a time for a given WF program instance is a pragmatic decision. It is possible to imagine concurrent dispatch of work items, but the benefits appear to be outweighed by the drawbacks.

One big advantage of a single-threaded execution model is the simplification of activity development. Activity developers need not worry about concurrent execution of an activity's methods. Locking, preemption, and other aspects of multi-threaded programming are not a part of WF activity development, and these simplifications are important given WF's goal of broad adoption by .NET developers.

Some readers might object to the fact that the threading model of the WF runtime eliminates the possibility of true, or fine-grained, concurrency (the simultaneous use of more than one machine processor). Let's be clear: What is precluded is the possibility of true concurrency *within an instance of a WF program*. In any application where the number of simultaneously executing (non-idle) WF program instances tends to be greater than the number of machine processors, true concurrency would not buy you much. The design-time overhead of a vastly more challenging programming model for activities weighs down this approach, and mightily so in our estimation. Computations that benefit from true concurrency are, for WF programs, best abstracted as features of a service; the service can be made available to activities (using the service chaining techniques we've already described). In this way, the service can be executed in an environment optimized for true concurrency, which may or may not be on the machine on which the WF program instance is running.

True concurrency is a rather simple concept to describe, but the techniques for synchronization that are available in most mainstream programming paradigms are difficult to master and, when not applied properly, are notorious for causing hard-to-find bugs that make programs defective (or, perhaps, in the eyes of their users, capricious). The WF programming model arguably has found a sweet spot, given the types of problems that WF is intended to solve. WF program instances clearly allow interleaved (pseudo-concurrent) execution of activities, and WF makes it *easy to write and use* the constructs that permit interleaving. We have seen an example of such an activity, `Interleave`, and how essentially similar it is to `Sequence`, in both its implementation and its usage in a WF program.

Just like the CLR virtualizes a set of operating system threads, the WF runtime can be said to virtualize CLR threads. The interleaved execution of activities within a WF program instance is therefore not unlike the interleaved execution of CLR threads within an operating system process. Each child activity of an `Interleave` can be thought of as executing on a separate **WF thread**, though in fact this WF thread is a purely conceptual entity and does not have any physical manifestation in the WF programming model. Figure 3.22 depicts the relationship between these shadowy WF threads and actual CLR threads.

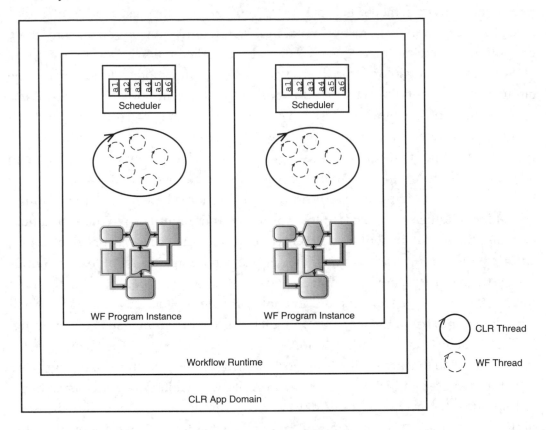

Figure 3.22   WF threads

This pattern of execution is sometimes called pseudo-concurrency or perceived parallelism.

Synchronized Access to State

Given the WF runtime's threading model, it should be clear that the synchronization primitives used in C# programs are not applicable in WF programs.

Synchronization primitives are not aware of the interleaved execution of WF threads. In fact, they can get you into quite a bit of trouble in a WF program and should be generally avoided. For example, if two activities in a WF program refer to some shared state (for instance, several fields of a third activity, accessed as properties of that activity), then CLR synchronization techniques will not be the right choice for ensuring synchronized access to the shared state. CLR locking primitives are generally not designed to survive and remain valid across passivation cycles of a WF program instance.

Put another way, since the WF programming model virtualizes threads of program execution, it must also carry the burden of providing synchronized access to shared data.

WF provides the ability to synchronize access to state shared by multiple WF threads in terms of a special composite activity defined in the `System.Workflow.ComponentModel` namespace. This activity is named `SynchronizationScopeActivity` and it executes its child activities sequentially.

`SynchronizationScopeActivity` is the WF programming model's synchronization primitive. It allows the developer of a WF program to draw boundaries around synchronization domains of (pseudo)concurrently executing activities, which, conceptually, run on different WF threads.

The `SynchronizationScopeActivity` type is shown in Listing 3.20.

Listing 3.20   `SynchronizationScopeActivity`

```
namespace System.Workflow.ComponentModel
{
  public sealed class SynchronizationScopeActivity : CompositeActivity
  {
    public ICollection<string> SynchronizationHandles { get; set; }

    /* *** other members *** */
  }
}
```

As you can see, the `SynchronizationScopeActivity` type carries a property called `SynchronizationHandles` of type `ICollection<string>`. This property holds a set of named **synchronization handles**. A synchronization handle is essentially a locking primitive.

The WF runtime guarantees that occurrences of `SynchronizationScope Activity` sharing a synchronization handle token will be executed serially without any interleaving of their contained activities. In other words, one `Synchronization ScopeActivity` will complete before the next one (that shares a synchronization handle with the first) begins. To avoid deadlocks, the WF runtime internally manages virtual locks (not CLR locks) corresponding to the synchronization handles specified by the occurrences of SynchronizationScopeActivity in a WF program. These virtual locks survive passivation of the WF program instance.

Before the execution of a SynchronizationScopeActivity begins, all of the virtual locks associated with that SynchronizationScopeActivity activity's set of synchronization handles are obtained.

Listing 3.21 shows a WF program that uses SynchronizationScopeActivity to provide synchronized execution of interleaving activities. Even though there is no actual shared data, the two occurrences of SynchronizationScopeActivity require the same virtual lock and therefore execute serially.

Listing 3.21   **Synchronization Using** SynchronizationScopeActivity

```
<Interleave xmlns="http://EssentialWF/Activities"
xmlns:x="http://schemas.microsoft.com/winfx/2006/xaml"
xmlns:wf="http://schemas.microsoft.com/winfx/2006/xaml/workflow" >
  <wf:SynchronizationScopeActivity SynchronizationHandles="h1">
    <WriteLine x:Name="w1" Text="One"/>
    <WriteLine x:Name="w2" Text="Two"/>
  </wf:SynchronizationScopeActivity>
  <wf:SynchronizationScopeActivity SynchronizationHandles="h1">
    <WriteLine x:Name="w3" Text="Three"/>
    <WriteLine x:Name="w4" Text="Four"/>
  </wf:SynchronizationScopeActivity>
</Interleave>
```

This WF program will always produce one of the following outputs:

```
One        Three
Two        Four
Three      One
Four       Two
```

There are only two possible outputs for the preceding program. The Interleave activity will schedule both of the SynchronizationScopeActivity activities. Whichever one is scheduled first acquires the virtual lock that protects the synchronization handle "h1". Once the lock is obtained, the second SynchronizationScopeActivity activity is not allowed to execute, even though it has a work item in the scheduler work queue. Only when the first `Synchro-nizationScopeActivity` transitions to the *Closed* state will the lock be released, and the second `SynchronizationScopeActivity` be permitted to execute.

In the preceding example, there is no interleaving of activity execution across the two occurrences of `SynchronizationScopeActivity`, due to the fact that they require the same lock. If we change the program by altering the value of the `SynchronizationHandles` property for one `SynchronizationScopeActivity` to "h2", then the presence of the two `SynchronizationScopeActivity` activities is meaningless because they are defining different synchronization domains. Interleaved execution of the activities contained within them can and will occur.

`SynchronizationScopeActivity` activities can be nested in a WF program. Each `SynchronizationScopeActivity` acts as a lock manager that is responsible for granting locks to its child activities and managing a wait list of activities waiting to acquire locks (the WF runtime acts as the lock manager for the root activity of the program).

`SynchronizationScopeActivity`, when it begins its execution, collects the locks corresponding to its synchronization handles as well as those for all nested `SynchronizationScopeActivity` activities.

Because a parent `SynchronizationScopeActivity` is guaranteed to start its execution before a `SynchronizationScopeActivity` nested within it, the parent acquires the locks needed for all of its nested child `SynchronizationScopeActivity` instances before executing them, and deadlocks are safely avoided.

For the WF program shown in Listing 3.22, either `SynchronizationScope-Activity` s1 or `SynchronizationScopeActivity` s4 will execute in its entirety before the other one begins executing. In this example, the locks required by s1 and s4 are the same (indicated by the synchronization handles "a", "b", and "c"). In fact, the execution of s1 and s4 will be serialized even if they share a single synchronization handle name in their respective subtrees.

Listing 3.22   Nested `SynchronizationScopeActivity` Declarations

```
<Interleave xmlns="http://EssentialWF/Activities"
  xmlns:x="http://schemas.microsoft.com/winfx/2006/xaml"
  xmlns:wf="http://schemas.microsoft.com/winfx/2006/xaml/workflow">
  <wf:SynchronizationScopeActivity x:Name="s1"
    SynchronizationHandles="a">
```

```
  <Interleave x:Name="i1">
    <wf:SynchronizationScopeActivity x:Name="s2"
      SynchronizationHandles="b">
      <WriteLine x:Name="w3" Text="One"/>
      <WriteLine x:Name="w4" Text="Two"/>
    </wf:SynchronizationScopeActivity>
    <wf:SynchronizationScopeActivity x:Name="s3"
      SynchronizationHandles="c">
      <WriteLine x:Name="w5" Text="Three"/>
      <WriteLine x:Name="w6" Text="Four"/>
    </wf:SynchronizationScopeActivity>
  </Interleave>
</wf:SynchronizationScopeActivity>
<wf:SynchronizationScopeActivity x:Name="s4"
  SynchronizationHandles="c">
  <Interleave x:Name="i2">
    <wf:SynchronizationScopeActivity x:Name="s5"
      SynchronizationHandles="b">
      <WriteLine x:Name="w9" Text="Five"/>
      <WriteLine x:Name="w10" Text="Six"/>
    </wf:SynchronizationScopeActivity>
    <wf:SynchronizationScopeActivity x:Name="s6"
      SynchronizationHandles="a">
      <WriteLine x:Name="w11" Text="Seven"/>
      <WriteLine x:Name="w12" Text="Eight"/>
    </wf:SynchronizationScopeActivity>
  </Interleave>
</wf:SynchronizationScopeActivity>
</Interleave>
```

SynchronizationScopeActivity provides a simple way to synchronize the inter-leaved execution of WF threads. Effectively, this synchronization technique orders the dispatch of operations in the scheduler work queue in accordance with the synchronization domains that are named by SynchronizationScopeActivity activities.

Where Are We?

This chapter introduced the activity automaton, which describes the lifecycle of any activity in a WF program instance. Our foray into custom activity development introduced the service-chaining capabilities of the WF runtime, as well as the use of bookmarks (and associated WF program queues) as a mechanism by which activities can receive stimulus from external entities.

We turned to composite activities next and discussed three—`Sequence`, `Interleave`, and `PrioritizedInterleave`—that provided insights into the flexibility of WF's model for control flow. Control flow patterns are a theme that will be continued in the next chapter.

We discussed the WF execution model and threading model, and specifically examined how the WF scheduler works. By looking at how the execution of various WF programs unfolds, we saw the nuts and bolts of how the scheduler performs its role as an intermediary for the dispatch of resumed bookmarks. As well, we learned that the WF runtime enforces the activity automaton and also protects the integrity of the containment relationships between activities in a WF program. Pseudo-concurrency within a WF program instance is caused by the interleaving of WF threads of execution.

The next chapter is a continuation of this one (feel free to bookmark it now). We will examine the *Canceling*, *Faulting*, and *Compensating* states of the activity automaton, and also introduce the WF programming model's support for explicit management of activity execution contexts.

4

Advanced Activity Execution

I N THE PREVIOUS CHAPTER, we learned about the basic lifecycle of an activity, which involves the *Initialized*, *Executing*, and *Closed* states of the activity automaton. We also explored the ramifications of the fact that the logical lifetime of activities differs from the lifetimes of CLR objects that transiently represent activities during those times that a WF program instance is not passivated. We developed several useful activities, including a few composite activities, and illustrated the central role of the `ActivityExecutionContext` as a facilitator of activity execution.

In this chapter, we will give more scrutiny to `ActivityExecutionContext` and introduce its vital role as a state boundary in WF programs. This will allow us to develop various iterative composite activities and other interesting control flow constructs. We will also learn about the other states of the activity automaton, and discuss activity cancellation, fault handling, and compensation.

Activity Execution Context

Until this point, we have straightforwardly used methods defined on `Activity ExecutionContext` (AEC), such as `GetService` and `ExecuteActivity`, in our activity examples. However, AEC has a larger role in the WF programming model that goes well beyond these methods. Arguably, AEC is overloaded with meanings and capabilities that could usefully be disentangled. Be that as it may, here we will catalog these meanings and capabilities, and provide a conceptual model for understanding and utilizing this key abstraction.

Let's begin with a brief summary of the functions of `ActivityExecution-Context` that we have already seen exercised.

The first role of AEC is as a container of services that is available to activities during their execution. This set of services is the same for all activities in all WF program instances (for a given application that hosts the WF runtime). Some services are provided by the WF runtime and are always obtainable from AEC; one such service we used in the `ReadLine` activity is the `WorkflowQueuingService`. Custom services can be offered by the application that hosts the WF runtime; such services are made available to activities, via AEC, by using the `AddService` method of `WorkflowRuntime`.

The fact that `ActivityExecutionContext` is a provider of services is made explicit by its implementation of the `System.IServiceProvider` interface, which defines the `GetService` method. `IServiceProvider` is a standard way to promote loose coupling between activities and the host application's implementations of services on which those activities depend.

The second role of `ActivityExecutionContext` is as an API surface through which activities can interact with the (internal) scheduler component of the WF runtime. For example, the `ExecuteActivity` method requests that a work item (corresponding to the invocation of the `Execute` method of a child activity) be added to the WF runtime's scheduler work queue. The `CloseActivity` method requests that the WF runtime finalize the current activity's transition to the *Closed* state, and resume the internal bookmark that notifies the parent composite activity of the activity's completion. AEC therefore abstracts the internal machinery of the WF runtime; even though we have explained the execution model of the WF runtime in terms of a scheduler and a work queue, these entities are not represented directly in the public API of the WF programming model.

To introduce the third, and subtlest, aspect of AEC, we need to return to the idea of WF program instances as continuations. The execution of a WF program instance is episodic, and at the end of each episode—when the WF program instance becomes idle—the instance can be persisted in durable storage as a continuation. This continuation, because it represents the entirety of the program instance's state that is necessary for resuming its execution, holds the relevant (internal) WF runtime execution state plus user-defined state, sometimes called the **application state**. The application state is nothing but the WF program instance's tree of activities (the actual CLR objects), which are usually stateful entities. The runtime state includes the state of the scheduler work queue, WF program queues, and book-keeping information about internally managed bookmarks (such as subscriptions to the `Activity.Closed` event).

The resumption point of a bookmark is called an **execution handler**, so we can refer to the (heap-allocated) execution state required by an execution handler as its **execution context**. Because an execution handler is typically a method on an activity, we will often refer to this execution context as **activity execution context**.

`ActivityExecutionContext` is a programmatic abstraction for precisely this execution context. `ActivityExecutionContext` is passed to every execution handler either as an explicit argument (as for `Activity.Execute`) or as the `sender` parameter in the case of execution handlers that conform to a standard .NET Framework event handler delegate type.

In the examples we've developed thus far in the previous chapters, this "execution context" aspect of AEC has not been apparent. When the host application calls the `WorkflowRuntime.CreateWorkflow` method, the WF runtime creates a new activity execution context that represents the execution context for the newly created WF program instance. This execution context is managed by the WF runtime because its lifecycle corresponds precisely to the lifecycle of the WF program instance. We call this execution context the **default execution context**.

The relationship between a WF program instance and its execution context is depicted in Figure 4.1.

The WF programming model might have stopped there, with a one-to-one mapping between every WF program instance and a corresponding execution context that is created and managed by the WF runtime. However, this leaves a gap in the execution model for activities.

Instead, the WF programming model allows a composite activity to explicitly create **subordinate execution contexts** during the execution of a WF program instance. A subordinate execution context, like the default execution context, consists of application state for a set of activities, along with the necessary runtime state. The application state of a subordinate execution context consists of (a copy of) a subtree of activities—a program fragment—the root of which is a child activity of the composite activity that created the subordinate AEC.

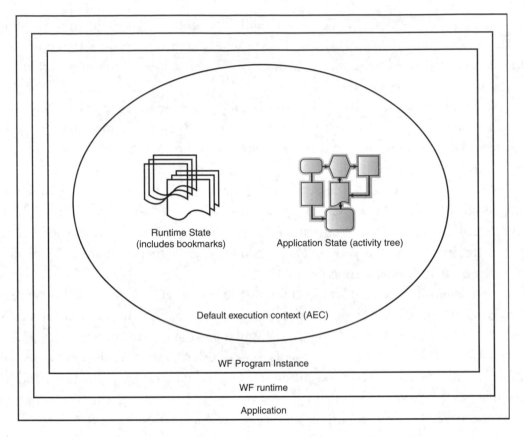

Figure 4.1   WF program instance and the default execution context

The API for creating and managing execution contexts is found in the `Activity-ExecutionContextManager` type, which we will refer to as the execution context manager, or `AECManager`. The capabilities of `AECManager` are the basis for a wide range of activity composition patterns, ranging from familiar iterative control flow to more exotic patterns including coroutine style-interleaved iterations, graphs of activities, fork and join patterns, state machines, and activity compensation.

Activity Execution Context Manager

The default execution context for a WF program instance is created and managed internally by the WF runtime. `AECManager`, which is shown in Listing 4.1, can be utilized by composite activities to explicitly create and manage subordinate execution contexts.

Listing 4.1   ActivityExecutionContextManager

```
namespace System.Workflow.ComponentModel
{
  public sealed class ActivityExecutionContextManager
  {
    public ActivityExecutionContext CreateExecutionContext(
      Activity activity);

    public ReadOnlyCollection<ActivityExecutionContext>
      ExecutionContexts { get; }

    public ActivityExecutionContext GetExecutionContext(
      Activity activity);

    public void CompleteExecutionContext(
      ActivityExecutionContext childContext);

    public void CompleteExecutionContext(
      ActivityExecutionContext childContext, bool forcePersist);

    public IEnumerable<Guid> PersistedExecutionContexts { get; }

    public ActivityExecutionContext GetPersistedExecutionContext(
      Guid contextGuid);
  }
}
```

AECManager is available to activity execution logic via the Execution-ContextManager property of ActivityExecutionContext, as shown in the following code fragment:

```
protected override ActivityExecutionStatus Execute(
  ActivityExecutionContext context)
{
    ActivityExecutionContextManager manager =
    context.ExecutionContextManager;

  ...
```

The role of AECManager is to allow a composite activity to create and manage subordinate execution contexts, which act as boundaries for the execution of subtrees of activities within a WF program. Activity subtrees are essentially program fragments whose roots are child activities of a composite activity within a WF program instance.

A new execution context is created by calling the `CreateExecutionContext` method of `AECManager`, passing as a parameter the child activity that is to be the root of the activity subtree that will be represented by the new AEC. This activity is called the **template activity** of the create operation. The state of the new AEC is essentially a deep copy of the application state of the activity subtree, of which the template activity is the root.

When a new execution context is created, it becomes a member of a collection of active execution contexts that are managed by the current composite activity. This collection is represented by the `ExecutionContexts` property of `AECManager`.

The execution state of the activity subtree within the new execution context (which is represented most visibly by the `ExecutionStatus` and `ExecutionResult` properties of all the activity objects, but also includes data managed internally by the WF runtime) is guaranteed to be pristine when the `CreateExecutionContext` method returns. To be specific, the activity objects that form the new instance of the subtree (within the new execution context) each have their `Initialize` method called so that they properly enter the activity automaton. This is exactly like the initialization of the WF program instance (the WF program's activity tree) that occurs within the default execution context when `WorkflowRuntime.CreateWorkflow` is called.

In this way, a running WF program instance actually can be viewed, from one vantage point, as a hierarchy (tree) of execution contexts, a simple example of which is shown in Figure 4.2.

All execution contexts except for the default AEC are explicitly created and managed by composite activities, so the execution context hierarchy will always structurally resemble the activity tree of the WF program. A new node in the execution context tree occurs precisely where a composite activity uses the `AECManager` to create a new execution context.

Rather than drilling deeper into the mechanics of execution context management, we will use some examples of composite activities that leverage `AECManager` to help bring this aspect of the WF programming model to life.

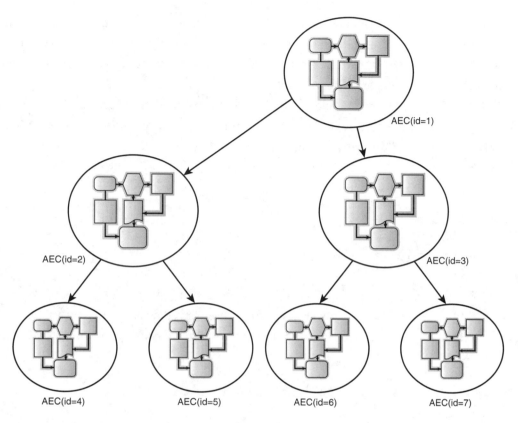

Figure 4.2   Hierarchy of execution contexts (the default AEC has an id of 1)

Iterative Control Flow

None of the composite activities we have encountered so far has had to exhibit iterative behavior. For example, Sequence and Interleave both execute each of their child activities once. However, many control flow constructs—such as the familiar while and foreach statements in C#—require repeated execution of a nested (child) statement.

The activity automaton appears to, and in fact does, preclude such repetition because there are no loops present in the state transition diagram. In particular, there is no path that takes an activity from the *Executing* state to another state and then back again to the *Executing* state. There are good reasons why the activity automaton has this characteristic, and they should become apparent in the examples we develop.

`AECManager` provides a composite activity with a way of repeating the execution of a child activity (actually, the subtree of activities rooted at a child activity, which is exactly what is required for iteration). We will use the mechanism to implement control flow constructs such as `while`.

Before going further, let's clarify terminology. By the term *activity iteration* (or, simply *iteration* in the context of WF), we are referring to any circumstance in which an activity within a WF program instance needs to execute more than one time. As a simple example, we need to be able to represent in a WF program, and then of course execute, iterative logic such as that in the following C# code snippet:

```
while (expression)
{
   string s = Console.ReadLine();
   Console.WriteLine(s);
}
```

Provided that we implement a `While` composite activity with the proper semantics, the representation of this Echo program in XAML is straightforward, as shown in Listing 4.2.

Listing 4.2   WF Program that Uses the `While` Activity

```
<While x:Name="while1" Condition="..."
xmlns="http://EssentialWF/Activities"
xmlns:x="http://schemas.microsoft.com/winfx/2006/xaml"
xmlns:wf="http://schemas.microsoft.com/winfx/2006/xaml/workflow">
  <Sequence x:Name="s1">
    <ReadLine x:Name="r1" />
    <WriteLine x:Name="w1" Text="{wf:ActivityBind r1,Path=Text}" />
  </Sequence>
</While>
```

In Chapter 7, "Advanced Authoring," we will show how the `While` activity can be associated with validation logic that limits its number of child activities to one. Here we will discuss how the `While` activity manages the repeated execution of its child activity.

The usual semantics of iteration requires a scoping boundary for data (which pulls along other requirements, such as variable binding rules, which we are ignoring here). This simply means that, within the scope of the construction governing the iteration, a given iteration does not see residual effects of the execution of the prior iterations. Iterations can certainly influence one another via shared data, but that data must be defined outside the scope of the iterative construction. Consider the following C# code:

```
while (expression)
{
  string s = "";
  Console.WriteLine(s);
  s = Console.ReadLine();
}
```

In order to compile this program with the C# compiler, the variable s must be assigned to prior to the WriteLine method call. More to the point, the value assigned to s by the ReadLine method call is lost when the first iteration finishes. The WriteLine will forever write the empty string, no matter what is entered at the console and read by the ReadLine.

The situation changes if the declaration of s occurs outside the while:

```
string s = "";
while (expression)
{
  Console.WriteLine(s);
  s = Console.ReadLine();
}
```

When s becomes shared data, any iterations of the while loop beyond the first one see the value that is assigned to s during the previous iteration.

In the case of a WF program, the activities (or, rather, the fields of activity objects) are the program's data. So, the WF program of Listing 4.2 must exhibit behavior similar to the C# program in which s is local to the scope within the while. The Write-Line activity's Text property takes its value from the Value property of the ReadLine activity *in the current iteration*.

If we rewrite the WF program by swapping the order of the WriteLine and ReadLine activities, the WriteLine will forever print the empty string. If this were not the case, there would be unexpected scoping of data and as a result the local maneuverings of one iteration of the While activity would influence (interfere with) the execution of subsequent iterations.

Thus, in order for iterative composite activities to work properly, there must be a way to provide a clean slate of local application data (and execution state) to each iteration. Practically speaking, for a WF program this conceptually amounts to either using (a) a freshly initialized activity subtree for each iteration, or (b) facilitating a reset of the activity subtree used in one iteration for use in the next iteration.

The "reset" approach is problematic. For one thing, if the WF scheduler were used to achieve the reset behavior, the resetting of an activity subtree would unfold asynchronously and necessitate a new "Resetting" state that doesn't correspond to any aspect of a real-world process. For another reason, it would complicate activity development, as activity writers would need to implement potentially difficult reset logic. Properties of an activity can be bound to fields and properties of other activities, so that an activity's reset logic might affect another executing activity adversely. Finally, the reset strategy would preclude (or at least make much more convoluted) certain use cases, including but not limited to interleaved execution of multiple instances of the same child activity, and activity compensation, both of which we will discuss later in this chapter.

The WF programming model therefore equates the normal semantics of a looping construct like `while` as one use case for subordinate execution contexts. Each iteration of an activity like `While` is housed within a distinct execution context that holds the state defined by the activity subtree over which the iteration is occurring. This scoping of state ensures the locality of the data, determines its lifetime, and establishes a framework for binding to data in other scopes. We will explore these aspects more fully in the examples to come.

It's time to write the `While` activity. We will assume that `While` has an associated validator component that assures only a single child activity is present within the `While` (this will be developed in Chapter 7).

The `While` activity is shown in Listing 4.3.

Listing 4.3   `While` **Activity**

```
using System;
using System.Workflow.ComponentModel;

namespace EssentialWF.Activities
{
  public class While : CompositeActivity
  {
    public static readonly DependencyProperty
```

```csharp
ConditionProperty = DependencyProperty.Register(
  "Condition",
  typeof(ActivityCondition),
  typeof(While),
  new PropertyMetadata(DependencyPropertyOptions.Metadata)
);

public ActivityCondition Condition
{
  get
  {
    return GetValue(ConditionProperty)
      as ActivityCondition;
  }

  set
  {
    SetValue(ConditionProperty, value);
  }
}

protected override ActivityExecutionStatus Execute(
  ActivityExecutionContext context)
{
  if (Condition != null && Condition.Evaluate(this, context))
  {
    ExecuteBody(context);
    return ActivityExecutionStatus.Executing;
  }

  return ActivityExecutionStatus.Closed;
}

void ExecuteBody(ActivityExecutionContext context)
{
  ActivityExecutionContextManager manager =
    context.ExecutionContextManager;

  ActivityExecutionContext newContext =
    manager.CreateExecutionContext(EnabledActivities[0]);

  Activity newActivity = newContext.Activity;

  newActivity.Closed += this.ContinueAt;
  newContext.ExecuteActivity(newActivity);
}

void ContinueAt(object sender,
    ActivityExecutionStatusChangedEventArgs e)
{
  e.Activity.Closed -= this.ContinueAt;
```

```
      ActivityExecutionContext context =
        sender as ActivityExecutionContext;

      ActivityExecutionContextManager manager =
        context.ExecutionContextManager;

      ActivityExecutionContext innerContext =
        manager.GetExecutionContext(e.Activity);

      manager.CompleteExecutionContext(innerContext);

      if ((this.ExecutionStatus ==
           ActivityExecutionStatus.Executing) &&
          Condition != null &&
          Condition.Evaluate(this, context))
      {
        ExecuteBody(context);
      }
      else
      {
        context.CloseActivity();
      }
    }
  }
}
```

The `While` activity has a `Condition` property of type `ActivityCondition`, and continues to execute iterations of its child activity until the condition evaluates to `false`. Evaluation of the condition occurs when the `While` begins its execution and, subsequently, upon the completion of each iteration.

The `ActivityCondition` type, which is in the `System.Workflow.Component-Model` namespace and is shown in Listing 4.4, represents a Boolean expression that can be evaluated by invoking `ActivityCondition.Evaluate`.

Listing 4.4   `ActivityCondition`

```
namespace System.Workflow.ComponentModel
{
  public abstract class ActivityCondition : DependencyObject
  {
    protected ActivityCondition();

    public abstract bool Evaluate(Activity activity,
      IServiceProvider provider);
  }
}
```

`ActivityCondition` is useful in other ways during the development of composite activities. For example, branching logic of the `if` or `switch` variety can be easily implemented with a composite activity that uses an attached property of type `ActivityCondition` on its ordered list of child activities. `ActivityCondition` is an abstract class. In Chapter 8, "Miscellanea," we will discuss the two generic derivatives of `ActivityCondition` provided by WF. You are also free to write your own custom derivative. If your activities requiring customizable conditional logic reference only the `ActivityCondition` base class, they are shielded from details of the various condition classes. This lets the user of the activity (the developer of the WF program) decide what is most appropriate for his solution. We can write a simplistic constant condition type that we can use throughout this chapter. This is shown in Listing 4.5.

Listing 4.5   `ConstantLoopCondition`

```
using System;
using System.Workflow.ComponentModel;

namespace EssentialWF.Activities
{
  public class ConstantLoopCondition : ActivityCondition
  {
    int counter = 0;

    public static readonly DependencyProperty
      MaxCountProperty = DependencyProperty.Register(
        "MaxCount",
        typeof(int),
        typeof(ConstantLoopCondition),
        new PropertyMetadata(DependencyPropertyOptions.Metadata)
      );

    public int MaxCount
    {
      get { return (int) GetValue(MaxCountProperty); }
      set { SetValue(MaxCountProperty, value); }
    }

    public override bool Evaluate(Activity activity,
      IServiceProvider provider)
    {
      return (counter++ < this.MaxCount);
    }
  }
}
```

Now we can rewrite Listing 4.2 by using `ConstantLoopCondition`. Listing 4.6 is an executable WF program (unlike Listing 4.2) and will loop through the `Sequence` three times.

Listing 4.6 An Executable Version of Listing 4.2

```
<While x:Name="while1" xmlns="http://EssentialWF/Activities"
xmlns:wf="http://schemas.microsoft.com/winfx/2006/xaml/workflow"
xmlns:x="http://schemas.microsoft.com/winfx/2006/xaml">
  <While.Condition>
    <ConstantLoopCondition MaxCount="3"/>
  </While.Condition>
  <Sequence x:Name="s1">
    <ReadLine x:Name="r1" />
    <WriteLine x:Name="w1" Text="{wf:ActivityBind r1,Path=Text}" />
  </Sequence>
</While>
```

Figure 4.3 shows the three execution contexts that are created, one for each of the iterations of the `While` activity.

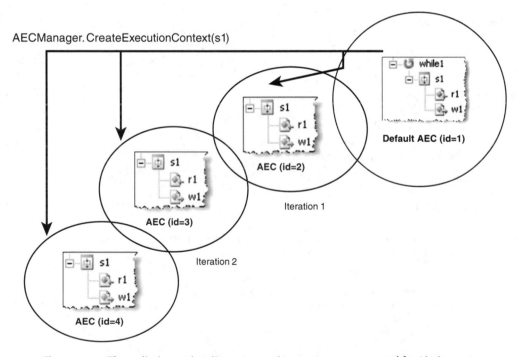

Figure 4.3   Three distinct subordinate execution contexts are created for Listing 4.6.

Returning to Listing 4.3, we see that in order to provide local state for each iteration, the `While` activity must use the `AECManager` to create a separate execution context for each iteration. The lone child activity of `While` is the template activity used in the creation of a new execution context. The newly created (subordinate) execution context contains a new instance of the template activity's subtree, and it is the root activity of this fresh subtree that is scheduled for execution. You can see that exactly the same pattern of subscribing to the `Closed` event of the scheduled activity that we used in `Sequence` and `Interleave` also is used here.

The subordinate AEC has an `Activity` property, which holds the new instance of the template activity. This new instance can be scheduled for execution, using the familiar `ExecuteActivity` method of AEC, so long as the AEC used to make the request is the execution context that corresponds to the newly created instance of the activity. The basic pattern is illustrated here:

```
ActivityExecutionContextManager manager =
    context.ExecutionContextManager;

Activity template = ...

ActivityExecutionContext newContext =
  manager.CreateExecutionContext(template);

Activity newInstance = newContext.Activity;

newInstance.Closed += this.ContinueAt;
newContext.ExecuteActivity(newInstance);
```

The important line of code is the last one; the newly created activity instance is scheduled for execution within the subordinate AEC.

The `IsDynamicActivity` property of `Activity` can be used to determine if a specific activity object is part of the default AEC, or instead has been manufactured as part of the creation of a dynamic execution context. In the preceding code, the `newInstance` object is a reference to an activity within a subordinate AEC. We can verify this fact by looking at the value of the `IsDynamicActivity` property:

```
System.Diagnostics.Debug.Assert(newActivity.IsDynamicActivity);
```

Because the `While` activity executes a new instance of the template activity for each iteration, the template activity itself (which is part of the default AEC) will always remain in the *Initialized* state. Only the instances of the template activity, which execute within subordinate execution contexts, move from the *Initialized* state to the *Executing* state and then to the *Closed* state.

This bookkeeping is not terribly difficult for the While activity to manage, but it does play a bit of havoc with the rest of the WF program's view of the While. There is no generalized way for code outside of While to locate the subordinate execution contexts that are dynamically created by While (or the activity objects within these execution contexts).

For this reason, it is a recommended practice for composite activities that dynamically create execution contexts to also provide helper properties or methods (depending upon what makes the most sense for a given composite activity) that assist external code in accessing appropriate iterations of a child activity. In the case of While, there is always at most one active iteration, so we can provide a property (as shown here) that returns the currently executing instance of the template activity:

```
public Activity CurrentIteration
{
  get
  {
    Activity template = EnabledActivities[0];
    Activity[] list = GetDynamicActivities(template);

    if (list.Length == 0) return null;
    return list[0];
  }
}
```

The GetDynamicActivities method is a protected method defined on the CompositeActivity class. It can be used to obtain the set of active instances of a child activity for which execution contexts have been dynamically created. In the case of While, there will always be at most one, but as we will see in the next section, this might not always be the case. GetDynamicActivities also by its nature implies that separate execution contexts could be created for different child activities (for those composite activities that allow multiple child activities).

Returning again to Listing 4.3, in its ExecuteBody method, the While activity subscribes for the Closed event of the newly created activity instance and schedules this activity for execution in its newly created AEC. As we have seen, the template activity never gets scheduled for execution and always remains in the ***Initialized*** state; it acts as a true declaration from which instances are manufactured at runtime. When a dynamic activity instance transitions to the ***Closed*** state, the `ContinueAt` method (of `While`) will be scheduled. `ContinueAt` retrieves the subordinate AEC using the `GetExecutionContext` method of `AECManager`, and then removes it from the list of active execution contexts by calling `CompleteExecutionContext`. In other words, when the execution of the activity subtree within a subordinate AEC is completed, the iteration is complete and that AEC can be discarded.

One additional aspect of subordinate execution contexts is related to activity databinding (the mechanics of which are discussed in Chapter 7). `ActivityBind` objects, though they reference a target activity by name, always implicitly reference an activity within a visible AEC. In other words, even though the instances of activities within the subtrees of different iterations carry the same values for their `Name` property, there is never any ambiguity about which activity instance an `Activity-Bind` object will use. This is depicted in Figure 4.4.

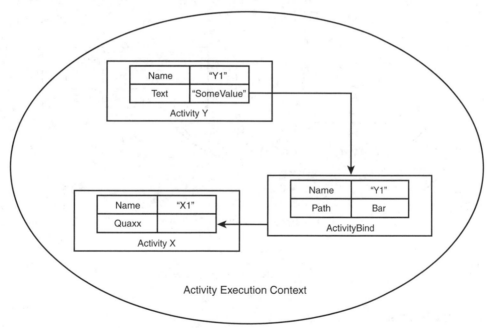

Figure 4.4   Activity execution context and `ActivityBind`

The current AEC and parent execution contexts (in the sense of the AEC hierarchy described earlier) are visible (as shown in Figure 4.5), but peer and subordinate AECs are not visible because this would introduce naming ambiguity. This is demonstrated in our example WF program (refer to Listing 4.6) that uses While, in which a property of the WriteLine activity is bound to a property of a peer Read-Line activity. In that example, resolution of the activity databinding expression always uses the ReadLine instance that is present within the same subordinate AEC as the WriteLine.

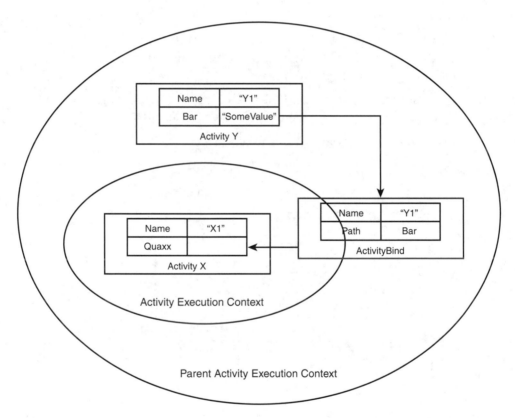

Figure 4.5 ActivityBind **across an activity execution context hierarchy**

Interleaved Iteration

The While activity demonstrates how the WF programming model enables scoped (iterative) execution of an activity subtree. Every iteration of While creates a new AEC, in which a new instance of the (template) child activity is executed.

There is nothing stopping us, though, from writing a composite activity that schedules more than one iteration of a child activity for execution at the same time. This does not make sense for `While`, but it is a quite natural and useful pattern when applied to the C# `foreach` construction. Instead of processing the items in a collection one after the other (for which use case we could write an ordinary `ForEach` activity that does what the C# `foreach` does), our `InterleavedForEach` activity will schedule the processing of all items in the collection simultaneously. Item processing is performed by a set of separately executed instances of the `Interleaved-ForEach` activity's single (template) child activity, with each instance comfortably ensconced within its own AEC.

Listing 4.7 shows an implementation of the `InterleavedForEach` activity.

Listing 4.7   `InterleavedForEach` **Activity**

```
using System;
using System.Collections;
using System.Workflow.ComponentModel;

namespace EssentialWF.Activities
{
  public class InterleavedForEach : CompositeActivity
  {
    int totalCount = 0;
    int closedCount = 0;

    public static readonly DependencyProperty
      IterationVariableProperty =
        DependencyProperty.RegisterAttached(
          "IterationVariable",
          typeof(object),
          typeof(InterleavedForEach)
        );

    public static object GetIterationVariable(object
      dependencyObject)
    {
      return ((DependencyObject)dependencyObject).
        GetValue(IterationVariableProperty);
    }

    public static void SetIterationVariable(object
      dependencyObject, object value)
    {
      ((DependencyObject)dependencyObject).SetValue(
        IterationVariableProperty, value);
    }
```

```
public static readonly DependencyProperty CollectionProperty =
  DependencyProperty.Register(
    "Collection",
    typeof(IEnumerable),
    typeof(InterleavedForEach)
  );

public IEnumerable Collection
{
  get { return (IEnumerable) GetValue(CollectionProperty); }
  set { SetValue(CollectionProperty, value); }
}

protected override ActivityExecutionStatus Execute(
  ActivityExecutionContext context)
{
  if (Collection == null)
    return ActivityExecutionStatus.Closed;

  Activity template = this.EnabledActivities[0];
  ActivityExecutionContextManager manager =
    context.ExecutionContextManager;

  foreach (object item in Collection)
  {
    totalCount++;
    ActivityExecutionContext newContext =
      manager.CreateExecutionContext(template);
    Activity newActivity = newContext.Activity;

    InterleavedForEach.SetIterationVariable(newActivity, item);

    newActivity.Closed += this.ContinueAt;
    newContext.ExecuteActivity(newActivity);
  }

  if (totalCount == 0)
    return ActivityExecutionStatus.Closed;

  return ActivityExecutionStatus.Executing;
}

void ContinueAt(object sender,
  ActivityExecutionStatusChangedEventArgs e)
{
  e.Activity.Closed -= this.ContinueAt;

  ActivityExecutionContext context =
    sender as ActivityExecutionContext;
  ActivityExecutionContextManager manager =
    context.ExecutionContextManager;
```

```
      ActivityExecutionContext innerContext =
        manager.GetExecutionContext(e.Activity);
      manager.CompleteExecutionContext(innerContext);

      if (totalCount == ++closedCount)
        context.CloseActivity();
    }

    public Activity[] ActiveIterations
    {
      get
      {
        if (this.EnabledActivities.Count > 0)
        {
          Activity template = EnabledActivities[0];
          return GetDynamicActivities(template);
        }
        return null;
      }
    }
  }
}
```

The code for `InterleavedForEach` is not unlike that of our `Interleave` activity. These two activities really are doing quite similar things, except that for `InterleavedForEach`, the number of iterations (number of instances of a *single* child activity) is determined dynamically (at runtime) by the size of the associated collection. In contrast, the list of child activities of an `Interleave` is described statically.

Just as with `While`, we should also implement a helper method on `InterleavedForEach` that provides external code with access to the currently running iterations. This is shown in Listing 4.8, which shows the implementation of an `ActiveIterations` property. In the case of the `InterleavedForEach`, because each iteration is effectively keyed by a data item (that was taken from the `Collection` property), we could also provide a useful lookup method that accepts this data item (or some representation of it) as a parameter and returns the activity of the appropriate iteration, if it is still executing.

After an iteration completes, the `InterleavedForEach` activity closes the corresponding subordinate execution context. That iteration's activity object is then no longer an element of the `ActiveIterations` array.

Listing 4.8   `InterleavedForEach.ActiveIterations`

```
public Activity[] ActiveIterations
{
  get
  {
    Activity template = EnabledActivities[0];
    return GetDynamicActivities(template);
  }
}
```

One important detail in the implementation of `InterleavedForEach` has to do with the handoff of data from the collection to an iteration of the template activity. A number of other viable strategies exist, but in this example we are taking a simple approach. The ith item in the collection is given to the ith iteration of the child activity in the form of an attached property, called `IterationVariable`. The item can then be easily retrieved programmatically, using the standard pattern for attached properties, by activity code within the corresponding AEC:

```
Activity a = ...
object o = InterleavedForEach.GetIterationVariable(a);
```

The `InterleavedForEach` activity is a useful construction for modeling real-world control flow. For example, the participants in a document review might be indicated as a list of names. For each participant, a document review task should be assigned and managed until it is completed. In many such situations, the assignees are allowed to complete their tasks simultaneously, making the management of a single task a natural fit for the template activity within an `InterleavedForEach`. The complexity of managing multiple subordinate execution contexts is entirely hidden from the WF program developer.

One requirement that `InterleavedForEach` places upon the underlying WF execution model (which we discussed earlier in this chapter) is that peer execution contexts are isolated and cannot interfere with each other. Just as we described earlier for `While`, each iteration must operate on local data. Stated differently, each iteration executes a local instance of the activity subtree.

The WF runtime enforces that all subordinate execution contexts must be completed (the `ExecutionContexts` collection is empty) in order for a composite activity to move to the *Closed* state. This is just an extension of the statement that all child activities of a composite activity must be in the *Initialized* state or the *Closed* state in order for the composite activity to move to the *Closed* state.

Completed Activity Execution Contexts

Our examples so far assume that after a subordinate AEC is completed, it can be discarded. This simple AEC lifecycle is sufficient for the implementation of many composite activities. But it is also possible to serialize a completed AEC for retrieval at a later time. A completed AEC will be serialized (as part of the state of the WF program instance) instead of discarded if you call the overload of `CompleteExecutionContext` that accepts two parameters, passing `true` as the value of the second parameter. The name of this parameter is `forcePersist` and, as its name indicates, it determines whether the state of the completed AEC should be saved or not. The overload of `CompleteExecutionContext` that takes one parameter simply calls the second overload passing a value of `false` for `forcePersist`.

A completed AEC will be saved automatically (regardless of the value of `forcePersist` parameter) if there are successfully executed *compensatable activities* within the completed activity subtree of that AEC. In order for activity compensation to work, it must be possible to resurrect a previously completed AEC and continue its execution by scheduling its compensation logic. Thus, the potential for compensation overrides a `false` value for the `forcePersist` parameter. Compensation will be discussed fully later in this chapter; for now, it is enough to appreciate that compensation logic requires the restoration of a previously completed AEC.

Additional use cases for this advanced feature will be discussed in Appendix B, "Control Flow Patterns."

AEC and WF Program Passivation

Because multiple instances of an activity can execute (each in a different AEC), there is a need to manage the lifecycle of those activity objects in an AEC-specific manner.

The WF runtime will invoke `Activity.OnActivityExecutionContextLoad` on the activities of a newly created AEC as part of a composite activity's invocation of the `AECManager.CreateExecutionContext` method. This allows the dynamically created activities within the new AEC a chance to allocate resources specific to

the lifetime of that AEC. Similarly, the WF runtime will invoke `Activity.`
`OnActivityExecutionContextUnload` on the activities in an AEC as part of the
`AECManager.CompleteExecutionContext` method.

Listing 4.9 shows the definition of these methods on the `Activity` class.

Listing 4.9   AEC Loading and Unloading

```
namespace System.Workflow.ComponentModel
{
  public class Activity
  {
    protected virtual void OnActivityExecutionContextLoad(
      IServiceProvider provider);

    protected virtual void OnActivityExecutionContextUnload(
      IServiceProvider provider);

    /* *** other members *** */
  }
}
```

The execution lifetime of an AEC (including the default AEC) does not necessarily match the in-memory lifetime of the activity objects that are executed within the AEC. Specifically, the lifetime of a subordinate AEC (bracketed by invocation of `CreateExecutionContext` and `CompleteExecutionContext`) may span multiple passivation cycles for the WF program instance. Consider again the program of Listing 4.6. Each iteration of the `While` executes the `Sequence` activity (and its nested `ReadLine` and `WriteLine` activities) in a separate subordinate AEC. Each iteration blocks until the hosting application enqueues an item into the WF program queue that is created by the active instance of the `ReadLine` activity. Because the scheduler's work queue might become empty at this point, the WF program instance can passivate. The program will be reactivated and resume the execution of the `ReadLine` activity after the external stimulus arrives.

Upon WF program passivation, the default AEC and all active subordinate execution context (which in the case of `While` will be at most one) will be saved. As a part of disposing the program instance, the WF runtime will invoke `OnActivity-ExecutionContextUnload` on the activities in each of the execution contexts, allowing all activity instances to clean up resources allocated for the in-memory lifecycle of the AEC. Correspondingly, the WF runtime will call

`OnActivityExecutionContextLoad` on the activities of all active execution contexts in the program instance each time the program is brought back into memory.

A sequence diagram that shows a single iteration of `While` is depicted in Figure 4.6.

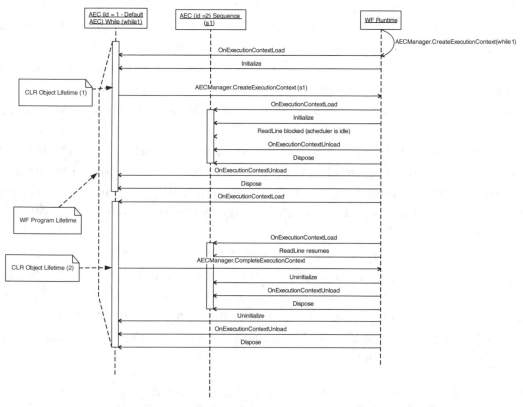

Figure 4.6 AEC lifetime, for a single iteration of the `While` activity in Listing 4.2

Cancellation

In real-world processes, it is common to begin two or more activities simultaneously, but then demand that only a subset of the activities need to complete in order to reach the desired goal. For example, when you are trying to sell your car, you might simultaneously buy a classified advertisement in the local newspaper, place a listing at the top Internet used car marketplaces, and put a sign in the window of your car. If a neighbor sees the sign and offers to buy the car, the other avenues used to locate buyers are no longer needed and should be abandoned.

In C# programs, it is certainly possible to create multiple threads in order to perform work concurrently. The basic capabilities of threads, though, do not directly provide patterns for orderly cancellation of work; custom solutions must be devised. After all, we don't want to pay for newspaper and Internet advertisements after the car is sold. Furthermore, if the actual work to be done is performed outside of the C# program—perhaps by remote web services or by an application that waits for input from people (a car can take weeks to sell)—then the use of threads to manage this work is not workable anyway (as we discussed in Chapter 1, "Deconstructing WF").

We will now see how easy it is to write a WF composite activity that implements exactly the semantic required in the car sale scenario. Once you are on the road to developing these kinds of composite activities, you will be able to more precisely translate the requirements of real-world processes to the control flow of the WF programs you write.

The `AnyOneWillDo` composite activity used in the program of Listing 4.10 is very similar to `Interleave` because `AnyOneWillDo` will schedule all of its child activities for execution in a single burst during the `AnyOneWillDo.Execute` method. `AnyOneWillDo` differs from `Interleave` in that after a *single* child activity reports its completion (moves to the *Closed* state from the *Executing* state), the `AnyOneWillDo` activity is logically ready to report its own completion.

Listing 4.10   **XAML that Uses an** `AnyOneWillDo` **Activity**

```
<AnyOneWillDo ... >
  <SellCarWithNewspaperAd />
  <SellCarOnline />
  <SellCarWithSignInWindow />
</AnyOneWillDo>
```

There is a catch, though. The WF runtime will not allow any composite activity to move to the *Closed* state while child activities within that composite activity are still in the *Executing* state. A composite activity cannot logically be done with its work if its child activities are still executing (and are therefore not finished with their work).

A composite activity can only transition to the *Closed* state if every one of its child activities is either in the *Initialized* state (which means it was never asked to do its work) or in the *Closed* state. Because this enforcement applies recursively to those child activities that themselves are composite activities, it is assured that the entire subtree of a composite activity is quiet (that is, *Initialized* or *Closed*) before the composite activity itself moves to the *Closed* state.

To get around this, `AnyOneWillDo` could wait for the completion of all child activities, but that would defeat the purpose and take us back to exactly what `Interleave` does. Instead, `AnyOneWillDo` can request *cancellation* of the executing child activities after one of the child activities completes.

The Canceling State

The cancellation of a child activity is requested via the `ActivityExecutionContext` in exactly the same way as the request to schedule the execution of a child activity. Cancellation is a scheduled dispatch to the `Cancel` method of the child activity.

Listing 4.11 shows the `CancelActivity` method of AEC, along with `ExecuteActivity`, which we have used already.

Listing 4.11   `ActivityExecutionContext.CancelActivity`

```
namespace System.Workflow.ComponentModel
{
  public sealed class ActivityExecutionContext : ...
  {
    public void CancelActivity(Activity activity);

    public void ExecuteActivity(Activity activity);

    /* *** other members *** */
  }
}
```

We will return in a moment to what the child activities might implement in their `Cancel` method; first let's look at the code in `AnyOneWillDo` that achieves the cancellation.

Listing 4.12 shows a modified version of the `ContinueAt` method that we first developed for `Interleave`. When `AnyOneWillDo` receives notification that a child activity has moved to the *Closed* state, it calls the `CompletionThresholdReached` method.

`CompletionThresholdReached` is assumed to be a private helper method that iterates through the child activities, checking their `ExecutionStatus` and `ExecutionResult` properties to see if the necessary condition for completion has been met. In the case of `AnyOneWillDo`, if one child activity has successfully completed its execution, then all other child activities that are not yet in the *Closed* state (the logic of the `Execute` method, which is the same as that of `Interleave`, ensures that no child activity is still in the *Initialized* state) are scheduled for cancellation.

Listing 4.12   `AnyOneWillDo.ContinueAt`

```
public class AnyOneWillDo : CompositeActivity
{
  ...

  void ContinueAt(object sender,
    ActivityExecutionStatusChangedEventArgs e)
  {
    e.Activity.Closed -= this.ContinueAt;

    ActivityExecutionContext context =
      sender as ActivityExecutionContext;

    if (CompletionThresholdReached())
    {
      bool okToClose = true;
      foreach (Activity child in this.EnabledActivities)
      {
        ActivityExecutionStatus status = child.ExecutionStatus;
        if (status == ActivityExecutionStatus.Executing)
        {
          okToClose = false;
          context.CancelActivity(child);
        }
        else if (status != ActivityExecutionStatus.Closed)
        {
          okToClose = false;
        }
      }

      if (okToClose)
        context.CloseActivity();
    }
  }
}
```

The call to `CancelActivity` immediately moves the child activity into the *Canceling* state from the *Executing* state. Just as with normal execution, it will be up to the child activity to decide when to transition to *Closed* from *Canceling*. When that transition does happen, the `AnyOneWillDo` activity will be notified of this change (it has already subscribed for the `Closed` event of the child activity, when it was scheduled for execution). Thus, only when all child activities are *Closed*, either by virtue of having completed their execution or by having been canceled, will the `AnyOneWillDo` activity report its own completion and move to the *Closed* state. At this point, only one of the child activities will have completed. The car has been sold, *and* the other work items that had started simultaneously have been canceled.

The `AnyOneWillDo` example illustrates how easily cancellation becomes a normal part of WF program execution. Cancellation is a natural and necessary characteristic of many real-world processes. In general, activities that begin their execution cannot assume that they will be allowed to complete their work (unless the work can be finished entirely within the `Execute` method).

In other words, real-world control flow has a natural notion of **early completion**. This stands in stark contrast to C# control flow. In composite activities that embody elements of real-world processes, the execution of some child activities must be canceled when the overall goal of the set of child activities has been met.

Let's now consider what happens to an activity that has been scheduled for cancellation. The relevant method of `Activity` is the `Cancel` method, which has the same signature as `Execute`:

```
namespace System.Workflow.ComponentModel
{
  public class Activity : DependencyObject
  {
    protected internal virtual ActivityExecutionStatus Cancel(
      ActivityExecutionContext context);

    /* *** other members *** */
  }
}
```

As we learned in the previous section, the `Cancel` method is the execution handler that is scheduled when a composite activity calls the `CancelActivity` method of AEC, passing the child activity to be canceled as the parameter.

The default implementation of the `Cancel` method, defined by the `Activity` class, is to immediately return a value of `ActivityExecutionStatus.Closed`, indicating that cancellation is complete. Activities needing to perform custom cancellation logic can override this method and add whatever cancellation logic is required.

Figure 4.7 depicts the *Canceling* state within the activity automaton.

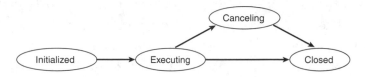

Figure 4.7 The Canceling state in the activity automaton

Just as with execution, activity cancellation logic might require interaction with external entities; an activity may therefore remain in the *Canceling* state indefinitely before reporting the completion of its cancellation logic and moving to the *Closed* state. This is exactly the same pattern as normal activity execution.

The `Wait` activity that we developed in Chapter 3, "Activity Execution," is a simple example of an activity that should perform custom cancellation work. If a `Wait` activity is canceled, it needs to cancel its timer because the timer is no longer needed. The `Wait` activity can also delete the WF program queue that is used to receive notification from the timer service. The cancellation logic of the `Wait` activity is shown in Listing 4.13.

Listing 4.13 `Wait` **Activity's Cancellation Logic**

```
using System;
using System.Workflow.ComponentModel;
using System.Workflow.Runtime;

namespace EssentialWF.Activities
{
  public class Wait : Activity
  {
    private Guid timerId;

    // other members per Listing 3.11
    ...

    protected override ActivityExecutionStatus Cancel(
      ActivityExecutionContext context)
```

```
  {
    WorkflowQueuingService qService =
      context.GetService<WorkflowQueuingService>();

    if (qService.Exists(timerId))
    {
      TimerService timerService =
        context.GetService<TimerService>();

      timerService.CancelTimer(timerId);
      qService.DeleteWorkflowQueue(timerId);
    }

    return ActivityExecutionStatus.Closed;
  }
 }
}
```

The `Cancel` method of the `Wait` activity does two things: It cancels the timer that was previously established using the `TimerService`, and it deletes the WF program queue that served as the location for the `TimerService` to deliver a notification when the timer elapsed.

When a canceled activity's transition to *Closed* occurs, its `ExecutionResult` property will from that point forward have a value of *Canceled*.

There is one subtle aspect to this cancellation logic, which is represented by the fact that the aforementioned cleanup is wrapped in a conditional check to see whether the WF program queue actually exists. The WF program queue will only exist if the `Execute` method of the `Wait` activity was executed. It would seem that this is an assertion we can make. But in fact it is not so. It is possible, though certainly not typical, for a `Wait` activity to move to the *Executing* state (when its parent schedules it for execution), and then to the *Canceling* state (when its parent schedules it for cancellation) without its `Execute` method ever being dispatched.

If the scheduler dequeues from its work queue an item representing the invocation of an activity's `Execute` method, but that activity has already moved to the *Canceling* state, then the work item corresponding to the `Execute` method is discarded. Invocation of the `Execute` execution handler would violate the activity automaton (because the activity is now in the *Canceling* state), and the reasonable expectation of the parent composite activity that had scheduled the cancellation of the activity. In short, the WF runtime enforces the activity automaton when scheduler work items are enqueued (for example, an activity cannot be canceled if it is already in the *Closed* state), and also when they are dequeued for dispatch.

In the case of the `Wait` activity, if the WF program queue does not exist, the `Execute` method was never actually invoked. If the `Execute` method was not invoked, no timer was established and hence there is no need to call the `Cancel-Timer` method of the `TimerService`.

We can illustrate the subtlety just described with a somewhat pathological composite activity, which schedules a child activity for execution and then requests its cancellation in consecutive lines of code. This activity's `Execute` method is shown in Listing 4.14.

Listing 4.14 Cancellation Overtakes Execution

```
using System;
using System.Workflow.ComponentModel;

public class ChangedMyMind : CompositeActivity
{
  protected override ActivityExecutionStatus Execute(
    ActivityExecutionContext context)
  {
    Activity child = this.EnabledActivities[0];
    child.Closed += this.ContinueAt;

    PrintStatus(child);
    context.ExecuteActivity(child);
    PrintStatus(child);
    context.CancelActivity(child);
    PrintStatus(child);

    return ActivityExecutionStatus.Executing;
  }

  void ContinueAt(object sender,
    ActivityExecutionStatusChangedEventArgs e)
  {
    PrintStatus(e.Activity);
  }

  void PrintStatus(Activity a)
  {
    Console.WriteLine(a.Name + " is " + a.ExecutionStatus +
      " : " + a.ExecutionResult);
  }
}
```

Though an extreme case, the ChangedMyMind activity suffices to illustrate the situation we have described. A request to schedule invocation of an activity's Cancel method is always made *after* a request to schedule invocation of that activity's Execute method; however, the dispatcher is not able to invoke Execute (dispatch the first work item) before the cancellation request comes in. Hence, when the Cancel work item lands in the scheduler work queue, the Execute work item will still also be in the work queue. The Execute work item has been logically overtaken because the enqueue of the Cancel work item moves the activity to the *Canceling* state. When the Execute work item is dequeued by the scheduler, it is ignored (and is not dispatched) because the target activity is already in the *Canceling* state.

Now let's consider the following WF program:

```
<ChangedMyMind ... >
  <Trace x:Name="e1" />
</ChangedMyMind>
```

Let's assume that the Trace activity prints a message when its Execute method and Cancel method is actually called:

```
using System;
using System.Workflow.ComponentModel;

public class Trace : Activity
{
  protected override ActivityExecutionStatus Execute(
    ActivityExecutionContext context)
  {
    Console.WriteLine("Trace.Execute");
    return ActivityExecutionStatus.Closed;
  }

  protected override ActivityExecutionStatus Cancel(
    ActivityExecutionContext context)
  {
    Console.WriteLine("Trace.Cancel");
    return ActivityExecutionStatus.Closed;
  }
}
```

When the WF program executes, we will see the following output:

```
e1 is Initialized : None
e1 is Executing  : None
e1 is Canceling  : None
Trace.Cancel
e1 is Closed : Uninitialized
```

The `Trace` activity never has the work item for invocation of its `Execute` method dispatched. Because it moves to the *Canceling* state before its `Execute` execution handler is dispatched, only the `Cancel` method is invoked.

When you write activities that have custom cancellation logic, it is probably not a bad idea to use a pathological composite activity (like the one shown previously) as a test case to help ensure the correctness of your cancellation logic.

Composite Activity Cancellation

We will now return to the execution logic of `Interleave` to see how it responds to cancellation. Listing 4.15 shows the implementation of its `Cancel` method. As you can see, the `Cancel` method of `Interleave`, unlike that of `Wait`, has no cleanup of private data to perform. It does, however, need to propagate the signal to cancel to any executing child activities because `Interleave` will not be able to report the completion of its cancellation logic if it has child activities that are still executing. The `Interleave` activity will therefore remain in the *Canceling* state until all previously executing child activities are canceled.

Listing 4.15 `Interleave` **Activity's Cancellation Logic**

```
using System;
using System.Workflow.ComponentModel;

namespace EssentialWF.Activities
{
  public class Interleave : CompositeActivity
  {
    ...
    protected override ActivityExecutionStatus Cancel(
      ActivityExecutionContext context)
    {
      bool okToClose = true;
      foreach (Activity child in EnabledActivities)
      {
        ActivityExecutionStatus status = child.ExecutionStatus;
        if (status == ActivityExecutionStatus.Executing)
        {
```

```
      context.CancelActivity(child);
      okToClose = false;
    }
    else if ((status != ActivityExecutionStatus.Closed)
      && (status != ActivityExecutionStatus.Initialized))
    {
      okToClose = false;
    }
  }

  if (okToClose)
    return ActivityExecutionStatus.Closed;

  return ActivityExecutionStatus.Canceling;
  }
 }
}
```

The cancellation logic shown in Listing 4.15 is correct for many composite activities, not just for `Interleave`. For example, it is a correct implementation for `Sequence` (and we will assume that the logic of our `Sequence` activity is updated to reflect this), though the cancellation logic for `Sequence` could be written slightly differently because at most one child activity of `Sequence` can be in the *Executing* state at a time. Any child activities in the *Executing* state are asked to cancel. When all child activities are in either the *Initialized* state or *Closed* state, then the composite activity may report its completion.

We've already alluded to the fact that just as for activity execution, activity cancellation is a scheduled request made via AEC. The `Interleave` activity (and the `Sequence` activity) must subscribe to the `Closed` event of any child activity for which it invokes the `CancelActivity` method of AEC. This in turn requires us to modify the logic of `ContinueAt`. We must selectively act upon the `Closed` event depending upon whether the composite activity is in the *Executing* state or the *Canceling* state. In other words, we are using the same bookmark resumption point to handle the `Closed` event that is raised by child activities that complete and also the `Closed` event that is raised by child activities that are canceled.

It is possible for a composite activity (call it "A") to detect that it is in the *Canceling* state before its `Cancel` method is invoked. This will happen if its parent activity schedules "A" for cancellation, but the notification for the `Closed` event of a child activity of "A" reaches "A" before the dispatch of its `Cancel` method.

The following code snippet shows a cancellation-aware implementation of `Interleave.ContinueAt`:

```
public class Interleave : CompositeActivity
{
  // other members same as earlier
  ...

  void ContinueAt(object sender,
    ActivityExecutionStatusChangedEventArgs e)
  {
    e.Activity.Closed -= ContinueAt;

    ActivityExecutionContext context =
      sender as ActivityExecutionContext;

    if (ExecutionStatus == ActivityExecutionStatus.Executing)
    {
      foreach (Activity child in EnabledActivities)
      {
        if (child.ExecutionStatus !=
          ActivityExecutionStatus.Initialized &&
            child.ExecutionStatus !=
          ActivityExecutionStatus.Closed)
          return;
      }

      context.CloseActivity();
    }
    else // canceling
    {
      bool okToClose = true;
      foreach (Activity child in EnabledActivities)
      {
        ActivityExecutionStatus status = child.ExecutionStatus;
        if (status == ActivityExecutionStatus.Executing)
        {
          // This happens if invocation of our Cancel method
          // has been scheduled but is still sitting in the
          // scheduler work queue
          okToClose = false;
          context.CancelActivity(child);
        }
        else if ((status != ActivityExecutionStatus.Closed) &&
          (status != ActivityExecutionStatus.Initialized))
        {
          okToClose = false;
```

```
      }
    }

    if (okToClose)
      context.CloseActivity();
  }
 }
}
```

Early Completion

The AnyOneWillDo activity that we developed earlier in this topic is so similar to Interleave we might consider just building the early completion capability directly into Interleave. While we are at it, we can also generalize how the completion condition is expressed. Imagine a variant of the Interleave activity that carries a property, PercentMustComplete, that indicates the percentage of child activities that must complete in order for the Interleave to be considered complete. If such an Interleave activity is given six child activities, and Percent-MustComplete is set to 50%, only three child activities need to complete before the Interleave activity can report its completion:

```
<Interleave PercentMustComplete="50%" ...>
  <A />
  <B />
  <C />
  <D />
  <E />
  <F />
</Interleave>
```

The Execute method of Interleave remains as we wrote it in Chapter 3; all child activities are immediately scheduled for execution. As the child activities complete their execution, the Interleave is notified via the ContinueAt callback. In the ContinueAt method, the Interleave can now check to see whether the PercentMustComplete threshold has been met (or exceeded), and based upon this check, decide whether to report its own completion.

It is easy to write many variants of Interleave in which the variation is confined to the criterion used to determine when a sufficient number of child activities have completed their execution. One way to generalize this idea of completion condition is to make it a customizable feature of the composite activity. It is easy to write a variant of `Interleave` that carries a property whose type is `ActivityCondition` (just like the `While` activity we developed has a property of type `ActivityCondition`).

The `Interleave` activity can evaluate this condition in its `Execute` method (in case no child activities need be executed), and again whenever the `ContinueAt` method is invoked, in order to decide when to complete. You can also imagine a variant of `Sequence`, or in fact a variant of just about any composite activity, that provides an early completion capability. Composite activities that create subordinate execution contexts (such as `InterleavedForEach`) need to perform cancellation of the activity instances within subordinate execution contexts as part of their early completion.

The actual syntax of condition types (derivatives of `ActivityCondition`) supported natively by WF is discussed in Chapter 8. Here we will use a stylized form of condition writing to communicate our intent. A completion condition allows composite activities to capture real-world control flow in a very flexible way:

```
<Interleave CompletionCondition="A OR (B AND (C OR D))" >
  <A />
  <B />
  <C />
  <D />
</Interleave>
```

This gives us the ability to model real-world processes that are a bit more involved in their completion logic than the simple car sale scenario we started with.

Cancellation Handlers

The composite activities we have written are general purpose in nature. In other words, when a `Sequence` activity or `Interleave` activity is used in a WF program, the developer of the program decides which child activities should be added to that occurrence of the composite activity. Although the execution logic of `Sequence` itself is unchanging, there are an infinite number of ways to use it because it accepts any list of child activities you wish to give it.

In this way, it may be said that both the developer of `Sequence` and the WF program developer who uses a `Sequence` activity have a say in what any particular occurrence of `Sequence` actually accomplishes. The WF programming model extends this same idea to activity cancellation, with the idea of a **cancellation handler**.

The concept is quite simple. When a composite activity is canceled by its parent, its `Cancel` method is scheduled for execution. As we know, this immediately moves the activity into the *Canceling* state. The composite activity remains in this state until all its child activities are quiet, at which time the composite activity reports the completion of its cancellation logic and moves to the *Closed* state. This much we have already covered. The extra step we are introducing here is that if the composite activity has an associated cancellation handler, that handler is executed as a final step prior to the activity's transition to the *Closed* state.

Any composite activity (unless its validation logic is written to explicitly prevent this) is allowed to have one special child activity of type `CancellationHandler-Activity`. This activity type is defined in the `System.Workflow.ComponentModel` namespace and is shown in Listing 4.16. The purpose of a cancellation handler is to allow the WF program developer to model what should happen in the case of an activity cancellation.

Listing 4.16   `CancellationHandlerActivity`

```
namespace System.Workflow.ComponentModel
{
  public sealed class CancellationHandlerActivity : CompositeActivity
  {
    public CancellationHandlerActivity();
    public CancellationHandlerActivity(string name);
  }
}
```

Because `CancellationHandlerActivity` is a composite activity, you may add whatever activities are required to represent the necessary cancellation logic. The child activities of a `CancellationHandlerActivity` will execute in sequential order.

In order to help prevent a composite activity (say, `Sequence`) from executing its `CancellationHandlerActivity` as part of normal execution logic, the `EnabledActivities` collection of `CompositeActivity` will never include the composite activity's cancellation handler. Only the WF runtime will schedule the execution of a cancellation handler.

Let's take a look at an example to see how `CancellationHandlerActivity` can be used. Listing 4.17 shows a simple WF program that starts two timers simultaneously.

Listing 4.17 `CancellationHandlerActivity`

```
<Interleave x:Name="i1" CompletionCondition="seq1 OR seq2"
xmlns="http://EssentialWF/Activities"
xmlns:x="http://schemas.microsoft.com/winfx/2006/xaml"
xmlns:wf="http://schemas.microsoft.com/winfx/2006/xaml/workflow">
  <Sequence x:Name="seq1">
    <Wait Duration="00:01:00" x:Name="delay1" />
    <wf:CancellationHandlerActivity x:Name="ch1">
      <WriteLine x:Name="w1" Text="Cancelling seq1" />
    </wf:CancellationHandlerActivity>
  </Sequence>
  <Sequence x:Name="seq2">
    <Wait Duration="00:00:10" x:Name="delay2" />
    <wf:CancellationHandlerActivity x:Name="ch2">
      <WriteLine x:Name="w2" Text="Cancelling seq2" />
    </wf:CancellationHandlerActivity>
  </Sequence>
</Interleave>
```

The `Interleave` activity carries a completion condition (expressed in stylized form), which says that either child activity must complete in order for the `Interleave` to complete. When the first timer fires, the corresponding `Wait` activity ("delay2" based on the `Duration` values in the example WF program) is notified and then reports its completion. `Sequence` "seq2" will be notified of the completion of "delay2", which will cause "seq2" to report its completion. When the `Interleave` activity is notified of the completion of "seq2", it will evaluate the completion condition and decide that it can report its own completion. Before doing this, though, it must cancel the execution of the other `Sequence`, "seq1". When "seq1" is canceled, it will propagate the cancellation to "delay1". After "delay1" cancels its timer and reports its cancellation, the cancellation handler associated with "seq1" will be scheduled for execution. Only when this cancellation handler moves to the *Closed* state will "seq1" finally move to the *Closed* state.

Figure 4.8 illustrates the same sequence of operations in diagrammatic form.

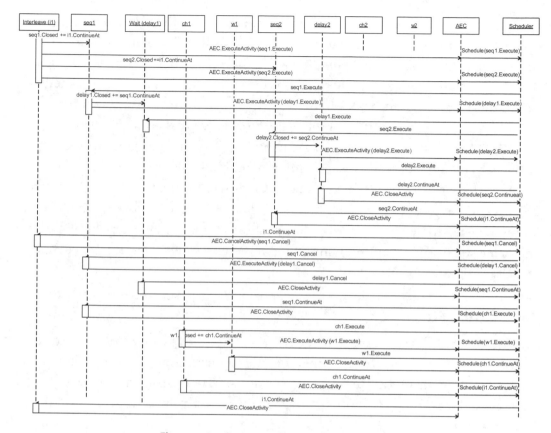

Figure 4.8   Sequence diagram for Listing 4.18

To summarize, we have seen that activity cancellation can be a common—indeed, essential—part of normal WF program execution. When a set of activities is executed in an interleaved manner, it is often the case that only some subset of these activities need to complete in order for the goal of that set of activities to be realized. The other in-progress activities must be canceled. Activity developers can add cancellation logic to their activities, and WF program developers can also have a say in what happens during cancellation by using a cancellation handler.

Fault Handling

The execution handlers that are invoked by the scheduler are just methods on activities, so each of them has the potential to throw an exception. An exception can occur in `Execute`, `Cancel`, `ContinueAt`, or any activity method that is scheduled for execution. If an exception does occur, and is not handled internally by the activity's code (which of course is free to employ `try-catch` constructs), then it is the scheduler that catches the exception (because it is the scheduler that invoked the method). When this happens, it indicates to the WF runtime that the activity that threw the exception cannot successfully complete the work it was asked to perform.

In the WF programming model, the handling of such an exception is an aspect of the activity automaton. Thus, exception handling in WF programs has an asynchronous flavor that exception handling in C# programs does not have. As we shall see, exceptions propagate asynchronously (via the scheduler work queue) and are therefore handled by activities asynchronously. It's important to keep this high-level characteristic of WF exception handling in mind as you write and debug activities and WF programs.

The Faulting State

The throwing of an exception by an activity is at some level comparable to an activity calling the `CloseActivity` method of AEC; both are signals from an activity to the WF runtime that indicate the activity's decision to transition from one state to another. In the case of an exception, the offending activity immediately moves to the *Faulting* state.

As shown in Figure 4.9, there are transitions to the *Faulting* state from both the *Executing* state and the *Canceling* state.

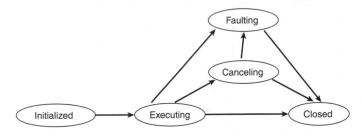

Figure 4.9   The Faulting state of the activity automaton

Activity initialization is a special case that we discussed in Chapter 3. The `Initialize` method of an activity is not a scheduled execution handler. Activity initialization occurs synchronously as part of the creation of a WF program instance.

If an exception is thrown by the `Initialize` method of an activity, the call to `Work-flowRuntime.CreateWorkflow` (within which activity initialization occurs) throws an exception indicating that the WF program instance failed to initialize properly.

A note about terminology: There is no notion of a fault in WF that is in any way different than a CLR exception—the terms are synonyms in WF. However, the term **fault handling** is favored in WF over exception handling because the mechanism by which faults (exceptions) are handled in WF does differ in important ways from the familiar exception handling constructs in CLR languages like C#. These differences are explored in the remainder of this section.

Figure 4.9 shows that after an activity enters the *Faulting* state, the only possible transition it can subsequently make is to the *Closed* state. When this transition occurs, the value of the activity's `ExecutionResult` property is *Faulted*. Figure 4.9 also implies that, if the *Faulting* state is like the *Executing* and *Canceling* states, an activity may remain in the *Faulting* state for an indefinite amount of time. Indeed this is the case. Only an activity can decide when it is appropriate to transition to the *Closed* state; this is true no matter whether an activity makes the transition to the *Closed* state via normal execution, cancellation, or the occurrence of a fault.

When an activity enters the *Faulting* state, its `HandleFault` method is scheduled by the WF runtime. The `HandleFault` method, like `Execute` and `Cancel`, is defined on the `Activity` class:

```
namespace System.Workflow.ComponentModel
{
  public class Activity : DependencyObject
  {
    protected internal virtual ActivityExecutionStatus HandleFault(
      ActivityExecutionContext context, Exception exception);

    /* *** other members *** */
  }
}
```

When the `HandleFault` execution handler is dispatched, it is expected that the activity will perform any cleanup work that is required prior to its transition to the *Closed* state. Just as with the `Execute` and `Cancel` execution handlers, the activity may (if the cleanup work is short-lived) return `ActivityExecution-Status.Closed` from this method. If the cleanup work is long-lived, the activity returns `ActivityExecutionStatus.Faulting` and waits for required callbacks before ultimately calling `ActivityExecutionContext.CloseActivity`.

To illustrate the mechanics of an activity's transitions from the *Executing* state to the *Faulting* state to the *Closed* state, consider the activity shown in Listing 4.18, which throws an exception in its `Execute` method, and then another exception in its `HandleFault` method.

Listing 4.18　An Activity that Always Faults

```
using System;
using System.Workflow.ComponentModel;

public class NeverSucceeds : Activity
{
  protected override ActivityExecutionStatus Execute(
    ActivityExecutionContext context)
  {
    throw new InvalidOperationException("told you so");
  }

  private bool beenHereBefore = false;

  protected override ActivityExecutionStatus HandleFault(
    ActivityExecutionContext context, Exception exception)
  {
    Console.WriteLine(exception.Message);

    if (beenHereBefore)
      return ActivityExecutionStatus.Closed;

    beenHereBefore = true;
    throw new InvalidOperationException("second time");
  }
}
```

If we run a WF program that consists of only a `NeverSucceeds` activity, we will see the following output at the console:

```
told you so
second time
```

When the program starts, the `Execute` method of the `NeverSucceeds` activity is scheduled, which moves it into the *Executing* state. When the `Execute` method is invoked, an exception is of course thrown and is caught by the WF scheduler. This moves the activity into the *Faulting* state, and also enqueues a work item corresponding to the activity's HandleFault method. When HandleFault is dispatched, the Message property of the current exception ("told you so") is written to the console and, because the beenHereBefore variable value is false, a new exception is thrown. This second exception is also caught by the WF scheduler, and again the HandleFault method of the NeverSucceeds activity is scheduled for execution. The second time through, the beenHereBefore variable value is true (having been set during the first invocation of HandleFault) and so the activity reports its completion (after again printing the Message property of the current exception, which now is "second time"). This moves the activity from the *Faulting* state to the *Closed* state.

This example does illustrate that care must be taken to avoid an infinite loop in which exceptions occurring within HandleFault cause repeated scheduling of additional calls to HandleFault. The potential for infinite looping is a byproduct of the fact that an activity must be allowed to remain in the *Faulting* state for an indefinite amount of time while it performs any necessary cleanup work.

The HandleFault method allows an activity to perform cleanup work when an exception occurs. However, the behavior of HandleFault is not the same as that of the catch block familiar to C# programmers. The WF runtime will schedule the propagation of the exception (to the parent of the faulting activity) only when the faulting activity transitions to the *Closed* state.

The faulting activity can choose to suppress the propagation of an exception by setting the ActivityExecutionContext.CurrentExceptionProperty to null:

```
protected override ActivityExecutionStatus HandleFault(
    ActivityExecutionContext context, Exception exception)
{
    this.SetValue(ActivityExecutionContext.CurrentExceptionProperty, null);

    return ActivityExecutionStatus.Closed;
}
```

The WF runtime automatically populates the AEC.CurrentExceptionProperty with the exception before calling HandleFault. It will clear the property when the faulting activity transitions to the *Closed* state. If the exception is not suppressed by the faulting activity, the exception will be made available to the parent activity.

The implementation of `HandleFault` that is provided by the `Activity` class simply returns `ActivityExecutionStatus.Closed`. Only when you need special cleanup to occur should you override this implementation. This is very similar to the situation for cancellation, which we previously discussed. In fact, in many cases it is useful to factor the cleanup logic for an activity like `Wait` into a helper method that is then called from both `Cancel` and `HandleFault`.

Composite Activity Fault Handling

As you might expect, things are a bit different for composite activities.

We saw previously that a composite activity will not be able to transition to the *Closed* state unless every child activity of that composite activity is either in the *Initialized* state or the *Closed* state. Therefore, when the `HandleFault` method of a composite activity is dispatched, the default implementation inherited from `Activity` will not be correct.

The implementation of the `HandleFault` method found in `CompositeActivity`, shown here, will call the `Cancel` method of the composite activity in order to ensure cancellation of all currently executing child activities:

```
ActivityExecutionStatus s = this.Cancel(context);

if (s == ActivityExecutionStatus.Canceling)
{
  return ActivityExecutionStatus.Faulting;
}

return s;
```

As we saw in the previous section, it is critical that composite activities implement appropriate cancellation logic. The simple implementation of the `Cancel` method defined by `Activity` immediately returns a status of `ActivityExecutionStatus.Closed`. This will not work for composite activities, and can lead to an infinite loop due to the fault that will be thrown by the WF runtime when a composite activity tries to report its completion if it has child activities still doing work.

Just as with cancellation, the composite activity must wait for all active child activities to move to the *Closed* state before it can report its completion. In the case of a composite activity that is handling a fault, the call to the `CloseActivity` method of AEC will move the composite activity from the *Faulting* state to the *Closed* state.

A composite activity will therefore, by default, see its `Cancel` method called (from `HandleFault`) when a fault needs to be handled. It is expected that for many composite activities, the logic of `Cancel` corresponds exactly to what must happen during the handling of a fault; specifically, all child activities in the *Executing* state are canceled, and the composite activity's call to `AEC.CloseActivity` occurs only when all child activities are in either the *Initialized* state or the *Closed* state. The implementations of `HandleFault` in `Activity` and `CompositeActivity` are just a convenience, however, and can be overridden in cases where they do not provide the appropriate behavior.

Fault Propagation

Thus far, we have only discussed the throwing and handling of a fault in the context of the activity whose execution handler produced an exception. For this activity, there is a transition to the *Faulting* state (from either the *Executing* state or the *Canceling* state) and a subsequent transition to the *Closed* state. But when this activity moves to the *Closed* state, the fault can hardly be considered to have been handled. After all, the default implementations of `HandleFault` provided by `Activity` and `CompositeActivity` essentially just enable an activity to move to the *Closed* state from the *Faulting* state as quickly as possible.

What actually happens when an activity transitions to the *Closed* state from the *Faulting* state is that (unless the fault is suppressed using the technique outlined earlier) the WF runtime automatically propagates the exception one level up the activity hierarchy. Specifically, the WF runtime schedules a work item for the `HandleFault` method of the parent of the activity that faulted; when this occurs, the parent activity moves to the *Faulting* state. Here we find the key point of difference between fault handling in WF and exception handling in the CLR. The WF fault does not propagate until the faulting activity moves to the *Closed* state; as we know this might take an arbitrary amount of time during which other scheduled execution handlers in the same WF program instance will be dispatched. The execution of other activities proceeds, unaffected by the fact that a fault has occurred.

When the exception propagates one level up, the parent composite activity eventually has a work item for its `HandleFault` method dispatched. As expected, the fault-handling logic of this composite activity will cause the cancellation of any executing child activities. Only when all child activities are quiet will the composite activity move to the *Closed* state; when this occurs, the exception will propagate yet one more level up the activity tree. In this way, the WF fault-handling model provides for the orderly cleanup of work as the exception propagates up the tree, one composite activity at a time.

WF's execution model is stackless and is driven by the activity automaton. Because activities are organized hierarchically in a WF program, the WF runtime must propagate exceptions according to the constraints of the activity automaton; this ensures *downward* propagation (and, indeed, completion) of cancellation (orderly cleanup of work) prior to the *upward* propagation of an exception. The WF program developer must be aware of the innately asynchronous nature of WF program execution. This is especially true when the fault-handling capabilities of activities are utilized.

Fault Handlers

We saw earlier in this chapter that the WF runtime schedules the execution of a cancellation handler, if one is present, when a composite activity transitions from the *Canceling* state to the *Closed* state. In a similar fashion, a FaultHandlers-Activity, if present, is scheduled for execution as part of a composite activity's transition from the *Faulting* state to the *Closed* state.

A FaultHandlersActivity (note the plural) is just an ordered list of child activities of type FaultHandlerActivity. A FaultHandlerActivity allows the WF program developer to model the handling of a fault of a specific type much like a catch handler in C#.

The FaultHandlerActivity type is shown in Listing 4.19.

Listing 4.19 FaultHandlerActivity

```
namespace System.Workflow.ComponentModel
{
  public sealed class FaultHandlerActivity : CompositeActivity
  {
    public Exception Fault { get; }
    public Type FaultType { get; set; }

    /* *** other members *** */
  }
}
```

The execution logic of `FaultHandlersActivity` is responsible for finding the child `FaultHandlerActivity` that can handle the current fault. If one is found, that activity is scheduled for execution, and the composite activity (whose `Fault-HandlersActivity` is being executed) remains in the *Faulting* state until the fault handler completes its execution. If no matching fault handler is found, the fault is propagated by the WF runtime to the next outer (parent) composite activity, and the composite activity handling the fault moves from the *Faulting* state to the *Closed* state.

When a `FaultHandlerActivity` executes, it sets the `CurrentException-Property` of the faulting composite activity to null in order to suppress the propagation of the (successfully handled) exception.

Unhandled Faults

If the root activity of a WF program moves from the *Faulting* state to the *Closed* state without having had a `FaultHandlerActivity` successfully handle the fault, the WF program terminates. The exception propagates to the application hosting the WF runtime in the form of an event.

The host application can subscribe to the `WorkflowRuntime.WorkflowTerminated` event to see the exception:

```
using (WorkflowRuntime runtime = new WorkflowRuntime())
{
  runtime.WorkflowTerminated += delegate(object sender,
    WorkflowTerminatedEventArgs e)
  {
    Exception exception = e.Exception;
    ...
  };

  ...
}
```

Modeled Faults

It is an inescapable fact that exceptions will sometimes be thrown by opaque activity code. Sometimes, though, it can be desirable to represent, or **model**, the throwing of a fault as an explicit part of a WF program.

A side effect of layering the WF runtime on top of the CLR is that the WF runtime must be able to recognize and deal with CLR exceptions raised, at the lowest level, via the Microsoft Intermediate Language (MSIL) throw instruction. Activities, after all, are compiled to MSIL instructions. Therefore, although the propagation of a fault and its eventual handling is governed by the laws of the WF runtime (and not the CLR's), the mechanism of throwing a fault is still the MSIL throw instruction.

In a more pristine architecture, wherein activities might be written with an exclusive reliance on WF APIs, WF could provide an API for activity writers to notify the WF runtime of the occurrence of a fault. This API would be used instead of the MSIL throw instruction. Rather than invent this duplicate API, though, WF pragmatically uses the throw statement of languages like C# as the mechanism by which activities signal a fault. Purists might object to the absence of a WF API for signaling a fault; this is an issue[1] that illustrates the design tradeoffs inherent in the building of a meta-runtime such as the WF runtime on top of the CLR.

That said, from the perspective of the WF program developer, it remains useful to hide this debate and provide an activity whose job is to raise a fault. An activity analog of the C# throw statement, a ThrowFault activity, is shown in Listing 4.20.

Listing 4.20   ThrowFault **Activity**

```
using System;
using System.Workflow.ComponentModel;

namespace EssentialWF.Activities
{
   public class ThrowFault : Activity
   {
     public static readonly DependencyProperty FaultProperty =
       DependencyProperty.Register("Fault",
         typeof(Exception),
         typeof(ThrowFault)
     );

     public Exception Fault
     {
       get { return GetValue(FaultProperty) as Exception; }
       set { SetValue(FaultProperty, value); }
     }

     protected override ActivityExecutionStatus Execute(
```

[1] The practicalities of activity object constructors and the Dispose method is another that we encountered earlier.

```
      ActivityExecutionContext context)
  {
    if (Fault == null)
      throw new InvalidOperationException ("Null Fault");

    throw Fault;
  }
}
}
```

Setting the `Fault` property prior to the execution of a `ThrowFault` activity is analogous to placing a reference to an object of type `System.Exception` on the stack prior to execution of the MSIL `throw`. If the exception object is `null`, an `InvalidOperationException` occurs.

The presence of `ThrowFault` in a WF program indicates precisely where the program is predictably going to fault. We don't even have to run the program in Listing 4.21. Just by looking at it, you can predict the result. The program will write `"hello, world"` but will then terminate without writing `"unreachable"` to the console.

Listing 4.21 WF Program That Throws an Exception

```
<Sequence x:Name="s1" xmlns="http://EssentialWF/Activities"
xmlns:x="http://schemas.microsoft.com/winfx/2006/xaml">
  <WriteLine x:Name="w1" Text="hello, world" />
  <ThrowFault x:Name="throw1" />
  <WriteLine x:Name="w2" Text="unreachable" />
</Sequence>
```

The `ThrowFault` activity is useful as written, but (outside of using a default `System.InvalidOperationException` if no other is provided) it takes no responsibility for creating the exception that it throws. Although the WF program developer could certainly resort to code to create a specialized exception, which `ThrowFault` can then throw, this more or less defeats the purpose of modeling the throwing of the exception. In other words, it is preferable to declaratively specify both the creation and the throwing of an exception.

One way to go about this would be to write a `CreateFault` activity that manufactures a `System.Exception` object based upon certain inputs (such as the type of the exception to be created, and any constructor parameter values that should be used). The `Fault` property of a `ThrowFault` activity could then be bound to the property of `CreateFault` that holds the manufactured exception.

This is a perfectly fine approach, but it makes reasoning about the types of exceptions thrown in a WF program a bit trickier because one must parse databinding expressions in order to determine the type of an exception that will be thrown. An alternative approach is to collapse both steps into a single activity that manufactures and throws an exception. A simple version of such an activity is shown in Listing 4.22.

Listing 4.22   ThrowTypedFault **Activity**

```
using System;
using System.Workflow.ComponentModel;

namespace EssentialWF.Activities
{
  public class ThrowTypedFault : Activity
  {
    public static readonly DependencyProperty FaultTypeProperty =
      DependencyProperty.Register("FaultType",
        typeof(System.Type),
        typeof(ThrowTypedFault),
        new PropertyMetadata(DependencyPropertyOptions.Metadata)
      );

    public static readonly DependencyProperty FaultMessageProperty =
      DependencyProperty.Register("FaultMessage",
        typeof(string),
        typeof(ThrowTypedFault)
      );

    public Type FaultType
    {
      get { return GetValue(FaultTypeProperty) as Type; }
      set { SetValue(FaultTypeProperty, value); }
    }

    public string FaultMessage
    {
      get { return GetValue(FaultMessageProperty) as string; }
      set { SetValue(FaultMessageProperty, value); }
    }

    protected override ActivityExecutionStatus Execute(
      ActivityExecutionContext context)
    {
      System.Reflection.ConstructorInfo c =
        FaultType.GetConstructor(new Type[]
          { typeof(System.String) }
        );

      Exception fault = c.Invoke(new object[] { FaultMessage } )
```

```
          as Exception;

      throw fault;
    }
  }
}
```

When it executes, the `ThrowTypedFault` activity creates a new exception object whose type is determined by the value of its `FaultType` metadata property. It is assumed that the exception type has a constructor that takes a single `string` parameter.

A `ThrowTypedFault` activity with a `FaultType` of `InvalidOperationException` and a `FaultMessage` of "nice try" is essentially equivalent to this C# statement:

```
throw new InvalidOperationException("nice try");
```

It is easy to augment the implementation of `ThrowTypedFault` to make it more robust, and to make it meet the needs of your own WF programs. Appropriate validation logic (discussed in Chapter 7) can ensure that the `FaultType` property holds a type reference to a derivative of `System.Exception`. Additional properties (for example, an `InnerException` property that becomes yet another constructor parameter for the manufactured exception) might be added as well.

When the throwing and handling of exceptions are both modeled in a WF program, it becomes possible to reason quite usefully about the behavior of the program without looking at any activity code. The WF program in Listing 4.23 shows such a program.

Listing 4.23 WF Program with Exceptions

```
<Sequence x:Name="s1" xmlns="http://EssentialWF/Activities"
xmlns:x="http://schemas.microsoft.com/winfx/2006/xaml"
xmlns:wf="http://schemas.microsoft.com/winfx/2006/xaml/workflow">

 ...

  <ThrowTypedFault x:Name="throw1" FaultMessage="oops" FaultType="{x:Type
System.InvalidOperationException}" />

 ...

  <wf:FaultHandlersActivity>
    <wf:FaultHandlerActivity x:Name="fh1" FaultType="{x:Type System.InvalidOpera-
tionException}">
```

```
      <WriteLine x:Name="w1" Text="{wf:ActivityBind fh1,Path=Fault.Message}" />
    </wf:FaultHandlerActivity>
    <wf:FaultHandlerActivity x:Name="fh2" FaultType="{x:Type System.Exception}">
      <ThrowFault x:Name="throw2" Fault="{wf:ActivityBind fh2,Path=Fault}" />
    </wf:FaultHandlerActivity>
  </wf:FaultHandlersActivity>
</Sequence>
```

Listing 4.23 is functionally similar to the following C# code:

```
try
{
  ...

  throw new InvalidOperationException("oops");

  ...
}
catch (InvalidOperationException e)
{
  Console.WriteLine(e.Message);
}
catch (Exception e)
{
  throw e;
}
```

The sequence diagram in Figure 4.10 shows the sequence of execution for the WF program shown in Listing 4.23.

Keep in mind that the exception propagation mechanism of the WF runtime ensures orderly cleanup of executing activities beginning at the origin of the exception. In WF, both the execution and exception models are fundamentally asynchronous. Only when the exception bubbles up to the composite activity with a fault handler that is able to handle the fault (has a matching fault type) will the fault be handled.

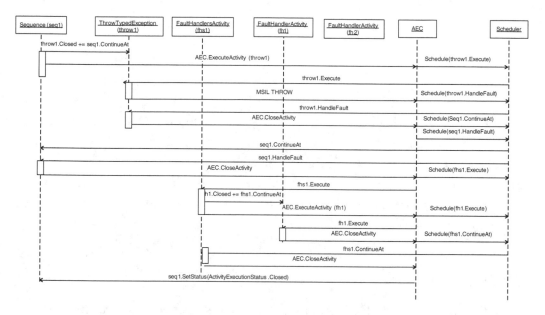

Figure 4.10   Sequence diagram for Listing 4.23

When an exception occurs in a C# program, the transfer of control to the appropriate exception handler (however many nested program statements need to be traversed) is effectively instantaneous. In a WF program, propagation of a fault to a fault handler will take an indeterminate amount of time, depending upon the time it takes to clean up (cancel) running activities within the activity subtrees of the composite activities that must move from the *Faulting* state to the *Closed* state.

ThrowActivity

The `System.Workflow.ComponentModel` namespace includes an activity named `ThrowActivity` (by convention, the names of activity types included with WF are suffixed with `"Activity"`). `ThrowActivity` combines the functionality of the two activities we've written in this chapter and thus is an easy way to model the throwing of exceptions in WF programs.

The following XAML snippets illustrate the usage of `ThrowActivity`:

```
<ThrowActivity FaultType="{x:Type System.InvalidOperationException}" />

<ThrowActivity Fault="{wf:ActivityBind SomeActivity,Path=SomeProp}" />
```

You can also specify both `FaultType` and `Fault` when using `ThrowActivity`, in which case a validation error occurs if the value of the `FaultType` property and the type of the object referenced by the `Fault` property do not match. Where `Throw-Activity` does not meet the needs of your WF programs, though, hopefully you have seen in this section how easy it is to craft variants that deliver the functionality you require.

Compensation

As we know, a typical WF program will perform work (execute activities) episodically. The effects of the execution of these activities are not necessarily, but often, visible outside of the boundaries of the WF program. To take a few concrete examples, one activity in a WF program might send an email, another activity might create and write to a file on the local hard drive, and yet another activity might call a web service.

If a WF program instance successfully executes these activities, but then later (perhaps a second later, or perhaps six months later) has its execution go awry, it might be desirable to try to undo the effects of the successfully completed activities. This is no different conceptually than what you might do in a C# program when you catch an exception. The logic of a C# `catch` block can attempt to undo the effects of the partially completed `try` block with which it is associated. For example, if the code in your `try` block created a file but failed during the writing of data to that file (and consequently threw an exception), the `catch` block might delete the file. Complicating this problem is the fact that your cleanup logic probably needs to figure out just how far the work in the `try` block proceeded before the exception occurred.

You are free to take this approach in WF programs. We have already discussed the fault-handling model of WF, and though you know now that the WF execution model differs from that of the CLR because of the asynchronous nature of the WF scheduler, it's nevertheless true that the purpose of a WF `FaultHandlerActivity` is essentially the same as that of a C# `catch` block. When a `FaultHandler-Activity` is executed, it means that something unexpected has happened in the execution of the WF program instance, and it also means that you have a chance to sort out the potentially messy state in which your program instance now finds itself.

Another strategy is to employ transactions so that work performed under the auspices of a transaction can be rolled back if the transaction cannot commit. Just as they do in CLR programs, transactions do play an important role in WF programs (and we will discuss transactions in Chapter 6, "Transactions"), but they are not a panacea. It is simply not practical to encompass long-running work (that spans episodes) in a single transaction; locks cannot be held for the required duration. Further complicating the situation is the fact that not all (or perhaps none) of the work represented by activities is performed locally—think of our activity that calls a web service; organizations will never give direct control of their transactional resources to external entities. Standards have emerged to address the transactional aspects of (short-lived) remote work, but such capabilities are not yet commonplace infrastructure. Use of transactions is therefore complementary to (and not a replacement for) other aspects of WF programming such as fault handling.

The Compensating State

The WF programming model permits the association of **compensation logic** with an activity. In a nutshell, the way compensation logic is expressed is very much the same as cancellation logic. An activity can implement a `Compensate` method if it wishes to express compensation logic in code.

Additionally, a composite activity can be given a `CompensationHandler-Activity`, so that the developer of a WF program can provide custom compensation logic for that composite activity.

The rules that govern the execution of compensation logic are a bit more complicated than those governing cancellation, and will be demonstrated in the examples of this section. At the level of the activity automaton, things are pretty simple. A compensatable activity that is in the *Closed* state with a result of *Succeeded* is allowed (but not required) to make a transition from the *Closed* state to the *Compensating* state. From the *Compensating* state, a transition can be made either to the *Faulting* state, or back to the *Closed* state.

The expected path is from the *Compensating* state back to the *Closed* state, which leaves the activity with an execution result of *Compensated* (thus precluding a second transition to the *Compensating* state). These transitions are shown in Figure 4.11.

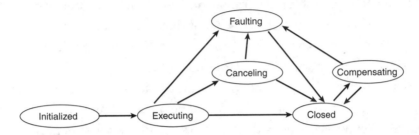

Figure 4.11 The Compensating state of the activity automatonCompensatable Activities

Not all activities are compensatable. In some cases, it might not be possible to describe reasonable compensation logic for an activity. Think of the `Wait` activity, which just waits for a timer to fire. After the timer fires, and the `Wait` activity completes, there is no way to undo the fact that the timer fired. In other cases it might not be desirable to utilize compensation (for example, if one takes the approach of doing best-effort cleanup within fault handlers).

In order to keep the WF programming model simple, compensation is an opt-in model. An activity must implement the `ICompensatableActivity` interface in order to be considered compensatable.

The `ICompensatableActivity` type is shown in Listing 4.24.

Listing 4.24 `ICompensatableActivity`

```
namespace system.Workflow.ComponentModel
{
  public interface ICompensatableActivity
  {
    ActivityExecutionStatus Compensate(
      ActivityExecutionContext context);
  }
}
```

`ICompensatableActivity` defines one method, `Compensate`. Like `Activity.Execute` and `Activity.Cancel`, this method takes an `Activity-ExecutionContext` as a parameter and returns `ActivityExecutionStatus`. Also like `Execute` and `Cancel`, `Compensate` is an execution handler whose dispatch is scheduled via the WF runtime.

Just as with cancellation and fault handling, an activity can complete its compensation logic within the `Compensate` method and return `ActivityExecution-Status.Closed`. An activity may alternatively implement long-running compensation logic, in which case a value of `ActivityExecutionStatus.Compensating` needs to be returned from the `Compensate` method.

As a simple example, consider the `SendEmail` activity shown in Listing 4.25.

Listing 4.25 `SendEmail` **Activity with Compensation Logic**

```
using System;
using System.Workflow.ComponentModel;

namespace EssentialWF.Activities
{
  public class SendMail : Activity, ICompensatableActivity
  {
    // To, From, Subject, and Body properties elided...

    protected override ActivityExecutionStatus Execute(
      ActivityExecutionContext context)
    {
      MailService mailService = context.GetService<MailService>();
      mailService.Send(To, From, Subject, Body);

      return ActivityExecutionStatus.Closed;
    }

    ActivityExecutionStatus ICompensatableActivity.Compensate(
      ActivityExecutionContext context)
    {
      MailService mailService = context.GetService<MailService>();
      mailService.Send(To, From, "IGNORE:" + Subject);

      return ActivityExecutionStatus.Closed;
    }
  }
}
```

The `SendEmail` activity's `Compensate` method simply sends a second email indicating that the original email should be ignored. A different approach might be to define a `Recall` method on the `MailService` type, and invoke that method from `Compensate`. In this manner, the `MailService` can decide the most appropriate action. In some situations, the second email might be sent, but in other cases (perhaps the original email had not been sent because the machine on which the WF program is executing is offline, or the destination mail server supported a recall mechanism for delivered but unread email), use of a full-featured email server might produce a more desirable outcome.

It is important to understand that we are not rolling back the work done by `SendEmail` in a transactional sense. We are logically undoing, or more accurately *compensating for*, that previously completed work. In the time that elapses between the first email and the second (or the recall), there may well have been side effects due to the visibility of the data. To take a different example, an `Insert` activity that inserts a row into a database could well have a `Compensate` method that deletes that row from the database. But, in the seconds, hours, or weeks that elapse before the row is deleted, any number of applications might have read and acted upon (even updated or deleted) the data in that row. For these reasons, it is important to carefully consider the requirements of the scenarios that are targeted by the compensation logic that you write.

Compensation Handlers

Composite activities can also implement `ICompensatableActivity` and provide custom compensation logic. More typically, though, the `Compensate` method of a composite activity will look like the example shown in Listing 4.26.

Listing 4.26   CompensatableSequence **Activity**

```
using System;
using System.Workflow.ComponentModel;

namespace EssentialWF.Activities
{
  public class CompensatableSequence : Sequence, ICompensatableActivity
  {
    ActivityExecutionStatus ICompensatableActivity.Compensate(
      ActivityExecutionContext context)
```

```
    {
      return ActivityExecutionStatus.Closed;
    }
  }
}
```

Clearly there is no actual compensation logic here.

However, by implementing ICompensatableActivity, the Compensatable-Sequence activity allows the WF program developer to associate a Compensation-HandlerActivity with any CompensatableSequence. When the Compensata-bleSequence transitions to the *Closed* state from the *Compensating* state, the WF runtime schedules the execution of the CompensationHandlerActivity.

CompensationHandlerActivity is similar in purpose to the cancellation handlers and fault handlers discussed earlier. A transition to the *Closed* state from the *Compensating* state made by the parent of a CompensationHandlerActivity does not actually occur until the CompensationHandlerActivity completes its execution.

Listing 4.27 shows how a CompensationHandlerActivity is used in the definition of a WF program. Two CompensatableSequence activities are executed simultaneously, and each one defines a compensation handler.

Listing 4.27 Modeling Compensation Logic Using
CompensationHandlerActivity

```
<Sequence x:Name="s1" xmlns="http://EssentialWF/Activities"
xmlns:x="http://schemas.microsoft.com/winfx/2006/xaml"
xmlns:wf="http://schemas.microsoft.com/winfx/2006/xaml/workflow">
  <Interleave x:Name="i1">
    <CompensatableSequence x:Name="seq1">

      . . .

      <wf:CompensationHandlerActivity x:Name="ch1">
        <WriteLine x:Name="w1" Text="In compensation handler 1" />
      </wf:CompensationHandlerActivity>
    </CompensatableSequence>
    <CompensatableSequence x:Name="seq2">
      . . .
      <wf:CompensationHandlerActivity x:Name="ch2">
        <WriteLine x:Name="w2" Text="In compensation handler 2" />
      </wf:CompensationHandlerActivity>
    </CompensatableSequence>
```

```
  </Interleave>
  <ThrowTypedFault x:Name="throw1" FaultMessage="oops" FaultType="{x:Type
System.InvalidOperationException}" />
</Sequence>
```

The two `CompensatableSequence` activities execute, and then a fault occurs. Now it is time to run compensation logic.

Default Compensation

Listing 4.27 illustrates how compensation handlers are defined, but we have not explained how they will be invoked. If we examine Listing 4.27, we see that an exception will be thrown by the `ThrowTypedFault` activity that follows the `Interleave` containing the two `CompensatableSequence` activities.

It is the default fault handling and compensation logic of `Sequence` and `Interleave`, inherited from `CompositeActivity`, which ensures that the compensation handlers for the two compensatable child activities are run. When the `ThrowTypedFault` activity moves to the *Closed* state (with a result of *Faulted*), the exception is propagated to its parent activity, the `Sequence`. The `Sequence` does not have a child `FaultHandlersActivity`, but even so, it will check to see if it contains any child activities that require compensation. Because this is indeed the case, the compensation handlers of the two `CompensatableSequence` activities will be scheduled. The order in which they are scheduled is the reverse order in which they completed their execution.

When executed, the WF program in Listing 4.27 will output one of the two following results, depending upon which `CompensatableSequence` finished first:

```
In compensation handler 1
In compensation handler 2
```

Or:

```
In compensation handler 2
In compensation handler 1
```

Only when the compensation handlers complete their execution will the exception propagate up from the `Sequence` activity. In this example, the `Sequence` is the root of the WF program, but if it were not, the exception would be propagated up the tree of activities one composite activity at a time. As the exception propagates up, compensation of any completed, compensatable activities (and cancellation of executing activities) occurs in an orderly (and sequential) fashion until an appropriate `FaultHandlerActivity` handles the exception or the WF program instance terminates.

Default compensation is also triggered for the child activities of a composite activity if the composite activity transitions from the *Canceling* state to the *Closed* state and does not have a `CancellationHandlerActivity`.

The program in Listing 4.28 illustrates default compensation of our `SendEmail` activity.

Listing 4.28　Default Compensation of a Primitive Activity

```
<Sequence xmlns="http://EssentialWF/Activities"
xmlns:x="http://schemas.microsoft.com/winfx/2006/xaml">
  <SendMail x:Name="send1" From="Bob" To="Dharma" Subject="Hello" />
  <ThrowTypedFault FaultMessage="oops" FaultType="{x:Type System.InvalidOpera-
tionException}" />
</Sequence>
```

The `Execute` method of `SendEmail` sends out the email message. After an exception is thrown and propagated by the `ThrowTypedFault` activity, the `Sequence` moves to the *Faulting* state. The `Sequence` does not have a fault handler to handle the exception, but it will schedule the `Compensate` method of the `SendMail` and wait for its *Closed* event before propagating the exception. The compensation logic of `SendEmail` will send the second email (or the recall). In this scenario, the exception is unhandled by the root of the WF program and hence the WF program instance will terminate.

If a compensatable activity such as `SendEmail` is executed more than one time (say, as a child activity of a `While`) then each of the iterations is independently compensatable. Compensation fundamentally relies upon the ability, discussed earlier in this chapter, to save and then retrieve a completed execution context. The compensation of such an activity entails the compensation (in reverse order of completion) of all the successfully completed iterations (execution contexts).

In the program shown in Listing 4.29, the `While` activity iterates over a `CompensatableSequence` three times. Subsequently, the `ThrowTypedFault` activity throws a fault that is not handled by the program. Just before it is propagated by the `Sequence`, the compensation of each of the iterations of `While` takes place.

Listing 4.29   Compensation and AECs

```
<Sequence x:Name="s1" xmlns="http://EssentialWF/Activities"
xmlns:x="http://schemas.microsoft.com/winfx/2006/xaml"
xmlns:wf="http://schemas.microsoft.com/winfx/2006/xaml/workflow">
  <While x:Name="while1" >
    <While.Condition>
      <ConstantLoopCondition MaxCount="3" />
    </While.Condition>
    <CompensatableSequence x:Name="body">
      <GetCurrentTime x:Name="t1" />
      <WriteLine x:Name="w1" Text="{wf:ActivityBind t1,Path=Time}" />
      <Wait x:Name="wait1" Duration="00:00:04" />
      <wf:CompensationHandlerActivity x:Name="ch1">
        <WriteLine x:Name="w2" Text="{wf:ActivityBind t1,Path=Time}" />
      </wf:CompensationHandlerActivity>
    </CompensatableSequence>
  </While>
  <ThrowTypedFault x:Name="throw1" FaultMessage="oops" FaultType="{x:Type
System.InvalidOperationException}" />
</Sequence>
```

The WF program of Listing 4.29 produces the following output:

```
6/10/2006 7:29:24 PM
6/10/2006 7:29:28 PM
6/10/2006 7:29:32 PM
6/10/2006 7:29:32 PM
6/10/2006 7:29:28 PM
6/10/2006 7:29:24 PM
```

Let's analyze the program in Listing 4.29. The `While` activity is configured to iterate over a `CompensatableSequence` three times. During each iteration, a `GetCurrentTime` activity (`t1`) is executed, followed by a `WriteLine` activity (`w1`), followed by a `Wait` activity (`wait1`). `GetCurrentTime` simply takes a snapshot of the current time in its `Execute` method (by calling `DateTime.Now.ToString()`) and sets its `Time` property to this value. The `WriteLine` activity's `Text` property is databound to the `GetCurrentTime` activity's `Time` property.

Within the compensation handler of the CompensatableSequence, the Text property of the WriteLine activity w2 is databound to the Text property of the WriteLine activity w1. Because the encompassing AEC of a compensation handler is restored during compensation, the application state that was saved at the time the AEC was persisted is available. Because the two WriteLine activities w1 and w2 reside within the same AEC, instances of w2 (the WriteLine inside the CompensationHandlerActivity) are able to print out values that were produced earlier (by instances of w1).

Because compensation of activities that implement ICompensatableActivity might not need to be triggered in a given program instance, compensatable activities that move to the *Closed* state with a result of *Succeeded* are not uninitialized until they are either compensated or until the WF program instance completes.

Custom Compensation

Default compensation unfolds naturally and implicitly as a part of fault handling and cancellation handling in a WF program instance. Of course, no compensation at all will ever happen if a WF program contains no compensatable activities (or, more precisely, if no compensatable activities in a WF program successfully complete their execution).

In some cases, the algorithm used by the WF runtime to implement default compensation does not correspond to the desired compensation logic. For these situations, WF includes an activity type named CompensateActivity that allows the WF program developer to exert a finer level of control over the compensation process.

The CompensateActivity type is shown in Listing 4.30.

Listing 4.30   CompensateActivity

```
namespace System.Workflow.ComponentModel
{
  public sealed class CompensateActivity : Activity
  {
    public string TargetActivityName { get; set; }

    /* *** other members *** */
  }
}
```

The most common usage of CompensateActivity occurs when a WF program developer wishes to specify custom compensation logic in a Compensation-HandlerActivity and *also* trigger default compensation as part of that composite activity's compensation logic. To meet this requirement, the Compensate-Activity is added to a CompensationHandlerActivity and the value of its TargetActivityName property is set to the name of the associated composite activity. This configuration indicates that when the CompensateActivity executes, the default (implicit) compensation algorithm should run. This will schedule the execution of the compensation logic for all appropriate (successfully completed) compensatable activities in the composite activity's subtree.

Listing 4.31 defines explicit compensation for the CompensatableSequence that, when all is said and done, does exactly what implicit compensation (a Compensat-ableSequence with no CompensationHandler at all) would do, except that it also writes two messages to the console, one on either side of the default compensation logic that is triggered by the execution of the CompensateActivity.

Listing 4.31   **Explicit Compensation Using** CompensateActivity

```
<CompensatableSequence x:Name="seq1"
xmlns="http://EssentialWF/Activities"
xmlns:x="http://schemas.microsoft.com/winfx/2006/xaml"
xmlns:wf="http://schemas.microsoft.com/winfx/2006/xaml/workflow">

  . . .

  <wf:CompensationHandlerActivity x:Name="ch1">
    <WriteLine x:Name="w1" Text="Time to run compensation" />
    <wf:CompensateActivity x:Name="c1" TargetActivityName="seq1"/>
    <WriteLine x:Name="w2" Text="Done compensating" />
  </wf:CompensationHandlerActivity>
</CompensatableSequence>
```

More advanced explicit compensation is also possible (for instance, in cases where it is not correct to initiate compensation sequentially in the reverse order of activity completion). For these cases, the CompensateActivity can be configured to reference a compensatable child activity of the associated composite activity. In this way, multiple CompensateActivity activities can be used to prescribe the order in which compensation unfolds. An example of such compensation logic is shown in Listing 4.32.

Listing 4.32 **Explicit Compensation Using** CompensateActivity

```
<Sequence x:Name="seq1" xmlns="http://EssentialWF/Activities"
xmlns:x="http://schemas.microsoft.com/winfx/2006/xaml"
xmlns:wf="http://schemas.microsoft.com/winfx/2006/xaml/workflow">

  <CompensatableInterleave x:Name="i1">
    <CompensatableSequence x:Name="cs1">
      <wf:CompensationHandlerActivity x:Name="ch1">
        <WriteLine Text="In compensator ch1" x:Name="w1" />
      </wf:CompensationHandlerActivity>
    </CompensatableSequence>
    <CompensatableSequence x:Name="cs2">
      <wf:CompensationHandlerActivity x:Name="ch2">
        <WriteLine Text="In compensator ch2" x:Name="w2" />
      </wf:CompensationHandlerActivity>
    </CompensatableSequence>
    <wf:CompensationHandlerActivity x:Name="ch4">
      <wf:CompensateActivity TargetActivityName="cs2"/>
      <wf:CompensateActivity TargetActivityName="cs1"/>
    </wf:CompensationHandlerActivity>
  </CompensatableInterleave>
  <wf:ThrowActivity FaultType="{x:Type System.InvalidOperationException}" />
</Sequence>
```

In contrast to the program in Listing 4.29, which used default compensation, the program in Listing 4.32 models compensation explicitly using CompensateActivity. In this way, the program in Listing 4.32 controls the order in which the compensation of child activities occurs. The preceding program will output the following:

```
In compensator ch2
In compensator ch1
```

The CompensatableInterleave activity used in Listing 4.32 is a simple modification of the Interleave activity: CompensatableInterleave needs to implement the ICompensatableActivity interface, just like the Compensatable-Sequence of Listing 4.26.

There are a couple of additional things to observe about CompensateActivity.

First, this activity can only appear (at any depth) within a fault handler, a cancellation handler, or a compensation handler. The validation logic of Compensate-Activity also ensures that the TargetActivityName property must refer to a compensatable activity.

Second, when `CompensateActivity` executes and its `TargetActivityName` property references a child activity that does not have a result of *Succeeded*, the `CompensateActivity` does nothing. This logic covers both the case of a target activity that did not compete successfully, as well as the case of a target activity that has already been compensated.

In summary, the examples shown in this section have illustrated how activity compensation can be used as one strategy within the broader implementation of fault handling and cancellation handling for WF programs. It is important to remember that compensation does not stand alone, but is rather a mechanism that might help you, in certain cases, implement the fault handling and cancellation handling that your WF programs need. If compensation logic is not helpful in this endeavor, it may be safely ignored due to the opt-in model for compensation adopted by the WF programming model.

Where Are We?

Chapters 3 and 4 together have presented the complete activity automaton, and the details of the execution model for activities. This asynchronous execution model rests firmly on the ideas of bookmarks and continuations, and goes hand in hand with the episodic execution of WF programs. The embodiment of the WF execution model is the activity automaton, along with a set of constraints, enforced by the WF runtime, that govern the runtime relationships between any composite activity and its child activities.

Because all WF programs are just compositions of activities, we have also come to see how, viewed from the inside, an in-memory WF program instance is a set of CLR objects, which transiently represent activities within various execution contexts.

In the next chapter, we will shift our perspective and take a look at WF programs from the outside—that is, from the vantage point of the application that hosts the WF runtime and manages the execution of WF program instances.

■ 5 ■
Applications

T HE PREVIOUS TWO CHAPTERS HAVE focused on the details of the execution model for activities. Now we will turn our attention to the larger-scale lifecycle of a WF program instance, which will lead us to examine the WF programming model from the perspective of the application that hosts the WF runtime. Along the way, we will introduce and discuss in detail a set of concepts related to WF program instance management including WF program instance passivation, suspension, and termination. We will also encounter several extensibility points offered by the WF runtime, which allow the character of the WF runtime to be tailored to the needs of the application in which it is being used. Finally, we will demonstrate that the WF runtime is source format agnostic and can accommodate WF programs that are represented in formats other than XAML.

The WF Runtime

The WF runtime is embodied by the `WorkflowRuntime` class, which not surprisingly is the central type in the `System.Workflow.Runtime` namespace. The methods, properties, and events of the `WorkflowRuntime` class fall into two general categories. The members shown in Listing 5.1 allow you to instantiate the WF runtime and manage it and the services it contains. We will discuss this functionality first. The remaining members of `WorkflowRuntime`, which we'll look at later in the chapter, allow you to create and manage instances of WF programs.

Listing 5.1 `WorkflowRuntime`

```
namespace System.Workflow.Runtime
{
  public class WorkflowRuntime : IServiceProvider, IDisposable
  {
    public WorkflowRuntime();
    public WorkflowRuntime(string configSectionName);
    public WorkflowRuntime(WorkflowRuntimeSection settings);

    public void StartRuntime();
    public void StopRuntime();
    public void Dispose();

    public bool IsStarted { get; }
    public string Name { get; set; }

    public void AddService(object service);
    public void RemoveService(object service);
    public T GetService<T>();
    public object GetService(Type serviceType);
    public ReadOnlyCollection<T> GetAllServices<T>();
    public ReadOnlyCollection<object> GetAllServices(
      Type serviceType);

    public event EventHandler<ServicesExceptionNotHandledEventArgs>
      ServicesExceptionNotHandled;

    /* *** other members *** */
  }
}
```

In order to run a WF program, you must first instantiate the WF runtime. The process of instantiating, configuring, and starting the WF runtime is called **hosting**. The WF runtime is represented in an application by a CLR object of type `WorkflowRuntime`, and as such can be hosted in any CLR application domain. As depicted in Figure 5.1, WF imposes no restriction on the number of `WorkflowRuntime` objects that can exist in any given application domain (though it is atypical to need more than one WF runtime in a given application domain).

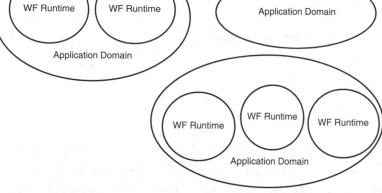

Figure 5.1   WF runtime hosted in CLR application domains

The simplest boilerplate code for hosting the WF runtime looks like this:

```
using (WorkflowRuntime runtime = new WorkflowRuntime())
{
  runtime.StartRuntime();

  ...

  runtime.StopRuntime();
}
```

Services

The WF runtime is a container of services. These services are actually just any CLR objects of your choosing; there are no special requirements that must be met in order to become a service (in the context of the WF runtime). As we have seen in examples of previous chapters (see the WriterService in Chapter 3, "Activity Execution"), you can develop custom services on which your activities depend and then add these services to the WF runtime. Activities obtain the services they need using the GetService method of ActivityExecutionContext.

WorkflowRuntime defines several simple methods (AddService, GetService, RemoveService) for managing its set of contained services.

The code to programmatically add a service to the WF runtime, thereby making it available to activities in WF program instances, is simple:

```
using (WorkflowRuntime runtime = new WorkflowRuntime())
{
  WriterService writer = new WriterService();
  runtime.AddService(writer);
  ...
  runtime.StartRuntime();
  ...
}
```

Services can also be added to the WF runtime via a configuration file. In some deployment scenarios it is more desirable to provide a configuration file for the application hosting the WF runtime than to perform programmatic addition of services. The WF programming model gives you both options. Please refer to the WF SDK for sample usage of configuration files.

WF Runtime Services

In addition to passively providing services to activities, the WF runtime relies upon a set of well-known services as it manages WF program instances. The core WF runtime is as lightweight as possible so that several aspects of its functionality can be customized by a host application. These well-known services, sometimes referred to as **WF runtime services**, are defined as types within the `System.Workflow.Runtime.Hosting` namespace. Following are the three WF runtime services that we will discuss here:

- `WorkflowLoaderService`
- `WorkflowSchedulerService`
- `WorkflowPersistenceService`

By abstracting these capabilities into standalone services, the core WF runtime remains lightweight and as a consequence can be utilized differently in different hosting applications. WF provides one or more useful implementations of each of these services, but as needed you can develop custom implementations that suit the needs of your specific solution. The three services listed previously are defined as abstract classes, which allow multiple concrete implementations to be written and interchanged without affecting the WF runtime.

Table 5.1 lists the WF-provided implementations of each WF runtime service. If no implementation of one of these services is added to the WF runtime (either programmatically or via a configuration file), the default implementation of that service is automatically added during the execution of the `StartRuntime` method of `WorkflowRuntime`. This ensures a valid WF runtime at the return of the `StartRuntime` method. All of the types mentioned in Table 5.1 are defined in the `System.Workflow.Runtime.Hosting` namespace.

Table 5.1   WF Runtime Services

Service	Default Implementation	Other Implementations
Loader	`DefaultWorkflowLoaderService`	
Scheduler	`DefaultWorkflowSchedulerService`	`ManualWorkflow-SchedulerService`
Persistence	n/a	`SqlWorkflowPersis-tenceService`

To summarize the information in Table 5.1, the WF runtime requires exactly one `WorkflowLoaderService`, and exactly one `WorkflowSchedulerService`. The WF runtime requires either zero or one service of type `WorkflowPersistenceService`, which means that it is possible to run WF programs without the possibility of passivation.

When you configure the WF runtime, you are free to mix and match the WF-provided service implementations with custom implementations of the abstract classes (within the constraints just mentioned) and, as we have already discussed, you are free to add whatever additional services are needed by your activities.

Unlike other services, the WF runtime services are used exclusively by the WF runtime, and are not available to activities in WF program instances. Calling `ActivityExecutionContext.GetService` returns `null` if the type of the requested service is any of the WF runtime service types.

WF Program Instances

Rather than examine each of the WF runtime services in isolation, we are going to turn next to the representation and management of WF program instances.

In the discussion of the lifecycle of a WF program instance, the roles of the WF runtime services will come into the picture. Our focus here is the lifecycle of a WF program instance because that is the context in which the runtime services are asked to perform their work.

As mentioned at the outset of the chapter, the `WorkflowRuntime` class contains a set of methods and properties related to the creation and management of WF program instances. These members are shown in Listing 5.2.

Listing 5.2 `WorkflowRuntime`

```
namespace System.Workflow.Runtime
{
  public class WorkflowRuntime : IServiceProvider, IDisposable
  {
    /* *** See Listing 5.1 for other members *** */

    public WorkflowInstance CreateWorkflow(XmlReader workflowReader);
    public WorkflowInstance CreateWorkflow(XmlReader workflowReader,
      XmlReader rulesReader,
      Dictionary<string, object> namedArgumentValues);
    public WorkflowInstance CreateWorkflow(XmlReader workflowReader,
      XmlReader rulesReader,
      Dictionary<string, object> namedArgumentValues,
      Guid instanceId);

    public WorkflowInstance CreateWorkflow(Type workflowType);
    public WorkflowInstance CreateWorkflow(Type workflowType,
      Dictionary<string, object> namedArgumentValues);
    public WorkflowInstance CreateWorkflow(Type workflowType,
      Dictionary<string, object> namedArgumentValues,
        Guid instanceId);

    public WorkflowInstance GetWorkflow(Guid instanceId);
    public ReadOnlyCollection<WorkflowInstance> GetLoadedWorkflows();

    public event EventHandler<WorkflowEventArgs> WorkflowAborted;
    public event EventHandler<WorkflowCompletedEventArgs>
      WorkflowCompleted;
    public event EventHandler<WorkflowEventArgs> WorkflowCreated;
    public event EventHandler<WorkflowEventArgs> WorkflowIdled;
    public event EventHandler<WorkflowEventArgs> WorkflowLoaded;
    public event EventHandler<WorkflowEventArgs> WorkflowPersisted;
    public event EventHandler<WorkflowEventArgs> WorkflowResumed;
    public event EventHandler<WorkflowEventArgs> WorkflowStarted;
    public event EventHandler<WorkflowSuspendedEventArgs>
```

```
      WorkflowSuspended;
    public event EventHandler<WorkflowTerminatedEventArgs>
      WorkflowTerminated;
    public event EventHandler<WorkflowEventArgs> WorkflowUnloaded;
  }
}
```

The return type of `WorkflowRuntime.CreateWorkflow` is `WorkflowInstance`, which represents an in-memory handle to an actual WF program instance. The `WorkflowInstance` type is defined in the `System.Workflow.Runtime` namespace and is shown in Listing 5.3.

Listing 5.3   `WorkflowInstance`

```
namespace System.Workflow.Runtime
{
  public sealed class WorkflowInstance
  {
    public Guid InstanceId { get; }

    public void Abort();
    public void Load();
    public void Resume();
    public void Start();
    public void Suspend(string error);
    public void Terminate(string error);
    public bool TryUnload();
    public void Unload();

    public Activity GetWorkflowDefinition();

    /* *** other members *** */
  }
}
```

`WorkflowInstance` wraps an underlying WF program instance (an actual set of `Activity` objects, if the instance is in memory) that is managed by the WF runtime.

When you need a durable handle to a WF program instance, you can use the value of the `InstanceId` property of `WorkflowInstance`. This globally unique identifier can always be used to obtain a `WorkflowInstance` that represents the WF program instance carrying that identifier. As shown here, `WorkflowRuntime` has a `GetWorkflow` method that accepts a `Guid` (which uniquely identifies a WF program instance) and returns a `WorkflowInstance`:

```
static void Main()
{
  using (WorkflowRuntime runtime = new WorkflowRuntime())
  {
    runtime.StartRuntime();

    WorkflowInstance instance = runtime.CreateWorkflow(...);
    Guid handle = instance.InstanceId;
    instance = null;

    // Get back a handle to the same instance
    instance = runtime.GetWorkflow(handle);

    ...
  }
}
```

Creating a WF Program Instance

The first step in running an instance of a WF program is actually creating the instance. This is the job of the CreateWorkflow method of WorkflowRuntime. As you can see from Listing 5.2, CreateWorkflow has several overloads, each of which returns a WorkflowInstance. The creation of an instance of a WF program involves a series of steps called **activation**.

In application code, activation simply amounts to calling CreateWorkflow. But inside the implementation of this method, a few interesting things happen.

First of all, a new WF program instance (an actual tree of Activity objects) needs to be manufactured from some representation of a WF program. To make things more concrete, consider the following Echo program:

```
<Sequence x:Name="Echo" xmlns="http://EssentialWF/Activities"
xmlns:x="http://schemas.microsoft.com/winfx/2006/xaml"
xmlns:wf="http://schemas.microsoft.com/winfx/2006/xaml/workflow">
  <ReadLine x:Name="r1" />
  <WriteLine x:Name="w1" Text="{wf:ActivityBind r1,Path=Text}" />
</Sequence>
```

Clearly, this is just a textual representation of a WF program, which happens to use XAML as the format of that text. Although it is common practice to call this XAML snippet a WF program (as we have done throughout this book), we can label it more precisely by calling it a WF program blueprint. A **WF program blueprint** is an artifact (or a set of artifacts) that *represents* a tree of activity declarations. It is something that can *become* an in-memory tree of activity objects.

A WF program blueprint is not something natively understood by the core of the WF runtime. A blueprint must be translated into an in-memory tree of activity objects by a runtime service called the **WF program loader** in order to be executed by the WF runtime. The job of a WF program loader is to accept a WF program blueprint as input and produce an activity tree as output. The activity tree produced by a WF program loader is called a **WF program prototype**, sometimes called a program definition. The program prototype consists of metadata—the values of activity properties that are immutable at runtime. This metadata includes the structure of the WF program (the `Activities` property of all composite activities in the program) and also the values of any properties that are registered as metadata properties (such as the `Name` property of `Activity`). Metadata properties were discussed briefly in Chapter 2, "WF Programs," and will be explored in more detail in Chapter 7, "Advanced Authoring."

A WF program prototype is held in memory by the WF runtime as a template, from which multiple instances can be manufactured (each resulting from a call to `CreateWorkflow`). A **WF program instance** is the entity (represented in memory by CLR objects and in durable storage as a continuation) that is actually executed by the WF runtime.

To run our Echo program, the default WF program loader translates the XAML into an in-memory tree of activity objects—a WF program prototype. If we run the program once, a single WF program instance is manufactured from the WF program prototype (and is eventually disposed when the instance completes its execution). If we run the program six times, six WF program instances come and go independently; all of these WF program instances share (a reference to) the same WF program prototype.

The relationship between a WF program prototype and the set of WF program instances manufactured from that prototype is depicted in Figure 5.2. All instances manufactured from the same prototype share the same metadata.

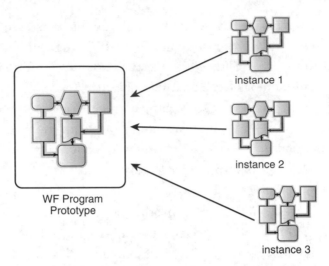

Figure 5.2 A WF program prototype and three WF program instances manufactured from that prototype

The situation depicted in Figure 5.2 is analogous to that which exists in the CLR between a type and objects of that type (see Figure 5.3). A typical CLR type acts as a template from which multiple objects can be instantiated. These objects share metadata (for example, CLR attributes that are applied to the type or inherited by it) but also hold unique instance-specific state (the values of nonstatic fields and properties defined by the type).

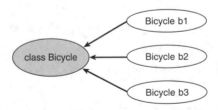

Figure 5.3 A CLR type and three objects of that type

The CLR does not care about the programming language used in source files that define a type, so long as the compiler of that language can translate the source code to MSIL. Similarly, the WF runtime does not care about WF program blueprint formats, so long as WF program prototypes can be realized from blueprints that use a particular format. The fact that WF does not have an underlying grammar, but is instead activity oriented, opens the door to programming in domain-specific languages (DSLs). XAML may be fine for general-purpose WF program authoring. However, DSLs offer the potential for more effective programming because the constructions of a DSL match the domain of the problem being solved and are usually more expressive (compared to a general-purpose language) in that domain. A set of activity types can be developed to exactly mirror the semantics of a chosen DSL.

There is a subtle but crucial difference here. What the WF runtime cares about is the in-memory representation of a WF program. Whereas the CLR loader is (for the most part) wedded to the assembly as a unit of packaging for MSIL and metadata, the WF runtime imposes no such restriction. WF program prototypes are not packaged; only the blueprints from which prototypes are loaded are packagable. As we shall see later, a WF program blueprint can be a CLR type that is packaged in an assembly. But as we already know, a WF program blueprint can also be XAML. XAML representing a WF program can be packaged as a file on disk, or as a blob in a database table, or might also be a stream of data (that is created dynamically by application code) without any packaging at all.

Figure 5.4 depicts the loading of WF program prototypes from several different formats and forms of packaging.

You can obtain a copy of the prototype for any WF program instance by calling the GetWorkflowDefinition method of WorkflowInstance. In order to preserve program execution robustness, the WF runtime does not provide access to actual prototypes; it only hands out copies thereof. Along the same lines, the WF runtime never provides direct access to the Activity objects that (transiently) represent underlying WF program instances while they are in memory. It is the Workflow-Instance wrapper that allows application code to interact with and manage WF program instances.

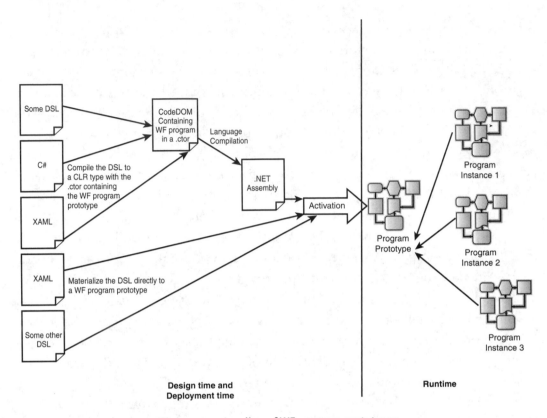

Figure 5.4   Loading of WF program prototypes

We will see in a minute, when we discuss custom loader services, exactly how different program representations are accommodated by the WF runtime. First, though, let's go through the capabilities that come for free with the default loader service.

`WorkflowRuntime` provides two flavors of `CreateWorkflow`. The first accepts a `System.Type` as the packaging for the WF program. The second accepts a `System.Xml.XmlReader`. There are three overloads of each, for a total of six distinct `CreateWorkflow` method signatures:

```
public WorkflowInstance CreateWorkflow(XmlReader reader);
public WorkflowInstance CreateWorkflow(XmlReader reader,
    XmlReader rulesReader,
    Dictionary<string, object> namedArgumentValues);
public WorkflowInstance CreateWorkflow(XmlReader reader,
    XmlReader rulesReader,
    Dictionary<string, object> namedArgumentValues,
```

```
      Guid instanceId);
   public WorkflowInstance CreateWorkflow(Type workflowType);
   public WorkflowInstance CreateWorkflow(Type workflowType,
      Dictionary<string, object> namedArgumentValues);
   public WorkflowInstance CreateWorkflow(Type workflowType,
      Dictionary<string, object> namedArgumentValues,
         Guid instanceId);
```

In the absence of a custom loader service, the overloads of `CreateWorkflow` that accept a `System.Type` will realize a WF program prototype by calling the constructor of the type. The type that is passed as a parameter to `CreateWorkflow` must therefore be a derivative of the `Activity` class because the constructor of any other kind of type will not yield a valid WF program prototype.

The first overload accepts only a `System.Type`.

A second overload accepts, in addition to a `System.Type`, a collection of name-value pairs that are used in the initialization of the WF program instance. Specifically, each name in the collection corresponds to the name of a settable public property of the root activity in the WF program. The value provided for that name is supplied as the value to that property's setter, as shown here:

```
using (WorkflowRuntime runtime = new WorkflowRuntime())
{
  runtime.StartRuntime();

  Dictionary<string, object> inputs =
    new Dictionary<string, object>();

  // The root activity must have public properties named
  // Assignee and DueDate, of the appropriate types
  inputs.Add("Assignee", "David");
  inputs.Add("DueDate", DateTime.Now.Add(new TimeSpan(1, 0, 0)));

  Type type = ...
  WorkflowInstance instance = runtime.CreateWorkflow(type, inputs);

  ...
}
```

This initialization of root activity properties, which may fairly be characterized as a way of providing "inputs" to the WF program instance, is entirely optional (hence the overload). As we will see later, when a WF program instance completes its execution, the values of the gettable public properties of the root activity will be readable by the application, and so may be considered the "outputs" of the instance.

The third overload of `CreateWorkflow` is exactly like the second except that you also provide a value for the globally unique identifier that will be used to identify the WF program instance being created. This overload can be useful when you need to map a WF program instance identifier to data that exists elsewhere in your application; sometimes it is helpful to represent the creation of a WF program instance before the call to `CreateWorkflow` is actually made. For the other overloads, the identifier will be generated by the WF runtime. In either case, the identifier is available via the `InstanceId` property of `WorkflowInstance`.

The second set of `CreateWorkflow` overloads accepts an `XmlReader` instead of a `Type`. The simplest of these overloads accepts a single `XmlReader` that (in the absence of a custom loader service) must contain a XAML representation of the WF program. We will see soon, when we discuss the details of the loader service, how formats other than XAML can be accommodated in a first-class manner. XAML, however, is what you get for free with the default loader.

The other two overloads accept, in addition to the first `XmlReader` representing the program, a second `XmlReader` expected to contain the definition of declarative rules (essentially, CodeDOM expressions serialized in XAML) that are part of the WF program. Rules will be discussed in detail in Chapter 8, "Miscellanea." And, just as with the `Type`-based overloads, there are `XmlReader`-based overloads that allow you to provide a collection of name-value pairs for root activity property initialization as well as a globally unique identifier for the WF program instance being created.

When the `CreateWorkflow` method returns, a brand new WF program instance exists in memory but it is not yet running. To run the instance, you must call the `Start` method of `WorkflowInstance`. It is the `Start` method that will enqueue (into the WF scheduler work queue) an item corresponding to the invocation of the `Execute` method of the root activity. Before examining the rest of the lifecycle of the WF program instance, though, let's summarize the instance creation process and discuss a few details we have missed so far.

Figure 5.5 depicts the internals of WF program instance creation.

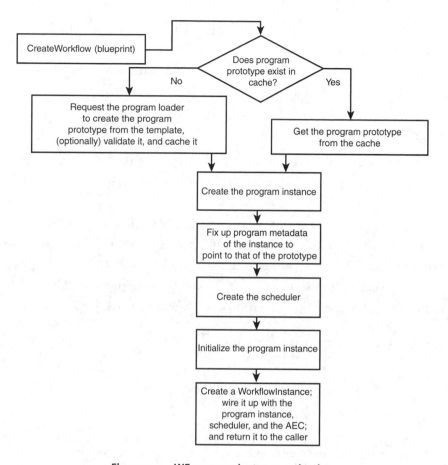

Figure 5.5   WF program instance activation

As you can see, there are a few steps in Figure 5.5 that we have not yet mentioned. The first is that the WF runtime maintains a cache of WF program prototypes. When a call to `CreateWorkflow` is made, the WF runtime first checks to see whether the relevant prototype is available. If a prototype is found, it is used to manufacture the instance. If no prototype is available, the loader service is invoked in order to obtain the prototype, and the resulting prototype is cached for future use.

After it has a new instance, the WF runtime prepares the instance for execution by creating its scheduler and the corresponding work queue, and providing the WF program instance with a default `ActivityExecutionContext`. The collection of name-value pairs (if provided to `CreateWorkflow`) is next used to set the values of properties of the root activity of the instance. The `Initialize` method of the root activity in the instance is called after the properties are set. Finally, a `Workflow-Instance` object that acts as a handle to the actual program instance is constructed and returned to the caller of `CreateWorkflow`.

The Program Loader Service

The important extensibility point that exists in the process of creating new WF program instances is the ability to provide the WF runtime with a custom loader service.

The WF runtime delegates the actual loading of a program to a runtime service called the **program loader service** (or simply the **loader**). The loader service is responsible for materializing an `Activity` object from a WF program blueprint.

The `WorkflowLoaderService` is the abstract base class for all loader service implementations. It defines two methods, as shown in Listing 5.4.

Listing 5.4   `WorkflowLoaderService`

```
namespace System.Workflow.Runtime.Hosting
{
   public abstract class WorkflowLoaderService
     : WorkflowRuntimeService
   {
     protected internal abstract Activity CreateInstance(
       XmlReader workflowDefinitionReader, XmlReader rulesReader);

     protected internal abstract Activity CreateInstance(
       Type workflowType);
   }
}
```

As indicated earlier in Table 5.1, the WF runtime will use a default loader if a custom implementation of `WorkflowLoaderService` is not provided.

The default loader implementation is named `DefaultWorkflowLoaderService` and is shown, with selected code snippets illustrating roughly how it works, in Listing 5.5. You can adapt this code as needed when writing a custom loader service.

Listing 5.5   DefaultWorkflowLoaderService

```
namespace System.Workflow.Runtime.Hosting
{
  public class DefaultWorkflowLoaderService : WorkflowLoaderService
  {
    // Error handling elided for clarity

    protected override Activity CreateInstance(
      Type workflowType)
    {
       return (Activity) Activator.CreateInstance(workflowType);
     }

    protected override Activity CreateInstance(
      XmlReader workflowDefinitionReader, XmlReader rulesReader)
    {
      Activity root = null;
      ServiceContainer serviceContainer = new ServiceContainer();
      ITypeProvider typeProvider =
        this.Runtime.GetService<ITypeProvider>();
      if (typeProvider != null)
        serviceContainer.AddService(typeof(ITypeProvider),
          typeProvider);

      DesignerSerializationManager manager = new
          DesignerSerializationManager(serviceContainer);
      using (manager.CreateSession())
      {
        WorkflowMarkupSerializationManager xamlSerializationManager =
          new WorkflowMarkupSerializationManager(manager);
        root = new WorkflowMarkupSerializer().Deserialize(
          xamlSerializationManager, workflowDefinitionReader)
          as Activity;

        if (root != null && rulesReader != null)
        {
          object rules = new WorkflowMarkupSerializer().Deserialize(
            xamlSerializationManager, rulesReader);
          root.SetValue(RuleDefinitions.RuleDefinitionsProperty,
            rules);
        }
      }

      return root;
    }
  }
}
```

The overload of `CreateInstance` that accepts a `System.Type` simply uses the `System.Activator` class to create a new instance of the specified type. The overload of `CreateInstance` that accepts two `XmlReader` objects deserializes the WF program and its associated rules using `WorkflowMarkupSerializer`.

The application that hosts the WF runtime can provide a custom loader implementation that materializes an `Activity` from any DSL. For example, we can write a loader that converts a simple Microsoft Visio file into a tree of activity objects. We start by creating a simple Visio file, say WriteLines.vdx, which is visualized in Figure 5.6. The content of the file is based on a custom domain-specific Visio stencil. Each `WriteLine` shape in WriteLines.vdx has a `Name` property and a `Value` property. The `Name` is the text on the shape, and will become the `Name` property of our `WriteLine` activity. The `Value` property of the `WriteLine` shape will become the `Text` property of the `WriteLine` activity. Let's assume that our WriteLines.vdx file specified four WriteLine shapes, with their values set to "one," "two," "three," and "four," respectively.

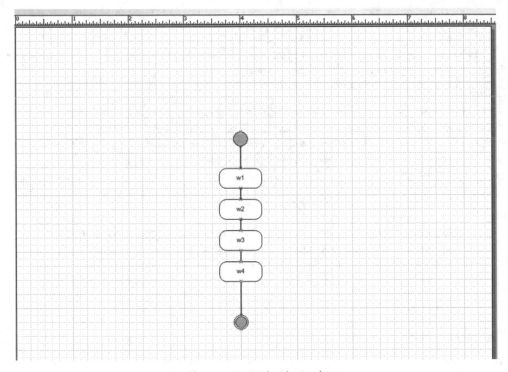

Figure 5.6   WriteLines.vdx

Next, we host the WF runtime in a console application that we've called `DiagramsCanExecuteToo`. You can pass a .vdx file to this application as an argument, like so:

```
> DiagramsCanExecuteToo.exe WriteLines.vdx
```

The result of executing WriteLines.vdx is

```
One
Two
Three
four
```

The implementation of the `DiagramsCanExecuteToo` application is shown in Listing 5.6.

Listing 5.6   The `DiagramsCanExecuteToo` **Application**

```
using System;
using System.Threading;
using System.Workflow.Runtime;
using System.Workflow.Runtime.Hosting;
using System.Xml;

namespace DiagramsCanExecuteToo
{
  class Program
    {
      static void Main(string[] args)
      {
        using (WorkflowRuntime runtime = new WorkflowRuntime())

        AutoResetEvent waitHandle = new AutoResetEvent(false);
        runtime.WorkflowCompleted += delegate(object sender,
          WorkflowCompletedEventArgs e)
        {
          waitHandle.Set();
        };

        if (args.Length != 1)
          throw new ArgumentException("expecting one vdx file");

        if (args[0].Contains(".vdx"))
          runtime.AddService(new VisioLoader());
        else
          throw new ArgumentException("we only support vdx files!");
```

```
          using (XmlReader reader = new XmlTextReader(args[0]))
          {
            WorkflowInstance instance = runtime.CreateWorkflow(reader);
            instance.Start();
            waitHandle.WaitOne();
          }
        }
      }
    }
  }
}
```

The custom Visio loader service upon which our solution depends is shown in Listing 5.7. There is no XAML here, and no compilation of the WF program to a CLR type either. The program is loaded directly from the Visio file.

Listing 5.7   Custom Loader that Reads Visio Files

```
using System;
using System.IO;
using System.Workflow.ComponentModel;
using System.Workflow.Runtime.Hosting;
using System.Xml;

using Microsoft.Office.Interop.Visio;
using EssentialWF.Activities;

public class VisioLoader : WorkflowLoaderService
{
  protected override Activity CreateInstance(XmlReader
    workflowReader, XmlReader rulesReader)
  {
    // Visio OM requires a file on disk
    // We create a temp file from the XmlReader

    workflowReader.MoveToContent();
    while (!workflowReader.EOF && !workflowReader.IsStartElement())
      workflowReader.Read();

    string tempPath = Environment.CurrentDirectory + @"\temp.vdx";
    string text = workflowReader.ReadOuterXml();

    using (StreamWriter sw = new StreamWriter(tempPath))
    {
      sw.Write(text);
    }
```

```
      // Create Visio Application Object
      Application app = new Application();

      // Open the Visio document that we just created
      Document doc = app.Documents.OpenEx(tempPath,
         (short)VisOpenSaveArgs.visOpenRO |
         (short)VisOpenSaveArgs.visOpenHidden |
         (short)VisOpenSaveArgs.visOpenMinimized |
         (short)VisOpenSaveArgs.visOpenNoWorkspace
      );

      // Translate Visio shapes to activities
      Sequence seq = new Sequence();
      foreach (Shape shape in doc.Pages[1].Shapes)
      {
        if (shape.Master.Name == "WriteLine")
        {
          WriteLine wl = new WriteLine();

          Cell cell1 = shape.get_Cells("Prop.Row_1");
          wl.Text = cell1.get_ResultStr(null);

          Cell cell2 = shape.get_Cells("Prop.Row_2");
          wl.Name = cell2.get_ResultStr(null);

          seq.Activities.Add(wl);
        }
      }

      // Close the document, quit the Visio app
      doc.Close();
      app.Quit();

      // Delete the temp file
      File.Delete(tempPath);

      // Return the activity tree to the WF runtime
      return seq;
    }

    protected override Activity CreateInstance(Type workflowType)
    {
      throw new NotSupportedException("Packaging a visio file in a .NET
        assembly is not supported");
    }
  }
```

Using the Visio automation model (API) works but is a bit heavyweight. Ideally, because Visio documents can be expressed as XML, one can envision writing a serializer (a class named `VisioSerializer`) that operates directly on this XML format, bypassing the automation API. With this improved design, the custom Visio loader service can simply delegate the job of materializing an `Activity` object from markup to the Visio serializer (just as the `DefaultWorkflowLoaderService` delegates work to `WorkflowMarkupSerializer`, which knows how to parse XAML). In Chapter 7, we will discuss custom serializers for activities.

Even our simplistic Visio loader demonstrates that the WF runtime is truly format agnostic. The currency of the WF runtime is in-memory trees of activities—actual CLR objects. What this means is that the WF runtime does not care how you choose to author a WF program so long as a custom loader implementation can translate your representations of WF programs to activities. This opens up avenues for directly executing programs of all kinds that are written in domain-specific languages.

Running a WF Program Instance

Now that we know how to create a new instance of a WF program, it's time to run it.

As we have already seen in some examples, calling `CreateWorkflow` is not enough; the `Start` method of `WorkflowInstance` must be called in order to begin the execution of the instance (and resume the initial, implicit, bookmark whose resumption point is the `Execute` method of the root activity).

It is here that the threading model employed by the WF runtime comes to the forefront. In Chapter 3, we learned that the scheduler (for a particular WF program instance) will only use a single CLR thread in its dispatcher loop. This ensures that within a WF program instance, the code for at most one activity can actually be executing at a given point in time. What is relevant to the application that hosts the WF runtime is where that CLR thread comes from.

The WF runtime never creates threads on its own, but instead relies upon a runtime service to obtain threads on which it can run WF program instances.

The relevant runtime service is called `WorkflowSchedulerService`, which provides an abstraction for a specific host-controllable threading policy (that drives the WF scheduler) and is shown in Listing 5.8.

Listing 5.8   `WorkflowSchedulerService`

```
namespace System.Workflow.Runtime.Hosting
{
  public abstract class WorkflowSchedulerService
    : WorkflowRuntimeService
  {
    protected internal abstract void Schedule(
      WaitCallback callback,
      Guid workflowInstanceId
    );

    /* *** other members *** */
  }
}
```

The default implementation of this service is the `DefaultWorkflowScheduler-Service`, which is shown in Listing 5.9.

Listing 5.9   `DefaultWorkflowSchedulerService`

```
namespace System.Workflow.Runtime.Hosting
{
  public class DefaultWorkflowSchedulerService
    : WorkflowSchedulerService
  {
    public DefaultWorkflowSchedulerService();

    public DefaultWorkflowSchedulerService(
      int maxSimultaneousWorkflows);

    public int MaxSimultaneousWorkflows { get; }

    /* *** other members *** */
  }
}
```

It is crucial to understand that the WF runtime does not create any CLR threads of its own. The threads that execute any code within the WF runtime (and WF program instances) are always threads that are owned and managed by the application that hosts the WF runtime. The host calls the methods of `WorkflowInstance` objects on any threads it wants. Not only can different program instances be created on different threads, but two or more `WorkflowInstance` objects representing the same WF program instance can be obtained on different threads.

Various operations of WorkflowInstance can be invoked on different threads—
the threads within a WorkflowInstance object are simply visitors, as depicted in
Figure 5.7.

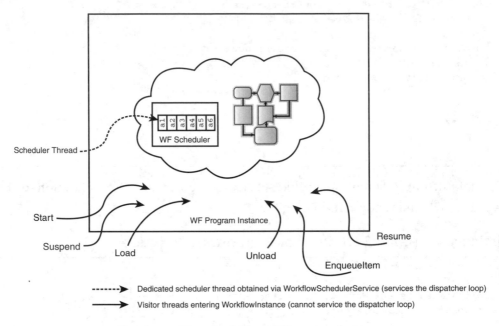

Figure 5.7 Threads visiting a WF program instance

Although operations on WorkflowInstance can be invoked on arbitrary threads,
the WF scheduler hosted within the program instance is serviced by a single thread.
The WF runtime guarantees that no other thread can interfere or service the scheduler while its dispatcher loop is actively processing work items. To be clear, the hosting application can invoke methods of WorkflowInstance on separate threads
concurrently—this does not affect the scheduler executing the activities on a dedicated thread (for an episode of execution).

Finally, although the scheduler of each WF program instance is serviced by a distinct CLR thread, a WF program instance can always run concurrently with other
instances, without any conflict.

Because WF programs typically run (in a logical sense) for a long time, with their
lifecycle potentially distributed across multiple application domains or machines, it
is natural that the Start method of WorkflowInstance does not block awaiting the
completion of the instance.

Instead, the `Start` method internally calls `AEC.ExecuteActivity`, passing the root activity as a parameter. Thus, the execution of the root activity is scheduled in exactly the same way as composite activities schedule the execution of their child activities. The `Start` method returns to the caller (the application hosting the WF runtime) after the work item for the root activity's execution has been scheduled.

At this point, the WF runtime requires a thread in order to dispatch the work item in the scheduler work queue. To obtain the thread, the `WorkflowScheduler-Service` is utilized. Specifically, the `Schedule` method of `Workflow-SchedulerService` is called, with the `WaitCallback` representing the scheduler dispatcher loop passed as a parameter. A typical implementation of the `Schedule` method invokes the callback on a distinct CLR thread using the CLR thread pool. This is essentially what the `DefaultWorkflowSchedulerService` does, so after the `Start` method returns, you will see the WF program instance running on a different thread obtained from the CLR thread pool. This asynchronous pattern is illustrated (simplistically) with the following snippet:

```
protected override void Schedule(WaitCallback callback,
  Guid workflowInstanceId)
{
  System.Threading.ThreadPool.QueueUserWorkItem(
    callback, workflowInstanceId);
}
```

Threads in Applications

In some scenarios, the application hosting the WF runtime has specific threading requirements dictated by the underlying programming model of the application. For instance, it may be desirable to have the host application explicitly provide the thread to be used by the scheduler in its dispatch loop, rather than having that thread come from the CLR thread pool. This is especially true for several popular UI programming models. Applications written using Windows Forms, Windows Presentation Foundation (WPF), and ASP.NET must follow the threading model of the chosen technology.

For example, Windows Forms requires that a UI control (say, a listbox) can only be accessed by the thread that created the control. This means that a background thread (perhaps in charge of obtaining data) cannot write values directly into the listbox. There is a requirement to explicitly switch what is known as the **synchronization context**, when operations are performed on background threads. When a Windows Forms application hosts the WF runtime and uses the `DefaultWorkflowSchedulerService` to run WF programs, we run into a problem if an activity calls a service that attempts to update a UI control. In this situation, we will see an `InvalidOperationException` stating

```
The calling thread may not access this object
because the object is owned by a different thread.
```

One simple way to get around this issue is to use a service like the `SynchContextSwitcher` that is shown in Listing 5.10.

Listing 5.10   `SynchContextSwitcher`

```
using System;
using System.Threading;

namespace EssentialWF.Services
{
  public sealed class SynchContextSwitcher
  {
    private SynchronizationContext originalContext = null;

    public SynchContextSwitcher()
    {
      // cache the SynchronizationContext.Current
      // on the host thread
      this.originalContext = SynchronizationContext.Current;
    }

    public SynchronizationContext SynchContext
    {
      get { return this.originalContext; }
    }
  }
}
```

The `SynchContextSwitcher` caches the `SynchronizationContext` associated with the thread on which its constructor is executed.

Assuming that the Windows Forms application creates an instance of this service on the UI thread, the `SynchronizationContext` of the UI thread will be cached.

The WF runtime can continue to use the `DefaultWorkflowSchedulerService` and execute WF program instances on CLR thread pool threads:

```
// The following code is executed on the UI thread
using (WorkflowRuntime runtime = new WorkflowRuntime())
{
  runtime.AddService(new SynchContextSwitcher());

  WorkflowInstance instance = runtime.CreateWorkflow(...);
  instance.Start();
}
```

A service upon which activities rely (let's call it `MyService`), and which updates the UI of the Windows Forms–based application in which it is running, can use the `SynchContextSwitcher` as shown here:

```
class MyService
{
  private WorkflowRuntime runtime;

  public void DoSomething(object o)
  {
    SynchContextSwitcher switcher =
      runtime.GetService<SynchContextSwitcher>();

    switcher.SynchContext.Post(ActualDoSomething, o);
  }

  public void ActualDoSomething(object o)
  {
    // update the UI here
  }
}
```

A better approach might be to implement a custom `WorkflowSchedulerService` that is intrinsically aware of the CLR `SynchronizationContext` and simply schedules the execution of activities under the synchronization context of the UI thread. Put differently, a custom `WorkflowSchedulerService` implementation can encapsulate synchronization context and eliminate the need to manually perform switching, which allows activity execution to proceed on the UI thread. This design frees up individual services from the burden of explicitly switching the synchronization context.

A custom `WorkflowSchedulerService` is shown is Listing 5.11.

Listing 5.11   SynchronizationContextSchedulerService

```
using System;
using System.Threading;
using System.Workflow.Runtime.Hosting;

namespace EssentialWF.Services
{
  public sealed class SynchronizationContextSchedulerService :
    WorkflowSchedulerService
  {
    bool synchronousDispatch = true;
    SynchronizationContext originalContext = null;

    public SynchronizationContextSchedulerService() : this(true){}
    public SynchronizationContextSchedulerService(
      bool synchronousDispatch)
    {
      this.originalContext = SynchronizationContext.Current;
      this.synchronousDispatch = synchronousDispatch;
    }

    public bool SynchronousDispatch
    {
      get { return this.synchronousDispatch; }
    }

    protected override void Schedule(WaitCallback callback, Guid
      workflowInstanceId)
    {
      // If the saved context from the thread that instantiated this
      // service is null, try obtaining the SynchronizationContext
      // of the current thread
      SynchronizationContext ctx = this.originalContext != null ?
        this.originalContext : SynchronizationContext.Current;

      if (ctx != null)
      {
        if (this.SynchronousDispatch)
          ctx.Send(delegate {callback(workflowInstanceId);}, null);
        else
          ctx.Post(delegate {callback(workflowInstanceId);}, null);
      }
      else // run the scheduler without SynchronizationContext
        callback(workflowInstanceId);
    }

    ...
```

```
    }

}
```

The approach outlined here works not just for Windows Forms but also for WPF and ASP.NET, because each of these technologies provides an implementation of `Synchronization Context` for their respective threading models. The technique works especially well in situations when the WF program instance runs in short bursts, in response to user input, and then waits for the next stimulus.

Because `SynchronizationContextSchedulerService.Schedule` uses the value of `Synchronization.Current`, it allows the host application to dictate the synchronization context explicitly by calling `SynchronizationContext.SetSynchronizationContext` before a call to `WorkflowInstance.Start` is made.

The application hosting the WF runtime must add the custom service to the `WorkflowRuntime`, like so:

```
using (WorkflowRuntime runtime = new WorkflowRuntime())
{
  runtime.AddService(new SynchronizationContextSchedulerService());

  ...

  WorkflowInstance instance = runtime.CreateWorkflow(...);

  // Execute on the current thread and its synchronization context
  instance.Start();
  ...
}
```

The implementation of the `SynchronizationContextSchedulerService` allows the host application to execute a WF program instance on a thread of its choosing. This is similar to the `System.Workflow.Runtime.Hosting.ManualWorkflowSchedulerService` that ships with WF, except that our implementation has an advantage in that it does not require the host application to explicitly call a special method (`ManualWorkflowSchedulerService.RunWorkflow`) to run the instance. Moreover, our implementation is aware of the CLR `SynchronizationContext`, whereas `ManualWorkflowSchedulerService` is not.

Passivating a WF Program Instance

Passivation is the process by which a WF program instance is persisted to a (typically durable) storage medium and removed from memory. At a later point in time, the instance can be brought back into memory and its execution is resumed. A passivated WF program instance can resume its execution in a different WF runtime, perhaps in a different CLR application domain (say, after a machine has crashed and restarted), or even on a different machine.

The WF runtime relies upon a runtime service called the persistence service in order to save and load instances to and from storage. It is possible to use the WF runtime with passivation disabled by not providing a persistence service. Although there is no default persistence service prescribed by the WF runtime, the `System.Workflow.Runtime.Hosting` namespace does include a `SqlWorkflowPersistenceService`, which we will use in some of our examples.

The standard reason for passivating a WF program instance is that the instance has become idle. A WF program instance is considered idle when there are no items in the work queue of its scheduler; no forward progress can be made without some external stimulus. When this occurs, the thread that the WF runtime obtained via `WorkflowSchedulerService` and used to dispatch work items is returned to the host. The WF program instance still lingers in memory, though. At this point, the WF runtime will raise the `WorkflowRuntime.WorkflowIdled` event. The host application can cause passivation to occur whenever a WF program instance becomes idle by subscribing for this event and calling the `Unload` method of the `WorkflowInstance`,[1] as shown here:

```
using (WorkflowRuntime runtime = new WorkflowRuntime())
{

  runtime.WorkflowIdled += delegate(object sender,
    WorkflowEventArgs e)
  {
    e.WorkflowInstance.Unload();
  };

  ...
}
```

[1] Because this is such a common pattern, you can automatically passivate idle WF program instances by giving the `UnloadOnIdle` property of `SqlWorkflowPersistenceService` a value of `true`.

The host application need not wait until a WF program instance is idle to unload it. For example, if a machine is running low on memory, the host may decide to proactively unload running instances while their execution is in progress. In other situations, running instances may be suspended and then unloaded. In order to preserve transaction guarantees, passivation cannot occur while the execution of `TransactionScopeActivity` (discussed in Chapter 6, "Transactions") is in progress. In such a situation, passivation will not occur until the transaction has completed.

As we have seen, `WorkflowInstance.Unload` is the method that the host application can call in order to passivate a WF program instance. `WorkflowInstance.TryUnload` differs from `Unload` in that it will succeed only if the instance is idle. If the instance is doing any work (the scheduler thread is active) when `TryUnload` is called, a value of `false` is returned and there is no effect on the instance.

Every WF program instance has a globally unique instance identifier associated with it. Thus, the host application can load a previously saved (passivated) WF program instance by calling `WorkflowRuntime.GetWorkflow` passing the required identifier. `GetWorkflow` causes the program instance to be loaded into memory from the store provided by the persistence service. If the host application already holds a `WorkflowInstance` for a passivated instance, the instance can be loaded by calling `WorkflowInstance.Load`, as shown here:

```
using (WorkflowRuntime runtime = new WorkflowRuntime())
{
  runtime.StartRuntime();

  WorkflowInstance instance =
    runtime.CreateWorkflow(type);

  instance.Start();
  ...
  instance.Unload();
  ...
  instance.Load();
  ...
}
```

There is no fundamental difference between `WorkflowRuntime.GetWorkflow` and `WorkflowInstance.Load`.

Typically, a passivated instance is loaded in order to deliver stimulus that has arrived from the external world:

```
Guid handle = ...
WorkflowInstance instance = runtime.GetWorkflow(handle);
instance.EnqueueItem(...);
```

`WorkflowInstance.EnqueueItem` enqueues an object in the specified WF program queue. This will typically trigger the resumption of a bookmark (the scheduling of an activity method) that was created by an activity that asked to be notified when data arrived in that WF program queue. This handoff of data from the host application to activities is illustrated later in this chapter and also explored fully (in the context of transactions) in Chapter 6.

As mentioned earlier, you can write a custom persistence service that utilizes whatever storage medium is appropriate for your solution. To do this, you extend an abstract base class, which is called `WorkflowPersistenceService`, and is shown in Listing 5.12.

Listing 5.12 `WorkflowPersistenceService`

```
namespace System.Workflow.Runtime.Hosting
{
  public abstract class WorkflowPersistenceService :
    WorkflowRuntimeService
  {
    protected static byte[] GetDefaultSerializedForm(
      Activity activity);
    protected static Activity RestoreFromDefaultSerializedForm(
      byte[] activityBytes, Activity outerActivity);

    protected internal abstract bool UnloadOnIdle(Activity activity);

    protected internal abstract Activity LoadWorkflowInstanceState(
      Guid instanceId);
    protected internal abstract void SaveWorkflowInstanceState(
      Activity rootActivity, bool unlock);
    protected internal abstract void UnlockWorkflowInstanceState(
      Activity rootActivity);

    protected internal abstract Activity LoadCompletedContextActivity(
      Guid scopeId, Activity outerActivity);
    protected internal abstract void SaveCompletedContextActivity(
```

```
        Activity activity);
    }
}
```

The `GetDefaultSerializedForm` and `RestoreFromDefaultSerializedForm` methods are static helpers that translate an `Activity` object to and from a default binary form. These methods rely upon the `Save` and `Load` methods of `Activity`, which in turn utilize a `System.Runtime.Serialization.Formatters.Binary.BinaryFormatter` by default to perform the serialization. There are overloads of `Save` and `Load` that accept any `IFormatter` (defined in the `System.Runtime.Serialization` namespace) so that a custom persistence service can use a formatter of its choosing. The `Save` and `Load` methods of `Activity` will only work properly when called on a **scheduler thread** (the thread running the WF program instance). Persistence services are the primary user of `Save` and `Load`. The other place in which these methods are utilized is in the `Clone` method of `Activity`, which (because it relies on `Save` and `Load`) should also only be called on a WF scheduler thread.

The `GetIsBlocked`, `GetSuspendOrTerminateInfo`, and `GetWorkflowStatus` methods are static helpers for obtaining information about the specified WF program instance. The values of the `WorkflowStatus` enumeration (see Listing 5.21) are discussed later in the chapter.

The `UnloadOnIdle` method must be overridden by a custom persistence service. This method is called by the WF runtime to determine whether a given WF program instance should be automatically unloaded when it becomes idle.

The real work of a persistence service is performed by the `SaveWorkflowInstanceState` and `LoadWorkflowInstanceState` methods. A custom persistence service will override these methods and provide the logic for saving and loading a WF program instance to the storage medium of choice. Whereas these methods are responsible for saving and loading an entire instance, the `LoadCompletedContextActivity` and `SaveCompletedContextActivity` methods perform a similar function for an activity that is the root of a dynamically created `ActivityExecutionContext`. A custom persistence service is expected to throw a `PersistenceException` (defined in the `System.Workflow.Runtime.Hosting` namespace) if an error occurs during loading or saving.

In some deployments of WF, there may be multiple WF runtimes (for example, on different machines) sharing a single storage medium for WF program instances (for example, a dedicated SQL Server installation). In such cases, the WF runtime and the persistence service collaborate to support a locking mechanism for WF program instances. If a persistence service supports this kind of multiruntime environment, it must lock the instance when a successful call to `LoadWorkflowInstanceState` is made. The instance is now under the control of a specific WF runtime. Likewise, when `SaveWorkflowInstanceState` is called, a Boolean parameter named `unlock` indicates whether the instance should then be unlocked. Finally, the persistence service defines an `UnlockWorkflowInstanceState` method that explicitly unlocks a given instance without actually saving it.

Listing 5.13 shows a custom persistence service that uses the `BinaryFormatter`[2] that is defined in the `System.Runtime.Serialization.Formatters.Binary` namespace to save and load WF program instances to and from files on disk.

Listing 5.13   Custom Persistence Service

```
using System;
using System.IO;
using System.Runtime.Serialization;
using System.Runtime.Serialization.Formatters;
using System.Runtime.Serialization.Formatters.Binary;
using System.Workflow.ComponentModel;
using System.Workflow.ComponentModel.Serialization;
using System.Workflow.Runtime;
using System.Workflow.Runtime.Hosting;

namespace EssentialWF.Services
{
  public class FilePersistenceService :
    WorkflowPersistenceService
  {
    private string location;
    private bool unloadOnIdle = false;

    public string Location
    {
      get { return this.location; }
    }
```

---

[2] Although WF runtime serialization architecture allows for plugging custom formatters, at the time of writing, only `BinaryFomatter` is fully supported by WF.

```
protected override bool UnloadOnIdle(Activity activity)
{
  return this.unloadOnIdle;
}

public FilePersistenceService(string location)
{
  this.location = location;
}

public FilePersistenceService(string location, bool unloadOnIdle)
{
  this.location = location;
  this.unloadOnIdle = unloadOnIdle;
}

string BuildFilePath(Guid ctxid)
{
  return Path.Combine(this.Location, ctxid.ToString() + ".bin");
}

protected override Activity LoadCompletedContextActivity(
  Guid ctxId, Activity outerActivity)
{
  return Load(ctxId, outerActivity);
}

protected override Activity LoadWorkflowInstanceState(
  Guid instanceId)
{
  return Load(instanceId, null);
}

protected override void SaveCompletedContextActivity(
  Activity ctxActivity)
{
  this.Save(ctxActivity, true);
}

protected override void SaveWorkflowInstanceState(
  Activity rootActivity, bool unlock)
{
  this.Save(rootActivity, unlock);
}

void Save(Activity activity, bool unlock)
{
  Guid ctxid = (Guid)activity.GetValue(
```

```
        Activity.ActivityContextGuidProperty);

    string filePath = this.BuildFilePath(ctxid);

    if (File.Exists(filePath))
      File.Delete(filePath);

    using (FileStream fs = new FileStream(filePath,
        FileMode.CreateNew))
    {
      IFormatter formatter = new BinaryFormatter();
      formatter.SurrogateSelector =
        ActivitySurrogateSelector.Default;

      activity.Save(fs, formatter);
    }

    if (!unlock)
      File.SetAttributes(filePath, FileAttributes.ReadOnly);
  }

  Activity Load(Guid ctxid, Activity outerActivity)
  {
    string filePath = this.BuildFilePath(ctxid);

    using (FileStream fs = new FileStream(filePath,
        FileMode.Open, FileAccess.Read, FileShare.Read))
    {
      fs.Seek(0, SeekOrigin.Begin);
      IFormatter formatter =new BinaryFormatter();
      formatter.SurrogateSelector =
        ActivitySurrogateSelector.Default;

      return Activity.Load(fs, outerActivity, formatter);
    }
  }

  protected override void UnlockWorkflowInstanceState(
    Activity rootActivity)
  {
    Guid ctxid = (Guid)rootActivity.GetValue(
        Activity.ActivityContextGuidProperty);
    string filePath = this.BuildFilePath(ctxid);
    using (FileStream fs = new FileStream(filePath, FileMode.Open))
      File.SetAttributes(filePath, FileAttributes.Normal);
  }
 }
}
```

Runtime Activity Serialization

As we learned in the previous section, the WF runtime can utilize a persistence serv-ice to store and retrieve WF program instances to and from a durable storage medium. The format used for **runtime serialization** should be optimized for effi-ciency (as opposed to, say, readability) and must also capture the state (values of activity object fields) of all activity instances within the executing WF program instance. For these reasons, the runtime serialization behavior of activities is not the same as the design-time serialization behavior of activities.

First, let's be clear about exactly what state must be serialized when a WF pro-gram instance is persisted to durable storage. The obvious data to serialize is the state of all activity instances in the WF program instance. As we learned earlier, there may be more than one activity instance for a given activity declaration, due to dynamic creation of execution contexts by a composite activity. Each activity instance is just a CLR object that contains fields representing the state of that activ-ity instance. Typically, all of these fields must be serialized, except for dependency property fields that specify activity metadata properties (which will be discussed in Chapter 7). Metadata properties do not need to be serialized because, by definition, they are shared by multiple WF program instances and their values are held in the WF program prototype managed by the WF runtime. This is a big win for runtime serialization efficiency.

Serializing the state of activity instances is necessary, but not sufficient. The WF runtime must also store bookkeeping data (such as the items in the work queue of the WF scheduler for the given WF program instance, and the internal bookmarks that are managed by the WF runtime on behalf of subscribers to the `Activity.Closed` event) when a WF program instance is persisted. This data ensures that the WF program instance about to be persisted can be loaded from durable storage at a later time, possibly in a different CLR application domain, and have its execution resumed.

Durability is an intrinsic property of WF program instances, and the WF pro-gramming model ensures that all WF programs have default serialization behavior. The details of runtime activity serialization, discussed in the remainder of this section, can typically be ignored by WF program authors using just XAML (or other declarative formats). Activity type developers should be aware of how their activities will be serialized at runtime so that they can, if necessary, utilize standard runtime serialization techniques—based on the types and services available in the `System.Runtime.Serialization` namespace—to improve serialization efficiency.

Surrogate-Based Serialization

The WF runtime serializes WF program instances, including all the activity instances within them, automatically. What this means is that you are not required to decorate activity types with the `System.SerializableAttribute` attribute.

```
// This is not required
[Serializable]
public class Widget : Activity { ... }
```

To achieve automatic serialization, the WF runtime uses what are known as serialization surrogates. A serialization surrogate is a type that is responsible for serializing objects of another type. A serialization surrogate must implement the `ISerializationSurrogate` interface, which is defined in the `System.Runtime.Serialization` namespace.

The WF runtime registers an internally implemented serialization surrogate for the `System.Workflow.ComponentModel.DependencyObject` type. Therefore, all derivatives of `DependencyObject` (including all activity types, because `Activity` inherits from `DependencyObject`) automatically have runtime serialization behavior. Details of serialization surrogates, and the types in the `System.Runtime.Serialization` namespace, are beyond the scope of this book but are discussed thoroughly in .NET Framework documentation.

The default serialization surrogate for activities relies upon `System.SerializableAttribute` to determine whether a field or dependency property of an activity is serializable. If the types of all of the fields and dependency properties declared by an activity type are marked `[Serializable]`, then as an activity developer, there is nothing else you need to do to make runtime serialization work. The following code snippet shows an activity type that is, by default, fully serializable:

```
public class CreateOrder : Activity
{
  public static readonly DependencyProperty SKUProperty
    = DependencyProperty.Register("SKU",
      typeof(string), typeof(CreateOrder));
```

```
public string SKU
{
  get { return (string) GetValue(SKUProperty); }
  set { SetValue(SKUProperty, value); }
}

private int quantity;

public int Quantity
{
  get { return this.quantity; }
  set { this.quantity = value; }
}

...
}
```

The System.String and System.Int32 types are both marked with [Serializable] so the SKUProperty dependency property field and the quantity field are both automatically serializable by the activity serialization surrogate.

However, consider a modified CreateOrder activity type that contains a field of a type Order which is not marked with System.SerializableAttribute:

```
public class CreateOrder : Activity
{
  public static readonly DependencyProperty OrderProperty =
    DependencyProperty.Register("Order",
      typeof(Order), typeof(CreateOrder));

  public Order Order
  {
    get { return (Order) GetValue(OrderProperty); }
    set { SetValue(OrderProperty, value); }
  }

  ...
}

public class Order
{
  private string sku;
  private int quantity;

  public Order(string sku, int quantity)
  {
    this.sku = sku;
```

```
      this.quantity = quantity;
    }

    public string SKU
    {
      get { return this.sku; }
      set { this.sku = value; }
    }

    public int Quantity
    {
      get { return this.quantity; }
      set { this.quantity = value; }
    }
  }
}
```

A type is not considered serializable unless it is marked with [Serializable].
Because the Order type is not marked with [Serializable], running a WF program that contains a CreateOrder activity will result in a runtime serialization exception (when the WF program instance is serialized):

```
A first chance exception of type 'System.Runtime.Serialization.Serialization-
Exception' occurred in mscorlib.dll

Additional information: Type 'Order' in Assembly 'Experiments, Version=1.0.0.0,
Culture=neutral, PublicKeyToken=null' is not marked as serializable.
```

The problem can be easily fixed by marking the Order type as serializable:

```
[Serializable]
public class Order
{
  ...
}
```

If certain fields of a type you develop should not participate in runtime serialization (for efficiency reasons), you can mark these fields with the System.NonSerialized-Attribute attribute:

```
[Serializable]
public class Order
{
  [NonSerialized]
```

```
        private string sku;

        ...
    }
```

In order to avoid serialization of a dependency property (that is not a metadata property), you must indicate this desired behavior when the dependency property is registered:

```
public static readonly DependencyProperty OrderProperty =
    DependencyProperty.Register("Order",
        typeof(Order),
        typeof(CreateOrder),
        new PropertyMetadata(DependencyPropertyOptions.NonSerialized)
    );
```

In certain cases, marking a type with `SerializableAttribute` may not be ideal. Because `[Serializable]` and `[NonSerialized]` are static decorations, all instances of the `Order` type (as implemented previously) are serialized in exactly the same way. Sometimes you might need to conditionally serialize fields of an object, or perform other custom processing. Implementing `System.Runtime.Serialization.ISerializable` gives you this kind of flexibility, illustrated here for the `Order` type:

```
[Serializable]
public class Order : ISerializable
{
    public Order(SerializationInfo info, StreamingContext context)
    {
        this.sku = info.GetString("sku");
        this.quantity = info.GetInt32("quantity");
    }

    void ISerializable.GetObjectData(SerializationInfo info,
        StreamingContext context)
    {

        // custom serialization logic
        info.AddValue("sku", ...);

        ...
    }
}
```

In the discussion so far, we are assuming that we have control over the source code of the Order type, and can therefore apply [Serializable] or implement ISerializable. There are situations, though, when you might utilize compiled types that do not have the serialization behavior that you require. In such cases, you can implement a custom serialization surrogate for a compiled type, whose behavior will effectively override whatever runtime serialization behavior was implemented by the author of the type.

Let's assume that our Order type is not marked with [Serializable] and does not implement ISerializable. To make the Order type serializable, we first implement a serialization surrogate:

```
public class OrderSurrogate :
  System.Runtime.Serialization.ISerializationSurrogate
{
  void ISerializationSurrogate.GetObjectData(object obj,
    SerializationInfo info, StreamingContext context)
  {
    Order order = obj as Order;
    if (order != null)
    {
      info.AddValue("sku", order.SKU);
      info.AddValue("quantity", order.Quantity);
    }
  }

  object ISerializationSurrogate.SetObjectData(object obj,
    SerializationInfo info, StreamingContext context,
    ISurrogateSelector selector)
  {
    Order order = obj as Order;
    if (order != null)
    {
      order.SKU = info.GetString("sku");
      order.Quantity = info.GetInt32("quantity");
    }

    return order;
  }
}
```

In order to have the `OrderSurrogate` type recognized by the WF runtime's serialization machinery, you need to write a serialization surrogate selector. A **surrogate selector** is a type that inherits from `System.Runtime.Serialization.SurrogateSelector` (or implements `System.Runtime.Serialization.ISurrogateSelector`) and allows you to associate a serialization surrogate with the type that it is responsible for serializing, as shown here:

```
public class OrderSurrogateSelector :
  System.Runtime.Serialization.SurrogateSelector
{
  private OrderSurrogate surrogate = new OrderSurrogate();

  public override ISerializationSurrogate GetSurrogate(
    Type type, StreamingContext context,
    out ISurrogateSelector selector)
  {
    if (type == typeof(Order))
    {
      selector = this;
      return this.surrogate;
    }

    return base.GetSurrogate(type, context, out selector);
  }

}
```

The final step is to register the custom surrogate selector with the WF runtime:

```
OrderSurrogateSelector selector =
  new OrderSurrogateSelector();

ActivitySurrogateSelector.Default.ChainSelector(selector);

using (WorkflowRuntime runtime = new WorkflowRuntime())
{

  ...
}
```

The `ActivitySurrogateSelector` type that is used to register custom surrogates is defined in the `System.Workflow.ComponentModel.Serialization` namespace and is shown in Listing 5.14.

Listing 5.14   `ActivitySurrogateSelector`

```
namespace System.Workflow.ComponentModel.Serialization
{
  public sealed class ActivitySurrogateSelector : SurrogateSelector
  {
    public ActivitySurrogateSelector();

    public static ActivitySurrogateSelector Default { get; }

    public override ISerializationSurrogate GetSurrogate(
      Type type,
      StreamingContext context,
      out ISurrogateSelector selector
    );
  }
}
```

There is a simple pattern that can help you reduce the serialization size of activities you develop. The WF runtime does not serialize dependency properties with a value of null. You can take advantage of this fact when you develop an activity type that defines private fields (that presumably hold data relevant only to the activity's execution and therefore must be serialized only while the activity is executing).

Clearly, we can develop an activity like this:

```
public class Widget : Activity
{
  private string str;

  ...
}
```

The field `str` will always be serialized, potentially long after a `Widget` activity has completed its execution. We can rewrite the `Widget` activity like this:

```
public class Widget : Activity
{
  private static readonly DependencyProperty StrProperty =
    DependencyProperty.Register("Str",
      typeof(string),
      typeof(Widget));

  // private getter/setter for Str
```

```
  protected override void Uninitialize(
    IServiceProvider provider)
  {
    base.Uninitialize(provider);
    this.SetValue(StrProperty, null);
  }

  ...

}
```

`StrProperty` is a private dependency property field that a `Widget` activity uses to keep track of some data while it is executing. When a `Widget` activity completes its execution, the data is not of any further use. By setting the value of the dependency property to `null` in the `Uninitialize` method, we avoid serialization of this data for all subsequent persistence points for the WF program instance. We could alternatively have used a standard `string` field, and set its value to `null` in the `Uninitialize` method, but the dependency property approach is nevertheless slightly more efficient (in terms of serialization size).

Suspending a WF Program Instance

A running WF program instance can be suspended by calling the `Suspend` method of the `WorkflowInstance` class. A running WF program instance will also be suspended if a `SuspendActivity` within the WF program is executed. `SuspendActivity` is defined in the `System.Workflow.ComponentModel` namespace and is shown in Listing 5.15.

Listing 5.15   `SuspendActivity`

```
namespace System.Workflow.ComponentModel
{
  public sealed class SuspendActivity : Activity
  {
    public string Error { get; set; }

    /* *** other members *** */
  }
}
```

Use of `SuspendActivity` in XAML looks like this:

```
<wf:SuspendActivity x:Name="s1" Error="Please fix xyz" />
```

A suspended WF program instance is not allowed to proceed further in its execution, even if there is work enqueued in its scheduler work queue. The instance remains in a suspended state until the `Resume` method of its `WorkflowInstance` is called. The `Error` property of `SuspendActivity` (and the equivalent string parameter of the `Suspend` method of `WorkflowInstance`) can be used to convey information about why the instance has been suspended.

The `WorkflowRuntime` has a `WorkflowSuspended` event, which is raised whenever a WF program instance is suspended. Listing 5.16 illustrates this process.

Listing 5.16   WF Program Instance Suspension

```
static void Main()
{
  WorkflowRuntime runtime = new WorkflowRuntime();
  runtime.StartRuntime();

  runtime.WorkflowSuspended  += delegate(object sender,
    WorkflowSuspendedEventArgs e)
  {
    Console.WriteLine("Instance suspended: " +
      e.WorkflowInstance.InstanceId);
    Console.WriteLine("Reason: " + e.Error);
  };

  WorkflowInstance instance = ...
  instance.Suspend("Need to suspend it");

  ...
}
```

`WorkflowInstance.Suspend` stops the execution of the WF program instance, and also causes the `WorkflowRuntime` to raise the `WorkflowSuspended` event. The suspended WF program instance remains in memory; if a host application wishes to unload the instance, the `Unload` method can be called as well (for example, from within the handler of the `WorkflowSuspended` event). A WF program instance that has been suspended must always be explicitly resumed in order for its execution to continue; it is not enough to simply load a suspended instance that was previously unloaded.

Calling `Resume` on `WorkflowInstance` will resume the program's execution from wherever it had left off. Calling `Resume` has no effect in causing the program execution to move forward if there are no items in the WF scheduler's work queue; it only removes a barrier to execution by moving the instance out of the suspended state.

Terminating a WF Program Instance

A WF program instance can be **terminated** by calling the `Terminate` method of the `WorkflowInstance` class. A WF program instance will also be terminated if an exception in the program propagates to the root activity and is not handled, or if a `TerminateActivity` within the WF program is executed. The `TerminateActivity` class is defined in the `System.Workflow.ComponentModel` namespace and is shown in Listing 5.17.

Listing 5.17 `TerminateActivity`

```
namespace System.Workflow.ComponentModel
{
  public sealed class TerminateActivity : Activity
  {
    public string Error { get; set; }

    /* *** other members *** */
  }
}
```

Use of `TerminateActivity` in XAML looks like this:

```
<wf:TerminateActivity x:Name="t1" Error="Cannot proceed" />
```

The `WorkflowRuntime` has a `WorkflowTerminated` event, which is raised whenever a WF program instance is terminated. Termination of a WF program instance is considered abnormal completion. Thus, the `WorkflowTerminated-EventArgs` that carries the data for the `WorkflowTerminated` event contains one property of type `Exception`. This exception is either an unhandled exception that occurred within the instance or, if the `Terminate` method of `WorkflowInstance` was called by the host application (or a `TerminateActivity` within the WF program executed) a special `WorkflowTerminatedException`, which carries the error string that was reported as part of the termination.

Listing 5.18 shows the `WorkflowTerminatedEventArgs` type.

Listing 5.18 `WorkflowTerminatedEventArgs`

```
namespace System.Workflow.Runtime
{
  public class WorkflowTerminatedEventArgs : WorkflowEventArgs
  {
    public Exception Exception { get; }
  }
}
```

Calling `WorkflowInstance.Terminate` causes the execution of the program instance to end immediately. As part of termination, the WF program instance is persisted and removed from memory. Although a WF program instance is persisted as part of termination, its execution can never be continued. The instance has irrevocably transitioned to the `Terminated` state. Instance termination is illustrated in Listing 5.19.

Listing 5.19 WF Program Instance Termination

```
static void Main()
{
    using(WorkflowRuntime runtime = new WorkflowRuntime())
  {
    runtime.StartRuntime();

    runtime.WorkflowTerminated += delegate(
      object sender, WorkflowTerminatedEventArgs e)
    {
      Console.WriteLine("Instance terminated: " +
        e.WorkflowInstance.InstanceId);
      Console.WriteLine("Exception message: " +
        e.Exception.Message);
    };

    WorkflowInstance instance = ...
    instance.Terminate("Need to terminate it");

    ...
  }
}
```

Aborting a WF Program Instance

`WorkflowInstance` also carries an `Abort` method. When a WF program instance is **aborted**, the progress of the instance since its most recent persistence point is discarded, and the instance is evicted from memory. Unlike `Terminate`, the `Abort` method does not persist the instance, and it leaves the program instance in the `Running` state; it is as if the execution of the instance since the last persistence point did not ever happen.

The `WorkflowRuntime` has a `WorkflowAborted` event, which is raised whenever a WF program instance is aborted, as shown in Listing 5.20.

Listing 5.20 `WorkflowInstance.Abort`

```
static void Main()
{
  using(WorkflowRuntime runtime = new WorkflowRuntime())
  {
    runtime.StartRuntime();

    runtime.WorkflowAborted += delegate(
      object sender, WorkflowEventArgs e)
    {
      Console.WriteLine("Instance aborted: " +
        e.WorkflowInstance.InstanceId);
    };

    WorkflowInstance instance = ...
    instance.Abort();

    ...
  }

}
```

The abort capability is perhaps best explained with an analogy. When you edit a document in an application such as Microsoft Word, it is typical to periodically save your work; this is analogous at some level to persisting a running WF program instance. When you close the Word document, you are asked whether the changes you have made to the document since the last time you saved it should be kept or discarded. If you discard the changes, the next time you open the document you will see it as it existed at the last point it was saved. So it is with the `Abort` method of

`WorkflowInstance`; it simply discards the progress that was made in the execution of the program instance since its last persistence point.

WF Program Instance Completion

When a WF program instance completes normally (the root activity moves to the *Closed* state of the activity automaton, and there is no unhandled exception), the `WorkflowCompleted` event is raised by `WorkflowRuntime`. In the handler of this event, the host is able to inspect the values of all gettable public properties of the root activity of the instance. This is shown in the following snippet, which uses the `OutputParameters` property of `WorkflowCompletedEventArgs`:

```
using (WorkflowRuntime runtime = new WorkflowRuntime())
{
  runtime.StartRuntime();

  runtime.WorkflowCompleted += delegate(
    object sender, WorkflowCompletedEventArgs e)
  {
    Dictionary<string, object> results =
      e.OutputParameters;

    foreach (string key in results.Keys)
    {
      object o = results[key];
      ...
    }
  };
  ...
}
```

As part of its completion, a WF program instance is unloaded if a persistence service is present.

WF Program Instance Lifecycle

We have thus far looked at the various aspects of WF program instance management in a somewhat piecemeal fashion. If we look at instance management holistically, we find that the lifecycle of any WF program instance is usefully described by a state diagram, shown in Figure 5.8.

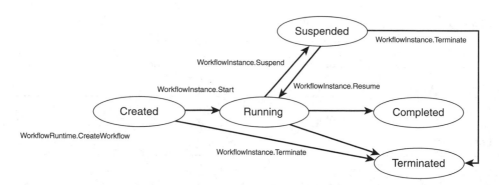

Figure 5.8   WF program instance lifecycle

Creating a new WF program instance leaves the instance in the `Created` state. Starting the instance moves it to the `Running` state. When it completes its execution, the instance is in a `Completed` state. A running instance can be suspended; a suspended instance can be resumed. An instance that is not completed can be terminated, which moves it to the `Terminated` state.

The states in Figure 5.8 correspond to the values of the `WorkflowStatus` enumeration, shown in Listing 5.21, and defined in the `System.Workflow.Runtime` namespace.

Listing 5.21   `WorkflowStatus`

```
namespace System.Workflow.Runtime
{
  public enum WorkflowStatus
  {
    Created,
    Running,
    Completed,
    Suspended,
    Terminated
  }
}
```

The values of the `WorkflowStatus` enum correspond to the values you will find in the Status column of the InstanceState table used by the `SqlWorkflowPersistenceService`. These values are summarized in Table 5.2.

Table 5.2 `WorkflowStatus` **Values**

WorkflowStatus	Value
Created	4
Running	0
Completed	1
Suspended	2
Terminated	3

One good way to get a feel for the control operations that allow a host to manage instances of WF programs it to write a simple application that lets you initiate these operations as commands at the console. Such an application is not hard to write, and is shown in Listing 5.22.

Listing 5.22   Application that Manages WF Program Instances

```
using System;
using System.Collections.ObjectModel;
using System.IO;
using System.Xml;
using System.Workflow.ComponentModel.Compiler;
using System.Workflow.Runtime;

namespace EssentialWF.Host.Chapter5
{
  class Program
  {
    // Nice and small WF program!
    // See Listing 5.24 for the Echo activity type

    static readonly string ECHO =
      "<Echo xmlns=\"http://EssentialWF/Activities\" />";

    static string ConnectionString =
      "Initial Catalog=SqlPersistenceService;Data Source=localhost;Integrated
Security=SSPI;";

    static void Main()
    {
      using (WorkflowRuntime runtime = new WorkflowRuntime())
      {
```

```
SqlWorkflowPersistenceService persistenceService =
  new SqlWorkflowPersistenceService(ConnectionString);
runtime.AddService(persistenceService);

TypeProvider typeProvider = new TypeProvider(null);
typeProvider.AddAssemblyReference("EssentialWF.dll");
runtime.AddService(typeProvider);

runtime.StartRuntime();

runtime.WorkflowAborted += WorkflowAborted;
runtime.WorkflowCompleted += WorkflowCompleted;
runtime.WorkflowCreated += WorkflowCreated;
runtime.WorkflowIdled += WorkflowIdled;
runtime.WorkflowLoaded += WorkflowLoaded;
runtime.WorkflowPersisted += WorkflowPersisted;
runtime.WorkflowResumed += WorkflowResumed;
runtime.WorkflowStarted += WorkflowStarted;
runtime.WorkflowSuspended += WorkflowSuspended;
runtime.WorkflowTerminated += WorkflowTerminated;
runtime.WorkflowUnloaded += WorkflowUnloaded;
runtime.ServicesExceptionNotHandled +=
  ServicesExceptionNotHandled;

WorkflowInstance instance = null;
string bookmarkName = null;

while (true)
{
  string s = Console.ReadLine();
  if (s.Equals("quit")) break;

  try
  {
    if (s.Equals("create"))
    {
      using(XmlReader reader = XmlReader.Create(new
        StringReader(ECHO)))
      {
        instance = runtime.CreateWorkflow(reader);
      }
      bookmarkName = instance.GetWorkflowDefinition().Name;
    }
    else if (s.StartsWith("get"))
    {
      string[] tokens = s.Split(new char[] { ' ' });
      Guid handle = new Guid(tokens[1]);  // InstanceId
      instance = runtime.GetWorkflow(handle);
```

```
                bookmarkName = instance.GetWorkflowDefinition().Name;
            }
            else if (s.Equals("abort")) instance.Abort();
            else if (s.Equals("load")) instance.Load();
            else if (s.Equals("resume")) instance.Resume();
            else if (s.Equals("start")) instance.Start();
            else if (s.Equals("suspend"))
              instance.Suspend("user says to suspend");
            else if (s.Equals("terminate"))
              instance.Terminate("user says to terminate");
            else if (s.Equals("tryunload")) instance.TryUnload();
            else if (s.Equals("unload")) instance.Unload();
            else instance.EnqueueItem(bookmarkName, s, null, null);
          }
          catch (Exception e)
          {
            Console.WriteLine(e.GetType().Name + ": " + e.Message);
          }
        }

      runtime.StopRuntime();
    }
  }

  /* *** see Listing 5.19 for event handlers *** */
  }
}
```

Our application subscribes to all of the events available on the `WorkflowRuntime`, so that we can see exactly when these events occur. The event handlers are shown in Listing 5.23.

Listing 5.23   Event Handlers for Application of Listing 5.22

```
static void WorkflowUnloaded(object sender, WorkflowEventArgs e)
{
  Console.WriteLine("WorkflowUnloaded");
}

static void WorkflowTerminated(object sender,
  WorkflowTerminatedEventArgs e)
{
  Console.WriteLine("WorkflowTerminated with " +
    e.Exception.GetType().Name + ": " + e.Exception.Message);
}
```

```
static void WorkflowSuspended(object sender,
  WorkflowSuspendedEventArgs e)
{
  Console.WriteLine("WorkflowSuspended: " + e.Error);
}

static void WorkflowStarted(object sender, WorkflowEventArgs e)
{
  Console.WriteLine("WorkflowStarted");
}

static void WorkflowResumed(object sender, WorkflowEventArgs e)
{
  Console.WriteLine("WorkflowResumed");
}

static void WorkflowPersisted(object sender, WorkflowEventArgs e)
{
  Console.WriteLine("WorkflowPersisted");
}

static void WorkflowLoaded(object sender, WorkflowEventArgs e)
{
  Console.WriteLine("WorkflowLoaded");
}

static void WorkflowIdled(object sender, WorkflowEventArgs e)
{
  Console.WriteLine("WorkflowIdled");
}

static void WorkflowCreated(object sender, WorkflowEventArgs e)
{
  Console.WriteLine("WorkflowCreated " +
    e.WorkflowInstance.InstanceId);
}

static void WorkflowAborted(object sender, WorkflowEventArgs e)
{
  Console.WriteLine("WorkflowAborted");
}

static void ServicesExceptionNotHandled(object sender,
  ServicesExceptionNotHandledEventArgs e)
{
  Console.WriteLine("ServicesExceptionNotHandled: " +
    e.Exception.GetType().Name);
}
```

```
static void WorkflowCompleted(object sender,
  WorkflowCompletedEventArgs e)
{
  Console.Write("WorkflowCompleted");
  foreach (string key in e.OutputParameters.Keys)
  {
    object o = e.OutputParameters[key];
    Console.Write(" " + key + "=" + o.ToString());
  }
  Console.Write("\n");
}
```

The application in Listing 5.22 uses a simple activity called `Echo`, and creates WF programs that are simply instances of this activity. The `Echo` activity is shown in Listing 5.24. Running the application will let you confirm the behavior of each of the control operations firsthand. Furthermore, you can get a feel for how persistence works by starting the application and starting some instances, and then quitting the application. At this point you can verify that the instances have been saved in your SQL Server database. Restarting the application will allow you to continue the execution of the instances that had previously been persisted.

Listing 5.24 The `Echo` Activity

```
using System;
using System.Workflow.ComponentModel;
using System.Workflow.ComponentModel.Serialization;
using System.Workflow.Runtime;

namespace EssentialWF.Activities
{
  public class Echo : Activity
  {
    // To illustrate WorkflowInstance.Abort
    private int n;

    public int NumEchoes
    {
      get { return this.n; }
    }

    protected override void Initialize(IServiceProvider provider)
    {
      n = 0;
      Console.WriteLine("Echo.Initialize");
```

```
    WorkflowQueuingService qService = provider.GetService(
      typeof(WorkflowQueuingService)) as WorkflowQueuingService;
    WorkflowQueue queue = qService.CreateWorkflowQueue(
      this.Name, false);
  }

  protected override ActivityExecutionStatus Execute(
    ActivityExecutionContext context)
  {
    Console.WriteLine("Echo.Execute");
    WorkflowQueuingService qService = context.GetService(
      typeof(WorkflowQueuingService)) as WorkflowQueuingService;
    WorkflowQueue queue = qService.GetWorkflowQueue(this.Name);
    queue.QueueItemAvailable += this.ContinueAt;

    return ActivityExecutionStatus.Executing;
  }

  void ContinueAt(object sender, QueueEventArgs e)
  {
    Console.WriteLine("Echo.QueueItemAvailable");
    ActivityExecutionContext context =
      sender as ActivityExecutionContext;
    WorkflowQueuingService qService = context.GetService(
      typeof(WorkflowQueuingService)) as WorkflowQueuingService;
    WorkflowQueue queue = qService.GetWorkflowQueue(this.Name);

    object o = queue.Dequeue();
    if (o is string)
    {
      // To illustrate termination via fault
      if ((o as string).Equals("fault"))
        throw new InvalidOperationException("thrown by Echo");

      else if ((o as string).Equals("complete"))
      {
        queue.QueueItemAvailable -= this.ContinueAt;
        context.CloseActivity();
        return;
      }
    }

    // else echo the item
    Console.WriteLine(o.ToString() + " {" + n++ + "}");
  }

  protected override void Uninitialize(IServiceProvider provider)
  {
```

```
      Console.WriteLine("Echo.Uninitialize");
      WorkflowQueuingService qService = provider.GetService(
        typeof(WorkflowQueuingService)) as WorkflowQueuingService;
      qService.DeleteWorkflowQueue(this.Name);
    }
  }
}
```

Running the application will confirm the behavior of the WF runtime and WF program instances. To begin, the following is the output of the program for a simple run in which we create an instance, start it, send it two strings ("hello" and "goodbye"), and then complete it. For clarity, we are showing the commands issued at the console in boldface:

```
create
Echo.Initialize
WorkflowCreated 14caf2b7-93f3-41ae-87c7-8342fb18ccf5
start
WorkflowStarted
Echo.Execute
WorkflowIdled
hello
Echo.QueueItemAvailable
hello {0}
WorkflowIdled
goodbye
Echo.QueueItemAvailable
goodbye {1}
WorkflowIdled
complete
Echo.QueueItemAvailable
Echo.Uninitialize
WorkflowPersisted
WorkflowCompleted NumEchoes=2
```

The instance is not automatically persisted when it becomes idle because we used the default value of false for the persistence service's UnloadOnIdle property.

If we call the same set of commands as the previous run except unload instead of complete and then quit the application, the one instance we've created will occupy a row in a database table managed by the SqlWorkflowPersistence-Service. The value in the status column of this row is set to 0 to indicate that the instance is still running (in a logical sense, of course, since it is nowhere in memory).

We can fire up our application again, and continue the execution of the instance using the `get` command, which accepts the `Guid` identifying the instance as a parameter:

```
get 919f2445-57a3-492e-a106-3bc619ca2ce9
WorkflowLoaded
all done now
Echo.QueueItemAvailable
all done now {2}
WorkflowIdled
complete
Echo.QueueItemAvailable
Echo.Uninitialize
WorkflowPersisted
WorkflowCompleted NumEchoes=3
```

When the instance completes, the value of `NumEchoes` is reported as 3. The instance retained the value of this data across the persistence point (and the application restart).

The following example shows termination of an instance; the `Echo` activity responds to an input of `fault` by throwing an exception:

```
create
Echo.Initialize
WorkflowCreated fbdec9c1-eb3a-413e-93ee-66c3798ddbc8
start
WorkflowStarted
Echo.Execute
WorkflowIdled
hello
Echo.QueueItemAvailable
hello {0}
WorkflowIdled
fault
Echo.QueueItemAvailable
Echo.Uninitialize
WorkflowPersisted
WorkflowTerminated with InvalidOperationException: thrown by Echo
```

And finally, here is an example that shows the abort capability of instances:

```
create
Echo.Initialize
WorkflowCreated 5bc7c2ee-ebad-4c99-8386-24d74a297e04
```

```
start
WorkflowStarted
Echo.Execute
WorkflowIdled
zero
Echo.QueueItemAvailable
zero {0}
WorkflowIdled
one
Echo.QueueItemAvailable
one {1}
WorkflowIdled
unload
WorkflowPersisted
WorkflowUnloaded
two
WorkflowLoaded
Echo.QueueItemAvailable
two {2}
WorkflowIdled
abort
WorkflowAborted
three
WorkflowLoaded
Echo.QueueItemAvailable
three {2}
WorkflowIdled
complete
Echo.QueueItemAvailable
Echo.Uninitialize
WorkflowPersisted
WorkflowCompleted NumEchoes=3
```

As you can see, the two input is forgotten (and the in-memory instance is discarded) at the point the abort command is issued. When the next input is provided, the instance continues executing based on the last persisted state. Thus, when the instance completes, NumEchoes is reported as 3 (not 4) because one of the four inputs had been discarded via the abort command.

We encourage you to experiment with this simple application. When you are comfortable with how it works, tweak it. For example, set the value of the Unload-OnIdle property of the SQL persistence service to true and see what changes. Use it to test a custom persistence service, or to run WF programs that are more complicated than a single Echo activity.

Where Are We?

WF provides a programming model for executing activity-based programs. The WF runtime is deliberately small, which allows it to be hosted in a variety of environments. Furthermore, the host application can adjust the capabilities and behavior of the WF runtime by selecting the most appropriate implementations of runtime services on which the WF runtime depends. WF provides one or more useful implementation of each of these services, but custom variants can be written as well.

WF program instances have a well-defined lifecycle, and can be created and managed using the `WorkflowRuntime` and `WorkflowInstance` classes. The WF runtime is format agnostic; this is perhaps the subtlest and also the most noteworthy lesson of this chapter. WF programs can be expressed as C# or Visual Basic code, XAML, or any other format that is translatable to activities, and directly loaded into the WF runtime for execution.

▌6▖
Transactions

W F ALIGNS WITH THE PROGRAMMING model for transactions that is provided by the `System.Transactions` namespace in the .NET Framework. There is plenty of documentation and additional explanatory material that has been written about this API—and we encourage you to familiarize yourself with the specifics—but the bottom line is that `System.Transactions` presents a simplified model for using transactions such that the nuts and bolts of managing a transaction (e.g., the selection of transaction managers, enlistment of resources, and transaction promotion) are, unless you need to get to them, agreeably out of sight.

Thus in C#, you just write the following:

```
using (TransactionScope ts = new TransactionScope())
{
  // use transactional resources...

  ts.Complete();
}
```

The use of a `System.Transactions.TransactionScope` object demarcates a block of C# code that participates in a transaction. Your code does not explicitly create an actual transaction object; that is taken care of for you by the `TransactionScope`.

Furthermore, resource managers that are compatible with `System.Transactions` will, when utilized within a `TransactionScope`, automatically detect the presence of what is known as the **ambient transaction** and enlist themselves appropriately. SQL Server is one example of such a resource manager. Thus, transactional programming against a database is as simple as this:

```
using (TransactionScope ts = new TransactionScope())
{
  using (System.Data.SqlClient.SqlConnection conn =
    new System.Data.SqlClient.SqlConnection(...))
  {
    ...
  }

  ts.Complete();
}
```

TransactionScopeActivity

In the WF programming model, the idea is to adopt the same simple model shown previously for `TransactionScope`. WF, like `System.Transactions`, uses the term **transaction** to always mean an ACID (Atomic, Consistent, Isolated, and Durable) transaction. Concepts such as *long-running transactions* (not a term that is used within the WF programming model) are accommodated by WF programming model features such as activity compensation (which was discussed in Chapter 4, "Advanced Activity Execution").

In this book, when we refer to transactions, we always mean ACID transactions.

`System.Workflow.ComponentModel.TransactionScopeActivity` is a composite activity that, when used within a WF program, behaves much like a (`System.Transactions`) `TransactionScope` in a C# program. `Transaction-ScopeActivity` is the root of a subtree of activities that all take part in the same transaction:

```
<wf:TransactionScopeActivity>
  <Sequence>
    ...
  </Sequence>
</wf:TransactionScopeActivity>
```

If an activity contained at any depth within a `TransactionScopeActivity` uses a resource manager in its execution logic, the resource manager automatically enlists in the ambient transaction. An activity that updates customer information in a database table might therefore look something like this:

```
using System;
using System.Workflow.ComponentModel;
using System.Workflow.ComponentModel.Compiler;

namespace EssentialWF.Activities
{
  public class UpdateCustomerInfo : Activity
  {
    ...

    protected override ActivityExecutionStatus Execute(
      ActivityExecutionContext context)
    {
      using (System.Data.SqlClient.SqlConnection conn =
        new System.Data.SqlClient.SqlConnection(...))
      {
        // update database tables
      }

      return ActivityExecutionStatus.Closed;
    }
  }
}
```

`TransactionScopeActivity` behaves in a WF program very much like a declarative variant of `TransactionScope`, so the execution logic of `UpdateCustomerInfo` does not need to create a `TransactionScope` object—when the `UpdateCustomerInfo` activity executes, an ambient transaction will be present, courtesy of `TransactionScopeActivity`.

As an activity writer, we may wish to stipulate that an activity like `UpdateCustomerInfo` should only be used within a `TransactionScopeActivity`. To do this, we need to write validation logic (a topic covered in more detail in Chapter 7, "Advanced Authoring") for `UpdateCustomerInfo` that ensures an `UpdateCustomerInfo` activity is always nested (at some depth) within a `TransactionScopeActivity`:

```
using System;
using System.Workflow.ComponentModel;
using System.Workflow.ComponentModel.Compiler;

namespace EssentialWF.Activities
{
  [ActivityValidator(typeof(UpdateCustomerInfoValidator))]
  public class UpdateCustomerInfo : Activity
  {
    ...
  }

  public class UpdateCustomerInfoValidator: ActivityValidator
  {
    public override ValidationErrorCollection Validate(
      ValidationManager manager, object obj)
    {
      ValidationErrorCollection errors =
        base.Validate(manager, obj);

      UpdateCustomerInfo activity = obj as UpdateCustomerInfo;
      CompositeActivity parent = activity.Parent;

      bool ok = false;
      while (parent != null)
      {
        if (parent is TransactionScopeActivity)
        {
          ok = true;
          break;
        }

        parent = parent.Parent;
      }

      if (!ok)
        errors.Add(new ValidationError("UpdateCustomerInfo must be nested within a
TransactionScopeActivity", 1000));

      return errors;
    }
  }
}
```

The `TransactionScopeActivity` type is shown in Listing 6.1.

Listing 6.1 `TransactionScopeActivity`

```
namespace System.Workflow.ComponentModel
{
  public sealed class TransactionScopeActivity
    : CompositeActivity
  {
    public WorkflowTransactionOptions TransactionOptions
      { get; set; }

    /* *** other members *** */
  }
}
```

Just as you can for a `System.Transactions.TransactionScope`, you can set the
isolation level and the timeout that are to be used for the transaction that is created
by a `TransactionScopeActivity`. The `TransactionScopeActivity.Transac-`
`tionOptions` property, of type `System.Workflow.ComponentModel.Workflow-`
`TransactionOptions`, is the place where these options are specified.

The `WorkflowTransactionOptions` type is shown in Listing 6.2.

Listing 6.2 `WorkflowTransactionOptions`

```
namespace System.Workflow.ComponentModel
{
  public sealed class WorkflowTransactionOptions
    : DependencyObject
  {
    public System.Transactions.IsolationLevel IsolationLevel
      { get; set; }

    public System.TimeSpan TimeoutDuration { get; set; }

    /* *** other members *** */
  }
}
```

Assignment of `TransactionScopeActivity.TransactionOptions` will appear in
XAML like so:

```
  <wf:TransactionScopeActivity>
    <wf:TransactionScopeActivity.TransactionOptions>
      <wf:WorkflowTransactionOptions TimeoutDuration="00:01:00"
IsolationLevel="Serializable" />
```

```
    </wf:TransactionScopeActivity.TransactionOptions>
    <Sequence>
    ...
    </Sequence>
</wf:TransactionScopeActivity>
```

In the preceding XAML snippet, a timeout of one minute has been set for the transaction, and the isolation level is `System.Transactions.IsolationLevel.Serializable`.

Within a WF program instance, when a `TransactionScopeActivity` begins its execution, only activities inside the `TransactionScopeActivity` will be allowed to execute until the `TransactionScopeActivity` completes. This is enforced by the WF runtime. Doing this ensures the consistency of data within the WF program by effectively serializing the execution of `TransactionScopeActivity` with respect to the rest of the activities in the WF program instance. Furthermore, during the execution of a `TransactionScopeActivity`, the WF program instance will not be allowed to persist or passivate (after all, a transaction is in progress).

To guarantee all-or-nothing semantics with respect to WF program instance state, `TransactionScopeActivity` takes a snapshot of the program instance state just before it creates a transaction. If an unhandled exception occurs (during the subsequent execution of its child activities), causing a `TransactionScopeActivity` to move to the *Faulting* state, the instance state snapshot is used by `TransactionScopeActivity` to revert the state of the WF program instance before the transaction is rolled back. The exception then propagates up the activity tree of the WF program.

TransactionScopeActivity Validation

`TransactionScopeActivity` has a custom validator component that imposes a few restrictions on its usage in WF programs.

Nesting of `TransactionScope` objects is allowed by `System.Transactions`. But in the WF programming model, you cannot nest a `TransactionScopeActivity` within another `TransactionScopeActivity`. This limitation precludes certain advanced scenarios; it is not unreasonable to expect the WF programming model to improve in this area in the future.

A `TransactionScopeActivity` in a WF program cannot have fault handlers. The point of a transaction is that its work either succeeds or fails. There is no such thing, in transaction programming, as a "failed, but successfully handled the exception" outcome for a transaction. That is why a composite activity that contains a `TransactionScopeActivity` can handle a transaction-related exception, but the `TransactionScopeActivity` itself cannot—it either succeeds or fails.

A `TransactionScopeActivity` in a WF program also cannot have a cancellation handler. Again, the point of a transaction is that its work either succeeds or fails. As all-or-nothing operations, transactions by definition do not need to support cancellation logic (which, in WF programs, is only invoked for a partially completed activity).

The WF runtime will not allow suspension of a WF program instance while a transaction is in progress. Consequently, the validation logic of `SuspendActivity` (discussed in Chapter 5, "Applications") will not allow the presence of `SuspendActivity`, at any depth, within a `TransactionScopeActivity`. Similarly, the WF runtime will not allow termination of a WF program instance while a transaction is in progress. The validation logic of `TerminateActivity` (also discussed in Chapter 5) will not allow the presence of `TerminateActivity`, at any depth, within a `TransactionScopeActivity`.

Persistence Points

When a `TransactionScopeActivity` successfully completes its execution, the ambient transaction is committed. As mentioned in the previous section, the WF runtime does not allow the execution of activities outside of a `TransactionScopeActivity` during the execution of that `TransactionScopeActivity`. So, when a `TransactionScopeActivity` completes, it is possible that other activities may be waiting in the wings, their execution handlers ready to be dispatched by the WF runtime.

Before moving on to the dispatch of these other execution handlers, though, the WF runtime persists the WF program instance. The WF program instance is not passivated here (which would include disposal of the activity objects representing the instance in memory), only persisted. This is a critical step because it means that the forward progress of the WF program instance is being indelibly recorded.

Furthermore, the persistence of the WF program instance takes place as part of the *same transaction* that was created for the `TransactionScopeActivity`. Only with this design can the WF runtime guarantee that the recorded forward progress of the WF program instance remains in lock-step with the transactional commitment of the program's side effects (which are caused by the execution of activities, such as an `UpdateCustomerInfo` activity, within a `TransactionScopeActivity`). As a consequence, a WF program containing a `TransactionScopeActivity` can be executed only by a WF runtime that is configured with a persistence service.

Consider what would happen if this were not the case (i.e., if WF program instance persistence did not occur as part of the completion of a `Transaction-ScopeActivity`). For our thought experiment, let's suppose that we use the `UpdateCustomerInfo` activity within a `TransactionScopeActivity` like this:

```
<Sequence>
  ...
  <Interleave>
    <wf:TransactionScopeActivity>
      <UpdateCustomerInfo ... />
      ...
    </wf:TransactionScopeActivity>
    <WriteLine Text="hello" />
    ...
  </Interleave>
</Sequence>
```

As part of the execution of the `TransactionScopeActivity`, `UpdateCustomer-Info` successfully updates data in some database tables. When the `Transaction-ScopeActivity` completes its execution (successfully), the transaction commits. Now, let's see what can happen if the WF runtime does *not* persist the WF program instance at this point in time. With the `TransactionScopeActivity` completed, the `WriteLine` activity is ready to run (its `Execute` method had already been scheduled for execution by its parent `Interleave` activity, but could not be dispatched while execution of `TransactionScopeActivity` was in progress).

Boom! The CLR application domain that is hosting the WF runtime now fails (maybe the machine crashes, or there is a power outage). It doesn't matter exactly how or when this failure occurs, so long as it happens before the next point in time at which the WF program instance is persisted. All is not lost, of course, because the WF runtime can be started again in a fresh CLR application domain, and WF program instances, including the one in our example, can have their execution resumed from their last persistence point.

But here we face the problem. The last persistence point for our example WF program instance occurred some arbitrary time before the `TransactionScopeActivity` began its execution. When this WF program instance resumes after the WF runtime is started again, the `TransactionScopeActivity` will execute *again*, and will in all likelihood fail when it tries to once again perform database operations. Remember, the database operations were previously committed in a transactional manner, but persistence of the instance was not part of this transaction. As we have shown, decoupling these actions is simply not viable.

Our thought experiment concluded, we now know why a WF program instance is always persisted by the WF runtime within the same transaction that is created for the execution of a `TransactionScopeActivity`.

Custom Persistence Points

Completion of a `TransactionScopeActivity` is not the only circumstance that leads to the persistence of a WF program instance. As we saw in Chapter 5, the application hosting the WF runtime can load and unload WF program instances as it pleases, using the methods available on the `System.Workflow.Runtime.Work-flowInstance` type. When a WF program instance is unloaded (passivated), it is persisted in addition to being disposed. A WF program instance is also persisted when its execution concludes.

Within a WF program, there are two ways to model persistence points. One is to use a `TransactionScopeActivity`, as we have already discussed. The second way is to use custom persistence points. Custom persistence points occur at the completion of any activity whose type is decorated with (or inherits) `PersistOnClose-Attribute`, an attribute type that is defined in the `System.Workflow.ComponentModel` namespace.

`PersistOnCloseAttribute` can be applied to any activity type that you develop, but for the simplest case you can write an activity whose sole purpose is to force a persistence point, as shown in Listing 6.3.

Listing 6.3 `SavePoint` **Activity that Models a Persistence Point**

```
using System;
using System.Workflow.ComponentModel;
```

```
namespace EssentialWF.Activities
{
  [PersistOnClose]
  public class SavePoint : Activity
  {
    protected override ActivityExecutionStatus Execute(
      ActivityExecutionContext context)
    {
      return ActivityExecutionStatus.Closed;
    }
  }
}
```

Persistence is not allowed to happen during execution of a `TransactionScope-Activity`. Thus, the validator of `TransactionScopeActivity` will flag as an error the presence of any activity whose type is decorated with (or inherits) `[PersistOn-Close]`.

Transactional Services

Let's summarize a few things we have learned in this chapter:

- WF program instance persistence occurs at the completion of a `TransactionScopeActivity` or any activity whose type carries `PersistOnCloseAttribute`.

- Persistence can also occur at arbitrary times, at the discretion of the host application, as part of WF program instance passivation (`WorkflowInstance.Unload`).

- In failure scenarios (or after `WorkflowInstance.Abort` is called by the host application), WF program instances resume their execution from their last persistence point.

As we have confirmed throughout the book, one of the distinguishing characteristics of WF programs is that they execute episodically. These episodes generally correspond to computation that is triggered by the arrival of data and ends when the WF program instance becomes idle (waiting for additional stimulus).

We can take a slightly different angle and alternatively classify an episode as *the computation that takes place between two persistence points of a WF program instance*. This is a slightly different definition (because this kind of episode can span idle points if a host application chooses not to persist when an instance becomes idle) but is arguably more precise. It is more precise because an episode cannot really be said to have "happened" until a persistence point is reached and the progress of the WF program instance is recorded in a transactional manner.

Let's explore this further. It is beneficial to use activities such as `Update-CustomerInfo` within a `TransactionScopeActivity` because the types they rely upon in their execution logic (such as the types defined in the `System.Data.Sql-Client` namespace) know how to enlist in the ambient transaction. The work of these activities occurs transactionally, and we have confirmed that the WF program instance is also always persisted as a part of the same transaction. So far, so good.

What about nontransactional work (like our `WriteLine` activity) that prints a message to the `System.Console` (which, alas, is not a `System.Transactions` resource manager)? Maybe it is all right for a message to be printed to the console more than once in the failure case we outlined earlier (wherein the same `WriteLine` activity might have its `Execute` method called more than once). In some scenarios, though, we may need to do better—for example, if we want the message to be printed exactly once.

Although a `WriteLine` activity may have its `Execute` method invoked more than once (as in the failure case), the execution of that `WriteLine` nevertheless must be said to "happen" exactly once if our source of truth is the data (WF program instance state) that is sent to the persistence service at persistence points. That is to say, a transaction is created (or borrowed from `TransactionScopeActivity`) when a persistence point occurs, and only when this transaction commits is a `WriteLine` activity executed (as part of the current episode), recorded, and said to have verifiably "happened."

The key insight here is that if we can delay the actual invocation of `Console.WriteLine` until a transaction (for the next persistence point) is available, the occurrence of the *actual* side effect (seeing a message appear at the console) and the WF runtime's recording of the completion of the program statement that *caused* this side effect (the completion of the `WriteLine` activity) will happen in the same transaction!

We can, in fact, achieve this splendid result quite simply. In Chapter 3, "Activity Execution," we discussed the benefits of factoring execution logic out of activities

and locating it in services that are added to the WF runtime. We already did this factoring very straightforwardly for `WriteLine` back in Chapter 3:

```
using System;
using System.Workflow.ComponentModel;

namespace EssentialWF.Activities
{
  public abstract class WriterService
  {
    public abstract void Write(string s);
  }

  public class WriteLine : Activity
  {
    // Text property elided for clarity

    protected override ActivityExecutionStatus Execute(
      ActivityExecutionContext context)
    {
      WriterService writer = context.GetService<WriterService>();
      writer.Write(Text);

      return ActivityExecutionStatus.Closed;
    }
  }
}
```

Our first implementation of a `WriterService` was very simple:

```
using System;
using EssentialWF.Activities;

namespace EssentialWF.Services
{
  public class SimpleWriterService : WriterService
  {
    public override void Write(string s)
    {
      Console.WriteLine(s);
    }
  }
}
```

The `SimpleWriterService` implementation does buy us a layer of abstraction
between the `WriteLine` activity and the actual assets used to write a message (which

is most definitely a good design practice), but it of course does not change the fact that the appearance of the message at the console is not occurring under the auspices of any transaction.

However, we can also implement a transaction-aware `WriterService` derivative that delays the call to `Console.WriteLine` until a transaction (associated with a persistence point in the WF program instance) is provided by the WF runtime. We do this by implementing the `System.Workflow.Runtime.IPendingWork` interface.

The `IPendingWork` type is shown in Listing 6.4.

Listing 6.4 `IPendingWork`

```
namespace System.Workflow.Runtime
{
  public interface IPendingWork
  {
    void Commit(System.Transactions.Transaction transaction,
      ICollection items);

    /* *** other members *** */
  }
}
```

A service that implements `IPendingWork` indicates that it is capable of processing work items in a transactional manner. Work items are handed to such a service (via invocation of the `IPendingWork.Commit` method) from what is known as a **work batch**. A work batch holds a set of work items for a specific WF program instance.

The work batch for the currently executing WF program instance can be obtained via the `WorkBatch` property of the `WorkflowEnvironment` type. `WorkflowEnvironment` is a static class defined in the `System.Workflow.Runtime` namespace, and is shown in Listing 6.5.

Listing 6.5 `WorkflowEnvironment`

```
namespace System.Workflow.Runtime
{
  public static class WorkflowEnvironment
  {
    public static IWorkBatch WorkBatch { get; }
    public static Guid WorkflowInstanceId { get; }
  }
}
```

A work batch is represented by an object of type `IWorkBatch`, which is defined in the `System.Workflow.Runtime` namespace and shown in Listing 6.6.

Listing 6.6   IWorkBatch

```
namespace System.Workflow.Runtime
{
  public interface IWorkBatch
  {
    void Add(IPendingWork service, object workItem);
  }
}
```

As you can see in Listing 6.6, when a work item (of type `object`) is added to a work batch, it is associated with a service (which must implement `IPendingWork`) that will later process the work item (when a transaction is available). When items in a work batch are processed—as part of the transaction that occurs at a WF program instance persistence point—each work item is handed to its associated service, along with the actual `System.Transactions.Transaction` that should be used in the performance of the work.

Here is our transaction-aware `WriterService` implementation:

```
using System;
using System.Collections;
using System.Transactions;
using System.Workflow.Runtime;
using EssentialWF.Activities;

namespace EssentialWF.Services
{
  public class TransactionalWriterService :
    WriterService, IPendingWork
  {
    public override void Write(string s)
    {
      IWorkBatch batch = WorkflowEnvironment.WorkBatch;
      batch.Add(this, s);
    }

    public void Commit(Transaction transaction, ICollection items)
    {
      foreach (object item in items)
      {
        string s = item as string;
```

```
      Console.WriteLine(s);
    }
  }

  // Called after the transaction succeeds or fails
  public void Complete(bool succeeded, ICollection items)
  {
  }

  // Called to see if Commit should be called
  public bool MustCommit(ICollection items)
  {
    return true;
  }
 }
}
```

In its implementation of the `Write` method, `TransactionalWriterService` adds a work item to the work batch of the currently executing WF program instance. The work item is simply the `string` passed as a parameter to `Write`. At some point in the future, when a transaction is available at a WF program instance persistence point, the `IPendingWork.Commit` method is called by the WF runtime. At this time, `TransactionalWriterServiceImpl` simply prints each work item (remember, in this case, each work item is a `string` that was passed earlier to the `Write` method, which could have been called more than one time if `WriteLine` executed more than once—for instance, inside a `While` activity).

All we have done is delay the execution of the invocation of `Console.Write-Line`. This may seem trivial (and the example is definitely contrived), but the benefit of having the actual work specified by an activity performed and committed in the same transaction that the WF runtime uses to record the successful execution of that activity is critical in some scenarios.

There is one rather serious consequence to this design. If an exception is thrown by the `Commit` method of `TransactionalWriterService`, the transaction under which the work (and the persistence of the WF program instance) is happening fails.

For this reason (and perhaps also for reasons of performance or scalability), the implementation of a transaction-aware service that is utilized by an activity might not choose to do the actual work requested by the activity as part of the transaction that occurs at a WF program instance persistence point, but instead can *transactionally record the fact that this work must occur*. In other words, there can be a transactional handoff of data from the service (and hence, logically, the WF program instance) to another system, using a transactional medium such as a database table or a Microsoft Message Queuing (MSMQ) queue. Unlike our simple example, in this more robust solution the `System.Transactions.Transaction` object that is passed as a parameter to the `IPendingWork.Commit` method will be needed by the transaction-aware service to perform the handoff of work.

Transactional Delivery of Data

The previous section explored how the progress of a WF program instance, which unfolds episodically, is recorded using transactions—and, significantly, also how transaction-aware services utilized by activities can participate in these transactions. Essentially, what we learned boils down to a model for how WF program instances can send data to external systems in a transactional manner.

Now we can turn our attention to the inbound direction. How can data be handed from an external system to a WF program instance in a transactional manner? To answer this question, we return to the `WorkflowInstance.EnqueueItem` method that we introduced back in Chapter 3 for our `ReadLine` activity. The signature of this method is shown here:

```
public void EnqueueItem(IComparable queueName,
                        object item,
                        IPendingWork service,
                        object workItem);
```

The `queueName` parameter is the name of a WF program instance queue where the WF program instance is ready to receive data. A WF program instance queue is nothing more than the data structure used by a bookmark—a named location where the execution of a WF program instance (or, more specifically, an activity within a WF program instance) can be resumed.

The `item` parameter is the data that is being enqueued.

When we used the `EnqueueItem` method in the code snippets of earlier chapters, we only used the first two parameters and passed a value of `null` for the other two. Now, though, you can guess that it is precisely these latter two parameters that give us the ability to enqueue data in a transactional manner.

When an item is enqueued into a WF program instance queue, it is available for processing by the WF program instance. However, just as we discussed earlier, the WF program instance—though it can consume this data—may not reach its next persistence point before some failure condition occurs.

If we pass `null` as the value of the latter two parameters of `EnqueueItem`, and a failure occurs before the next WF program instance persistence point, the enqueued data is lost. Instead, if we provide a transaction-aware service and a work item when we enqueue the data, our service will get called when the next persistence point in the WF program instance is reached. A transaction will then be available so that our service can transactionally record the fact that the data was successfully handed to the WF program instance.

Where Are We?

In this chapter, we learned how WF program instances are executed in a durable and transactional manner. Because the execution progress of a WF program instance is recorded transactionally, it is possible to keep the state of the program consistent with the state of the external world, with which the program is interacting.

The `TransactionScopeActivity` activity allows us to explicitly model transactional boundaries in a WF program. The transaction used by a `TransactionScopeActivity` is the same transaction that is used to persist the WF program instance at the end of the execution of the `TransactionScopeActivity`.

We saw how to write an activity that lets us declaratively specify persistence points in WF programs, and we were also reminded that a host application can initiate passivation (which entails persistence) at any time (except if a `TransactionScopeActivity` is executing). Transactional services used by activities can participate in the transaction used for persistence, regardless of whether a `TransactionScopeActivity` is employed in a WF program. And, external entities that enqueue items into WF program queues can also do work within the transaction that is used to persist the newly enqueued item as part of the WF program instance state—in this way, we can achieve transaction handoff of data from external entities to WF program instances.

7

Advanced Authoring

$\mathbf{L}$IKE OTHER PROGRAMS YOU HAVE WRITTEN, a WF program is a set of program statements that solves some problem. You can write an Open, Sesame program in XAML just like you can write such a program in C#. But, as we saw in Chapters 3, "Activity Execution," and 4, "Advanced Activity Execution," WF programs execute differently than regular C# programs because WF program statements—activities—are resumable.

In this chapter, we will take a closer look at how activity types and WF programs are defined. We will begin by focusing on the capabilities of `DependencyObject`, the class from which `Activity` derives. This will lead us to discussions of activity metadata, activity databinding, and attached properties.

Additionally, an activity type can be associated with a set of other classes that define different aspects of the activity's functionality. The canonical example of this factoring, in the context of the .NET Framework, is the association of a designer (a class that implements `IDesigner`) with an `IComponent`, so that the `IComponent` can have a visual representation in Visual Studio and in other design environments. Every activity is an `IComponent` and therefore can be associated with a designer, but the more general point is that this "separation of concerns" approach is a useful design pattern that the WF programming model relies upon to associate different pieces of functionality with any activity type. In the fullest sense, then, an activity is not just a class that derives from `Activity`. Such a class is certainly the core of any activity you develop, but an activity type is also associated with a designer and other components that collectively define the full capabilities of the activity.

Dependency Properties

In earlier chapters, we have seen example activity types with properties whose implementations differ from the standard "store the property value in a private field" approach. These properties have getters and setters that call `GetValue` and `SetValue` methods inherited from the base class of `Activity`, which is a type called `DependencyObject`.

The inheritance hierarchy for activity types is shown in Figure 7.1.

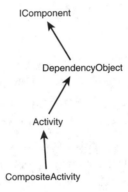

Figure 7.1   Activity inheritance hierarchy

To get us started, the `DependencyObject` type is shown in Listing 7.1.

Listing 7.1   `DependencyObject`

```
namespace System.Workflow.ComponentModel
{
  public abstract class DependencyObject :
    System.ComponentModel.IComponent
  {
    public object GetValue(DependencyProperty property);
    public void SetValue(DependencyProperty property,
      object value);

    public ActivityBind GetBinding(DependencyProperty property);
    public void SetBinding(DependencyProperty property,
      ActivityBind bind);

    protected internal bool DesignMode { get; }
```

```
    /* *** other members *** */
  }
}
```

In the sections that follow, we will focus on the details of how `DependencyObject` helps activities manage their property values. Specifically, we will look at three special, and distinct, kinds of properties that `DependencyObject` supports:

- Metadata properties
- Databinding-enabled properties
- Attached properties

Activity Metadata

When we develop a C# program, such as the simple one shown here, we can compile it and run it any number of times:

```csharp
using System;

class Program
{
  static void Main()
  {
    string s = Console.ReadLine();
    Console.WriteLine(s);
  }
}
```

Every time we run this Echo program, the same program statements execute, according to the program logic that is defined in our source code.

If we wish to comment out the `Console.WriteLine` statement, we modify the source code like this:

```csharp
// Console.WriteLine(s);
```

Once that program statement is commented out, it remains commented out unless and until we return to the source code and uncomment it. All of this is very obvious for a C# program.

WF programs are hierarchies of activities. When a WF program instance is executed, the WF runtime needs instances of activity types—actual CLR objects—on which it can invoke methods such as `Activity.Execute`. As we explored in depth in Chapters 1, "Deconstructing WF," and 2, "WF Programs," the representation of program statements as objects goes hand in hand with the WF approach to bookmarking that supports the development of resumable programs.

But the fact that program statements are objects (within an executing WF program instance) presents some challenges.

As we have seen, `Activity` defines properties such as `Name` and `Enabled`. What would happen if the execution logic of an activity decides to change the value of its `Enabled` property, or even its `Name`? Changing `Enabled` to `false` would imply that the activity, in that specific WF program instance, is now commented out. But this makes no sense. Changing the `Name` property is problematic too because the execution logic of other activities in the WF program (and also activity databinding) can depend vitally on an assumption that activity names are unchanging.

Let's take the `Enabled` property as our example, and see exactly what is going on.

When we comment out a C# `Console.WriteLine` statement, we are removing this program statement from the definition of our C# program. For a comparable WF program expressed in XAML, we could use an XML comment to do the same thing, but really what we need is a Boolean value associated with `WriteLine` because a WF program can be expressed in a number of different ways—not just as XAML—and we would like a single way of expressing the fact that an activity is "commented out of" a WF program. Because WF programs can be represented in various formats at design-time, and equivalently as an in-memory activity tree at runtime, we do not want to devise format-specific notation for indicating that an activity is commented out.

One way that WF could have tackled this problem would have been to define a CLR attribute type (let's hypothetically call it `EnabledAttribute`) that could be applied to activities. But CLR attributes (a form of CLR metadata) are applied to types, not objects (instances of types), so that means we would need two versions of our `WriteLine` activity:

```
[Enabled(true)]
public class WriteLine : Activity { ... }

[Enabled(false)]
public class DisabledWriteLine : Activity { ... }
```

Clearly this is not a desirable solution. In order to comment out a `WriteLine` activity, we need to switch to a `DisabledWriteLine`, which is an altogether different activity type! And this approach is doomed as soon as we introduce the need for associating other, similar pieces of metadata with activities. The combinatorial explosion of the number of activity types would quickly overwhelm us.

Let's go another direction, then, and try using a Boolean property whose value will determine whether or not a `WriteLine` activity is commented out of a WF program:

```
using System;
using System.Workflow.ComponentModel;

namespace EssentialWF.Activities
{
  public class WriteLine : Activity
  {
    private bool enabled;
    public bool Enabled
    {
      get { return this.enabled; }
      set { this.enabled = value; }
    }

    ...
  }
}
```

This approach appears to work much better because we express whether or not an activity is commented out simply by setting the value of the `Enabled` property. In XAML it looks like this:

```
<WriteLine Enabled="false" Text="hello, world" />
```

We seem to have hit upon the right solution. We can easily comment and uncomment this WF program statement by changing the value of its `Enabled` property.

However, as we mentioned earlier, when we comment out a program statement in our C# program, that statement remains commented out for all instances of the program that are executed. The fact that a program statement is commented out cannot change unless you go back to the definition of the program and uncomment the statement.

Because `Enabled` is just a property, it is possible for its value to change during the execution of a WF program instance (as we said earlier, the WF runtime will require an object of type `WriteLine` when we run our WF program). For the `Text` property defined by the `WriteLine` activity, this is exactly the behavior we want. The value of the `Text` property can be set during the execution of the WF program instance (just as the variable `s` is assigned at runtime in the C# Echo program). For the `Enabled` property, however, this is a fiasco. Program statements cannot be allowed to change from being uncommented to being commented out (or vice versa) during the execution of a WF program instance!

The `Enabled` property is what we described in Chapter 3 as a metadata property. The values of activity metadata properties are established at design-time (when a WF program is developed), and cannot change during the execution of instances of a WF program.

It may be helpful to consider another analogy. In C#, when you define a static read-only field for a type, at runtime that field is given a value exactly once within a particular CLR application domain (which is the boundary for access to a loaded type). The value, once set, is immutable and is effectively shared by all objects of that type within that application domain.

We encountered the same idea in Chapter 5, "Applications," when we learned that a WF program prototype is shared by multiple WF program instances. The value of a metadata property is shared by all instances of that activity (across instances of that WF program), and it is the program prototype that holds the actual value of the property.

Now we come to the implementation of metadata properties. How is it that the `Enabled` property is settable at design-time but is immutable for an activity within a running WF program instance? If we assume the presence of a Boolean property—hypothetically called `IsRunning`—that indicates whether or not an activity instance is part of an executing WF program instance, the property implementation might look like this:

```
private bool enabled;
public bool Enabled
{
  get { return this.enabled; }
  set
  {
```

```
      if (this.IsRunning)
        throw new InvalidOperationException(...);
      else
        this.enabled = value;
  }
}
```

This implementation gives us exactly the behavior we are seeking.

As an activity writer, it would be nice to not have to remember to implement this pattern for every activity metadata property. If a standard implementation could somehow be inherited, this would serve the cause of consistency (for example, ensuring that the message associated with the System.InvalidOperationException is a standard one, used by all activity types) and also make the job of developers easier. In fact, the WF programming model does provide exactly this pattern to developers of activity types via DependencyObject.

The pattern shown here is the standard implementation of a metadata property:

```
using System;
using System.Workflow.ComponentModel;

public class Widget : Activity
{
  public static readonly DependencyProperty SizeProperty
    = DependencyProperty.Register("Size",
        typeof(int), typeof(Widget),
        new PropertyMetadata(
          DependencyPropertyOptions.Metadata)
      );

  public int Size
  {
    get { return (int) GetValue(SizeProperty); }
    set { SetValue(SizeProperty, value); }
  }

  ...
}
```

This pattern is utilized by the Activity type in its implementation of metadata properties such as Name and Enabled and can also be utilized by any derivative of DependencyObject that you develop, including, of course, any activity types.

The implementation of the `Widget.Size` property has a couple of interesting aspects.

First, the `Widget` class does not (as might typically be expected) declare a private field of type `int` to store the value of the `Size` property. Instead, the `Widget` class has a static read-only field of type `System.Workflow.ComponentModel.Dependency-Property`. A dependency property is essentially the declaration of a special kind of property. `DependencyProperty` supports the definition of several special kinds of properties, one of which is a metadata property.

The `Register` method that is invoked to initialize the `SizeProperty` field basically declares four things:

- There is a special property called `"Size"`.
- The type of this property is `int`.
- This property is being defined on the `Widget` type.
- This property is a metadata property.

The second interesting part of the implementation of the `Size` property is that the property getter and setter invoke inherited methods, `GetValue` and `SetValue`, in order to get and set the actual value of the property. The `GetValue` and `SetValue` methods are defined by the abstract `System.Workflow.ComponentModel.Dependency-Object` type, which, as we saw in Figure 7.1, is the base class of `Activity`.

Dependency objects are entities in WF programs that support dependency properties, which as we know now are just special kinds of properties. The kind of special property we are defining here is a metadata property—but there are other kinds, which we will discuss in the sections that follow. Dependency properties can be used profitably in the design of types other than just activity types, so support for them is not found directly within `Activity` but instead is implemented in the `Dependency-Object` type from which `Activity` inherits.

Conceptually, what happens at runtime in our `Widget` example is that `Dependency-Object` provides storage for the actual value of a `Widget` object's `Size` property. In the context of WF, we say that the `Size` property is "backed by" `SizeProperty`, which is a field of type `DependencyProperty`. The association between `Size` and `SizeProperty` is twofold. First, there is a naming convention, which must be followed for all dependency properties: The name of the dependency property field (`SizeProperty`) must be the name of the property (`Size`) suffixed with `"Property"`. Additionally, the first parameter of the `Register` method (`"Size"` in the example code snippet) confirms the name of the property that will be backed by the dependency property being registered.

The `GetBinding` and `SetBinding` methods of `DependencyObject` will be discussed later in this chapter, in the context of activity databinding.

The `System.Workflow.ComponentModel.DependencyProperty` type is shown in Listing 7.2.

Listing 7.2   `DependencyProperty`

```
namespace System.Workflow.ComponentModel
{
  public sealed class DependencyProperty
  {
    public static DependencyProperty Register(string name,
      Type propertyType, Type ownerType);

    public static DependencyProperty Register(string name,
      Type propertyType, Type ownerType,
      PropertyMetadata propertyMetadata);

    public string Name { get; }
    public Type OwnerType { get; }
    public Type PropertyType { get; }

    /* *** other members *** */
  }
}
```

As we saw earlier, the registration of a `DependencyProperty` specifies the name of the property, the type of the property, and the type that is declaring the property (this is sometimes called the **owner type** of the dependency property). The overload of the `Register` method that we used in the definition of the `Widget` activity type has a fourth parameter of type `System.Workflow.ComponentModel.PropertyMetadata` that explicitly specifies the nature of the special property being registered.

To summarize what we have learned in this section, `DependencyObject` is the type from which `Activity` derives, and from which all activity types inherit an ability to define special kinds of properties. One special kind of property is a metadata property; the value of a metadata property is set (on an activity declaration within a WF program) at design-time and is then immutable across instances of that activity within running instances of the WF program.

The `Activity` class defines an `Enabled` property that is a metadata property. Its purpose is exactly what we described earlier: If the value of this property is `false` (the default value is `true`), the activity is considered commented out of the WF program in which it has been declared.

The `Activity` class also defines a `Name` property, which, like `Enabled`, is a metadata property. This means that every activity declaration (program statement) in a WF program can be given a name, which can be used thereafter to refer to that activity. If activities were not named, we would have to resort to referring to them by position. Because `Name` is a metadata property, we know that its value is supplied at design-time and then cannot change during the execution of instances of the WF program. As we will see shortly, we will rely upon the fact that `Name` is an activity metadata property when we use activity databinding to implement the WF version of our C# Echo program.

Activity Databinding

Let's return now to our C# Echo program that we want to implement as a WF program. This program contains the following program statements within its `Main` method:

```
string s = Console.ReadLine();
Console.WriteLine(s);
```

To implement this program we are going to need a `ReadLine` activity with a `Text` property that holds the string that is provided by an external entity (which can read from the console). The implementation of `ReadLine` was shown and explained in Chapters 2 and 3. What we are interested in probing here is how the `Text` property of a `WriteLine` activity can take its value, at runtime, from the `Text` property of a `ReadLine` activity.

The answer is activity databinding.

In the first implementation of `WriteLine` way back in Chapter 2, we implemented the `Text` property in the standard way, using a private field of type `string`. `WriteLine.Text` is not a metadata property because its value *can* differ, for a given `WriteLine` activity, across instances of a WF program. So, using a private field is a perfectly legitimate way of implementing the `Text` property; unfortunately, it does not help us solve our data flow problem.

`DependencyObject` helps us. The second kind of special property that is supported by any dependency object is a **databinding-enabled property**. A databinding-enabled property can be assigned a databinding expression that is evaluated at runtime in order to obtain the actual value of the property. A databinding-enabled property can also be assigned a regular value (of the appropriate type) in lieu of a databinding expression; in this way, use of activity databinding is a choice made by the user of the activity.

Metadata properties and databinding-enabled properties are mutually exclusive sets. If a property is a metadata property, its value is supplied at design-time. The whole point of a databinding-enabled property is that the value will be procured at runtime by evaluation of a databinding expression. Thus, `Activity.Name` is not a databinding-enabled property; the `Text` property of `WriteLine`, however, is a perfect candidate for us to enhance with this databinding capability.

A reimplementation of the `WriteLine.Text` property, which turns it into a databinding-enabled property, is shown here:

```
using System;
using System.Workflow.ComponentModel;

namespace EssentialWF.Activities
{
  public class WriteLine : Activity
  {
    public static readonly DependencyProperty TextProperty
      = DependencyProperty.Register("Text",
        typeof(string), typeof(WriteLine));
```

```
    public string Text
    {
      get { return (string) GetValue(TextProperty); }
      set { SetValue(TextProperty, value); }
    }

    ...

  }
}
```

The implementation of the `Text` property's getter and setter have changed; they now look very much like our earlier implementation of the `Widget.Size` property. A dependency property field, `TextProperty`, has been declared, and is being used to back the `Text` property.

The parameters to the `DependencyProperty.Register` method are in this case *not* indicating that `Text` is a metadata property. When a dependency property is registered using the overload of `Register` that only accepts three parameters (as is the case here), it is presumed that the kind of property being specified is a databinding-enabled property (in other words, this is the default). We could equivalently use the same overload of `Register` that we had used for `Widget.Size` with the following value for the fourth parameter:

```
new PropertyMetadata(DependencyPropertyOptions.Default)
```

Now that we have implemented `WriteLine.Text` as a databinding-enabled property, we can assign to it an activity-databinding expression, like so:

```
<ReadLine x:Name="r1" />
<WriteLine x:Name="w1" Text="{wf:ActivityBind r1,Path=Text}" />
```

To declare an activity-databinding expression, we require the use of the `Activity-Bind` type, which is shown in Listing 7.3.

Listing 7.3   ActivityBind

```
namespace System.Workflow.ComponentModel
{
  public sealed class ActivityBind : MarkupExtension
  {
    public ActivityBind();
```

```
    public ActivityBind(string name);
    public ActivityBind(string name, string path);

    public string Name { get; set; }
    public string Path { get; set; }

    public object GetRuntimeValue(Activity activity);
    public void SetRuntimeValue(Activity activity, object value);

    /* *** other members *** */
  }
}
```

The `Name` property of `ActivityBind` names an activity within the same WF program. The `Path` property indicates a field or property on the activity indicated by the `Name` property. In our previous example XAML snippet, the value of the `Path` property is simply `"Text"` (indicating a binding to the `Text` property of the `ReadLine`) but the value can also be a dotted path such as `"PropA.PropB.PropC"` that indicates the location of a nested property (or field) within a compound property (or field) defined on the activity type.

The `WriteLine.Text` property getter is called by the `Execute` method of `WriteLine`. When this happens, the `GetValue` method (inherited from `DependencyObject`) is called by the implementation of the `Text` property's getter. Because `Text` is a databinding-enabled property, the `DependencyObject` type's implementation of `GetValue` knows that it will find *either* a `string` object (the type of the `Text` property is `string`, as indicated by the `Register` method) or an `ActivityBind` object in its internal table of dependency property values when it looks for a value to return. If a `string` is found, that value is returned. If an `ActivityBind` object is found, the `ActivityBind.GetRuntimeValue` method is invoked in order to evaluate the databinding expression. The result of evaluation is then returned. This process is depicted in Figure 7.2. To clarify, what we have just described are a few of the internals of the `DependencyObject` type. The developer of the `WriteLine` activity type, as well as the developer of WF programs that utilize `WriteLine`, needn't worry about the underlying mechanics of how databinding expressions are evaluated.

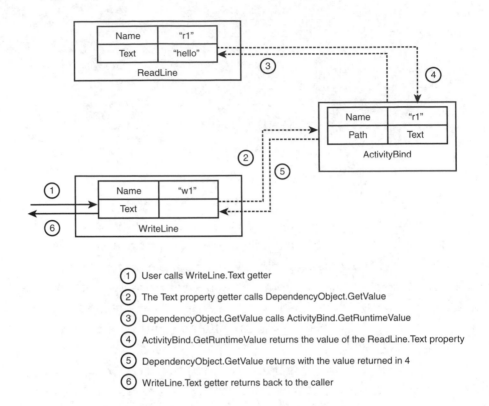

1. User calls WriteLine.Text getter

2. The Text property getter calls DependencyObject.GetValue

3. DependencyObject.GetValue calls ActivityBind.GetRuntimeValue

4. ActivityBind.GetRuntimeValue returns the value of the ReadLine.Text property

5. DependencyObject.GetValue returns with the value returned in 4

6. WriteLine.Text getter returns back to the caller

Figure 7.2   Evaluation of an activity-databinding expression

In our example XAML snippet, we specify the databinding expression as the value of the Text property using a special syntax, Text="{wf:ActivityBind r1,Path=Text}". What happens beneath the surface, in this example, is that an ActivityBind object is created, its Name property is set to "r1", and its Path property is set to "Text". The ActivityBind object is then associated with the Text property of the WriteLine activity using the DependencyObject.SetBinding method (refer to Listing 7.1), which allows a databinding-enabled property to be assigned a databinding expression.

It is critical here that the Name property of ReadLine (inherited from Activity) is a metadata property; if it were not, activity names would be able to change at runtime. Because activity-databinding expressions refer to activities by name, their evaluation yields predictable results only if Activity.Name cannot change at runtime.

To complete our WF program, we use the `Sequence` composite activity as a container of a `ReadLine` and a `WriteLine`:

```
<Sequence xmlns="http://EssentialWF/Activities"
xmlns:x="http://schemas.microsoft.com/winfx/2006/xaml"
xmlns:wf="http://schemas.microsoft.com/winfx/2006/xaml/workflow">
  <ReadLine x:Name="r1" />
  <WriteLine x:Name="w1" Text="{wf:ActivityBind r1,Path=Text}" />
</Sequence>
```

The preceding XAML is a complete WF program and, when executed by the WF runtime, will produce the same result as the C# Echo program we saw earlier in the chapter.

Attached Properties

There is a third kind of dependency property that is known as an **attached property**. Attached properties are a general-purpose capability of dependency objects, but are particularly useful in the development of composite activities that must be provided with special information about each of their child activities.

To illustrate how attached properties work, we will return to the `Prioritized-Interleave` activity that we introduced in Chapter 3. `PrioritizedInterleave` executes its child activities in priority order. First, all child activities with a priority of 1 are executed (in an interleaved fashion); when those are all completed, child activities with a priority of 2 are executed (again, in an interleaved fashion). This continues until all child activities have completed their execution. We would like this composite activity to be general-purpose so that activities of any type can be contained within it. This seems a tall order because we know that not all activities (in fact, none of the ones we've developed) define a property called `Priority`.

This is precisely where an attached property can help us out. Essentially, an **attached property** is a property that is defined by one type (the owner type), but is applied to other types, which then act as if they had defined such a property.

Listing 7.4 shows the `PrioritizedInterleave` activity implementation.

Listing 7.4 `PrioritizedInterleave` **Activity that Uses an Attached Property**

```
using System;
using System.Workflow.ComponentModel;

namespace EssentialWF.Activities
{
  public class PrioritizedInterleave : CompositeActivity
  {
    public static readonly DependencyProperty PriorityProperty
      = DependencyProperty.RegisterAttached("Priority",
          typeof(Int32),
          typeof(PrioritizedInterleave),
          new PropertyMetadata(
            DependencyPropertyOptions.Metadata)
    );

    public static object GetPriority(object dependencyObject)
    {
      return ((DependencyObject)
        dependencyObject).GetValue(PriorityProperty);
    }

    public static void SetPriority(object dependencyObject,
      object value)
    {
      ((DependencyObject)dependencyObject).SetValue(
        PriorityProperty, value);
    }

    // Execution logic...
  }
}
```

Listing 7.4 shows the standard boilerplate code for an attached property, which is somewhat larger than the code for the other kinds of dependency properties we have seen. First of all, we are using the `RegisterAttached` method (not `Register`) of `DependencyProperty` to register the attached property. Second, we provide `public static` methods for getting and setting the value of the attached property. These methods take the place of the strongly typed (and nonstatic) getter and setter that exist for standard properties. Such a strongly typed property is by definition not possible for an attached property because the property will be attached to objects of already-compiled types. There is a requirement that an object to which the property is being attached is a derivative of `DependencyObject`.

With the `PriorityProperty` dependency property defined and registered, we can define WF programs that use the `PrioritizedInterleave` composite activity. Such a program is shown in Listing 7.5. In our example implementation, we've chosen to make `Priority` a metadata property but this needn't be the case; attached properties can also carry values that are determined at runtime.

Listing 7.5 A WF Program that Uses the `PrioritizedInterleave` **Activity**

```
<PrioritizedInterleave x:Name="i1"
xmlns="http://EssentialWF/Activities"
xmlns:x="http://schemas.microsoft.com/winfx/2006/xaml"
xmlns:wf="http://schemas.microsoft.com/winfx/2006/xaml/workflow">

  <Sequence x:Name="s1" PrioritizedInterleave.Priority="2" >
  ...
  </Sequence>
  <Sequence x:Name="s2" PrioritizedInterleave.Priority="1" >
  ...
  </Sequence>
  <Sequence x:Name="s3" PrioritizedInterleave.Priority="3" >
  ...
  </Sequence>
  <Sequence x:Name="s4" PrioritizedInterleave.Priority="2" >
  ...
  </Sequence>
  <Sequence x:Name="s5" PrioritizedInterleave.Priority="3" >
  ...
  </Sequence>
</PrioritizedInterleave>
```

Using XAML to Define Activity Types

Thus far in our examples, we have drawn a crisp distinction between WF programs and activity types. What happens, though, if we want to reuse the logic of a WF program in a larger WF program?

If we tackle this problem in the context of a C# program, the result might look something like this:

```
using System;

public class Echo
{
  public void DoEcho()
  {
    string s = Console.ReadLine();
    Console.WriteLine(s);
  }
}

class Program
{
  static void Main()
  {
    Echo echo1 = new Echo();
    echo1.DoEcho();

    ...

    Echo echo2 = new Echo();
    echo2.DoEcho();
  }
}
```

The echo functionality is factored out into a separate type, Echo. Now we can instantiate objects of type Echo and invoke their DoEcho method, as shown in the Main method of the preceding simple code snippet.

With what we know so far of the WF programming model, we are stuck. Here is our WF Echo program:

```
<Sequence xmlns="http://EssentialWF/Activities"
xmlns:x="http://schemas.microsoft.com/winfx/2006/xaml"
xmlns:wf="http://schemas.microsoft.com/winfx/2006/xaml/workflow">
  <ReadLine x:Name="r1" />
  <WriteLine x:Name="w1" Text="{wf:ActivityBind r1,Path=Text}" />
</Sequence>
```

As it stands, there is no way for us to reuse this logic as-is in a larger WF program. The problem is that activity declarations in WF programs are typed, and the preceding XAML is not defining a type—it is just an XML document that is a blueprint for an activity tree.

In fact, XAML supports the use case in which we are interested quite elegantly. The use of a single special XML attribute turns the WF Echo program into the definition of an activity type:

```
<Sequence x:Class="EssentialWF.Activities.Echo" xmlns="http://EssentialWF/Activities"
xmlns:wf="http://schemas.microsoft.com/winfx/2006/xaml/workflow"
xmlns:x="http://schemas.microsoft.com/winfx/2006/xaml">
  <ReadLine x:Name="r1" />
  <WriteLine x:Name="w1"Text="{wf:ActivityBind r1,Path=Text}"/>
</Sequence>
```

The Class attribute is defined in the special XML namespace for XAML constructs, which we have mapped (according to XAML convention) to the XML namespace prefix "x". Using the x:Class attribute in our XAML means that we are actually specifying

```
namespace EssentialWF.Activities
{
  public class Echo : Sequence
  {
    ...
  }
}
```

That's right, the XAML is now equivalent to a C# type definition. The namespace-qualified name of the type is "EssentialWF.Activities.Echo", which is the value of the Class attribute in the root element of the XAML document. The Echo type derives from Sequence, which is the activity type of the root element of the XAML.

There are many interesting details and implications of the underlying mechanics of this approach; we will explore these in just a moment. But first, let's appreciate the fact that this solution gives us precisely the capability we were seeking. We can now write another WF program that uses the Echo activity type, even though Echo was defined in XAML:

```
<Sequence x:Name="s1" xmlns="http://EssentialWF/Activities"
xmlns:x="http://schemas.microsoft.com/winfx/2006/xaml">
  <Echo x:Name="echo1" />
  <Echo x:Name="echo2" />
</Sequence>
```

One implication of the preceding XAML snippet is that each of the two `Echo` activities has exactly the same substructure—both contain a `ReadLine` followed by a `WriteLine`. As a consequence, the value of the `Activity.Name` property for the two `ReadLine` activities is the same. Because of this use case, activities cannot assume that the value of their `Name` property is unique within a WF program. `Name` is only guaranteed to be unique among the immediate child activities of a given composite activity. This is a problem for the `ReadLine` activity because our current implementation of `ReadLine` uses the value of its `Name` property as the name of its WF program queue.

The `Activity.QualifiedName` property can help us. `Activity.QualifiedName` uniquely identifies each activity within a WF program. The qualified name of an activity is a computed value (the `QualifiedName` property has no setter). This value is a concatenation of the `Name` of the activity and the values of the `Name` properties of all activity name scopes in the activity's chain of parent activities (with a '.' character separating each name). An activity name scope is a composite activity whose type definition specifies one or more child activities. `Echo` is an activity name scope, but `Sequence` is not (because a `new Sequence()` has no child activities but a `new Echo()` does). Thus, in the preceding XAML snippet, the two `ReadLine` activities have the qualified names `"echo1.r1"` and `"echo2.r1"`. We can now refer to them unambiguously, and we can update the implementation of `ReadLine` to use the value of `QualifiedName` as the name of its bookmark (WF program queue).

The first WF Echo program that we wrote, which did not use the XAML `x:Class` attribute, is an artifact from which a WF program prototype can be directly loaded. When we changed our WF program by adding the `x:Class` attribute, though, we changed the meaning of the XAML. Rather than simply representing a tree of activities, the updated XAML represents the specification of a new activity type.

A XAML document that defines a new activity type is compiled using the WF program compiler. The WF program compiler is available programmatically as the `WorkflowCompiler` type (details of which will be discussed later in this chapter) or by using `wfc.exe`, which is a command-line wrapper around `WorkflowCompiler` that is available as part of the WF SDK.

The WF program compiler accepts a XAML document, turns it into the equivalent C# code (or VisualBasic.NET code), and then passes this code to the C# (or VisualBasic.NET) compiler. The result of compilation is, of course, an assembly.

Let's go ahead and compile our WF Echo program, which is shown in Listing 7.6, and which we will assume resides in a file "echo.xoml":

```
wfc /r:EssentialWF.dll echo.xoml
```

Listing 7.6 WF Echo Program in Echo.xoml

```
<Sequence x:Class="EssentialWF.Activities.Echo"
xmlns="http://EssentialWF/Activities"
xmlns:x="http://schemas.microsoft.com/winfx/2006/xaml"
xmlns:wf="http://schemas.microsoft.com/winfx/2006/xaml/workflow">
  <ReadLine x:Name="r1" />
  <WriteLine x:Name="w1" Text="{wf:ActivityBind r1,Path=Text}" />
</Sequence>
```

XAML File Extensions

WF uses ".xoml" as the file extension for XAML files that represent WF programs. This allows applications and tools to easily distinguish between XAML files that have meaning in WF, and XAML files that are meant for use in other frameworks such as WPF.

The "/r:EssentialWF.dll" command-line parameter indicates an assembly reference to the assembly that contains the WriteLine, ReadLine, and Sequence activity types.

To see descriptions of all wfc.exe options, you can type the following:

```
wfc /help
```

The result of compilation is a new assembly, echo.dll. If we examine this assembly, we will see that it contains compiled code for a single type, Echo, that has been defined like this:

```
namespace EssentialWF.Activities
{
  public class Echo : Sequence
  {
    private ReadLine r1;
    private WriteLine w1;
```

```
public Echo()
{
  InitializeComponent();
}

private void InitializeComponent()
{
  this.CanModifyActivities = true;

  this.w1 = new WriteLine();
  this.w1.Name = "w1";

  this.r1 = new ReadLine();
  this.r1.Name = "r1";

  ActivityBind bind1 = new ActivityBind();
  bind1.Name = "r1";
  bind1.Path = "Text";
  this.w1.SetBinding(WriteLine.TextProperty, bind1);

  this.Activities.Add(this.r1);
  this.Activities.Add(this.w1);

  this.Name = "Echo";
  this.CanModifyActivities = false;
  }
 }
}
```

As you can see, the constructor logic of Echo builds the same tree of activities that we had represented earlier in XAML. The Echo type, in the assembly echo.dll, is a WF program blueprint—it is just a different form of packaging for the representation of our activity tree!

There are a few things to observe about the Echo type:

- The logic to construct the activity tree is factored into a private method called InitializeComponent, which is called by the WriteLine constructor. This is merely a convention that is also followed in other programming models such as Windows Forms. There are situations in which the Visual Studio Workflow Designer relies upon this convention, so it is good practice to follow it.

- The CanModifyActivities property controls the window of time in which it is legal to add child activities to a composite activity.

The default WF program loader recognizes both XAML documents (that do not use the x:Class attribute) and compiled types that derive from Activity as valid WF program blueprints. Thus, any activity type, packaged in an assembly, will be recognized by the default WF program loader as a WF program blueprint. Hence, even the WriteLine type is a WF program blueprint; if you point the default WF program loader at this blueprint, it will load a WF program prototype (an activity tree) that has exactly one node—a WriteLine activity.

From the preceding discussion, we can infer that compilation of XAML—at a high level—involves conversion of XAML to code, and then compilation of the code using a language compiler. This is indeed the case. A WF program that is expressed in XAML can be deserialized into an in-memory tree of activity objects. This tree of activities can also be serialized back into XAML. The WorkflowMarkupSerializer type, which is shown in Listing 7.7 and is defined in the System.Workflow. ComponentModel.Serialization namespace, allows any object (not just any activity object) to be serialized to and deserialized from XAML.

Listing 7.7   WorkflowMarkupSerializer

```
namespace System.Workflow.ComponentModel.Serialization
{
  public class WorkflowMarkupSerializer
  {
    public WorkflowMarkupSerializer();

    public object Deserialize(XmlReader reader);
    public void Serialize(XmlWriter writer, object obj);

    /* *** other members *** */
  }
}
```

Using WorkflowMarkupSerializer, it is easy to programmatically create the XAML for the WF Echo program we earlier wrote by hand:

```
using System;
using System.Xml;
using System.Text;
using System.Workflow.ComponentModel;
using System.Workflow.ComponentModel.Serialization;
using EssentialWF.Activities;
```

```
class Program
{
  static void Main()
  {
    ReadLine read = new ReadLine();
    read.Name = "r1";

    WriteLine write = new WriteLine();
    write.Name = "w1";

    ActivityBind bind = new ActivityBind();
    bind.Name = "r1";
    bind.Path = "Text";

    write.SetBinding(WriteLine.TextProperty, bind);

    Sequence seq = new Sequence();
    seq.Activities.Add(read);
    seq.Activities.Add(write);

    using (XmlWriter writer = new XmlTextWriter("echo.xoml",
      System.Text.Encoding.Default))
    {
      WorkflowMarkupSerializer serializer =
        new WorkflowMarkupSerializer();

      serializer.Serialize(writer, seq);
    }
  }
}
```

Later in this chapter, we will get a much closer look at how activity serialization unfolds, and how serialization to and from custom formats is accommodated by the WF programming model.

Those of you who are already familiar with WF may have been wondering when we would get around to explaining what is sometimes known as *code-beside*. We left this topic aside (so to speak) because the association of code with WF programs is not central to the WF programming model, but is merely—as you probably now realize— a WF program-authoring convenience.

Because a WF program can be defined as a type (textually as C# or VisualBasic.NET code or as XAML that uses x:Class), there is nothing stopping us from adding additional custom code to this type. From there it is a simple enhancement to have activities (within a running WF program instance) raise events that are handled by this custom code.

We don't want the presence of such custom code to prevent us from authoring WF programs in XAML. To meet this requirement, we will rely upon a feature of the C# and VisualBasic.NET compilers called partial types. **Partial types** allow the definition of a type (such as a WF program) to be split across multiple physical files, such as two different C# source files or a C# source file and a XAML file. In the case of WF, the sweet spot is to allow an activity tree to be specified as XAML (utilizing the x:Class attribute) while allowing custom code, which accompanies that XAML, to reside in a separate C# or VisualBasic.NET source file.

Let's enhance our `WriteLine` activity so that it raises an event, by adding the following event declaration:

```
public event System.EventHandler BeforeWrite;
```

We express the subscription to this event in the XAML of our WF Echo program like so:

```
<WriteLine BeforeWrite="OnBeforeWrite" />
```

We handle the `BeforeWrite` event in code, where we assign the value of the `WriteLine.Text` property:

```
using System;
using System.Workflow.ComponentModel;

namespace EssentialWF.Activities
{
  public partial class Echo : Sequence
  {
    void OnBeforeWrite(object sender, EventArgs e)
    {
      WriteLine write = sender as WriteLine;
      CompositeActivity parent = write.Parent;
      ReadLine read = parent.GetActivityByName("r1") as ReadLine;

      write.Text = read.Text;
    }
  }
}
```

There are a few things to observe about the preceding XAML and code snippets:

- The `Echo` class is declared using the `partial` type modifier.
- The `sender` parameter to the `OnBeforeWrite` method is the activity object—in this case, the `WriteLine` activity instance—that is raising the event. This is a convention that should be adhered to by the execution logic of all activity types that raise events.
- The `WriteLine` activity declaration (in XAML) no longer specifies an activity databinding expression for the `Text` property. The logic of `OnBeforeWrite` takes its place, and achieves exactly the same result.

Because our WF program is now represented in two different files, we must provide both of these files to the WF program compiler:

```
wfc /r:EssentialWF.dll echo.xoml echo.cs
```

Figure 7.3 depicts the WF compilation process. First, the XAML plus either a C# or VisualBasic.NET partial class definition are merged into a single type within a temporary assembly managed by the WF program compiler. This temporary type is validated (a topic discussed later in this chapter) and then there is a special WF-specific code generation step (also a topic discussed later in this chapter). Finally, the C# or VisualBasic.NET language compiler is asked to produce an assembly.

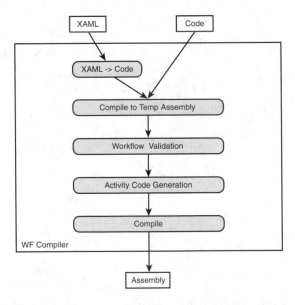

Figure 7.3   WF program compilation

As a final demonstration of the equivalence of XAML and code as specifications of a WF program, we can represent our new version of the WF Echo program entirely as code:

```
using System;
using System.Workflow.ComponentModel;

namespace EssentialWF.Activities
{
  public class Echo : Sequence
  {
    public Echo()
    {
      InitializeComponent();
    }

    private void InitializeComponent()
    {
      this.CanModifyActivities = true;

      WriteLine write = new WriteLine();
      write.Name = "w1";

      ReadLine read = new ReadLine();
      read.Name = "r1";

      this.Activities.Add(read);
      this.Activities.Add(write);

      write.BeforeWrite += this.OnBeforeWrite;

      this.Name = "Echo";
      this.CanModifyActivities = false;
    }

    void OnBeforeWrite(object sender, EventArgs e)
    {
      WriteLine w = sender as WriteLine;
      CompositeActivity parent = w.Parent;
      ReadLine r = parent.GetActivityByName("r1") as ReadLine;

      w.Text = r.Text;
    }
  }
}
```

Our WF program is now represented in a single C# source file. We still compile it using the WF program compiler in order to ensure that proper validation of the WF program takes place before the handoff to the C# language compiler:

```
wfc /r:EssentialWF.dll echo.cs
```

As a WF program author, you can decide when to use just XAML, when to combine XAML with code, and when to develop WF programs entirely in code. Of course, as we learned in Chapter 5, we can also ignore all of this and declare WF programs using a custom domain-specific language of our choosing.

Activity Component Model

An activity type is more than just a class that derives, directly or indirectly, from `Activity`.

Table 7.1 lists five standard components that can be associated with any activity type. The `Activity` class carries defaults for all of these, and therefore when you define an activity type, you only need to develop custom versions of one or more of these components if a specific requirement of your activity demands it.

Table 7.1   Activity Components

Name	Description
Validator	Validates the correctness of an activity within a WF program
Code Generator	Emits code into the CLR type resulting from compilation of the WF program in which the activity resides
Designer	Renders the activity within a visual design environment
Toolbox Item	Represents the activity in the toolbox of a visual design environment
Designer Serializer	Serializes an activity to a specific format, such as XAML or CodeDOM

Before we move into deeper discussion of the component types, though, let's first consider the specific benefits of the design approach that allows these pieces of orthogonal functionality to be factored into different classes that are associated with an activity.

The basic principle behind the factoring of activity functionality into separate components is **modularity**—the separation of code into different modules among which there are well-defined relationships. This approach allows orthogonal pieces of functionality to be developed independently and to then be associated with one another in such a way as to improve the understandability (and the maintainability) of both the individual parts as well as the ways in which the parts relate. If WF did not embrace this principle, activity classes would be larger, more cumbersome and difficult to develop, and harder to understand.

There are several reasons that support the adoption of this design approach, beginning with the fact that it allows selective instantiation of an activity's capabilities. For example, the WF runtime does not care about the designer associated with an activity and therefore never needs to deal with this component. Aside from the cleanliness of the design, this helps keep the runtime (binary) serialization size of activity objects small, which can help the performance of an application that is executing WF program instances that travel to and from persistent storage.

Additionally, component attributes are inheritable, which means that an activity will inherit associations with components. For example, an activity writer only needs to develop a toolbox item component if the toolbox item of the activity's base class is not adequate. Also, the separation of orthogonal pieces of functionality allows the activity developer to get around restrictions on multiple inheritance by separately inheriting different activity components from the required base classes.

To summarize, every activity has an associated family of components that collectively determines its capabilities. The class that defines an activity type has two major purposes. The first is to specify the activity's properties. The second is to define the execution logic of the activity (as discussed in Chapters 3 and 4). Components associated with the activity provide additional aspects of the activity's functionality.

Table 7.2 lists the attribute types that are used to associate components with an activity. Only the `ActivityValidatorAttribute` and the `ActivityCodeGenerator-Attribute` are defined in a WF namespace; the other three are defined under `System.ComponentModel`.

Table 7.2   Attribute Types for Activity Components

Name	Attribute Type
Validator	`System.Workflow.ComponentModel.Compiler.ActivityValidatorAttribute`
Code Generator	`System.Workflow.ComponentModel.Compiler.ActivityCodeGeneratorAttribute`
Designer	`System.ComponentModel.DesignerAttribute`
Toolbox Item	`System.ComponentModel.ToolboxItemAttribute`
Designer Serializer	`System.ComponentModel.Design.Serialization.DesignerSerializerAttribute`

Table 7.3 displays the values of the `ValidOn`, `AllowMultiple`, and `Inherited` properties of each of the attribute types listed in Table 7.2. These are standard properties of all attributes, as defined by `System.AttributeUsageAttribute`. As you can see, an activity class can be associated with exactly one validator, one code generator, and one toolbox item (associations can also be inherited from the base class of the activity and interfaces implemented by the activity). And, an activity can be associated with any number of designers and serializers (which, again, may be inherited).

Table 7.3   Standard Properties of Attribute Types of Table 7.2

Attribute Type	ValidOn	AllowMultiple	Inherited
`ActivityValidatorAttribute`	Interface, Class	false	true
`ActivityCodeGeneratorAttribute`	Interface, Class	false	true
`DesignerAttribute`	Interface, Class	true	true
`ToolboxItemAttribute`	All	false	true
`DesignerSerializerAttribute`	Interface, Class	true	true

As you might expect, the `Activity` class has associations with a set of components, which act as default components for any activity. Custom activities only need to provide custom component associations when the defaults are not sufficient. If, for example, a custom toolbox item is not directly associated with an activity type, an association with the default activity toolbox item will be inherited from `Activity`. Listing 7.8 shows the `Activity` class's component associations.

Listing 7.8 `Activity` **Components**

```
namespace System.Workflow.ComponentModel
{
  [ActivityValidator(typeof(ActivityValidator))]
  [ActivityCodeGenerator(typeof(ActivityCodeGenerator))]
  [Designer(typeof(ActivityDesigner), typeof(IDesigner))]
  [Designer(typeof(ActivityDesigner), typeof(IRootDesigner))]
  [ToolboxItem(typeof(ActivityToolboxItem))]
  [DesignerSerializer(typeof(ActivityMarkupSerializer),
    typeof(WorkflowMarkupSerializer))]
  [DesignerSerializer(typeof(ActivityCodeDomSerializer),
    typeof(CodeDomSerializer))]
  [DesignerSerializer(typeof(ActivityTypeCodeDomSerializer),
    typeof(TypeCodeDomSerializer))]
  public class Activity : DependencyObject
  {
    ...
  }
}
```

As expected, Listing 7.8 confirms that `Activity` has a validator, a code generator, and a toolbox item. Additionally, there are two default designer associations—one for an `IDesigner` and a second for an `IRootDesigner` (both of these designer interfaces are defined in the `System.ComponentModel.Design` namespace). Finally, there are three default serializers—one for XAML, a second for standard CodeDOM, and a third for CodeDOM type serialization.

Listing 7.9 shows that `CompositeActivity`, which inherits from `Activity`, provides its own validator and code generator components, and also its own XAML serializer. Of course, based upon what we just learned, `CompositeActivity` will inherit associations with a toolbox item component, two designers, and two Code-DOM serializers from `Activity`.

Listing 7.9 `CompositeActivity` **Components**

```
namespace System.Workflow.ComponentModel
{
  [ActivityValidator(typeof(CompositeActivityValidator))]
```

```
[ActivityCodeGenerator(typeof(CompositeActivityCodeGenerator))]
[DesignerSerializer(typeof(CompositeActivityMarkupSerializer),
  typeof(WorkflowMarkupSerializer))]
public class CompositeActivity : Activity
{
  ...
}
}
```

In the remainder of this chapter, we will examine the details of three of the five components—validator, code generator, and designer serializer. We will begin with the two topics that are specific to the WF programming model: activity validation and code generation. The designer and toolbox item components will be given lighter treatment in Chapter 8, "Miscellanea," because here the WF programming model builds upon established elements of the .NET Framework.

Validation

Compilers for languages like C# determine the validity of programs written in these languages. They establish that a program is legal by parsing the program's textual representation and checking that it conforms to the language grammar. This conformance check is somewhat analogous to ensuring that an XML document obeys the rules of a particular XML schema.

A WF program is a tree of activities. There is no WF grammar that restricts how activities can be arranged within a WF program, other than the rules that an activity must be composite in order to contain other activities, and an activity can only be contained by one other activity. The need for assessing the validity of a WF program, however, is arguably just as important as that for other kinds of programs. Many activities are meant to be used within WF programs in specific ways.

The fundamental (and liberating) difference between the WF programming model and traditional program validation is that in WF the activities themselves define relevant validation logic. There is no grammar in WF, but you have the freedom (as an activity author) to decide exactly how your activities can be used within WF programs. You can write activities that impose few, if any, restrictions on their usage. You can also write more restrictive activities; a set of such activities might implement a "grammatically closed" domain-specific language.

To this end, one of the components that can optionally be associated with any activity is a **validator**. The purpose of a validator component is to ensure that the companion activity is correctly used within a WF program. For example, a validator component will complain if the properties of the activity do not have values (at the time of validation) that are collectively an acceptable basis for that activity's participation in the WF program. The set of validators for the activities in a WF program together ensure the validity of the program.

Earlier in this chapter, we learned about the difference between activity metadata and instance data. Validation often is limited to metadata; the values of metadata properties *must* be supplied when the WF program is being designed, because metadata cannot be changed once an instance of the WF program is running. Activity metadata includes properties of `Activity` such as `Name` and `Enabled`, plus any custom activity properties that are registered as metadata properties. A composite activity's set of child activities (to be precise, a composite activity's containment relationship with each child activity) is also metadata because it is established as part of the definition of the program. A validator component for an activity should in general validate all of the metadata for that activity.

Values for normal properties of an activity are not generally required at design-time. The distinguishing feature of a normal property (compared to a metadata property) is that its value can be different across different instances of the same WF program. The `Text` property of `WriteLine`, for example, can be set dynamically (at runtime) just before a `WriteLine` activity executes. It *may* be supplied statically at design-time but if `WriteLine` required this, it would be a far less useful activity. A validator component for an activity should usually not require the values of normal properties to be set (because they are expected to be set at runtime); however, if values for such properties *are* supplied statically, they may become subject to validation at the discretion of the activity author.

A validator is associated with an activity by applying `ActivityValidator-Attribute` to the activity class definition. Listing 7.10 defines a custom activity, called `Simple`, and an associated validator, called `SimpleValidator`. The `Simple` activity defines a metadata property named `Amount`, of type integer. The `Simple-Validator` casts the `obj` parameter of the `Validate` method to a `Simple` object, and checks to make sure that the value of the `Amount` property is between 50 and 100. If it is not, a validation error is created and added to the collection of errors that is returned by the `Validate` method.

Listing 7.10 Custom Activity with a Validator Component

```
using System;
using System.Workflow.ComponentModel;
using System.Workflow.ComponentModel.Compiler;

namespace EssentialWF.Activities
{
  [ActivityValidator(typeof(SimpleValidator))]
  public class Simple : Activity
  {
    public static readonly DependencyProperty AmountProperty =
      DependencyProperty.Register("Amount",
        typeof(int),
        typeof(Simple),
        new PropertyMetadata(DependencyPropertyOptions.Metadata)
      );

    public int Amount
    {
      get { return (int)base.GetValue(AmountProperty); }
      set { base.SetValue(AmountProperty, value); }
    }

    ...
  }

  public class SimpleValidator : ActivityValidator
  {
    public override ValidationErrorCollection Validate(
      ValidationManager manager, object obj)
    {
      ValidationErrorCollection errors =
        base.Validate(manager, obj);

      Simple simple = obj as Simple;

      if (simple.Amount > 100 || simple.Amount < 50)
      {
        ValidationError error = new ValidationError(
          "Simple.Amount must be between 50 and 100", 7000);
        errors.Add(error);
      }
```

```
      CompositeActivity parent = simple.Parent;
      Sequence seq = parent as Sequence;

      if (parent == null || seq == null)
      {
        ValidationError error = new ValidationError(
          "Simple must be a child activity of a Sequence", 7001);
        errors.Add(error);
      }

      return errors;
    }
  }
}
```

The validator for the `Simple` activity also performs a second validation check, which ensures that the `Simple` activity is always part of a WF program in which a `Sequence` activity is its parent; `Sequence`, of course, has no knowledge of the `Simple` activity. Although this example is contrived, it illustrates an important principle: All activities can participate in the validation of the containment relationships in an activity tree.

Because a validator component can inspect the entire WF program in which its companion activity is located, more sophisticated validation logic can be written. This allows for the development of sets of activities that have meaningful relationships above and beyond what is conveyed in the tree structure of a WF program. To take one example, if you are modeling a request-response operation with two distinct activities (say, `Request` and `Response`), these activities can perform special validation: You should not be able to use a `Response` in a WF program without a corresponding `Request`; and, if the activities are used within a `Sequence`, a `Request` should occur before its `Response`.

Activity developers can write whatever validation logic is necessary to ensure that a given activity is appropriately related to other activities within the WF program—the context for performing validation is a fully instantiated tree of activities. One common example is a validation check in which a composite activity validates that all of its child activities are of some specific type or types (or, perhaps, that all child activities implement some interface). Similarly, an activity may validate that its parent activity is always of a particular type (as we demonstrated with the `Simple` activity). An activity may validate that it is always at the root of a WF program by checking that its `Parent` property is `null`.

Turning to Listing 7.10, you can see that the `SimpleValidator` class derives from `ActivityValidator`, which is the base class for all activity validator components. `ActivityValidator` is a derivative of `DependencyObjectValidator`, which in turn derives from `Validator`. The chain of base classes is depicted in Figure 7.4. As you might guess, not all validators need to be associated with activities; more on this later.

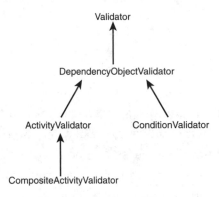

Figure 7.4 Validator base classes

The `Validator` class, which (along with the other validator base classes shown in Figure 7.4) is part of the `System.Workflow.ComponentModel.Compiler` namespace, is shown in Listing 7.11.

Listing 7.11 `Validator`

```
namespace System.Workflow.ComponentModel.Compiler
{
  public class Validator
  {
    public virtual ValidationErrorCollection Validate(
      ValidationManager manager, object obj);

    public virtual ValidationErrorCollection ValidateProperties(
      ValidationManager manager, object obj);

    /* *** other methods *** */
  }
}
```

The method relevant to all activity validators is `Validate`, which returns a collection of validation errors produced in the analysis of the object being validated, the `obj` parameter. The `ValidationErrorCollection` and `ValidationError` classes are shown in Listings 7.12 and 7.13, respectively.

Listing 7.12 `ValidationErrorCollection`

```
namespace System.Workflow.ComponentModel.Compiler
{
  public sealed class ValidationErrorCollection :
    Collection<ValidationError>
  {
    public ValidationErrorCollection();
    public ValidationErrorCollection(
      ValidationErrorCollection errors);
    public ValidationErrorCollection(
      IEnumerable<ValidationError> errors);

    public void AddRange(IEnumerable<ValidationError> errors);
    public ValidationError[] ToArray();

    protected override void InsertItem(int index,
      ValidationError item);
    protected override void SetItem(int index,
      ValidationError item);

    public bool HasErrors { get; }
    public bool HasWarnings { get; }
  }
}
```

A validation error is identified by a number, `ErrorNumber`, and carries a string property, `ErrorText`, that described the error. A `ValidationError` object can be marked as an error (this is the default) or as a warning. The `IsWarning` property is used to distinguish between validation issues that *must* be corrected and those that are not vital to fix (or, situations where the validator cannot be sure of an error). The `ToString` method override returns a formatted string containing the text and number of the error, and also an indication of whether or not the error is a warning.

Listing 7.13 `ValidationError`

```
namespace System.Workflow.ComponentModel.Compiler
{
```

```
public sealed class ValidationError
{
  public ValidationError(string errorText, int errorNumber);
  public ValidationError(string errorText, int errorNumber,
    bool isWarning);

  public int ErrorNumber { get; }
  public string ErrorText { get; }
  public bool IsWarning { get; }
  public IDictionary UserData { get; }

  public override string ToString();

  /* *** other members *** */

}
}
```

ValidationError is a sealed class, but you may use the UserData dictionary to store any custom data that you need to associate with a validation error.

Now let's look at how to perform validation of a WF program (actually, any tree of activity objects). The console application in Listing 7.14 performs validation of two different activity trees—one tree is an Interleave activity containing a freshly constructed Simple activity; the other tree is a Sequence activity containing a Simple activity that has had several of its properties set.

Listing 7.14 Validation of WF Programs

```
using System;
using System.Workflow.ComponentModel;
using System.Workflow.ComponentModel.Compiler;
using EssentialWF.Activities;

namespace Chapter7
{
  class Program
  {
    static void Main()
    {
      Simple simple1 = new Simple();
      Interleave i = new Interleave();
      i.Activities.Add(simple1);
      Console.WriteLine("—— Validating Interleave containing a Simple activity ——");
      Validate(i);
```

```
        Simple simple2 = new Simple();
        simple2.Amount = 70;
        simple2.Name = "$simple";
        Sequence seq = new Sequence();
        seq.Activities.Add(simple2);
        Console.WriteLine("\n-- Validating Sequence containing a Simple activity --");
        Validate(seq);
    }

    static void Validate(Activity activity)
    {
        System.ComponentModel.Design.ServiceContainer container =
          new System.ComponentModel.Design.ServiceContainer();

        ValidationManager manager = new ValidationManager(container);

        foreach (Validator validator in
          manager.GetValidators(activity.GetType()))
        {
          ValidationErrorCollection errors =
            validator.Validate(manager, activity);

          foreach (ValidationError error in errors)
            Console.WriteLine(error.ToString());
        }
    }
  }
}
```

We use the `ValidationManager` type to obtain the validators associated with the root activity in an activity tree, and then call the `Validate` method of each. There typically will be just a single validator for the root activity in a WF program, which, as part of its validation logic, will recursively propagate the call to `Validate` down the hierarchy of activities in the tree.

When we run the program in Listing 7.14, we see the following result:

```
-- Validating Interleave containing a Simple --
error 7000: Simple.Amount must be between 50 and 100
error 7001: Simple must be a child activity of a Sequence

-- Validating Sequence containing a Simple --
error 281: Property 'Name' has invalid value. The identifier '$simple' is not a
valid name.
```

Validation of the first activity tree yields two errors, both of which arise, as expected, due to the validator component we associated with the `Simple` activity. The second activity tree yields neither of these errors because the `Simple` activity in this case is a child activity of a `Sequence`, and also has its `Amount` metadata property set to a value deemed appropriate. However, validation of the second activity tree does produce one validation error. You may have noticed that the value of the `Name` property of the `simple2` object is set to a value of `"$simple"` in the console application before the validation of the second activity tree occurs. It is the call to `base.Validate` within the `Validate` method of `SimpleValidator` that checks the value of the `Name` property and produces this validation error. All validator components should derive from an appropriate base class and call `base.Validate` as part of their implementation of the `Validate` method.

ActivityValidator

`ActivityValidator` is the base class for all validators associated with activities. The validation that is performed by `ActivityValidator` ensures the following:

- If the activity is the root activity in the activity tree, `Enabled` is `true`.
- The value of the `Name` property is a legal identifier.
- The value of the `QualifiedName` property is unique within the activity tree.
- Standard validation (based upon validation options, discussed later) of all metadata properties takes place.
- Invocation of the associated validator occurs for all properties (metadata and instance) whose type has a custom `Validator` component.

Validation of properties entails a call to the `ValidateProperties` method defined on the `Validator` class. We will see a bit later how the default property validation logic utilizes the `ValidationOption` enumeration in the validation of metadata properties.

Composite Activity Validation

As we have seen, composite activities are analogous in purpose to control flow constructs found in familiar programming languages (though given the degrees of freedom in the WF programming model, not all composite activities will have familiar analogs in languages like C#). As one example, the `Sequence` composite activity maps closely in meaning to a C# { } program statement block. The `Interleave` composite activity, on the other hand, doesn't have an analog in the grammar of a language like C#.

Without validation logic that ensures the legitimacy of the containment relationships it has with its child activities, a composite activity cannot claim to represent a well-defined control flow construction. Let's look at a familiar and simple example. Consider the *while* construction in the C# language:

```
while (boolean-expression)
    embedded-statement
```

The `while` statement is an element of the C# language grammar. The compiler for the C# language enforces the correctness of any usage of the `while` keyword; a C# `boolean-expression` (which governs the looping) is required along with exactly one C# `embedded-statement` (which can be a compound statement such as a { } program statement block).

Because the WF runtime has no special knowledge of any control flow constructs, each composite activity is responsible for enforcing its semantics by providing a validator component. Consider the `While` composite activity and its associated validator, shown in Listing 7.15.

Listing 7.15 Custom `While` Activity and Associated Validator

```
using System;
using System.Workflow.ComponentModel;
using System.Workflow.ComponentModel.Compiler;

namespace EssentialWF.Activities
{
  [ActivityValidator(typeof(WhileValidator))]
  public class While : CompositeActivity
  {
    public static readonly DependencyProperty ConditionProperty
      = DependencyProperty.Register("Condition",
        typeof(ActivityCondition), typeof(While),
        new PropertyMetadata(
          DependencyPropertyOptions.Metadata,
          new Attribute[] { new ValidationOptionAttribute(
            ValidationOption.Required) }
        )
```

```
      );

  public ActivityCondition Condition
  {
    get
    {
      return GetValue(While.ConditionProperty)
        as ActivityCondition;
    }
    set
    {
      SetValue(While.ConditionProperty, value);
    }
  }

  ...

}

public class WhileValidator : CompositeActivityValidator
{
  public override ValidationErrorCollection Validate(
    ValidationManager manager, object obj)
  {
    ValidationErrorCollection errors = base.Validate(manager, obj);
    While loop = obj as While;

    if (loop.EnabledActivities.Count != 1)
    {
      errors.Add(new ValidationError(
        "While must have exactly one child activity", 7002));
    }

    return errors;
  }
}
}
```

We are using the `ActivityCondition` type here, which is an abstract class defined in the `System.Workflow.ComponentModel` namespace. `ActivityCondition` was briefly discussed in Chapter 4, where we wrote a simple derivative of it. In Chapter 8, we will dig into the details of rules and conditions; for now it is enough to understand that the runtime evaluation of an object of type `ActivityCondition` will return a `boolean` value. This is just what we will need to drive the execution logic of `While`.

The `WhileValidator` must enforce that our `While` composite activity has a single child activity. We do not want the user of `While` to arbitrarily add child activities; we want exactly one, in order to exactly match the familiar C# language construction. The job of `While` is to iterate; it should not also provide sequential (or other) execution of a set of child activities.

Clearly a composite activity may decide to raise validation errors based upon the number and type of child activities it is given. But it is not necessary to always write validation logic. For instance, the `Sequence` composite activity permits an empty `Activities` collection. This is effectively equivalent to allowing an empty `{}` statement block as a legal construction in C#.

As expected, `WhileValidator` derives from `CompositeActivityValidator`, and calls `base.Validate` as part of its validation logic. The validation that is performed by `CompositeActivityValidator`, which derives from `Activity-Validator`, ensures the following:

- Recursive validation of all enabled child activities.
- At most one child `CancellationHandler` activity is present.
- At most one child `FaultHandlers` activity is present.
- At most one child `CompensationHandler` activity is present.

`CancellationHandler`, `FaultHandlers`, and `CompensationHandler` are special modeling constructs that were discussed in Chapter 4.

Validation Options

You may have noticed that in the registration of the `ConditionProperty` dependency property in the `While` class, an extra piece of information—a validation option—was specified as part of the `PropertyMetadata`:

```
public static readonly DependencyProperty ConditionProperty
  = DependencyProperty.Register("Condition",
    typeof(ActivityCondition),
    typeof(While),
    new PropertyMetadata(
      DependencyPropertyOptions.Metadata,
      new Attribute[] { new ValidationOptionAttribute(
        ValidationOption.Required) })
  );
```

The validation option that is specified as part of the `PropertyMetadata` object is utilized by the validation logic of `ActivityValidator`. This reduces the need for writing custom validation logic. The `ValidationOption` enumeration is shown in Listing 7.16. If no validation option is used in the registration of a metadata property, a value of `ValidationOption.Optional` is assumed.

Listing 7.16 `ValidationOption`

```
public enum ValidationOption
{
  None,
  Optional,
  Required
}
```

The `ValidationOptionAttribute` is utilized (by validator base classes) only in the validation of *metadata* properties. A value of `ValidationOption.Optional` indicates that a value for the associated metadata property does not need to be specified, but if a value is specified and its type has an associated validator component, then validation will occur. We will see an example of this soon when we discuss validation of databinding. A value of `ValidationOption.Required` means that a value must be specified, and if the type of the property has an associated validator component, that validation will, of course, also occur. A value of `ValidationOption.None` means that validation is disabled; even if a value is present, and the type of the property has an associated validator, that validator will not be given a chance to validate the property value.

We can demonstrate how `ValidationOption` is used by base class validation logic with an example that validates an activity tree with a `While` activity at the root. The following code snippet can be added to the console application we developed earlier (refer to Listing 7.14):

```
While loop = new While();
loop.Activities.Add(new Sequence());

Console.WriteLine("\n— Validating While —");
Validate(loop);
```

The result of validation of the While is, as expected:

```
-- Validating While --
error 278: Property 'Condition' is not set.
```

Because the registration of the Condition property by While (refer to Listing 7.15) used ValidationOption.Required, we did not need to write any custom validation logic to ensure that the Condition property must be set.

Compilation

As mentioned earlier, it is not necessary to compile all WF programs. Only some kinds of WF programs require packaging as a type in a CLR assembly. To be specific, WF programs that are specified using code, as well as WF programs whose XAML uses the x:Class attribute (these are overlapping, but distinct, categories), must be compiled using the WF program compiler. The constructor of the type resulting from compilation can then be used, on demand, to realize the tree of activities that constitutes the WF program. The WF program compiler is available programmatically as the WorkflowCompiler class, which is the central type in the System.Workflow.ComponentModel.Compiler namespace. Listing 7.17 shows that WorkflowCompiler is a simple class, containing just a single Compile method.

Listing 7.17   WorkflowCompiler

```
namespace System.Workflow.ComponentModel.Compiler
{
  public sealed class WorkflowCompiler
  {
    public WorkflowCompiler();

    public WorkflowCompilerResults Compile(
      WorkflowCompilerParameters parameters,
      params string[] files);
  }
}
```

Included with the WF SDK is an executable, wfc.exe, which provides the same functionality as WorkflowCompiler only at the command line. The choice of when to use WorkflowCompiler and when to use wfc.exe is entirely up to you.

The WF program compiler is a simple class. Its purpose is to accept one or more source files as input, ensure the validity of the WF programs that are defined in these files, and produce CLR types that package these program definitions. There are two kinds of files passed as parameters to the WF program compiler—code files and XAML files. There can be any number of either kind of file. Code files must contain either C# or Visual Basic code. Other languages may be supported in future versions of WF.

The root element of all XAML files presented to the WF program compiler must map to a CLR type that derives from `Activity`. Additionally, each XAML document must use the `x:Class` attribute in order to specify the namespace and name of the type that will be produced by compilation. There is no analogous restriction on code files; you are free to define types in code that are not WF programs and they will become a part of the assembly or code compile unit (CCU) that results from WF program compilation.

The process of WF program compilation includes the following steps:

1. XAML deserialization and code generation
2. Activity validation
3. Activity code generation
4. Code compilation

After an activity tree is realized in memory from the source files of a WF program, the WF program compiler uses the WF validation infrastructure, discussed in the previous section, to perform validation of the program. The WF program compiler relies upon language compilers (the C# and Visual Basic compilers) to perform the final step in the compilation process, which produces the assembly or code compile unit.

Compiler Parameters

The `WorkflowCompilerParameters` class, shown in Listing 7.18, carries properties that can be set in order to influence the WF program compilation process. The `Compile` method of `WorkflowCompiler` accepts a parameter of type `Workflow-CompilerParameters`.

Listing 7.18 WorkflowCompilerParameters

```
namespace System.Workflow.ComponentModel.Compiler
{
  public sealed class WorkflowCompilerParameters : CompilerParameters
  {
    public WorkflowCompilerParameters();
    public WorkflowCompilerParameters(string[] assemblyNames);
    public WorkflowCompilerParameters(string[] assemblyNames,
      string outputName);
    public WorkflowCompilerParameters(string[] assemblyNames,
      string outputName, bool includeDebugInformation);

    public string CompilerOptions { get; set; }
    public bool GenerateCodeCompileUnitOnly { get; set; }
    public string LanguageToUse { get; set; }
    public StringCollection LibraryPaths { get; }
    public IList<CodeCompileUnit> UserCodeCompileUnits { get; }
  }
}
```

WorkflowCompilerParameters derives from the CompilerParameters class in the System.CodeDom.Compiler namespace. All properties that are inherited from CompilerParameters are available to help you manage the compilation of WF programs.

Among the more frequently used properties inherited from CompilerParameters are OutputAssembly, which defines the location and name of the assembly that results from successful compilation, and ReferencedAssemblies, which is a collection of strings specifying the locations of assemblies referenced by the WF program code being compiled.

> ### Compilation Base Classes
>
> Please consult .NET Framework documentation for descriptions of the CompilerParameters, CompilerResults, and CompilerError classes, which are part of the System.CodeDom.Compiler namespace.

The `LanguageToUse` property specifies the language used in any code files being compiled. The value must be either `"VB"` or `"CSharp"` in the current version of WF; it is taken as `"CSharp"` by default. The `LibraryPaths` property specifies the set of paths on the file system that should be searched for assemblies that are referenced only by name.

The `UserCodeCompileUnits` property specifies additional compilation inputs, in the form of `System.CodeDom.CodeCompileUnit` objects. The `GenerateCode-CompileUnitOnly` property indicates whether the WF program compiler should suppress the production of an assembly and only produce a `CodeCompileUnit` as the result of WF program compilation.

Compiler Results

The results of WF program compilation are returned as a `WorkflowCompiler-Results` object. Not surprisingly, `WorkflowCompilerResults` (shown in Listing 7.19) inherits from the `CompilerResults` class that is defined in the `System.CodeDom.Compiler` namespace.

Listing 7.19   `WorkflowCompilerResults`

```
namespace System.Workflow.ComponentModel.Compiler
{
  public sealed class WorkflowCompilerResults : CompilerResults
  {
    CodeCompileUnit CompiledUnit { get; }
  }
}
```

The `CompiledUnit` property will contain the result of WF program compilation (as a `CodeCompileUnit`). If the `GenerateCodeCompileUnitOnly` property is set to `true` in the `WorkflowCompilerParameters` object used for compilation, an assembly is not produced and the code compile unit is the only tangible result of a successful compilation.

The `Errors` property, inherited from `CompilerResults`, will contain a set of zero or more `WorkflowCompilerError` objects that represent errors or warnings that resulted from WF program compilation. `WorkflowCompilerError` is a simple class. Its most useful properties are inherited from `CompilerError`. Inherited properties include `IsWarning`, `FileName`, `Line`, `Column`, `ErrorNumber`, and `ErrorText`.

Collectively, they provide information about a specific warning or error that has occurred during compilation.

Validation and Compilation

Now we can try to compile an invalid WF program to confirm that activity validation occurs automatically during the compilation process. The following WF program is invalid because it uses the activity name "write1" twice:

```
<Sequence x:Class="Chapter7.Workflow1" x:Name="Workflow1" xmlns="http://Essen-
tialWF/Activities" xmlns:x="http://schemas.microsoft.com/winfx/2006/xaml">
  <WriteLine x:Name="write1" Text="hello" />
  <WriteLine x:Name="write1" Text="goodbye" />
</Sequence>
```

A simple console application, shown in Listing 7.20, can be used to programmatically compile our WF program.

Listing 7.20   Programmatic WF Program Compilation

```
using System;
using System.Workflow.ComponentModel;
using System.Workflow.ComponentModel.Compiler;

namespace Ch7
{
  class Program
  {
    static void Main()
    {
      WorkflowCompiler compiler = new WorkflowCompiler();
      WorkflowCompilerParameters parameters =
        new WorkflowCompilerParameters(
          new string[] { "EssentialWF.dll" },
          "test.dll"
        );

      WorkflowCompilerResults results = compiler.Compile(
        parameters, "test.xoml");

      for (int i = 0; i < results.Errors.Count; i++)
        Console.WriteLine(results.Errors[i].ToString());
    }
  }
}
```

The output of running the console application of Listing 7.20 reports a validation error due to the use of a duplicate activity name:

```
test.xoml : error WF1538: Activity 'write1' validation failed: There is already an
activity named 'write1'. Activity names must be unique.
```

Let's return now to our `While` composite activity, which validates that exactly one child activity is present. To simplify things, let's assume now that we've changed the definition of `While` so that its `Expression` property is not required (and is presumed by `While` to take a value of `true` if not present). We can try to compile the `While` source code using wfc.exe:

```
>wfc.exe While.cs
Microsoft (R) Windows Workflow Compiler version 3.0.0.0
Copyright (C) Microsoft Corporation 2005. All rights reserved.

The compiler generated the following message(s):

error WF7002: Activity 'While' validation failed: While must have exactly one
child activity


Compilation finished with 0 warning(s), 1 error(s).
```

As we can see from the output, the compilation fails. This must mean that the validator component associated with `While` has been invoked. Validation, of course, fails because the `Activities` collection of a newly instantiated `While` object is empty. For this reason, composite activity types such as `While` can be compiled using the language compiler—in this case, the C# compiler.

Now, all we are really saying with the previous experiment is that `While` is not a valid WF program on its own. Nor was it ever intended to be. In fact, if we try to load a WF program (expressed in XAML) that consists entirely of an empty `While` activity, we will see exactly the same validation failure because the default loader service invokes validation as part of its loading of a WF program.

Activity Code Generation

Now that we understand WF program compilation, we can discuss how activities can participate in the compilation process (beyond validation). Activities can generate code that will become part of the assembly or code compile unit that results from compilation. The use cases for code generation are much narrower than those for validation, so it is fair to consider this an advanced feature that can be safely ignored by the majority of activity developers.

As with validation, custom code generation is an opt-in model in which you first need to associate a **code generator** component with an activity by decorating the activity class with the `ActivityCodeGeneratorAttribute`, as shown here:

```
[ActivityCodeGenerator(typeof(MyActivityCodeGenerator))]
public class MyActivity : Activity
{
  ...
}

public class MyActivityCodeGenerator : ActivityCodeGenerator
{
  public override void GenerateCode(CodeGenerationManager manager,
    object obj)
  {
    ...
  }
}
```

An activity code generator component will always derive from `ActivityCodeGenerator` or, in the case of a composite activity, `CompositeActivityCodeGenerator`. The `ActivityCodeGenerator` class contains a single public method, and is shown in Listing 7.21. `CompositeActivityCodeGenerator` simply derives from `ActivityCodeGenerator` and overrides the `GenerateCode` method in order to recursively involve all enabled child activities in the code generation process.

Listing 7.21 `ActivityCodeGenerator`

```
namespace System.Workflow.ComponentModel.Compiler
{
  public class ActivityCodeGenerator
  {
    public ActivityCodeGenerator();

    public virtual void GenerateCode(CodeGenerationManager manager,
      object obj);
  }
}
```

`ActivityCodeGenerator` defines a single public virtual method called `Generate-Code`. It is in this method that you will be allowed to generate code for an activity. If you are unfamiliar with the types in the `System.CodeDom` namespace, you will need to consult .NET Framework documentation in order to proceed without puzzlement.

Essentially, the code generator component of an activity can obtain a reference to the `CodeTypeDeclaration` for the WF program being compiled, and add new `CodeTypeMembers` to it. Let's dig into this with an example. Suppose we wanted the ability to declare local variables *in markup*, much as we can do in code like this:

```
private string s;
```

This will give us an avenue for pursuing "markup only" WF programs (though it will force us to compile these programs in order for code generation to occur). So, let us begin by creating a variant of the `Sequence` activity (call it `SequenceWith-Vars`) that supports declarative variables. We will then define a code generator component for `SequenceWithVars` that generates fields or properties within the compiled type representing a WF program.

First let's quickly define a type that can act as a variable declaration within markup:

```
public class VariableDeclaration : DependencyObject
{
  // Implementations use metadata dependency properties
  public string Name { ... }
  public Type Type { ... }
  public bool IsProperty { ...}

  public VariableDeclaration() { }
  public VariableDeclaration(string name, Type type, bool isProperty)
    :base()
  {
    this.Name = name;
    this.Type = type;
    this.IsProperty = isProperty;
  }
}
```

`VariableDeclaration` conceptually allows us to define the equivalent of a CLR field using markup.

```
<VariableDeclaration Name="s" Type="{x:Type System.String}" />
```

Listing 7.22 shows how we can allow the `SequenceWithVars` activity to support a list of declarative variables, modeled as a property.

Listing 7.22   Sequence that Supports Declarative Variables

```
using System;
using System.CodeDom;
using System.Collections.Generic;
using System.ComponentModel;
using System.Text;
using System.Workflow.ComponentModel;
using System.Workflow.ComponentModel.Compiler;

namespace EssentialWF.Activities
{
  [ActivityCodeGenerator(typeof(SequenceWithVarsCodeGenerator))]
  public class SequenceWithVars : CompositeActivity
  {
    public static readonly DependencyProperty VariableDeclsProperty
      = DependencyProperty.Register(
        "VariableDecls",
        typeof(List<VariableDeclaration>),
        typeof(SequenceWithVars),
        new PropertyMetadata(
          DependencyPropertyOptions.Metadata |
          DependencyPropertyOptions.ReadOnly,
          new Attribute[] { new DesignerSerializationVisibilityAttribute(Designer-
SerializationVisibility.Content) }
        )
      );

    public SequenceWithVars()
      : base()
    {
      base.SetReadOnlyPropertyValue
        (SequenceWithVars.VariableDeclsProperty,
         new List<VariableDeclaration>());
    }

    [DesignerSerializationVisibility
       (DesignerSerializationVisibility.Content)]
    public List<VariableDeclaration> VariableDecls
    {
      get
      {
```

```
      return base.GetValue(
        SequenceWithVars.VariableDeclsProperty)
          as List<VariableDeclaration>;
    }
  }
 }
}
```

Now we can turn our attention to the code generator component for Sequence-WithVars. We override the GenerateCode method and, based upon the collection of variable declarations associated with the SequenceWithVars being compiled, we generate the appropriate private fields and public variables. This is shown in Listing 7.23.

Listing 7.23 **Code Generator Component for** Sequence

```
public class SequenceWithVarsCodeGenerator :
CompositeActivityCodeGenerator
  {
    public override void GenerateCode(
      CodeGenerationManager manager, object obj)
    {
      base.GenerateCode(manager, obj);

      SequenceWithVars s = obj as SequenceWithVars;
      CodeTypeDeclaration codeTypeDecl =
        this.GetCodeTypeDeclaration(manager,
          s.GetType().FullName);

      foreach (VariableDeclaration decl in s.VariableDecls)
      {
        if (decl.IsProperty)
        {
          CodeMemberField field =
           new CodeMemberField(decl.Type, "_" + decl.Name);
          field.Attributes = MemberAttributes.Private;

          CodeMemberProperty prop = new CodeMemberProperty();
          prop.Name = decl.Name;
          prop.Type = new CodeTypeReference(decl.Type);
          prop.Attributes = MemberAttributes.Public | MemberAttributes.Final;

          prop.GetStatements.Add(new CodeMethodReturnStatement(new CodeFieldRefer-
enceExpression(new CodeThisReferenceExpression(), "_" + decl.Name)));
          prop.SetStatements.Add(new CodeAssignStatement(new CodeFieldReference-
Expression(new CodeThisReferenceExpression(), "_" + decl.Name), new CodeProperty-
```

```
SetValueReferenceExpression()));

        codeTypeDecl.Members.Add(field);
        codeTypeDecl.Members.Add(prop);
      }
      else  // field only
      {
        CodeMemberField field = new CodeMemberField(
          decl.Type, decl.Name);
        field.Attributes = MemberAttributes.Private;

        codeTypeDecl.Members.Add(field);
      }
    }
  }
}
```

Now we can run a simple example. Here is some markup that is valid based upon the types we have defined:

```
<SequenceWithVars x:Class="Workflow2" xmlns="http://EssentialWF/Activities"
xmlns:x="http://schemas.microsoft.com/winfx/2006/xaml">
  <SequenceWithVars.VariableDecls>
    <VariableDeclaration Name="StringProp" Type="{x:Type System.String}"
IsProperty="True" />
    <VariableDeclaration Name="n" Type="{x:Type System.Int32}" IsProperty="False"
/>
  </SequenceWithVars.VariableDecls>
</SequenceWithVars>
```

Compilation of this markup yields a CLR type with one field and one property, the code for which was created by the code generator component of SequenceWith-Vars:

```
public partial class Workflow2 : SequenceWithVars
{
  private int n;
  private string stringProp;

  public string StringProp
  {
    get
    {
      return this.stringProp;
    }
```

```
    set
    {
      this.stringProp = value;
    }
  }

  public Workflow2() { ... }

  ...
}
```

Perhaps the strongest use case for activity code generators is a situation where compilation-time code generation can avoid reflection at runtime (during the execution of the activity). You won't come across this circumstance every day, but when you do you'll benefit from the code generation capability of activities.

Designer Serialization

Serialization is a process that translates objects from object form (in memory) into a format that can be persisted (for example, to a file) or transmitted over a network. Subsequently, the object can be reconstituted from the serialized form. The .NET Framework supports several serialization mechanisms, some of which are most appropriate for design-time and others of which are optimized for use at runtime.

In this section, we will be discussing the **design-time serialization** of activities. This is the kind of serialization that is utilized within design environments (such as Visual Studio) in order to allow the user to manipulate serialized representations of the components being authored. Design environments typically allow the user to manipulate components visually, but authors almost always find it convenient to view or edit the component in some textual format as well.

A component can have any number of different serialized formats including uncompiled code, various forms of XML markup, or any other format. This is depicted in Figure 7.5. By extension then, a WF program (a tree of activities, which are components) also can be serialized into multiple formats. We came across this fact in the earlier section on compilation, where we saw two equivalent WF programs—one expressed using C# code and the other written entirely as XAML.

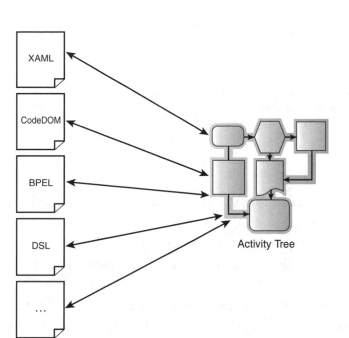

Figure 7.5 Isomorphism of activity tree formats

You are free to develop an entirely custom serialization capability for your activities, which can translate your WF programs to and from a custom serialization format of your choosing. More than likely, you will find the designer serialization infrastructure of the WF programming model sufficient (in both its assets and its extensibility) to meet your needs as an activity writer as it builds on the established patterns and types that are found in the `System.ComponentModel.Design.Serialization` namespace.

The WF serialization framework includes types that serialize activities to XAML and to code. Essentially, these are the two serialization formats you get for free as an activity writer. As we mentioned, though, it is perfectly reasonable to develop custom serializers for activities that translate to and from formats other than XAML and code. The WF types related to serialization of WF programs and activities are defined in the `System.Workflow.ComponentModel.Serialization` namespace.

At the outset of the chapter, we saw that the `Activity` class has three associated designer serializer components:

```
[DesignerSerializer(typeof(ActivityMarkupSerializer),
  typeof(WorkflowMarkupSerializer))]
[DesignerSerializer(typeof(ActivityCodeDomSerializer),
  typeof(CodeDomSerializer))]
[DesignerSerializer(typeof(ActivityTypeCodeDomSerializer),
  typeof(TypeCodeDomSerializer))]
public class Activity : DependencyObject
{
  ...
}
```

As you can see, the `DesignerSerializerAttribute` type, which is defined in the `System.ComponentModel.Design.Serialization` namespace, is used to associate a designer serializer component with an activity. Other facets of the serialization process are also codified by attributes and services present in this .NET Framework namespace.

The constructor of `DesignerSerializerAttribute` accepts two arguments. The first argument indicates the designer serializer type that is being associated with the activity. The second argument indicates the base type from which the designer serializer inherits and can be thought of as answering the question "To what format does this serializer serialize?"

Thus, `ActivityMarkupSerializer` is responsible for serializing an activity to XAML, which is the format utilized by `WorkflowMarkupSerializer`. Both of these types are defined in the `System.Workflow.ComponentModel.Serialization` namespace.

`ActivityCodeDomSerializer` and `ActivityTypeCodeDomSerializer`, in turn, are responsible for serializing an activity to two different forms of CodeDOM, which are defined by `CodeDomSerializer` and `TypeCodeDomSerializer`. `CodeDomSerializer` and `TypeCodeDomSerializer` are standard .NET Framework serialization components defined in the `System.ComponentModel.Design.Serialization` namespace.

It should be clear that multiple designer serializers can be associated with an activity. The one restriction that is necessary to avoid ambiguity, though, is that the base type specified for these serializers (the second constructor argument for `DesignerSerializerAttribute`) must be unique among the serializers associated with the activity. For an entirely new serialization format, you simply need to associate a designer serializer component using a base serialization type that you implement:

```
[DesignerSerializer(typeof(WidgetCustomFormatSerializer),
  typeof(CustomFormatSerializer))]
public class Widget : Activity
{
...
}
```

Code Serialization

TypeCodeDomSerializer serializes a component into a new code type declaration with a well-known method (InitializeComponent) that contains its initialization logic. Because the Activity class is associated with a serializer that derives from TypeCodeDomSerializer, we can write a simple program to illustrate this kind of serialization for a WF program. This is shown in Listing 7.24.

Listing 7.24 Serialization Using TypeCodeDomSerializer

```
using System;
using System.CodeDom;
using System.CodeDom.Compiler;
using System.ComponentModel.Design;
using System.ComponentModel.Design.Serialization;
using System.IO;
using System.Text;
using System.Workflow.ComponentModel;
using System.Workflow.ComponentModel.Serialization;
using Microsoft.CSharp;
using EssentialWF.Activities;

class Program
{
  static void Main()
  {
    Sequence seq = new Sequence();
    seq.Activities.Add(new ReadLine());
    seq.Activities.Add(new WriteLine());

    seq.SetValue(WorkflowMarkupSerializer.XClassProperty,
      "Sequence1");

    SerializeToCode(seq, new CSharpCodeProvider(),
      "C:\\wfprogram.cs");
  }
```

```
static void SerializeToCode(Activity rootActivity,
  CodeDomProvider domProvider, string csharpFilePath)
{
  CodeCompileUnit ccu = new CodeCompileUnit();

  DesignerSerializationManager mgr =
    new DesignerSerializationManager(new ServiceContainer());

  using (mgr.CreateSession())
  {
    ActivityCodeDomSerializationManager codeMgr =
      new ActivityCodeDomSerializationManager(mgr);

    TypeCodeDomSerializer typeCodeDomSerializer =
      codeMgr.GetSerializer(rootActivity.GetType(),
        typeof(TypeCodeDomSerializer)) as TypeCodeDomSerializer;

    ...

    CodeTypeDeclaration activityTypeDeclaration =
    typeCodeDomSerializer.Serialize(codeMgr, rootActivity,
      allActivities);

    CodeNamespace activityCodeNamespace = new CodeNamespace();
    activityCodeNamespace.Types.Add(activityTypeDeclaration);
    ccu.Namespaces.Add(activityCodeNamespace);
  }

  CodeGeneratorOptions options = new CodeGeneratorOptions();
  options.BracingStyle = "C";
  Stream temp = new FileStream(csharpFilePath, FileMode.Create,
    FileAccess.Write, FileShare.Read);

  using (StreamWriter sw = new StreamWriter(temp, Encoding.UTF8))
  {
    domProvider.GenerateCodeFromCompileUnit(ccu, sw, options);
  }
}
}
```

We must set the `WorkflowMarkupSerializer.XClassProperty` on the `Sequence` activity object in order to indicate the namespace-qualified name of the type to be generated. The `SerializeToCode` method contains standard code for manipulating `TypeCodeDomSerializer`. The result of running our program is a C# code file:

```
//wfprogram.cs
//─────────────────────────────────────//  <auto-generated>
//      This code was generated by a tool.
//      Runtime Version:2.0.50727.42
//
//      Changes to this file may cause incorrect behavior
//      and will be lost if the code is regenerated.
// </auto-generated>
//─────────────────────────────────────

public class Sequence1 : Sequence
{
    private ReadLine readLine1;
    private WriteLine writeLine1;
    public Sequence1()
    {
        this.InitializeComponent();
    }

    private void InitializeComponent()
    {
        this.CanModifyActivities = true;
        this.readLine1 = new ReadLine();
        this.writeLine1 = new WriteLine();
        //
        // readLine1
        //
        this.readLine1.Name = "readLine1";
        //
        // writeLine1
        //
        this.writeLine1.Name = "writeLine1";
        //
        // Sequence1
        //
        this.Activities.Add(this.readLine1);
        this.Activities.Add(this.writeLine1);
        this.Name = "Sequence";
        this.CanModifyActivities = false;
    }
}
```

As a custom activity writer, you generally do not need to associate custom Code-DOM serializer components with your activities. For situations where this is necessary, the .NET Framework documentation should be consulted.

XAML Serialization

XAML is a general-purpose markup format for initializing object trees. Consider the following code to initialize an object:

```
Album album = new Album();
album.Artist = "Eric Clapton";
album.Title = "Crossroads";
```

The essence of XAML is that the preceding code can be expressed in markup like this:

```
<Album Artist="Eric Clapton" Title="Crossroads" />
```

Earlier in the chapter, we saw how the `WorkflowMarkSerializer` class makes it easy to serialize and deserialize a tree of activity objects. The following code snippet illustrates XAML serialization with a simple example that uses the `WriteLine` and `Sequence` activities:

```
Sequence seq = new Sequence();
seq.Name = "s1";
WriteLine w1 = new WriteLine();
w1.Name = "w1";
WriteLine w2 = new WriteLine();
w2.Name = "w2";
seq.Activities.Add(w1);
seq.Activities.Add(w2);

WorkflowMarkupSerializer serializer =
  new WorkflowMarkupSerializer();

using (XmlWriter writer = new XmlTextWriter(
  new StreamWriter("test.xaml")))
{
  serializer.Serialize(writer, seq);
}
```

The `WriteLine` and `Sequence` activities do not define any custom XAML serializers; they inherit these components from `Activity` and `CompositeActivity`. Execution of the preceding code results in the following XAML:

```
<ns0:Sequence x:Name="s1" xmlns:x="http://schemas.microsoft.com/winfx/2006/xaml"
xmlns:ns0="http://EssentialWF/Activities">
  <ns0:WriteLine Text="{x:Null}" x:Name="w1" />
```

```
  <ns0:WriteLine Text="{x:Null}" x:Name="w2" />
</ns0:Sequence>
```

We can easily deserialize the contents of the file test.xaml back into an in-memory activity tree by calling `WorkflowMarkupSerializer.Deserialize`:

```
Sequence seq2 = null;
using (XmlReader reader = new XmlTextReader(
  new StreamReader("test.xaml")))
{
  seq2 = serializer.Deserialize(reader) as Sequence;
}
```

As with CodeDOM serialization, you generally do not need to associate custom XAML serializer components with your activities. For situations where this is necessary, the .NET Framework documentation should be consulted.

Collection Serialization

Designer serializer components can establish and enforce their own rules and conventions governing serialization to the format they understand. Where possible, though, it is useful to utilize patterns and types already established in the .NET Framework. A good example of this is the way in which collections are serialized.

Properties that are collections are obviously serialized differently in CodeDOM and XAML formats. But the CodeDOM and XAML serializers both utilize, in a consistent way, the `DesignerSerializationVisibilityAttribute` type (which is defined in the `System.ComponentModel` namespace). This attribute can be used to control whether, and how, a collection property is serialized. Consider the following activity type:

```
public class Widget : Activity
{
  private ArrayList list1 = new ArrayList();
  private IList list2;

  [DesignerSerializationVisibility(
    DesignerSerializationVisibility.Content)]
  public IList List1
  {
      get { return list1; }
  }
```

```
[DesignerSerializationVisibility(
  DesignerSerializationVisibility.Visible)]
public IList List2
{
    get { return list2; }
    set { list2 = value; }
}
}
```

The `List1` property is read-only. It returns an internally instantiated `ArrayList` object that can be manipulated by the user of a `Widget`. But the `List1` property cannot be assigned because it has no property setter. The `List2` property has a getter and a setter, so the user of a `Widget` can (and is expected to) assign a new list in its entirety.

Here is some code that manipulates the two collection properties of a `Widget`:

```
Widget widget = new Widget();

IList list = widget.List1;
list.Add("one");
list.Add("two");

StringCollection sc = new StringCollection();
sc.Add("three");
sc.Add("four");

widget.List2 = sc;
```

If we use the `WorkflowMarkupSerializer` to serialize the activity to XAML, the markup we find illustrates the difference in the way the collections are treated (XML namespaces have been omitted for clarity):

```
<Widget>
    <Widget.List1>
        <String>one</String>
        <String>two</String>
    </Widget.List1>
    <Widget.List2>
        <StringCollection>
            <String>three</String>
            <String>four</String>
        </StringCollection>
    </Widget.List2>
</Widget>
```

The items of the first list are represented as subelements of the `MyActivity.List1` element. When deserialization of this XAML occurs, each of the strings "one" and "two" will be added to the `IList` object that is obtained using the `List1` getter. Conceptually, the `List1` collection has not been serialized; only its contents have been serialized, as indicated by the `DesignerSerializationVisibility.Content` option with which we attributed the property definition.

For the second list, things are different. The entire `StringCollection` object is serialized to markup. Upon deserialization, this `StringCollection` object will be realized, and the value of the `List2` property will be set to be this `StringCollec-tion`. This behavior reflects the fact that the serializer is using the *value* of the `List2` collection property (as indicated by the `DesignerSerializationVisibility.Visible` option) instead of merely the *contents* of the collection.

If we choose to instead serialize a `MyActivity` object to code, the CodeDOM serializer will also use the `DesignerSerializationVisibilityAttribute` during its serialization to produce code that, for `List1`, adds items to the object obtained from the property getter and, for `List2`, assigns a `StringCollection` object using the property setter. This practice of sharing serialization semantics where possible reduces the proliferation of format-specific attributes on activity classes and their properties.

To summarize this section, the `System.Workflow.ComponentModel.Serial-ization` namespace builds upon patterns and types in the .NET Framework to provide serialization of activities to code and to XAML. This infrastructure is extensible, and allows for custom serializer components that translate activity objects to and from custom formats. Though we have focused on some of the details of the XAML and CodeDOM serializers, we would like to stress that these formats are in no way required by the WF programming model (or by the WF runtime which, as we have seen, is format agnostic).

In Chapter 3, we made the point that it is easy to write custom activities that function as domain-specific opcodes in WF programs. Now we can broaden that statement to say that you can *express* your WF programs in the domain-specific *format* of your choosing, so long as your activities are associated with serializer components that understand that format.

Where Are We?

In this chapter, we began by exploring the three kinds of dependency properties that are supported by `DependencyObject`—metadata properties, databinding-enabled properties, and attached properties—and why these special kinds of properties are helpful when defining activity types and WF programs.

Next, we showed how WF programs can, using XAML, be compiled into activity types that are usable within other WF programs. WF programs that are compiled into .NET assemblies can therefore be expressed using XAML, XAML plus code, or entirely with code.

Finally, we broadened the notion of what an activity is to include a set of components associated with the class that defines the activity. Modularizing the definition of an activity has several benefits, which originate from the fact that different aspects of an activity's functionality can be described and manipulated as discrete elements. The WF programming model introduces validation and code generation components that can be associated with any activity. Validation allows activities to participate in the determination of whether a tree of activity objects is a legal WF program. We also discussed XAML and CodeDOM as serialization formats for activities, which are two formats supported by WF natively. The WF runtime is not dependent upon these formats, so it is possible to specify WF programs using domain-specific languages (DSLs) by associating custom designer serializer components with activity types.

8.
Miscellanea

W E HAVE ARRIVED AT THE FINAL CHAPTER of this book. In Chapters 3, "Activity Execution," and 4, "Advanced Activity Execution," we discussed the execution model and learned how to write the execution logic for resumable programs. The focus of Chapter 5, "Applications," was on how to write applications that host the WF runtime. Chapter 6, "Transactions," focused on how transactions relate to the execution of WF programs. In Chapter 7, "Advanced Authoring," we explored the aspects related to authoring WF programs. At certain points along the way, we have made reference to other features of the WF programming model that would have been a distraction to delve into at that moment. The purpose of this chapter is to visit several important parts of the WF programming model that have not been covered in previous chapters. This exploration will round out your understanding of the capabilities provided by Windows Workflow Foundation.

The (disparate) topics covered in this chapter are

- Declarative conditions and rules
- Making changes to running WF program instances
- WF program tracking
- Designers
- Designer hosting

Conditions and Rules

In earlier chapters, we alluded to rules functionality that would let more of the logic of WF programs be expressed declaratively to allow WF program authors to rely on code minimally or not at all. The rules capabilities of WF greatly strengthen the case to be made for fully declarative WF programs, for which markup alone carries sufficient expressive power to capture real-world processes.

The following discussion of rules capabilities in WF (essentially, the types defined in the `System.Workflow.Activities.Rules` namespace) is predicated upon a basic understanding of CodeDOM because rule conditions and actions are generally specified using `System.CodeDom` expressions and statements.

A broader discussion of rule-based systems is beyond the scope of this book. Inferencing engines—both forward-chaining and backward-chaining varieties—and the algorithms that underlie them are an active area of work in academia as well as in industry. Software products that include inferencing engines are in the marketplace today. WF provides simple but powerful ways of melding program logic that is expressed using rules with the activity-oriented approach, which is at the heart of the WF programming model. This section provides a brief but pragmatic exploration of the rules capabilities of WF. We encourage you to consult the .NET Framework documentation and SDK—as well as industry literature—to develop your expertise in this important domain.

Conditions

Before we get to WF rules, we must begin with conditions. A **condition** is an expression that, when evaluated, yields a Boolean value. We employed a condition in Chapter 4 as part of the activity metadata of our `While` composite activity. The concept of a condition is a fundamental abstraction that you will find useful again and again as an activity developer, wherever you require conditional logic to be expressed by the author of the WF program. Branching, looping, conditional transitions, and conditional (early) completion are a few examples of how conditions can be utilized by activities.

`System.Workflow.ComponentModel.ActivityCondition` is the base type for conditions that are associated with activities. `ActivityCondition` is an abstract class with a single method, `Evaluate`, as shown in Listing 8.1. The first parameter of the

`Evaluate` method is the activity that is associated with the condition; the second parameter is a `System.IServiceProvider` that can be used by derivatives of `ActivityCondition` to obtain services required to complete the evaluation of the condition.

Listing 8.1   `ActivityCondition`

```
namespace System.Workflow.ComponentModel
{
  public abstract class ActivityCondition : DependencyObject
  {
    public abstract bool Evaluate(Activity activity,
      IServiceProvider provider);
  }
}
```

As an activity developer, when you require a condition property for an activity you are developing, you can define a property of type `ActivityCondition`. Listing 8.2 defines a new composite activity called `Conditional`, with such a property.

Listing 8.2   `Conditional` **Activity**

```
using System;
using System.Workflow.ComponentModel;
using System.Workflow.ComponentModel.Compiler;

namespace EssentialWF.Activities
{
  public class Conditional : CompositeActivity
  {
    public static readonly DependencyProperty ConditionProperty =
      DependencyProperty.Register(
        "Condition",
        typeof(ActivityCondition),
        typeof(Conditional),
        new PropertyMetadata(
          DependencyPropertyOptions.Metadata,
          new Attribute[] { new ValidationOptionAttribute(
            ValidationOption.Required) }
        )
      );

    public ActivityCondition Condition
    {
      get { return GetValue(ConditionProperty)
              as ActivityCondition; }
```

```
      set { SetValue(ConditionProperty, value); }
    }

    ...

  }
}
```

With this implementation of the `Condition` property, users of the `Conditional` composite activity are free to utilize whatever derivative of `ActivityCondition` is most appropriate for their WF program; meanwhile, the `Conditional` activity is shielded from the details of this choice because the activity execution logic (of `Conditional`) will only need to invoke the condition's `Evaluate` method.

WF includes two condition types that derive from `ActivityCondition`: `System.Workflow.Activities.CodeCondition` and `System.Workflow.Activities.Rules.RuleConditionReference`. We will look at these two classes next. Of course, you are also free to develop a custom condition type; so long as your custom condition type derives from `ActivityCondition`, WF program authors will be able to use it interchangeably with the two condition types that WF provides.

Code Conditions

The purpose of `CodeCondition` is to allow a WF program author to express conditional logic in terms of C# or VB.NET code compiled into a delegate. `CodeCondition` is shown in Listing 8.3.

Listing 8.3   `CodeCondition`

```
namespace System.Workflow.Activities
{
  public class CodeCondition : ActivityCondition
  {
    public CodeCondition();

    public event EventHandler<ConditionalEventArgs> Condition;

    public override bool Evaluate(Activity activity,
      IServiceProvider provider);

    /* *** other members *** */
  }
}
```

The `CodeCondition.Condition` event is raised during the execution of the `Evaluate` method. The result of condition evaluation (the return value of `Evaluate`) will be the value of the `Result` property of the `System.Workflow.Activities.ConditionalEventArgs` (see Listing 8.4) at the conclusion of the event handler invocation.

Listing 8.4 `ConditionalEventArgs`

```
namespace System.Workflow.Activities
{
  public sealed class ConditionalEventArgs : System.EventArgs
  {
    public ConditionalEventArgs();
    public bool Result { get; set; }
  }
}
```

A `CodeCondition` is expressed in XAML as shown in Listing 8.5 (using the `Conditional` activity we defined previously as the context for the example).

Listing 8.5 Condition Expressed in Terms of Imperative Code Using `x:Code`

```
<Conditional x:Name="c1" x:Class="Chapter8.Program1"
xmlns="http://EssentialWF/Activities"
xmlns:x="http://schemas.microsoft.com/winfx/2006/xaml"
xmlns:wf="http://schemas.microsoft.com/winfx/2006/xaml/workflow">
  <Conditional.Condition>
    <wf:CodeCondition Condition="LoopCondition" />
  </Conditional.Condition>
  <x:Code>
    <![CDATA[
        void LoopCondition(object sender, ConditionalEventArgs e)
        {
          e.Result = true;
        }
    ]]>
  </x:Code>
</Conditional>
```

In the preceding simple example, the condition always evaluates to true, but in general your code can execute whatever logic (and whatever examination of WF program instance state) is required to determine the outcome of condition evaluation.

The XAML program in Listing 8.5 uses the `x:Code` feature of XAML in order to directly embed code within a XAML document. This is entirely equivalent to (in other words, the result of compilation is the same as) separating the code into a separate file that defines a partial type, just as we have shown in previous examples. For this reason, use of `x:Code` requires use of `x:Class`.

There is a validator component associated with the `CodeCondition` type, which ensures that the `Condition` event is always handled. The event handler subscription must be established at design-time and therefore is part of the metadata of the WF program.

Declarative Conditions

The second derivative of `ActivityCondition` provided by WF is `System.Workflow.Activities.Rules.RuleConditionReference`. The purpose of `RuleConditionReference` is to allow a WF program author to express conditional logic without writing any imperative code. `RuleConditionReference` is shown in Listing 8.6.

Listing 8.6   `RuleConditionReference`

```
namespace System.Workflow.Activities.Rules
{
  public class RuleConditionReference : ActivityCondition
  {
    public RuleConditionReference();

    public string ConditionName { get; set; }

    public override bool Evaluate(Activity activity,
      IServiceProvider provider);

    /* *** other members *** */
  }
}
```

`RuleConditionReference` is just a simple level of indirection. Its `ConditionName` property names a `System.Workflow.Activities.Rules.RuleCondition` that is found within an associated `System.Workflow.Activities.Rules.RuleDefinitions` object, which acts as a container for all of the declarative conditions and rules associated with a WF program. This is depicted in Figure 8.1.

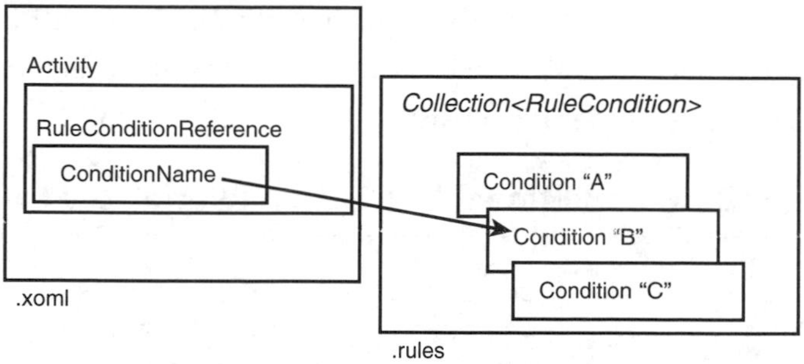

Figure 8.1 A `RuleConditionReference` **points to a** `RuleCondition`.

The `RuleDefinitions` type is shown in Listing 8.7. The `Conditions` property of `RuleDefinitions` is where we find the actual condition named by a `RuleConditionReference`; we will discuss the `RuleSets` property of `RuleDefinitions` in the next section.

Listing 8.7 `RuleDefinitions`

```
namespace System.Workflow.Activities.Rules
{
public sealed class RuleDefinitions
{
  public RuleDefinitions();

  public RuleConditionCollection Conditions { get; }
  public RuleSetCollection RuleSets { get; }

/* *** other members *** */
}
```

A `RuleConditionReference` is expressed in XAML like this (using the `Conditional` activity we defined previously):

```
<Conditional>
  <Conditional.Condition>
  <wf:RuleConditionReference ConditionName="LoopCondition" />
  </Conditional.Condition>
  ...
</Conditional>
```

The `RuleDefinitions` data for the WF program (which, when authoring a WF program, is specified in a separate file that by convention has an extension of .rules) will contain the actual condition definition, as shown in Listing 8.8.

Listing 8.8 CodeDOM Conditional Expressions Serialized to XAML

```
<RuleDefinitions
xmlns="http://schemas.microsoft.com/winfx/2006/xaml/workflow" xmlns:ns0="clr-name-
space:System.CodeDom;Assembly=System, Version=2.0.0.0, Culture=neutral, PublicKey-
Token=b77a5c561934e089" xmlns:ns1="clr-namespace:System;Assembly=mscorlib,
Version=2.0.0.0, Culture=neutral, PublicKeyToken=b77a5c561934e089">
  <RuleDefinitions.Conditions>
    <RuleExpressionCondition Name="LoopCondition">
      <RuleExpressionCondition.Expression>
        <ns0:CodePrimitiveExpression>
          <ns0:CodePrimitiveExpression.Value>
            <ns1:Boolean>true</ns1:Boolean>
          </ns0:CodePrimitiveExpression.Value>
        </ns0:CodePrimitiveExpression>
      </RuleExpressionCondition.Expression>
    </RuleExpressionCondition>
  </RuleDefinitions.Conditions>
</RuleDefinitions>
```

The `RuleDefinitions.Conditions` property is a collection of objects of type `System.Workflow.Activities.Rules.RuleCondition`. `RuleCondition` is the base class for declarative condition implementations. WF provides a single derivative of `RuleCondition`, `System.Workflow.Activities.Rules.RuleExpression-Condition`.

Shown in Listing 8.9, `RuleExpressionCondition` is simply a wrapper around a `System.CodeDom.CodeExpression`. Specifically, it is XAML serialization of the CodeDOM expression tree. In the preceding XAML snippet, which is functionally equivalent to the `CodeCondition` implementation we provided earlier (because it always evaluates to `true`), we use a `System.CodeDom.CodePrimitiveExpression` to express the constant `System.Boolean` value `true`. The markup is verbose, but it is actually specifying the initialization of a very simple object:

```
CodePrimitiveExpression expression =
  new CodePrimitiveExpression(true);
```

```
RuleExpressionCondition condition =
  new RuleExpressionCondition("LoopCondition", expression);

RuleDefinitions definitions = new RuleDefinitions();
definitions.Conditions.Add(condition);
```

Listing 8.9   `RuleExpressionCondition`

```
namespace System.Workflow.Activities.Rules
{
  public sealed class RuleExpressionCondition : RuleCondition
  {
    public RuleExpressionCondition();
    public RuleExpressionCondition(CodeExpression expression);
    public RuleExpressionCondition(string conditionName);
    public RuleExpressionCondition(string conditionName,
      CodeExpression expression);

    public CodeExpression Expression { get; set; }
    public override string Name { get; set; }

    /* *** other members *** */
  }
}
```

To summarize, condition properties on activities are of type `ActivityCondition`. A condition can be implemented as an event handler in terms of imperative code, or declaratively using markup that specifies CodeDOM expressions. You may also develop custom condition types that derive from `ActivityCondition`.

In general, activities can expose properties that represent either expressions in textual form or compiled code (delegates). We just saw how CodeDOM expressions, serialized as XAML, can be associated with activities but it is also possible to associate other expression representations with activities, including XPath or `System.Expression` based expressions. If activities in a WF program do not rely upon compiled code, but instead are provided with any necessary expressions in some textual form, then execution of the program can occur without a compilation step.

Rules

In the previous section, we learned that a `RuleConditionReference` is a markup-based alternative to a `CodeCondition`. More broadly, though, rules are a markup-based alternative to expressing program logic in code. A rule in WF is just a statement (requiring no compilation) that is expressed according to the following pattern:

```
IF condition THEN actions ELSE other-actions
```

A **rule set** is a collection of rules that act in concert to form a single computational unit.

Expressing program logic as a set of rules instead of as compiled code has two important advantages. First, by embracing rules, you can build design environments for WF programs that do not require the author to do any coding. Second, by expressing logic declaratively (rules are just part of the metadata of a WF program) you allow that logic to be modified on the fly, in the context of a single WF program instance. Making changes to running instances of WF programs is a topic we will discuss later in this chapter.

For the WF program developer, the `System.Workflow.Activities.Policy-Activity` activity type is the gateway to rules functionality. A **policy** is a wrapper around a rule set. The `PolicyActivity` type is shown in Listing 8.10.

Listing 8.10   `PolicyActivity`

```
namespace System.Workflow.Activities
{
  public sealed class PolicyActivity : Activity
  {
    public PolicyActivity();
    public PolicyActivity(string name);

    public RuleSetReference RuleSetReference { get; set; }

    /* *** other members *** */
  }
}
```

When a `PolicyActivity` executes, it simply executes the rule set that is named by its `RuleSetReference` property. Thus, the purpose of `PolicyActivity` is to allow the execution of a rule set to be modeled as an activity within any WF program.

`System.Workflow.Activities.Rules.RuleSetReference`, shown in Listing 8.11, names a rule set that is found in the collection of rule sets held by the `Rule-Definitions` object (refer to Listing 8.7) associated with the WF program. This is depicted in Figure 8.2.

Listing 8.11 RuleSetReference

```
public sealed class RuleSetReference : DependencyObject
{
  public RuleSetReference();
  public RuleSetReference(string ruleSetName);

  public string RuleSetName { get; set; }

  /* *** other members *** */
}
```

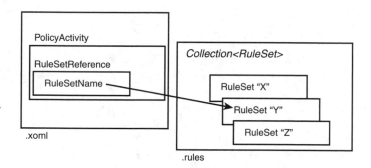

Figure 8.2 A RuleSetReference **points to a** RuleSet.

A WF rule set holds a collection of System.Workflow.Activities.Rules.Rule objects. The System.Workflow.Activities.Rules.RuleSet type is shown in Listing 8.12.

Listing 8.12 RuleSet

```
namespace System.Workflow.Activities.Rules
{
  public class RuleSet
  {
    public RuleSet();
    public RuleSet(string name);
    public RuleSet(string name, string description);

    public string Name { get; set; }
    public string Description { get; set; }
    public ICollection<Rule> Rules { get; }
    public RuleChainingBehavior ChainingBehavior { get; set; }
```

```
    /* *** other members *** */
  }
}
```

The `Rule` type is shown in Listing 8.13. A **WF rule** is a condition implementation—
of type `RuleCondition`, discussed earlier—plus a set of actions (the `Rule.Then-Actions` property) to be taken if the condition evaluates to `true`. A WF rule can also
specify a set of actions (the `Rule.ElseActions` property) to be taken if the condition
evaluates to `false`.

Listing 8.13   `Rule`

```
namespace System.Workflow.Activities.Rules
{
  public class Rule
  {
    public Rule();
    public Rule(string name);
    public Rule(string name, RuleCondition condition,
      IList<RuleAction> thenActions);
    public Rule(string name, RuleCondition condition,
      IList<RuleAction> thenActions, IList<RuleAction> elseActions);

    public string Name { get; set; }
    public string Description { get; set; }
    public int Priority { get; set; }
    public RuleReevaluationBehavior ReevaluationBehavior { get; set; }

    public RuleCondition Condition { get; set; }
    public IList<RuleAction> ThenActions { get; set; }
    public IList<RuleAction> ElseActions { get; set; }
  }
}
```

Thus, a WF rule is essentially a construction that takes the following form:

```
if (rule.condition == true)
  execute rule.then-actions
else
  execute rule.else-actions
```

As a simple illustration of the concept of a rule, consider the following code snippet
which, functionally, does exactly what a single rule can do:

```
if (package.Urgency == "High")
{
  package.ShippingType = "Overnight";
  DoSpecialPreparation(package);
}
else
{
  package.ShippingType = "Ground";
}
```

The `(package.Urgency == "High")` expression is a condition, and each of the statements within the first set of { } braces is an action to be performed if the condition evaluates to `true`. The statements within the second set of { } braces are the actions to be performed if the condition evaluates to `false`.

A rule set, as we know, is a collection of rules. Because the rules in a rule set can influence one another (by modifying shared data), there are several different ways in which a rule set can be executed. Before we discuss the choices you have that govern WF rule set execution, though, let's take a look at the kinds of actions that can be associated with a rule.

The `System.Workflow.Activities.Rules.RuleAction` type is the base class for rule actions, and WF provides three derivatives, `RuleHaltAction`, `Rule-UpdateAction`, and `RuleStatementAction`, all of which are also defined in the `System.Workflow.Activities.Rules` namespace.

If you use a `RuleHaltAction` in a rule, execution of this action will cause the execution of the current rule set to immediately end.

`RuleUpdateAction` is used to achieve explicit chaining of rules, which will be discussed shortly. Essentially, execution of this kind of action explicitly tells the rules engine that a specific piece of data (indicated by the `Path` property of `RuleUpdate-Action`) should be considered to have had its value changed as a consequence of the execution of that action.

`RuleStatementAction` is the general-purpose action type. A `RuleStatement-Action` wraps a `System.CodeDom.CodeStatement`, which is executed when the action executes. Among other things, a `RuleStatementAction` can be used to set the value of a field or property of a WF program (or of an activity within the program), invoke a method available on the WF program (or on an activity within the program), or invoke a static method. Essentially, a `RuleStatementAction` specifies what otherwise might be expressed as a line of code.

Rule Set Execution

Rules in a rule set are evaluated one at a time—by default, in priority order according to the value of `Rule.Priority`—until there are no more rules to evaluate, but there a couple of ways in which you can influence the manner in which a rule set is executed. The `ChainingBehavior` property of `RuleSet` indicates whether the rule set should execute without chaining, with explicit chaining only, or with full chaining. The kind of chaining we are referring to here is called **forward chaining** because the basic idea is that the execution of a rule can change some data that then prompts reevaluation of other (previously evaluated) rules in the rule set whose conditions depend upon that data.

If a rule set executes *without chaining*, each of its rules is evaluated once. The order of evaluation is determined by the value of the `Priority` property of each `Rule` object. If two or more rules carry the same priority, their ordering is not guaranteed. Because you will typically be using actions of type `RuleStatementAction` in your rule set, this option basically amounts to execution of an ordered list of CodeDOM expressions.

If a rule set executes *with explicit chaining* only, the execution of an action of type `RuleUpdateAction` (which indicates the data that should be considered changed) can cause chaining to occur. Specifically, if a rule "E" modifies data that is read by the condition of a previously evaluated rule "B" (a rule with higher priority), then "B" will be the next rule (after "E") to be evaluated.

If a rule set is configured to execute *with full chaining*, then, in addition to chaining via `RuleUpdateAction`, chaining can occur implicitly (when the WF rules engine infers that a rule condition's dependent data has changed) or based upon the presence of CLR attributes that serve as hints to the rules engine about when reevaluation of specific rules is needed.

To achieve implicit chaining, the WF rules engine parses the CodeDOM statements underlying each rule's `RuleCondition` along with each rule's set of `RuleStatementAction` objects so that it knows what data that rule depends upon and what data that rule changes.

To realize chaining based upon CLR attributes, you simply decorate methods (that are called by actions of type `RuleStatementAction` or by the code expression of a `RuleCondition`) to indicate what data that method reads, what data it writes, and what other methods it calls. The `RuleReadAttribute`, `RuleWriteAttribute`, and `RuleInvokeAttribute` types are defined (in the `System.Workflow.Activi-ties.Rules` namespace) for this purpose. By default, parameters of a method are assumed to be read by the method (unless they are `out` or `ref` parameters in which case they are assumed to be written).

As an example of a rule set that uses forward chaining, consider the following set of rules:

```
Rule1 (Priority=3)

  if (x==2)
  then z++
  else y+=4


Rule2 (Priority=2)

  if (y==6)
  then z++, x++
  else x=0


Rule3 (Priority=1)

  if (z==5)
  then output="red"
  else output="green"
```

Let's evaluate this rule set (using forward chaining) with the following input data:

```
x = 1
y = 2
z = 3
output = " "
```

The rule evaluation proceeds as follows:

```
Rule1 (else-actions are executed, y is now 6)
Rule2 (then-actions are executed, z is now 4, x is now 2)
Rule1 since x changed (then-actions are executed, z is now 5)
Rule3 (then-actions are executed, output is now "red")
```

To familiarize yourself with the mechanism of rule evaluation, try to work out how rule evaluation unfolds for different sets of input values.

There is one additional lever for controlling the execution behavior of a rule set, and that is the `ReevaluationBehavior` property of `Rule`. If this property carries a value of `Never`, reevaluation of the rule will never happen once the `ThenActions` (or the `ElseActions`, if present) of such a rule has executed. If the `Reevaluation-Behavior` property carries a value of `Always`, there is no restriction on how many times the rule can be reevaluated.

Dynamic Editing of Running WF Program Instances

WF programs can describe real-world processes. Typically, however, a WF program can really only capture a set of most probable paths along which a process may unfold. A great deal of flexibility can be built into WF programs using control flow activities that are crafted to meet the requirements of a specific problem domain. But because people are involved in processes, processes inevitably change. Steps are added, skipped, restarted, or canceled, and the logic that governs transitions from one step to another can certainly change too. We are not referring here to gradual refinement of a process definition. Most change comes from the realities of having to constantly adjust—on the fly, in the context of an instance of the process—to special circumstances: a difficult but important customer, an employee who changes jobs, a shifting deadline, a supplier that goes out of business, a rush order, a lost order, a duplicate order, a power outage, new requirements from a partner, or an unexpected spike in demand.

This is one reason why software is not as pervasive as it might be. No one will use a program to help coordinate her work if the program shackles her with rigid definitions of processes. The software cannot propose to help 25% or even 50% of the time. It should be useful all of the time. To do this, it must have a degree of malleability— at the level of process instances—that is rare in software today.

The approach taken by WF is simple. The activity tree that constitutes a WF program prototype is available for inspection at runtime. Furthermore, a request can be made to perform changes to a prototype, in the context of a single running WF program instance (which was manufactured from that prototype). The WF runtime will enforce certain inherent constraints on what changes are allowed, and the activities in the tree also vote on whether a proposed set of changes is acceptable. The crucial point here is that the WF runtime, and the activities, make their determination based

upon the full current state of the running WF program instance that is being
changed. Thus it is possible for a WF program instance to evolve, as it is running,
subject to fine-grained state-based constraints, and in this way can enjoy some of the
same nimbleness that the people who are involved in a process typically exhibit as
they steer the process, and tweak it, with the goal of reaching a successful outcome.

Here is a simple but functional code snippet that shows how to dynamically add
one child activity, of type WriteLine, to the root activity of a WF program:

```
// Obtain the instance that we wish to change
WorkflowInstance instance = ...

// Get the prototype for this instance
Activity definition = instance.GetWorkflowDefinition();

// Create a wrapper for proposing changes
WorkflowChanges changes = new WorkflowChanges(definition);

// Obtain the writeable copy of the prototype
Interleave root = changes.TransientWorkflow as Interleave;

// Create and add our new activity
WriteLine write = new WriteLine();
write.Name = "write1";
write.Text = "added dynamically!";
root.Activities.Add(write);

// Apply the changes, for this instance
instance.ApplyWorkflowChanges(changes);
```

In order to propose changes to a WF program instance, we first obtain from the WF
runtime a System.Workflow.Runtime.WorkflowInstance object representing
that instance. The WorkflowInstance type was discussed in Chapter 5; the WorkflowInstance methods used in the preceding code snippet are shown in Listing
8.14.

Listing 8.14 WorkflowInstance **Revisited**

```
namespace System.Workflow.Runtime
{
  public sealed class WorkflowInstance
  {
    public Activity GetWorkflowDefinition();
    public void ApplyWorkflowChanges(WorkflowChanges changes);
```

```
  /* *** other members *** */
  }
}
```

The `GetWorkflowDefinition` method returns a copy of the WF program prototype from which the instance was manufactured. Because this activity tree is a prototype, the activity objects in the tree will not carry any instance-specific property values—it is effectively all metadata.

We use this copy of a WF program prototype, obtained from `WorkflowInstance`, to create a `System.Workflow.ComponentModel.WorkflowChanges` object. A `WorkflowChanges` object is conceptually just a container for a set of proposed changes to a specific WF program instance. The `WorkflowChanges` type is shown in Listing 8.15.

Listing 8.15   `WorkflowChanges`

```
namespace System.Workflow.ComponentModel
{
  public sealed class WorkflowChanges
  {
    public WorkflowChanges(Activity root);

    public CompositeActivity TransientWorkflow { get; }
    public ValidationErrorCollection Validate();

    public static readonly DependencyProperty ConditionProperty;

    /* *** other members *** */
  }
}
```

From the `WorkflowChanges.TransientWorkflow` property getter, we obtain a writeable *instance-specific* activity tree. We can cast the object returned to the actual type of the root activity of our WF program. In our preceding example, the root activity of the WF program instance being changed is assumed to be of type `EssentialWF.Activities.Interleave`. Our preparatory work is done.

Because we now hold an updateable activity tree for the WF program instance, we are free to navigate up and down the hierarchy of activities and make changes. Here we simply add a `WriteLine` activity to the `Interleave` activity at the root of the WF program, but (subject to restrictions discussed shortly) we can actually add and remove activities anywhere in the tree, just as we could at design-time.

Once we are done proposing changes, we apply these changes to the instance by calling the `ApplyWorkflowChanges` method of the `WorkflowInstance` object from which we obtained the WF program prototype.

Restrictions on Dynamic Editing of a Program Instance

There are three forms of restrictions on the kinds of changes to a WF program instance that can be made. Some limitations are inherent to the WF programming model. Other restrictions can be imposed by the WF program author; this can include turning off update capability. Still other restrictions can be dictated by composite activity writers; this logic too can go so far as to reject any proposed changes. Of course the application hosting the WF runtime also can play a part in determining what changes are permissible, and who can propose them, but such layers of application code are outside the scope of the WF programming model.

The first set of restrictions on what changes can be made to a running WF program instance are inherent to the WF programming model. These are

- **Granularity-based.** Activities can be added to or removed from a WF program but properties on an existing activity (with the exception of declarative conditions and rule sets, which can be updated) cannot be changed.

- **Composition-based.** A composite activity whose type constructor defines its set of child activities cannot have activities dynamically added or removed (at any depth). Thus, you can dynamically add and remove child activities to and from a `Sequence` activity within a WF program instance but you cannot do this to an `Echo` activity (a derivative of `Sequence` that always contains a `ReadLine` and a `WriteLine`) within a WF program. This protects the integrity of custom composite activity types.

- **Automaton-based.** An activity with one or more instances in the *Executing* state (or *Faulting* state, or *Canceling* state, or *Compensating* state) cannot be removed from a WF program instance.

The author of a WF program can also participate in the determination of whether a set of proposed changes is allowed. An `ActivityCondition` can be attached to the root activity of a WF program, which at runtime is used by the WF runtime as a conditional check on whether a dynamic change can take place for a specific WF program instance. The condition is an attached dependency property named `Condition` that is defined by the `WorkflowChanges` class (see Listing 8.15). The following XAML snippet shows how the property is attached to the root activity in a WF program:

```
<Interleave x:Class="Ch8.Workflow1"
xmlns:x="http://schemas.microsoft.com/winfx/2006/xaml"
xmlns:wf="http://schemas.microsoft.com/winfx/2006/xaml/workflow"
xmlns="http://EssentialWF/Activities">
  <wf:WorkflowChanges.Condition>
    ...
  </wf:WorkflowChanges.Condition>
  ...
</Interleave>
```

Like any condition, this attached condition can be realized as a `CodeCondition` or as a `RuleConditionReference`, or even as a custom derivative of `Activity-Condition`. As an example of a custom condition type, Listing 8.16 shows a simple derivative of `ActivityCondition` that holds a constant Boolean value.

Listing 8.16 ConstantCondition

```
using System;
using System.Workflow.ComponentModel;

namespace EssentialWF.Activities
{
  public class ConstantCondition : ActivityCondition
  {
    public static readonly DependencyProperty
      BooleanValueProperty = DependencyProperty.Register(
        "BooleanValue",
        typeof(bool),
        typeof(ConstantCondition),
        new PropertyMetadata(DependencyPropertyOptions.Metadata)
      );

    public bool BooleanValue
    {
      get { return (bool) GetValue(BooleanValueProperty);}
      set { SetValue(BooleanValueProperty, value); }
    }
```

```
   public override bool Evaluate(Activity activity,
     IServiceProvider provider)
   {
     return this.BooleanValue;
   }
 }
}
```

If `WorkflowChanges.Condition` is configured as a `ConstantCondition` that always evaluates to `false`, any proposed change (to an instance of this WF program type) will be rejected. For example, here is the implementation of a `Constant-Condition` that always rejects proposed changes to the WF program:

```
<Interleave x:Name="i1" xmlns="http://EssentialWF/Activities"
xmlns:x="http://schemas.microsoft.com/winfx/2006/xaml"
xmlns:wf="http://schemas.microsoft.com/winfx/2006/xaml/workflow">
  <wf:WorkflowChanges.Condition>
    <ConstantCondition BooleanValue="false" />
  </wf:WorkflowChanges.Condition>

  ...

</Interleave>
```

If we attempt to make dynamic changes to an instance of this WF program, we need to be prepared to handle a `System.InvalidOperationException` when we try to apply the changes (this is a slight modification to the code snippet shown at the beginning of this topic):

```
// Apply the changes, for this instance
try
{
  instance.ApplyWorkflowChanges(changes);
}
catch (InvalidOperationException e)
{
  Console.WriteLine(e.Message);
}
```

When the `WorkflowInstance.ApplyWorkflowChanges` method is called, our `ConstantCondition` is invoked as part of the validation of the proposed changes. Because our condition implementation always evaluates to `false`, the proposed changes are always rejected.

The value of the `Message` property of the `InvalidOperationException` that we catch will look like this:

```
Workflow changes can not be applied to instance 'c762f961-548b-464e-a898-
2fbe627f6845' at this time. The WorkflowChanges Condition property on the root
activity has evaluated to false.
```

Activity developers can also participate in the validation of proposed changes. As we learned in Chapter 7, activities are associated with validator components. When a set of changes is proposed for a WF program instance, the entire activity tree is validated—just as at design-time—to ensure that the WF program remains valid after the changes. Additionally, the validator component of each composite activity to which a child activity is being added (or from which a child activity is being removed) will have its `ValidateActivityChange` method called.

Here is a simple validator component for `Interleave` that allows dynamic removal of child activities (subject to aforementioned constraints) but disallows dynamic addition of child activities:

```
using System;
using System.Workflow.ComponentModel;
using System.Workflow.ComponentModel.Compiler;

namespace EssentialWF.Activities
{
  public class InterleaveValidator : CompositeActivityValidator
  {
    public InterleaveValidator()
      : base()
    {
    }

    public override ValidationError ValidateActivityChange(
      Activity activity, ActivityChangeAction action)
    {
      if (action is AddedActivityAction)
        return new ValidationError("Interleave won't allow dynamic addition of
child activities!", 1000);

      return base.ValidateActivityChange(activity, action);
    }
  }

  [ActivityValidator(typeof(InterleaveValidator))]
  public class Interleave : CompositeActivity
```

```
  {
    ...
  }
}
```

The `action` parameter to the `ValidateActivityChange` method is either of type `AddedActivityAction` or of type `RemovedActivityAction` (both of which are defined in the `System.Workflow.ComponentModel` namespace). These types provide information about the activity that is being dynamically added or removed from the composite activity. In our simple example, we reject all proposed additions of child activities to `Interleave`.

Now, when we call `WorkflowInstance.ApplyWorkflowChanges` in our host application, we must also be prepared to handle an exception of type `Workflow-ValidationFailedException` (this type is defined in the `System.Workflow.ComponentModel.Compiler` namespace):

```
// Apply the changes, for this instance
try
{
  instance.ApplyWorkflowChanges(changes);
}
catch (InvalidOperationException e)
{
  Console.WriteLine(e.Message);
}
catch (WorkflowValidationFailedException e)
{
  foreach (ValidationError error in e.Errors)
    Console.WriteLine(error);
}
```

Let's assume that we change the logic of the `ConstantCondition` associated with the WF program to allow dynamic changes (evaluate to `true`). When we propose to dynamically add a child activity to an `Interleave`, the WF program logic allows it, but the `InterleaveValidator` logic rejects it. We will see the following output at the console:

```
error 1000: Interleave won't allow dynamic addition of child activities!
```

There is one more detail to take care of. When the dynamic addition of a `WriteLine` activity to our `Interleave` composite activity succeeds, the `WriteLine` needs to be scheduled for execution if the `Interleave` itself happens to be executing. We can accomplish this by overriding, in our implementation of the `Interleave` activity (see Chapter 5 for the rest of the implementation), the `OnActivityChangeAdd` method defined by `CompositeActivity`:

```
namespace EssentialWF.Activities
{
  public class Interleave : CompositeActivity
  {

    ...

    protected override void OnActivityChangeAdd(
      ActivityExecutionContext context,
      Activity addedActivity)
    {
      if (this.ExecutionStatus == ActivityExecutionStatus.Executing)
      {
        addedActivity.Closed += this.ContinueAt;
        context.ExecuteActivity(addedActivity);
      }
    }
  }
}
```

In general, composite activity developers must (if their activities allow dynamic changes) determine the appropriate implementation of the `OnActivityChangeAdd` (and related `OnActivityChangeRemove`) method when developing their execution logic.

Tracking

It is generally useful, and in some scenarios critical, for the application that is hosting the WF runtime to obtain information about WF program instances as they are executing. Here we are not talking about the sending of data as modeled in the WF program; instead, what we are after are generic events that inform us of lifecycle transitions for WF program instances and the activities within them.

To this end, you can add one or more **tracking services** to the WF runtime, and these services will receive data, via the WF runtime, about WF program instances that are executing. There is no burden placed here upon the WF program author; the events that are tracked are generic in nature (though as we shall see there is also a notion of a custom tracking event).

All tracking services must derive from the `TrackingService` type (shown in Listing 8.17) and implement several abstract methods. `TrackingService`, along with the rest of the WF tracking infrastructure, is defined in the `System.Workflow.Runtime.Tracking` namespace.

Listing 8.17   `TrackingService`

```
namespace System.Workflow.Runtime.Tracking
{
  public abstract class TrackingService : WorkflowRuntimeService
  {
    protected abstract bool TryGetProfile(
      Type workflowType, out TrackingProfile profile);

    protected abstract TrackingChannel GetTrackingChannel(
      TrackingParameters parameters);

    /* *** other members *** */
  }
}
```

Tracking services utilize **tracking profiles** to express to the WF runtime which events they care to receive. The WF runtime calls the `TryGetProfile` method of `TrackingService` to obtain a tracking profile for each new WF program instance that is created. `TryGetProfile` returns a Boolean value that indicates whether or not tracking should occur at all for the specified instance; if the return value is `true`, the `out` parameter named `profile` is the tracking profile that will be used for the WF program instance.

The `System.Workflow.Runtime.Tracking.TrackingProfile` type is shown in Listing 8.18.

Listing 8.18   `TrackingProfile`

```
namespace System.Workflow.Runtime.Tracking
{
  public class TrackingProfile
  {
    public TrackingProfile();
```

```
    public ActivityTrackPointCollection ActivityTrackPoints { get; }
    public WorkflowTrackPointCollection WorkflowTrackPoints { get; }
    public UserTrackPointCollection UserTrackPoints { get; }

    public System.Version Version { get; set; }
  }
}
```

A **tracking channel** is the conduit along which tracking events flow from the WF runtime to a tracking service. This is depicted in Figure 8.3.

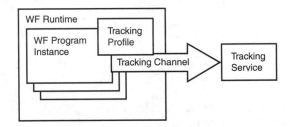

Figure 8.3   A tracking service receives data from a tracking channel.

The `System.Workflow.Runtime.Tracking.TrackingChannel` type is shown in Listing 8.19. A tracking service must manufacture its own tracking channels; typically, a unique tracking channel object will be provided for every executing WF program instance. The `System.Workflow.Runtime.Tracking.TrackingParameters` type carries information that can be used to identify the WF program instance with which a tracking channel is associated.

Listing 8.19   `TrackingChannel`

```
namespace System.Workflow.Runtime.Tracking
{
  public abstract class TrackingChannel
  {
    protected abstract void Send(TrackingRecord record);
    protected abstract void InstanceCompletedOrTerminated();
  }
}
```

As you can see from the definition of `TrackingProfile` (refer to Listing 8.17), there are three kinds of tracking points. An activity tracking point is at the granularity of a single activity. A workflow tracking point is at the level of a WF program instance. A custom tracking point represents the receipt of custom tracking data from an activity.

Activity tracking events occur when an activity makes a transition from one state of the activity automaton to another. A tracking profile can therefore specify an interest in the events corresponding to any or all of the values of the `Activity-ExecutionStatus` enumeration (defined in the `System.Workflow.Component-Model` namespace), which was discussed in Chapter 3.

WF program tracking events occur when the WF program instance makes a life-cycle transition. The set of WF program tracking events is established by the `Track-ingWorkflowEvent` enumeration, defined in the `System.Workflow.Runtime.Tracking` namespace and shown in Listing 8.20.

Listing 8.20   `TrackingWorkflowEvent`

```
namespace System.Workflow.Runtime.Tracking
{
  public enum TrackingWorkflowEvent
  {
    Created,
    Completed,
    Idle,
    Suspended,
    Resumed,
    Persisted,
    Unloaded,
    Loaded,
    Exception,
    Terminated,
    Aborted,
    Changed,
    Started
  }
}
```

Custom tracking events occur when activity execution logic calls the `TrackData` method that is defined by the `Activity` type, as shown in Listing 8.21.

Listing 8.21   `Activity.TrackData`

```
namespace System.Workflow.ComponentModel
{
  public class Activity : DependencyObject
```

```
{
    protected void TrackData(object userData);
    protected void TrackData(string userDataKey, object userData);

    /* *** other members *** */
  }
}
```

The object that is passed by the activity as a parameter to TrackData is the data that
is received by the tracking channel and can be any System.Object.

As part of activity and WF program tracking events, a tracking service can receive
the values of activity fields and properties by utilizing derivatives of System.Work-
flow.Runtime.Tracking.TrackingExtract in the specification of tracking points
within a tracking profile. Tracking points can also be made conditional in order to
limit the volume of data that you receive on a tracking channel to be precisely that
data in which you are interested.

Tracking data arrives on a tracking channel in the form of a tracking record. The
System.Workflow.Runtime.Tracking.TrackingRecord base class has three
derivatives—ActivityTrackingRecord, WorkflowTrackingRecord, and User-
TrackingRecord—that correspond to the three previously discussed kinds of tracking points (activity level, WF program instance level, and custom) that can be
specified within a tracking profile.

A comprehensive examination of the WF tracking infrastructure, including the
nuts and bolts of the System.Workflow.Runtime.Tracking.SqlTracking-
Service that stores tracking data in a SQL Server database, is outside the scope of
this book; we suggest that you consult .NET Framework documentation and the WF
SDK samples for more information. The basic ideas of WF program instance tracking, though, can be illustrated with a simple implementation of a custom tracking
service that listens for all possible tracking events:

```
using System;
using System.Workflow.ComponentModel;
using System.Workflow.Runtime;
using System.Workflow.Runtime.Tracking;

public class SimpleTrackingService : TrackingService
{
    private TrackingProfile profile;
```

```csharp
public SimpleTrackingService()
  : base()
{
  profile = CreateTrackingProfile();
}

private TrackingProfile CreateTrackingProfile()
{
  // Listen for activity status changes
  ActivityTrackingLocation loc =
    new ActivityTrackingLocation(typeof(Activity));
  loc.ExecutionStatusEvents.Add(ActivityExecutionStatus.Initialized);
  loc.ExecutionStatusEvents.Add(ActivityExecutionStatus.Executing);
  loc.ExecutionStatusEvents.Add(ActivityExecutionStatus.Canceling);
  loc.ExecutionStatusEvents.Add(ActivityExecutionStatus.Faulting);
  loc.ExecutionStatusEvents.Add(ActivityExecutionStatus.Closed);
  loc.ExecutionStatusEvents.Add(
    ActivityExecutionStatus.Compensating);
  loc.MatchDerivedTypes = true;

  ActivityTrackPoint atp = new ActivityTrackPoint();
  atp.MatchingLocations.Add(loc);

  // Listen for workflow status events
  WorkflowTrackPoint wtp = new WorkflowTrackPoint();
  wtp.MatchingLocation = new WorkflowTrackingLocation();
  wtp.MatchingLocation.Events.Add(TrackingWorkflowEvent.Aborted);
  wtp.MatchingLocation.Events.Add(TrackingWorkflowEvent.Changed);
  wtp.MatchingLocation.Events.Add(TrackingWorkflowEvent.Completed);
  wtp.MatchingLocation.Events.Add(TrackingWorkflowEvent.Created);
  wtp.MatchingLocation.Events.Add(TrackingWorkflowEvent.Exception);
  wtp.MatchingLocation.Events.Add(TrackingWorkflowEvent.Idle);
  wtp.MatchingLocation.Events.Add(TrackingWorkflowEvent.Loaded);
  wtp.MatchingLocation.Events.Add(TrackingWorkflowEvent.Persisted);
  wtp.MatchingLocation.Events.Add(TrackingWorkflowEvent.Resumed);
  wtp.MatchingLocation.Events.Add(TrackingWorkflowEvent.Started);
  wtp.MatchingLocation.Events.Add(TrackingWorkflowEvent.Suspended);
  wtp.MatchingLocation.Events.Add(TrackingWorkflowEvent.Terminated);
  wtp.MatchingLocation.Events.Add(TrackingWorkflowEvent.Unloaded);

  // Listen for custom tracking data
  UserTrackingLocation loc2 = new UserTrackingLocation();
  loc2.ActivityType = typeof(Activity);
  loc2.MatchDerivedActivityTypes = true;
  loc2.ArgumentType = typeof(object);
  loc2.MatchDerivedArgumentTypes = true;
```

```
    UserTrackPoint utp = new UserTrackPoint();
    utp.MatchingLocations.Add(loc2);

    // Return tracking profile
    TrackingProfile profile = new TrackingProfile();
    profile.Version = new Version(1, 0, 0, 0);
    profile.ActivityTrackPoints.Add(atp);
    profile.WorkflowTrackPoints.Add(wtp);
    profile.UserTrackPoints.Add(utp);

    return profile;
  }

  protected override bool TryGetProfile(Type workflowType,
    out TrackingProfile profile)
  {
    profile = this.profile;
    return true;
  }

  protected override TrackingChannel GetTrackingChannel(
    TrackingParameters parameters)
  {
    return new SimpleTrackingChannel(parameters);
  }

  ...
}
```

Our custom tracking channel dutifully reports all tracking events that it receives to the console:

```
public class SimpleTrackingChannel : TrackingChannel
{
  private TrackingParameters parameters;

  public SimpleTrackingChannel(TrackingParameters parameters)
    : base()
  {
    this.parameters = parameters;
  }

  protected override void Send(TrackingRecord record)
  {
    ActivityTrackingRecord r1 = record as ActivityTrackingRecord;
    WorkflowTrackingRecord r2 = record as WorkflowTrackingRecord;
    UserTrackingRecord r3 = record as UserTrackingRecord;
```

```
      if (r1 != null)
        Console.WriteLine(r1.QualifiedName + " (" + r1.ActivityType.Name + ") -> " +
r1.ExecutionStatus);
      else if (r2 != null)
        Console.WriteLine(r2.TrackingWorkflowEvent);
      else if (r3 != null)
        Console.WriteLine(r3.QualifiedName + " (" + r3.ActivityType.Name + ") " +
r3.UserDataKey + "= " + r3.UserData);
    }

  ...
}
```

To illustrate a custom tracking event, we can develop a very simple activity that uses the `Activity.TrackData` method to issue a string:

```
using System;
using System.Workflow.ComponentModel;

namespace EssentialWF.Activities
{
  public class CallsTrackData : Activity
  {
    protected override ActivityExecutionStatus Execute(
      ActivityExecutionContext context)
    {
      base.TrackData("Inside the CallsTrackData activity");
      return ActivityExecutionStatus.Closed;
    }
  }
}
```

Before we execute a WF program that contains a `CallsTrackData` activity, we add an instance of our tracking service to the WF runtime:

```
  runtime.AddService(new SimpleTrackingService());
```

When we run a WF program, designed using the ensemble of custom activities we've developed during the course of this book, the console output looks like this:

```
Created
Started
root (SimpleWFProgram) -> Executing
par1 (Interleave) -> Executing
seq1 (Sequence) -> Executing
```

```
seq2 (Sequence) -> Executing
w1 (WriteLine) -> Executing
w3 (WriteLine) -> Executing
One
w1 (WriteLine) -> Closed
Three
w3 (WriteLine) -> Closed
wait1 (Wait) -> Executing
wait2 (Wait) -> Executing
Idle
wait2 (Wait) -> Closed
w4 (WriteLine) -> Executing
Four
w4 (WriteLine) -> Closed
seq2 (Sequence) -> Closed
Idle
wait1 (Wait) -> Closed
w2 (WriteLine) -> Executing
Two
w2 (WriteLine) -> Closed
seq1 (Sequence) -> Closed
par1 (Interleave) -> Closed
track1 (CallsTrackData) -> Executing
track1 (CallsTrackData) = Inside the CallsTrackData activity
track1 (CallsTrackData) -> Closed
root (SimpleWFProgram) -> Closed
Completed
```

See if you can work out, from the tracking data reported by our tracking service, what the WF program must look like.

Designers

A WF program is a hierarchical arrangement of activities. It is easy to write and utilize packages of domain-specific activities rather than building WF programs from a fixed set of modeling constructs and adding imperative code. This opens the door for domain experts to participate directly in the authoring of WF programs without having to do any coding. Domain experts can be WF program authors simply by composing activities within a visual design environment.

Application and tool vendors can therefore build visual design environments that are targeted at specific kinds of WF program authors. Because the WF programming model for activities is public, you are free to create whatever WF program authoring applications that you require. You are limited only by your creativity in how you map UI (or other) gestures to the manipulation of an activity object tree.

Rather than starting from scratch, though, it may be helpful to utilize the visualization framework for activities that is provided by the WF programming model. This is the same framework used in the implementation of the **Visual Studio Workflow Designer**. This framework (the `System.Workflow.ComponentModel.Design` namespace), however, is not tied in any way to Visual Studio. As we will see in the next section, WF program design elements can be hosted directly in design environments other than Visual Studio.

The WF visualization framework is layered upon the design-time infrastructure used by Windows Forms and ASP.NET. All three technologies—WF, Windows Forms, and ASP.NET—base their design-time architectures on `System.Component-Model.Design`, an established part of the .NET Framework. Figure 8.4 should give you a sense of what a visual design environment for WF programs can look like, and also points out several design-time concepts that we will discuss in this section.

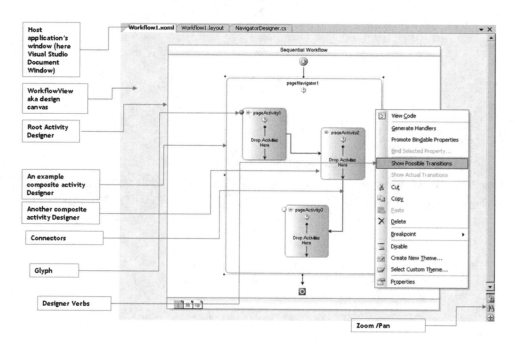

Figure 8.4   Visual WF program designer

At a high level, the `System.Workflow.ComponentModel.Design` namespace contains two kinds of assets. There is a set of types used by activity developers to build **activity designer** components; we will discuss this use case first. There are also a set of types that can be used in the development of custom WF program design environments (in addition to being utilized within the Visual Studio Workflow Designer); these are discussed in a subsequent section.

The `Activity` class implements the `IComponent` interface defined in the `System.ComponentModel` namespace (as depicted in Figure 8.5). Because of this, activities can associate themselves with designer components, and can participate in design environments, in much the same way as Window Forms controls.

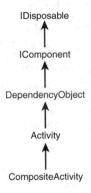

Figure 8.5   Activity type inheritance

A designer component holds specialized logic that renders a visual representation of the activity and allows it to be manipulated within a design environment. The base `Activity` class is associated with a designer, named `ActivityDesigner`:

```
namespace System.Workflow.ComponentModel
{
  [Designer(typeof(ActivityDesigner), typeof(IDesigner))]
  [Designer(typeof(ActivityDesigner), typeof(IRootDesigner))]
  public class Activity : DependencyObject
  {
    ...
  }
}
```

ActivityDesigner is defined in the System.Workflow.ComponentModel.Design namespace, and is shown in Listing 8.22. This is a mandatory base class for all activity designers. The IDesigner and IRootDesigner interfaces, both of which are implemented by ActivityDesigner, are defined in the System.ComponentModel.Design namespace.

Listing 8.22   ActivityDesigner

```
namespace System.Workflow.ComponentModel.Design
{
  public class ActivityDesigner : IWorkflowRootDesigner, ...
  {
    public Activity Activity { get; }
    public CompositeActivityDesigner ParentDesigner { get; }
    ...
  }
}
```

The ActivityDesigner class implements a set of interfaces, the most vital of which is System.Workflow.ComponentModel.Design.IWorkflowRootDesigner. IWorkflowRootDesigner, shown in Listing 8.23, inherits from System.ComponentModel.IRootDesigner (see Listing 8.24), which in turn inherits from System.ComponentModel.Design.IDesigner (see Listing 8.25). A root designer is simply a designer that can function at the top (root) of a hierarchy of designers and exhibits some special behaviors that are accorded only to the designer in this position.

Listing 8.23   IWorkflowRootDesigner

```
namespace System.Workflow.ComponentModel.Design
{
  public interface IWorkflowRootDesigner : IRootDesigner
  {
    CompositeActivityDesigner InvokingDesigner { get; set; }

    bool SupportsLayoutPersistence { get; }

    ReadOnlyCollection<WorkflowDesignerMessageFilter>
      MessageFilters { get; }

    bool IsSupportedActivityType(Type activityType);
  }
}
```

Listing 8.24 `System.ComponentModel.Design.IRootDesigner`

```
namespace System.ComponentModel.Design
{
  public interface IRootDesigner : IDesigner
  {
    ViewTechnology[] SupportedTechnologies { get; }
    object GetView(ViewTechnology technology);
  }
}
```

`IDesigner` does not mandate any specific rendering or visualization technology. In fact, `IDesigner` is just an abstraction representing the visualization of an `IComponent`. As we will see later in this section, `ActivityDesigner` provides concrete support for default rendering and visualization behavior. In order to provide consistent visualization services across various activities, the WF programming model demands that any activity's designer component inherits from `ActivityDesigner`.

Listing 8.25 `System.ComponentModel.Design.IDesigner`

```
namespace System.ComponentModel.Design
{
  public interface IDesigner : IDisposable
  {
    IComponent Component { get; }
    DesignerVerbCollection Verbs { get; }

    void DoDefaultAction();
    void Initialize(IComponent component);
  }
}
```

Although all activity designers implement `IRootDesigner`, for a given WF program being edited in a design environment, only the designer of the root activity is queried for its view. The view object is obtained by the design environment using the `GetView` method, which returns the actual user interface control with which the user interacts.

A **root designer** is free to return any view object that represents a design surface on which individual activity designers will be rendered. The `GetView` method of `ActivityDesigner` returns an object of type `WorkflowView` (shown in Listing 8.26).

Listing 8.26 `WorkflowView`

```
namespace System.Workflow.ComponentModel.Design
{
  public class WorkflowView : System.Windows.Forms.UserControl,
    System.Windows.Forms.IMessageFilter,
    System.IServiceProvider,
    IDesignerVerbProviderService
  {
    ...
  }
}
```

As Listing 8.26 shows, `WorkflowView` is a Windows Forms `UserControl` and there-fore can be hosted in any application. The Visual Studio Workflow Designer hosts this control in the Visual Studio document window. Think of this control as a design canvas that hosts individual designer components corresponding to the activities within the WF program being designed. Each activity designer renders the activity it represents within specific rectangular bounds inside the `WorkflowView`. The `WorkflowView` acts as a window manager and provides window management func-tionality including scrolling, hit testing, coordinate management, and other func-tions. Additionally, the `WorkflowView` provides a set of specialized capabilities for visualizing WF programs, including scrolling, zooming, panning, undo and redo, drag and drop, clipboard management, print and preview, and layout negotiation. We will discuss the `WorkflowView` in detail in the next section.

Because creating a USER32 HWND via `CreateWindow` is a performance hit, and because visualization of a WF program may often require tens or even hundreds of activity designers, making the WF program design surface windowless tremen-dously boosts overall designer performance.

As you can see from Listing 8.22, every `ActivityDesigner` holds a reference to its parent designer in the property named `ParentDesigner`. `CompositeActivity-Designer`, shown in Listing 8.27, inherits from `ActivityDesigner` and refers to a collection of contained designers that are the designer components associated with the child activities of the composite activity.

Listing 8.27   CompositeActivityDesigner

```
namespace System.Workflow.ComponentModel.Design
{
  public abstract class CompositeActivityDesigner : ActivityDesigner
  {
    public virtual ReadOnlyCollection<ActivityDesigner>
      ContainedDesigners { get; }

    ...
  }
}
```

Designer Base Classes

ActivityDesigner is the base class for all activity designers, but there are a number of derivatives of ActivityDesigner with which you should familiarize yourself in order to save time when developing custom designers. In many cases, you may be able to inherit behavior from the appropriate base class instead of developing it from scratch. Figure 8.6 shows the set of designer base classes found in the System.Workflow.ComponentModel.Design namespace.

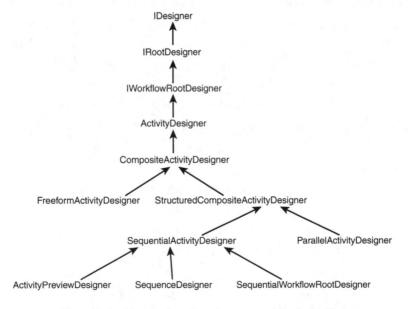

Figure 8.6   ActivityDesigner **and its derivatives**

The development of a custom designer is typically needed only for composite activities (the association of a custom theme with a noncomposite activity—discussed later in this section—is one other situation in which a custom designer is required). Even for composite activities, sometimes you need not develop a custom designer at all but instead can associate the activity with one of the base designer types. For instance, the `Sequence` activity that we had developed earlier can simply use the `SequenceDesigner` by specifying it as a parameter to the `System.ComponentModel.DesignerAttribute`. This is shown in Listing 8.28.

Listing 8.28   Applying `SequenceDesigner` **to the Sequence Activity**

```
using System;
using System.ComponentModel;
using System.ComponentModel.Design;
using System.Workflow.ComponentModel;
using System.Workflow.ComponentModel.Design;

namespace EssentialWF.Activities
{
  [Designer(typeof(SequenceDesigner),typeof(IDesigner))]
  public class Sequence : CompositeActivity
  {
    ...
  }
}
```

The program in Listing 8.29 shows two `WriteLine` activities within a `Sequence`.

Listing 8.29   Program with a Sequence Containing Two `WriteLine`**s**

```
<Sequence x:Name="Sequence1"
xmlns="http://EssentialWF/Activities"
xmlns:x="http://schemas.microsoft.com/winfx/2006/xaml">
  <WriteLine x:Name="WriteLine1" Text="One" />
  <WriteLine x:Name="WriteLine2" Text="Two" />
</Sequence>
```

WF programs like the one shown in Listing 8.29 can be visually represented by any application or tool that knows how to host activity designers; we will discuss designer hosting later in this chapter. Figure 8.7 shows the visual representation of the program in Listing 8.29. The `SequenceDesigner` automatically renders the two `WriteLine` activities in sequential order.

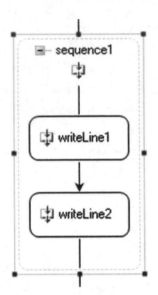

Figure 8.7   Visual representation of program in Listing 8.29

As we know, a WF program is a hierarchical arrangement of activities. In the context of a design environment, this hierarchy will be mirrored by a hierarchy of activity designers. Figure 8.8 illustrates the correspondence between an activity hierarchy and its hierarchy of designer components. As depicted, the `WriteLine` activity does not define its own designer (that is why it renders as a simple rectangle in Figure 8.7), and defaults to using `ActivityDesigner` (which is specified by the base class `Activity`).

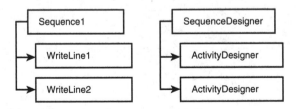

Figure 8.8   WYSIWYG hierarchy of designers for a WF program

Consider another example: the `PrioritizedInterleave` activity (discussed in Chapter 3). We can begin by associating the `ParallelActivityDesigner` provided by WF (see Figure 8.6) with `PrioritizedInterleave`:

```
using System;
using System.ComponentModel;
using System.ComponentModel.Design;
using System.Workflow.ComponentModel;
using System.Workflow.ComponentModel.Design;

namespace EssentialWF.Activities
{
  [Designer(typeof(ParallelActivityDesigner), typeof(IDesigner))]
  public class PrioritizedInterleave: CompositeActivity
  {
  ...
  }
}
```

The association between an activity (that implements IComponent) and its designer is made using the DesignerAttribute type, defined in the System.Component-Model.Design namespace. This is no different than associating a Windows Forms control (or other IComponent) with a designer.

The result of the association of the ParallelActivityDesigner with PrioritizedInterleave activity is shown in Figure 8.9.

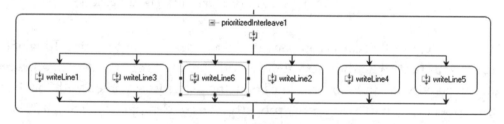

Figure 8.9 ParallelActivityDesigner to visualize PrioritizedInterleave

As you can see in Figure 8.9, the choice of ParallelActivityDesigner as the designer component is unsatisfying (and perhaps even misleading) because it does not visually convey the special prioritization scheme employed by this composite activity. This presents a perfect opportunity to develop a custom designer.

As we discussed in Chapter 3, PrioritizedInterleave attaches an integer property called Priority to each of its child activities. Child activities with the same priority execute in an interleaved manner. Thus, it would be helpful for the designer component of `PrioritizedInterleave` to arrange the child activities (more accurately, the child activity designers) in a way that groups them by priority. Figure 8.10 illustrates one such approach, in which horizontal bands within the design area of `PrioritizedInterleave` contain child activities with the same priority.

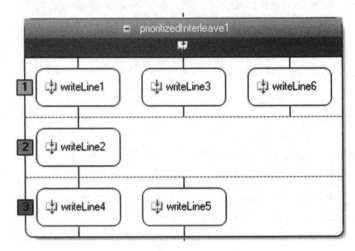

Figure 8.10 `PrioritizedInterleave` **designer component**

One nice feature that can accompany this visual design is automatic setting of the `Priority` property when a child activity is added to the `PrioritizedInterleave`. When an activity is added to a specific band, the priority associated with that band is used to set the activity's `Priority` property. The code snippet in Listing 8.30 is the starting point for `PrioritizedInterleaveDesigner`, which inherits from `CompositeActivityDesigner`.

Listing 8.30 `PrioritizedInterleaveDesigner`

```
using System;
using System.ComponentModel;
using System.ComponentModel.Design;
using System.Collections;
using System.Collections.Generic;
using System.Drawing;
using System.Drawing.Drawing2D;
using System.Workflow.ComponentModel;
using System.Workflow.ComponentModel.Design;
using System.Windows.Forms;
```

```
namespace EssentialWF.Activities
{
  public class PrioritizedInterleaveDesigner :
    CompositeActivityDesigner, IDesignerVerbProvider
  {
    ...
  }
}
```

We will also need to modify PrioritizedInterleave to specify its association with PrioritizedInterleaveDesigner, as shown in Listing 8.31.

Listing 8.31 Associating PrioritizedInterleaveDesigner **with** PrioritizedInterleave

```
using System;
using System.ComponentModel;
using System.ComponentModel.Design;
using System.Workflow.ComponentModel;

namespace EssentialWF.Activities
{
  [Designer(typeof(PrioritizedInterleaveDesigner), typeof(IDesigner))]
  public class PrioritizedInterleave: CompositeActivity
  {
    ...
  }
}
```

The (incomplete) implementation of PrioritizedParallelDesigner shown in the next section is for illustration purposes only. It makes several simplifying assumptions (for instance, it supports only noncomposite designers for its child activities) and provides only a cursory overview of all the steps involved in writing a custom composite designer. Our goal with this example is to give you a taste of the richness of capabilities you can build into designer components and not delve into details (which are beyond the scope of this book).

Attached Properties

The PrioritizedInterleave activity attaches a Priority property to its child activities by calling DependencyProperty.RegisterAttached. This is shown in Listing 8.32.

Listing 8.32   Priority as an Attached Property of PrioritizedInterleave

```
using System;
using System.ComponentModel;
using System.ComponentModel.Design;
using System.Workflow.ComponentModel;

namespace EssentialWF.Activities
{
  [Designer(typeof(PrioritizedInterleaveDesigner), typeof(IDesigner))]
  public class PrioritizedInterleave: CompositeActivity
  {
    public static DependencyProperty PriorityProperty =
      DependencyProperty.RegisterAttached("Priority", typeof(int),
        typeof(PrioritizedInterleave), new PropertyMetadata(1,
        DependencyPropertyOptions.Metadata));

    public static object GetPriority(object dependencyObject)
    {
      return ((DependencyObject)dependencyObject).
        GetValue(PriorityProperty);
    }

    public static void SetPriority(object dependencyObject,
      object priority)
    {
      ((DependencyObject)dependencyObject).
        SetValue(PriorityProperty, priority);
    }
  }
}
```

Because Priority is an attached property, it is not available as a standard property on child activities of PrioritizedInterleave. The PrioritizedInterleaveDesigner must do some extra work in order to have Priority appear in the property grid (of the design environment) when a child activity is selected, as shown in Figure 8.11.

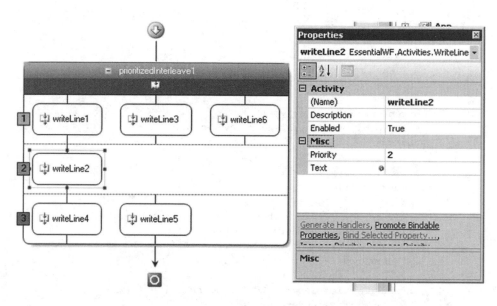

Figure 8.11 `Priority` **property on child activities of** `PrioritizedInterleave`

Specifically, `PrioritizedInterleaveDesigner` registers an extender provider for the `Priority` property by overriding `ActivityDesigner.Initialize`. This is shown in Listing 8.33.

Listing 8.33 `PrioritizedInterleaveDesigner.Initialize`

```
// namespace imports same as Listing 8.30

namespace EssentialWF.Activities
{
  public class PrioritizedInterleaveDesigner : ...
  {
    protected override void Initialize(Activity activity)
    {
      base.Initialize(activity);

      IDesignerVerbProviderService verbProviderService =
          (IDesignerVerbProviderService)GetService(
            typeof(IDesignerVerbProviderService));
      if (verbProviderService != null)
        verbProviderService.AddVerbProvider(this);

      IExtenderListService extenderListService =
        (IExtenderListService)GetService(
            typeof(IExtenderListService));
```

```
      if (extenderListService != null)
      {
        bool foundExtender = false;
        foreach (IExtenderProvider extenderProvider in
            extenderListService.GetExtenderProviders())
        {
          if (extenderProvider.GetType() ==
                  typeof(PriorityExtenderProvider))
            foundExtender = true;
        }

        if (!foundExtender)
        {
          IExtenderProviderService extenderProviderService =
              (IExtenderProviderService)GetService(
                typeof(IExtenderProviderService));
          if (extenderProviderService != null)
          {
              extenderProviderService.AddExtenderProvider(new
                  PriorityExtenderProvider());
          }
        }
      }
    }
  }
}
```

Listing 8.34 shows the `PriorityExtenderProvider` class, which provides a custom implementation of the `System.ComponentModel.IExtenderProvider` interface.

Listing 8.34   `PriorityExtenderProvider`

```
// namespace imports same as Listing 8.30

namespace EssentialWF.Activities
{
  public class PrioritizedInterleaveDesigner : ...
  {
    // initial number of levels (rows)
    internal readonly int MaxPriorityLevel = 3;

    ...

    [ProvideProperty("Priority", typeof(Activity))]
    private class PriorityExtenderProvider : IExtenderProvider
    {
      public int GetPriority(Activity activity)
```

```
    {
      if (activity.Parent is PrioritizedInterleave)
        return
          (int)activity.GetValue(
              PrioritizedInterleave.PriorityProperty);
      else
        return 0;
    }
    public void SetPriority(Activity activity, int priority)
    {
      if (activity.Parent is PrioritizedInterleave)
        activity.SetValue(
          PrioritizedInterleave.PriorityProperty, priority);
    }
    bool IExtenderProvider.CanExtend(object extendee)
    {
      return ((extendee != this) &&
            (extendee is Activity) &&
            (((Activity)extendee).Parent is PrioritizedInterleave));
    }
  }
 }
}
```

The `System.ComponentModel.ProvidePropertyAttribute` is applied to the `PriorityExtenderProvider`. Doing so informs the design environment that the designer is interested in exposing an extended property whose name is `Priority`.

`PriorityExtenderProvider` implements `IExtenderProvider.CanExtend` and returns `true` for any activity whose `Parent` property is the `Prioritized-Interleave` activity object associated with the designer. The property grid control (which is the typical consumer of the `IExtenderProvider`) will look for `Set<PropertyName>` and `Get<PropertyName>` methods on the extender class when the user tries to configure the property. To meet that requirement, the `PriorityExtender-Provider` implements `GetPriority` and `SetPriority` methods.

Designer Verbs

Designer verbs are essentially menu commands that represent actions to be taken in the context of a designer. An activity designer can override the `Activity-Designer.Verbs` property to provide its verbs to the design environment. These verbs will appear as items in the context menu of the activity. In some cases, an activity designer may need to apply verbs on behalf of other activity designers. In this situation, the activity designer that applies the verbs is required to implement `IDesignerVerbProvider`, an interface that is defined in the `System.Workflow.ComponentModel.Design` namespace.

`PrioritizedInterleaveDesigner` implements the `IDesignerVerbProvider` interface. The implementation of the `GetVerbs` method adds two verbs, `"Increase Priority"` and `"Decrease Priority"`, to the context menu of each child activity (see Listing 8.35).

Listing 8.35 `PrioritizedInterleaveDesigner.GetVerbs`

```
// namespace imports same as Listing 8.30

namespace EssentialWF.Activities
{
  public class PrioritizedInterleaveDesigner : ...
  {
    ...
    ActivityDesignerVerbCollection IDesignerVerbProvider.
        GetVerbs(ActivityDesigner activityDesigner)
    {
      ActivityDesignerVerbCollection extendedVerbs = new
            ActivityDesignerVerbCollection();
      if (ContainedDesigners.Contains(activityDesigner))
      {
        ActivityDesignerVerb verb = new
              ActivityDesignerVerb(
                activityDesigner, DesignerVerbGroup.Actions,
                 "Increase Priority", new
                      EventHandler(OnIncreasePriority));

        verb.Properties["Activity"] = activityDesigner.Activity;
        extendedVerbs.Add(verb);
        verb = new ActivityDesignerVerb(activityDesigner,
          DesignerVerbGroup.Actions, "Decrease Priority", new
              EventHandler(OnDecreasePriority));
        verb.Properties["Activity"] = activityDesigner.Activity;
        extendedVerbs.Add(verb);
      }

      return extendedVerbs;
    }
```

```
    private void OnIncreasePriority(object sender, EventArgs e)
    {
      ActivityDesignerVerb verb = sender as ActivityDesignerVerb;

      if (verb != null)
      {
        PrioritizedInterleave interleave = Activity as
               PrioritizedInterleave;
        Activity activity = verb.Properties["Activity"] as Activity;
        int newPriority =
           (int)PrioritizedInterleave.GetPriority(activity) - 1;
        if (newPriority < MaxPriorityLevel) {
          PrioritizedInterleave.SetPriority(activity, newPriority);
          PerformLayout();
        }
      }
    }

    private void OnDecreasePriority(object sender, EventArgs e)
    {
      ActivityDesignerVerb verb = sender as ActivityDesignerVerb;
      if (verb != null)
      {
        Activity activity = verb.Properties["Activity"] as Activity;
        int newPriority =
           (int)PrioritizedInterleave.GetPriority(activity) + 1;
        if (newPriority >= 0)
        {
          PrioritizedInterleave.SetPriority(activity, newPriority);
          PerformLayout();
        }
      }
    }
  }
}
```

PrioritizedInterleaveDesigner can register itself as a verb provider by adding
the following logic to its Initialize method (which we previously used to register the extender provider for the Priority property):

```
IDesignerVerbProviderService verbProviderService =
  (IDesignerVerbProviderService)GetService(
    typeof(IDesignerVerbProviderService));

if (verbProviderService != null)
  verbProviderService.AddVerbProvider(this);
```

As proper cleanup for this initialization logic, `PrioritizedInterleaveDesigner` should override the `Dispose` method and call `IDesignerVerbProvider-Service.RemoveVerbProvider`.

The result of this work is shown in Figure 8.12, which displays the context menu for a child activity of `PrioritizedInterleave`.

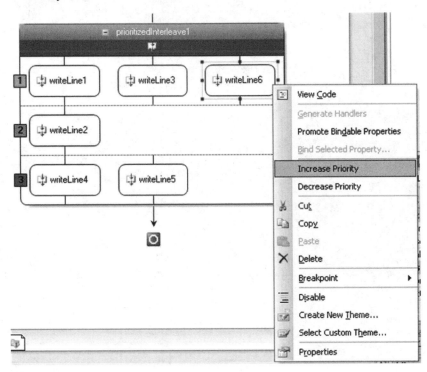

Figure 8.12   Context menu for child activities of `PrioritizedInterleave`

Designer Glyphs

Another helpful feature we can add to `PrioritizedInterleaveDesigner` is a visual indication of the priority associated with each band of child activities (see the left edge of the `PrioritizedInterleave` designer as shown in Figure 8.11). We can achieve this using a designer adornment called a **designer glyph**. As shown in Listing 8.36, `PrioritizedInterleaveDesigner` overrides the `ActivityDesigner.Glyphs`.

Listing 8.36 `PrioritizedInterleaveDesigner.Glyphs`

```
// namespace imports same as Listing 8.30

namespace EssentialWF.Activities
{
  public class PrioritizedInterleaveDesigner : ...
  {
    protected override ActivityDesignerGlyphCollection Glyphs
    {
      get
      {
        ActivityDesignerGlyphCollection glyphs = base.Glyphs;

        if (Expanded)
        {
          PrioritizedInterleave interleave = this.Activity as
              PrioritizedInterleave;

          for (int i = 0; i < MaxPriorityLevel; i++)
            glyphs.Add(new PriorityIndicatorGlyph(i + 1));
        }

        return glyphs;
      }
    }
  }
}
```

The `PriorityIndicatorGlyph` that is added to the collection of glyphs is a simple
derivative of the base `System.Workflow.ComponentModel.Design.Designer-`
`Glyph` type. `PriorityIndicatorGlyph` overrides the `GetBounds` method to return
the rectangular bounds of the glyph circle and overrides the `OnPaint` method to perform the requisite graphics functions (see Listing 8.37).

Listing 8.37 `PriorityIndicatorGlyph`

```
// namespace imports same as Listing 8.30

namespace EssentialWF.Activities
{
  public class PriorityIndicatorGlyph : DesignerGlyph
  {
    private int priorityLevel;
    public PriorityIndicatorGlyph(int priorityLevel)
    {
```

```
      this.priorityLevel = priorityLevel;
    }

    public override Rectangle GetBounds(ActivityDesigner designer,
      bool activated)
    {
      PrioritizedInterleaveDesigner interleaveDesigner =
          designer as PrioritizedInterleaveDesigner;
      Rectangle bounds = new Rectangle(Point.Empty, new Size(16, 16));
      bounds.X = interleaveDesigner.Bounds.Left - bounds.Width / 2;
      bounds.Y = interleaveDesigner.Bounds.Top +
        interleaveDesigner.CellOffset.Height +
        ((this.priorityLevel - 1) *
            interleaveDesigner.CellSize.Height) +
          (interleaveDesigner.CellSize.Height / 2 - bounds.Height / 2);

      return bounds;
    }

    protected override void OnPaint(Graphics graphics, bool activated,
      AmbientTheme ambientTheme, ActivityDesigner designer)
    {
      Rectangle bounds = GetBounds(designer, activated);

      int priorityLevels =
          ((PrioritizedInterleaveDesigner)designer).MaxPriorityLevel;
      int increment = 255 / Math.Max(1, priorityLevels);

      Color fillColor = Color.FromArgb(Math.Min(255,
          (this.priorityLevel - 1) * increment),
        Math.Max(0, 255 - (increment *
            (this.priorityLevel - 1))), 48);

      using (Brush fillBrush = new SolidBrush(fillColor))
        graphics.FillRectangle(fillBrush, bounds);

      graphics.DrawRectangle(designer.DesignerTheme.BorderPen, bounds);
      ActivityDesignerPaint.DrawText(graphics,
        designer.DesignerTheme.BoldFont,
        this.priorityLevel.ToString(),
          bounds, StringAlignment.Center,
          TextQuality.Aliased, Brushes.Black);
    }
  }
}
```

Designer Layout Management

A composite activity designer is responsible for arranging the designers of its child activities. So, as part of this management of canvas real estate, `PrioritizedInterleaveDesigner` overrides the `OnLayoutSize` and `OnLayoutPosition` methods that are defined by `ActivityDesigner`. `OnLayoutSize` returns the total size of the designer (in this case, by adding up the sizes of its contained bands). The `OnLayoutPosition` method calculates the offset of a child activity designer (see Listing 8.38).

Listing 8.38 `PrioritizedInterleaveDesigner.Glyphs`

```
// namespace imports same as Listing 8.30

namespace EssentialWF.Activities
{
  public class PrioritizedInterleaveDesigner : ...
  {
    internal Size CellOffset
    {
      get
      {
        int headerHeight = TextRectangle.Height +
            ImageRectangle.Height + 3 *
            WorkflowTheme.CurrentTheme.AmbientTheme.Margin.Height;

        return new Size(0, headerHeight);
      }
    }

    internal Size CellSize
    {
      get
      {
        Size margin = WorkflowTheme.CurrentTheme.AmbientTheme.Margin;
        Size size = DesignerTheme.Size;
        size.Width += 6 * margin.Width;
        size.Height += 6 * margin.Height;

        return size;
      }
    }

    protected override Size OnLayoutSize(
      ActivityDesignerLayoutEventArgs e)
    {
```

```
    Size baseSize = base.OnLayoutSize(e);

  if (Expanded)
  {
    PrioritizedInterleave interleave = Activity as
              PrioritizedInterleave;
    Size designerSize = new Size(
        CellSize.Width * 3, CellSize.Height * MaxPriorityLevel);
    designerSize.Width += CellOffset.Width;
    designerSize.Height += CellOffset.Height;
    return designerSize;
  }
  else
    return baseSize;
}

protected override void OnLayoutPosition(
  ActivityDesignerLayoutEventArgs e)
{
  base.OnLayoutPosition(e);

  foreach (ActivityDesigner designer in ContainedDesigners)
  {
    int priority =
        (int)PrioritizedInterleave.GetPriority(designer.Activity);

    int position = (int)designer.Activity.GetValue(
        PrioritizedInterleave.PositionProperty);

    designer.Location = new Point(Location.X +
        CellOffset.Width + (position * CellSize.Width) +
        (3 * e.AmbientTheme.Margin.Width),
        Location.Y + CellOffset.Height +
          ((priority-1) * CellSize.Height) +
        (3 * e.AmbientTheme.Margin.Height));
    }
  }
 }
}
```

The logic for layout of child activities relies on the value of `PrioritizedInter-leave.PositionProperty`. The property represents the horizontal position of a child activity within a priority band. This is an internal attached property registered by the `PrioritizedInterleave` for each child. Each time a child activity is added to the `PrioritizedInterleave`, it updates the value of this property (see Listing 8.39).

Listing 8.39 **Setting** PrioritizedInterleave.PositionProperty

```
// namespace imports same as Listing 8.30

namespace EssentialWF.Activities
{
  [Designer(typeof(PrioritizedInterleaveDesigner), typeof(IDesigner))]
  public class PrioritizedInterleave : CompositeActivity
  {
    internal static DependencyProperty PositionProperty =
      DependencyProperty.RegisterAttached("Position",
        typeof(int),
        typeof(PrioritizedInterleave));

    public PrioritizedInterleave() {
      if(this.DesignMode)
      this.Activities.ListChanged += new
        EventHandler<ActivityCollectionChangeEventArgs>
          (Activities_ListChanged);
    }

    void Activities_ListChanged(object sender,
            ActivityCollectionChangeEventArgs e)
    {
      foreach (Activity child in e.AddedItems)
      {
        int priority = (int)child.GetValue(
              PrioritizedInterleave.PriorityProperty);
        int count = FindChildActivitiesOfSamePriority(priority);
        child.SetValue(PositionProperty, count - 1);
      }
    }

    int FindChildActivitiesOfSamePriority(int priority)
    {
      int count = 0;
      foreach (Activity child in this.Activities)
      {
        if (priority == (int)child.GetValue(
            PrioritizedInterleave.PriorityProperty))
          count++;
      }
      return count;
    }
  }
}
```

Designer Themes

When a designer component renders itself on a design surface, it utilizes types in the System.Drawing namespace (such as Color, Pen, Font, and Image). But rather than fixing the choice of colors, pens, fonts, and images as part of the implementation of a designer, the WF design-time programming model allows the association of a separate component, called a **designer theme**, with an activity designer. The theme component holds the set of drawing-related resources to be used by the designer during its rendering.

Separation of resource selection from the activity designer component enables activity designer components to inherit the look and feel of the ambient design environment. The look and feel of an activity designer can be customized simply by changing the thematic elements in use within the broader design environment. This is a big help when you are trying to create domain-specific tooling experiences. Additionally, this approach allows the WF designer infrastructure to efficiently manage drawing-related resources.

A theme component is associated with an activity designer using the Activity-DesignerThemeAttribute, which is defined in the System.Workflow.ComponentModel.Design namespace. We can illustrate use of this attribute by associating a theme component with a designer for our WriteLine activity (see Listing 8.40).

Listing 8.40   **Associating a** DesignerTheme **with a Designer**

```
// namespace imports same as Listing 8.30

namespace EssentialWF.Activities
{
  [Designer(typeof(WriteLineDesigner), typeof(IDesigner))]
  public class WriteLine : Activity {...}

  [ActivityDesignerTheme(typeof(WriteLineDesignerTheme))]
  public class WriteLineDesigner : ActivityDesigner { }

  public class WriteLineDesignerTheme : ActivityDesignerTheme
  {
    public WriteLineDesignerTheme(WorkflowTheme theme)
      : base(theme)
    {
      this.ForeColor = Color.FromArgb(0xFF, 0x00, 0x00, 0x00);
      this.BorderColor = Color.FromArgb(0xFF, 0xA5, 0x79, 0x73);
```

```
      this.BorderStyle = DashStyle.Solid;
      this.BackColorStart = Color.FromArgb(0xFF, 0xFF, 0xFF, 0xDF);
      this.BackColorEnd = Color.FromArgb(0xFF, 0xFF, 0xFF, 0x95);
      this.BackgroundStyle = LinearGradientMode.Horizontal;
    }
  }
}
```

The `WriteLineDesignerTheme` class inherits from `ActivityDesignerTheme` as all theme components for activities must.

The designer's theme component is made available to the designer within its methods, notably the `ActivityDesigner.OnPaint`. Listing 8.41 (which presumes a `PrioritizedInterleaveDesignerTheme` associated with `PrioritizedInterleaveDesigner`) illustrates how the designer component of `PrioritizedInterleave` can make use of the drawing-related resources defined by the theme.

Listing 8.41   `PrioritizedInterleaveDesigner.OnPaint`

```
// namespace imports same as Listing 8.30

namespace EssentialWF.Activities
{
  [ActivityDesignerTheme(typeof(PrioritizedInterleaveDesignerTheme))]
  public class PrioritizedInterleaveDesigner : ...
  {
    ...
    protected override void OnPaint(ActivityDesignerPaintEventArgs e)
    {
      base.OnPaint(e);

      PrioritizedInterleave interleave = Activity as
            PrioritizedInterleave;
      PrioritizedInterleaveDesignerTheme interleaveTheme =
          e.DesignerTheme as PrioritizedInterleaveDesignerTheme;

      Rectangle titleRectangle = new Rectangle(
          Location.X, Location.Y, Size.Width, CellOffset.Height);
      e.Graphics.FillRectangle(
            interleaveTheme.TitleBrush, titleRectangle);

      Rectangle glassShadowRectangle = new
          Rectangle(titleRectangle.Left, titleRectangle.Top,
            titleRectangle.Width, titleRectangle.Height / 2);
```

```
e.Graphics.FillRectangle(
        interleaveTheme.GetGlassShadowBrush(
    glassShadowRectangle), glassShadowRectangle);

ActivityDesignerPaint.DrawText(e.Graphics,
        interleaveTheme.Font, Text,
    TextRectangle, StringAlignment.Near,
        e.AmbientTheme.TextQuality,
        interleaveTheme.ForegroundBrush);

ActivityDesignerPaint.DrawImage(e.Graphics, Image,
    ImageRectangle, DesignerContentAlignment.Fill);

 ActivityDesignerPaint.DrawExpandButton(e.Graphics,
    ExpandButtonRectangle, !Expanded, interleaveTheme);

if (Expanded)
{
  Rectangle layoutRectangle = new Rectangle(
      Location.X + CellOffset.Width,
      Location.Y + CellOffset.Height,
      Size.Width - CellOffset.Width, Size.Height -
          CellOffset.Height);

  e.Graphics.DrawLine(interleaveTheme.BorderPen,
      layoutRectangle.Left, layoutRectangle.Top,
      layoutRectangle.Right, layoutRectangle.Top);

  for (int i = 1; i < MaxPriorityLevel; i++)
    e.Graphics.DrawLine(interleaveTheme.PrioritySeparatorPen,
        layoutRectangle.Left, layoutRectangle.Top +
      CellSize.Height * i,
      layoutRectangle.Right,
       layoutRectangle.Top + CellSize.Height * i);

  foreach (ActivityDesigner containedDesigner in
      ContainedDesigners)
  {
    Rectangle bounds = containedDesigner.Bounds;
    e.Graphics.DrawLine(interleaveTheme.BorderPen,
        bounds.Left + bounds.Width / 2,
        bounds.Top - 3 * e.AmbientTheme.Margin.Height,
        bounds.Left + bounds.Width / 2, bounds.Top);

    e.Graphics.DrawLine(interleaveTheme.BorderPen,
        bounds.Left + bounds.Width / 2, bounds.Bottom,
```

```
                    bounds.Left + bounds.Width / 2,
                    bounds.Bottom + 3 * e.AmbientTheme.Margin.Height - 1);
            }
          }
        }
      }
}
```

Toolbox Items

A **toolbox item** is associated with a component using the `ToolboxItemAttribute`
type defined in the `System.ComponentModel` namespace. Its job is to represent the
component within the toolbox of a design environment, as shown in Figure 8.13.
Listing 8.42 confirms that there is a toolbox item, named `ActivityToolboxItem`,
associated with the `Activity` class.

Listing 8.42   `Activity` **Has an Associated** `ActivityToolboxItem`

```
namespace System.Workflow.ComponentModel
{
  [ToolboxItem(typeof(ActivityToolboxItem))]
  public class Activity : DependencyObject
  {
    ...
  }
}
```

`ActivityToolboxItem` derives from the `ToolboxItem` class defined in the
`System.Drawing.Design` namespace.

Within a design environment, users will drag items from the toolbox onto their
design surface. When this occurs during the design of a WF program, an activity
toolbox item has an opportunity to configure the activity being added to the WF program. In the case of a composite activity, it is sometimes desirable to configure a set
of child activities. For example, the `Conditional` composite activity might for convenience be automatically given two child activities, each of type `Sequence`. We can
easily implement a toolbox item for `Conditional` that will automatically add these
two child activities when a `Conditional` activity is added to a WF program via the
toolbox.

Figure 8.13   Toolbox containing toolbox items

First we attribute `Conditional` to refer to the custom toolbox item:

```
using System;
using System.Workflow.ComponentModel;
using System.ComponentModel;
using System.Drawing.Design;

namespace EssentialWF.Activities
{
  [ToolboxItem(typeof(ConditionalToolboxItem))]
  public class Conditional : CompositeActivity
  {
    ...
  }
}
```

The `ConditionalToolboxItem` (see Listing 8.43) class overrides the `CreateCompo-`
`nentsCore` method.

Listing 8.43   `ConditionalToolboxItem`

```
using System;
using System.Workflow.ComponentModel;
using System.ComponentModel;
using System.Drawing.Design;
using System.Runtime.Serialization;
```

```
namespace EssentialWF.Activities
{
  [Serializable]
  public class ConditionalToolboxItem : ActivityToolboxItem
  {
    public ConditionalToolboxItem(Type type)
      : base(type) {}

    private ConditionalToolboxItem(SerializationInfo info,
      StreamingContext context)
    {
      base.Deserialize(info, context);
    }

    protected override IComponent[] CreateComponentsCore(
      IDesignerHost designerHost)
    {
      CompositeActivity cond = new Conditional();
      cond.Activities.Add(new Sequence());
      cond.Activities.Add(new Sequence());

      return new IComponent[] { cond };
    }
  }
}
```

The bitmap that is shown on the toolbox (refer to Figure 8.13) for a particular activity can be customized using the System.Drawing.ToolboxBitmapAttribute (see Listing 8.44).

Listing 8.44   Associating a Toolbox Bitmap with an Activity

```
using System;
using System.Workflow.ComponentModel;
using System.Drawing;
using System.Drawing.Design;

namespace EssentialWF.Activities
{
  [ToolboxBitmap(typeof(Conditional), "conditional.png")]
  public class Conditional : CompositeActivity
  {
    ...
  }
}
```

Designer Hosting

As mentioned earlier, one of the goals of the WF programming model is to enable WF programs to be authored by non-developers. Because WF programs can be developed using domain-specific sets of activities, it often makes sense to offer custom domain-specific design environments to WF program authors who are not developers. On the other hand, Visual Studio will be the first choice of many developers who build programs and applications using WF. The purpose of this section is to explore some territory that lies between these two ends of a spectrum—Visual Studio at the one end, and entirely custom design environments built from scratch at the other. To be specific, the WF visualization framework (supporting both activities and declarative conditions and rules) has been designed so that visualization components can be hosted in design environments other than Visual Studio. Thus, you do not need to start from scratch—unless your scenario warrants it—when building design environments for your WF program authors.

The *WorkflowView* Control Revisited

As we learned in the previous section, every activity type has a designer component with which it is associated. The base class of these activity designer components is `ActivityDesigner`. **Activity designer components** are windowless entities. The designer component of each activity in a WF program renders itself within the bounds allotted to it on a design canvas. All activity designer components inherit from the `ActivityDesigner` type an implementation of the `System.Component-Model.Design.IRootDesigner` interface. Of interest to us in this section is the fact that this implementation's `IRootDesigner.GetView` method returns an object of type `System.Workflow.ComponentModel.Design.WorkflowView`.

The `WorkflowView` type is a derivative of `System.Windows.Forms.User-Control`. The WF extensions for Visual Studio host this control in the Visual Studio document window (as shown in Figure 8.14). `WorkflowView` is the design canvas on which individual activity designers are rendered. `WorkflowView` is responsible for dispatching messages to individual activity designers and also provides window management, command routing, scrolling, drag and drop, rubber banding and connection management, zooming, panning, layout management, glyphs, and print and preview support. We will see a sample of how to use `WorkflowView` outside of Visual Studio a little later in this section.

Workflow Outline Control →

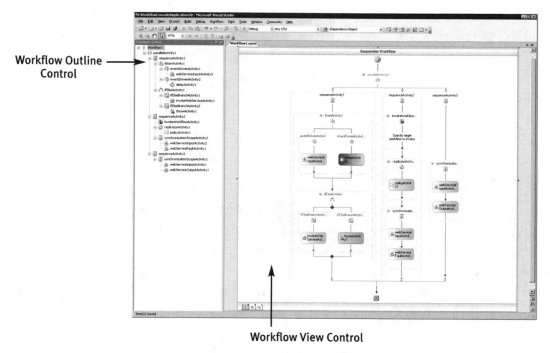

Workflow View Control

Figure 8.14 The `WorkflowView` control hosted in Visual Studio

`System.Workflow.ComponentModel.Design.WorkflowOutline` is another Windows Forms user control (also shown in Figure 8.14) that can be used outside of Visual Studio. This control visualizes the structure of a WF program in its true form—as a tree.

Hosting activity designers in a custom design environment carries some responsibilities. The design environment must associate components (activities) with instances of their designer components, and must also support the designer components in specific ways. Types in the `System.ComponentModel.Design` namespace provide off-the-shelf capabilities that can help you build custom design environments. Specifically, `System.ComponentModel.Design` introduces the concept of a **designer host** that is responsible for managing the interaction between an `IComponent` (such as an activity) and an associated `IDesigner` (in the case of an activity, a derivative of `ActivityDesigner`).

A designer host is a component that implements the `IDesignerHost` interface, which is defined in the `System.ComponentModel.Design` namespace. `IDesigner-Host` is a service container, and as such can be configured to provide support for undo operations, clipboard functions, and many other capabilities that activity designer components rely upon to deliver their visualization functionality.

An activity designer component can access the ambient `IDesignerHost` via the associated activity's `Site` property, like so:

```
// Get the designer host
IComponent component = this.Activity as IComponent;
IDesignerHost host = component.Site.GetService(
    typeof(IDesignerHost)) as IDesignerHost;
```

Every design environment that hosts activity designers can provide a specific implementation of `IDesignerHost`. Thus, activity components must not rely upon the details of any specific implementation of `IDesignerHost`.

A designer host is also responsible for design-time serialization of components (activities) and their associated designers. To do this, the designer host relies on a **designer loader**. The designer loader may, in turn, utilize individual serializers (discussed in Chapter 4) to serialize components (activities). The `System.Workflow.ComponentModel.Design` namespace includes an abstract class, `WorkflowDesignerLoader`, which provides standard design-time serialization capabilities for WF programs. Included is the serialization of designer-specific layout information (into a file with a .layout extension), which is leveraged by activity designers that inherit from `FreeFormActivityDesigner` (one of the base types for activity designers defined in the `System.Workflow.ComponentModel.Design` namespace).

Within a design environment, a **design surface** manages a designer host, and presents a self-contained user interface with which the user interacts (a design environment may have multiple design surfaces). `System.ComponentModel.Design.DesignSurface` is the base class for design surfaces. The design surface is not the same thing as the canvas (`WorkflowView`) that manages the rendering of activity designers. The canvas is obtained via the `View` property of `DesignSurface`, which in its getter implementation invokes the `GetView` method of the current `IRootDesigner` (obtained from the designer host). As mentioned previously,

`ActivityDesigner` implements `IRootDesigner`, and in its implementation of the `IRootDesigner.GetView` method returns a `WorkflowView` object.

The relationships between a design surface, its designer host, and a designer loader are depicted in Figure 8.15.

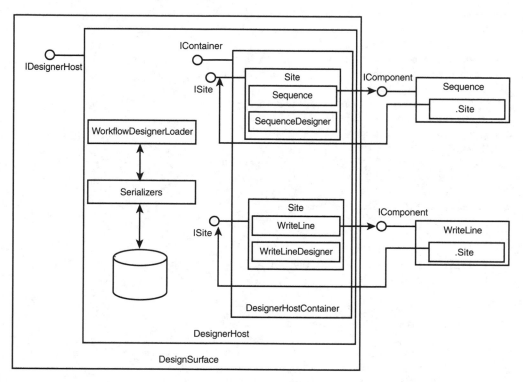

Figure 8.15   A design surface with a designer host and a designer loader

With this information, we can write a Windows Forms application that hosts the designer component of the `Sequence` composite activity. We subscribe to the `Form.Load` event within the `InitializeComponent` method (not shown), and in the event handler for this event, we create and configure the design surface (see Listing 8.45).

Listing 8.45   Hosting the Designer in a Windows Form Application

```
using System;
using System.Data;
using System.Drawing;
using System.Text;
using System.IO;
using System.Collections.Generic;
using System.ComponentModel;
using System.ComponentModel.Design;
using System.ComponentModel.Design.Serialization;
using System.Windows.Forms;
using System.Workflow.ComponentModel;
using System.Workflow.ComponentModel.Design;
using System.Workflow.ComponentModel.Compiler;
using EssentialWF.Activities;

namespace DesignerHosting
{
  public partial class Form1 : Form
  {
    public Form1()
    {
      // Will subscribe to the Form.Load event
      InitializeComponent();
    }

    private void Form1_Load(object sender, EventArgs e)
    {
      // Set up the design surface
      DesignSurface surface = new DesignSurface();
      DesignerLoader loader = new WorkflowLoader();

      surface.BeginLoad(loader);

      // Get the designer host
      IDesignerHost host = surface.GetService(
        typeof(IDesignerHost)) as IDesignerHost;

      // Build a WF program
      Sequence sequence = host.CreateComponent(
        typeof(Sequence)) as Sequence;

      WriteLine wl = new WriteLine();
      sequence.Activities.Add(wl);
      host.RootComponent.Site.Container.Add(wl);
```

```
      // Set up the canvas
      Control canvas = surface.View as Control;
      canvas.Parent = this;
      canvas.Dock = DockStyle.Fill;
      canvas.Refresh();
      host.Activate();
      surface.EndLoad();
    }
  }

  public class WorkflowLoader : WorkflowDesignerLoader
  {
    public override TextReader GetFileReader(string filePath)
    {
      return new StreamReader(
        new FileStream(filePath, FileMode.Open));
    }

    public override TextWriter GetFileWriter(string filePath)
    {
      return new StreamWriter(
        new FileStream(filePath, FileMode.OpenOrCreate));
    }

    ...
  }
}
```

The `Form.Load` event handler creates a design surface and passes a designer loader to the `DesignSurface.BeginLoad` method. This initializes the services required by activity designer components. Next, we obtain the designer host from the design surface and use it to create a `Sequence` activity. We add a couple of `WriteLine` activities to the `Sequence` in the usual manner. The `WriteLine` activities are also added to the container associated with the `Site` of the designer host's root component. Finally, we obtain the `WorkflowView` from the design surface and prepare it for rendering.

When we run our application, we see our form as shown in Figure 8.16.

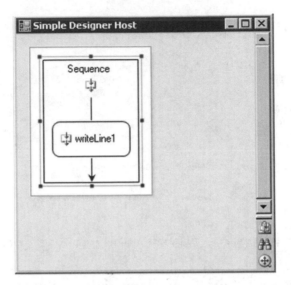

Figure 8.16 A form that hosts activity designer components

Dynamic Resolution of Activity Designers

As we have learned, an activity type is associated with a designer component using `DesignerAttribute`. There are situations, though, in which a design environment may need to override this association and dynamically provide a custom activity designer component for an activity. The mechanism for doing this is not specific to the WF visualization infrastructure; dynamic resolution of an `IDesigner` to be used with an `IComponent` is achieved using `ITypeDescriptorFilterService`, which is found in the `System.ComponentModel` namespace.

In the following code snippet, we dynamically replace the activity designer for the `WriteLine` activity type:

```
// Set up the design surface
DesignSurface surface = new DesignSurface();
DesignerLoader loader = new WorkflowLoader();

surface.BeginLoad(loader);

// Get the designer host
IDesignerHost host = surface.GetService(
  typeof(IDesignerHost)) as IDesignerHost;
```

```
ITypeDescriptorFilterService oldFilter =
  (ITypeDescriptorFilterService) designerhost.GetService(
    typeof(ITypeDescriptorFilterService));

if (oldFilter != null)
  host.RemoveService(typeof(ITypeDescriptorFilterService));

host.AddService(typeof(ITypeDescriptorFilterService),
  new CustomDesignerFilterService(oldFilter));
```

A custom `ITypeDescriptorFilterService`, shown next, can effectively replace the `DesignerAttribute` associated with `WriteLine` with a new `Designer-Attribute` that indicates a custom designer component:

```
namespace DesignerHosting
{
  public class CustomDesignerFilterService :
    ITypeDescriptorFilterService
  {
    private ITypeDescriptorFilterService oldService = null;

    public CustomDesignerFilterService(
      ITypeDescriptorFilterService service)
    {
      this.oldService = service;
    }

    bool ITypeDescriptorFilterService.FilterAttributes(
      IComponent component, IDictionary attributes)
    {
      this.oldService.FilterAttributes(component, attributes);

      if (component is WriteLine)
      {
        DesignerAttribute da = new DesignerAttribute(
          typeof(CustomWriteLineDesigner));

        attributes[da.TypeId] = da;
      }

      return true;
    }

    ...
  }
}
```

Where Are We?

In this chapter, we rounded out our exploration of the WF programming model by discussing conditions and rules, making changes to running WF program instances, tracking, activity designers, and designer hosting.

This brings us to the end of our journey. We began this book by putting the concepts of bookmarking and continuations under a microscope, and then using these abstractions to build a resumable program statement. The WF programming model is built around this idea, which has its essence captured in the `Activity`, `CompositeActivity`, and AEC types. We have explored in great detail how activity types and WF programs are authored, and how they are executed. Finally, we have surveyed the WF programming model by highlighting useful abstractions that will let you build activity types, WF programs, and applications quickly and effectively.

We hope that you can gainfully apply the ideas explored herein—as well as the Windows Workflow Foundation technology—in your software engineering endeavors.

■ A.
Activity Automaton

I N CHAPTERS 3, "ACTIVITY EXECUTION," AND 4, "Advanced Activity Execution," we discussed the activity automaton that describes the execution lifecycle of activities within WF programs. The WF programming model presents a somewhat simplified view of this automaton by representing the full set of actual states using the two enumerations `ActivityExecutionStatus` and `ActivityExecutionResult`. For the sake of clarity, the full activity automaton as understood by the WF runtime is shown in Figure A.1.

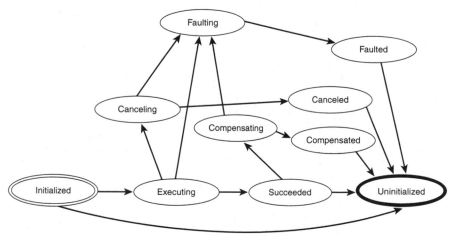

Figure A.1   Activity Automaton

For activities that do not implement the `ICompensatableActivity` interface, the *Compensating* and *Compensated* states are not applicable.

◾ B ◾
Control Flow Patterns

IN CHAPTERS 1 THROUGH 8, we developed several useful composite activities in order to illustrate concepts and features of the WF programming model. The purpose of this appendix is to explore different kinds of control flow patterns that composite activities can support.

A composite activity effectively has two parts:

- A set of child activities
- Information used to manage the execution of the child activities

The `Sequence` activity, discussed in Chapter 3, "Activity Execution," schedules the execution of its child activities one by one. `Sequence` therefore functions like a C# {} program statement block. The ordering of its child activities within the `Composite-Activity.EnabledActivities` list is metadata that the `Sequence` activity uses to determine the execution order.

The `Interleave` activity, discussed in Chapter 3, schedules the execution of its child activities all at once, which allows them to execute in an interleaved fashion. `Interleave` requires no metadata unless we decide to give it an `ActivityCondition` that governs early completion of the `Interleave`. Conditions might also be applied (as attached metadata properties) to individual child activities of `Interleave` in order to make their execution order interdependent (for example, child activity A executes only after child activities B and C are complete) or dependent upon WF program instance state (for example, child activity D executes only if the purchase order amount is greater than $1,000).

The `PrioritizedInterleave` activity is a functional superset of `Sequence` and `Interleave`. The ordering and interleaving of child activity execution is made explicit with a `Priority` property that is attached to child activities. Activities with the same priority execute in an interleaved manner; all activities given a priority n must complete their execution prior to the execution of activities with priority $n+1$.

There are a number of valid designs for composite activities that correspond to familiar branching constructs (such as C# `if` and `switch`). These composite activities will generally associate conditions with a number of potential paths of execution that are represented as child activities. Evaluation of the conditions will determine which path is taken.

The `While` activity, discussed in Chapter 4, "Advanced Activity Execution," offers an `ActivityCondition` that governs how many times its lone child activity (validation logic limits the number of child activities to one) is executed. This is exactly like a C# `while` loop.

It is easy to write a `ForEach` activity that works like a C# `foreach`, executing independent instances of a lone child activity (validation logic limits the number of child activities to one) for each item in a collection. In Chapter 4, we discussed a variant, `InterleavedForEach`, which schedules the instances of the child activity all at once, which allows them to execute in an interleaved fashion. As with `Interleave`, a condition governing early completion can be offered.

Some of these composite activities' functionality maps straightforwardly to the familiar control flow found in languages like C#. If you stick to these constructs, your WF program will read a lot like a C# program. However, the concepts of interleaved execution and early completion clearly go beyond what is offered by the control flow constructs of most general-purpose programming languages, and are indicative of WF's flexible approach to control flow.

It is crucial to understand that unlike the approach taken by "workflow languages," the WF runtime does not have any intrinsic bias toward, or knowledge of, *any* control flow patterns—even sequencing. Because of this, the activities that are shipped with WF in the `System.Workflow.Activities` namespace are not privileged in any way relative to activities that you might develop.

If you exploit the power of composite activities and develop control flow constructs that capture—with high fidelity—the patterns in real-world processes, you will have a much easier time modeling those processes in your programs.

Pick

Let's begin with a specific (and useful) pattern that is hard to capture using familiar control flow constructs available in general-purpose programming languages like C#. The `Pick` activity shown in Listing B.1 uses an attached metadata property to classify each of its child activities as a leader or a follower. When a `Pick` executes, its leaders are scheduled for execution first and only the followers of the first leader to complete are subsequently executed.

Listing B.1 `Pick` Activity

```
using System;
using System.Workflow.ComponentModel;
using System.Workflow.ComponentModel.Compiler;

namespace EssentialWF.Activities
{
  [ActivityValidator(typeof(PickValidator))]
  public class Pick : CompositeActivity
  {
    public static readonly DependencyProperty
      FollowerOfProperty = DependencyProperty.RegisterAttached(
        "FollowerOf",
        typeof(string),
        typeof(Pick),
        new PropertyMetadata(DependencyPropertyOptions.Metadata),
        typeof(FollowerOfAttachedPropertyValidator)
      );

    public static object GetFollowerOf(object dependencyObject)
    {
      DependencyObject o = dependencyObject as DependencyObject;
      return o.GetValue(Pick.FollowerOfProperty);
    }

    public static void SetFollowerOf(object dependencyObject,
      object value)
    {
      DependencyObject o = dependencyObject as DependencyObject;
      o.SetValue(Pick.FollowerOfProperty, value);
    }

    internal static bool IsLeader(Activity a)
    {
      return (Pick.GetFollowerOf(a) == null);
```

```
      }

      private bool firstLeaderDone;
      protected override void Initialize(
        IServiceProvider provider)
      {
        firstLeaderDone = false;
        base.Initialize(provider);
      }

      protected override ActivityExecutionStatus Execute(
        ActivityExecutionContext context)
      {
        if (EnabledActivities.Count == 0)
          return ActivityExecutionStatus.Closed;

        // schedule execution of the leaders
        foreach (Activity child in EnabledActivities)
        {
          if (Pick.IsLeader(child))
          {
            child.Closed += this.ContinueAt;
            context.ExecuteActivity(child);
          }
        }

        return ActivityExecutionStatus.Executing;
      }

      void ContinueAt(object sender,
        ActivityExecutionStatusChangedEventArgs e)
      {
        e.Activity.Closed -= this.ContinueAt;
        ActivityExecutionContext context =
          sender as ActivityExecutionContext;

        if (!firstLeaderDone)
        {
          // first leader is now completed
          firstLeaderDone = true;
          string leaderName = e.Activity.Name;

          // cancel the other leaders, if any
          int leadersCanceled = 0;
          foreach (Activity child in EnabledActivities)
          {
            if (child.ExecutionStatus ==
              ActivityExecutionStatus.Executing)
```

```
        {
          context.CancelActivity(child);
          leadersCanceled++;
        }
      }

      // schedule execution of the followers, if any
      int followersExecuted = 0;
      foreach (Activity child in EnabledActivities)
      {
        string s = Pick.GetFollowerOf(child) as string;
        if (leaderName.Equals(s))
        {
          child.Closed += this.ContinueAt;
          context.ExecuteActivity(child);
          followersExecuted++;
        }
      }
      if ((leadersCanceled + followersExecuted) == 0)
      {
        // no canceled leaders, and also no followers
        context.CloseActivity();
      }
    }
    else  // a follower has completed
    {
      foreach (Activity child in EnabledActivities)
      {
        ActivityExecutionStatus status =
          child.ExecutionStatus;

        if ((status != ActivityExecutionStatus.Closed) &&
          (status != ActivityExecutionStatus.Initialized))
        {
          // there is still at least 1 follower executing
          return;
        }
      }

      // all followers are done
      context.CloseActivity();
    }
  }

  // Cancellation logic
  ...
  }
}
```

The `Pick` activity uses the standard attached property pattern to define an attached property called `FollowerOf`, of type `string`. When the `FollowerOf` property is registered, a custom validator called `FollowerOfAttachedPropertyValidator` is specified. In this example, `Pick` is also associated with a validator component, `Pick-Validator`.

Every child activity of `Pick` is either a leader or a follower. A child activity is a leader by default; a child activity is a follower if it has the `FollowerOf` property attached to it. The value of the `FollowerOf` property must be the name of a peer activity (a different child activity of the same `Pick`) whose execution will precede that of the activity to which the `FollowerOf` property has been attached. In its `Execute` method, `Pick` schedules the execution of all leaders. When the first leader finishes, the `Pick` cancels the other leaders and executes any followers of the leader that completed first. There is no restriction on the type of child activity allowed as either leader or follower.

As an example, in the following WF program, there are two leaders (the `Wait` activities) and two followers (the `WriteLine` activities):

```
<Pick x:Name="pick1" xmlns="http://EssentialWF/Activities"
xmlns:x="http://schemas.microsoft.com/winfx/2006/xaml">
  <Wait Duration="00:00:06" x:Name="d1" />
  <Wait Duration="00:00:02" x:Name="d2" />
  <WriteLine Pick.FollowerOf="d1" x:Name="w1" Text="one" />
  <WriteLine Pick.FollowerOf="d2" x:Name="w2" Text="two" />
</Pick>
```

The output of the program is determined by which leader completes first. In this case, the `Wait` `"d2"` has a shorter duration, so the follower `"w2"` will execute and the output is

```
two
```

There is an interesting amount of validation logic to be written in order to ensure that the `FollowerOf` property is used correctly. For example, if all child activities are followers, none by definition can ever get executed. The `PickValidator` component, shown next, ensures that at least one child activity of a `Pick` is a leader:

```
using System;
using System.Workflow.ComponentModel;
using System.Workflow.ComponentModel.Compiler;
```

```
namespace EssentialWF.Activities
{
  public class PickValidator : CompositeActivityValidator
  {
    public override ValidationErrorCollection Validate(
      ValidationManager manager, object obj)
    {
      ValidationErrorCollection errors =
        base.Validate(manager, obj);

      Pick pick = obj as Pick;
      foreach (Activity child in pick.EnabledActivities)
      {
        // if we find a leader, we can return
        if (Pick.IsLeader(child))
          return errors;
      }

      errors.Add(new ValidationError("At least one child of Pick must not carry
the FollowerOf attached property", 200));

      return errors;
    }
  }
}
```

Next we come to `FollowerOfAttachedPropertyValidator`, which is the validator component specified in the registration of the `FollowerOf` attached property. As shown next, this validation logic ensures that the `FollowerOf` property, as applied to a specific child activity of a `Pick`, has a legal value:

```
using System;
using System.Workflow.ComponentModel;
using System.Workflow.ComponentModel.Compiler;

namespace EssentialWF.Activities
{
  public class FollowerOfAttachedPropertyValidator : Validator
  {
    public override ValidationErrorCollection Validate(
      ValidationManager manager, object obj)
    {
      ValidationErrorCollection errors =
        base.Validate(manager, obj);
```

```
      string activityName = obj as string;
      if (activityName == null ||
          activityName.Equals(string.Empty))
      {
        errors.Add(new ValidationError("FollowerOf has null or empty value
specified", 201));
        return errors;
      }

      Activity activity = manager.Context[typeof(Activity)] as Activity;
      Pick pick = activity.Parent as Pick;

      if (pick == null)
      {
        errors.Add(new ValidationError("FollowerOf must be applied to a child
activity of Pick", 202));
        return errors;
      }

      Activity target = pick.Activities[activityName];
      if (target == null)
      {
        errors.Add(new ValidationError("FollowerOf must be the name of a child
activity of Pick", 203));
        return errors;
      }

      if (target.Name.Equals(activity.Name))
      {
        errors.Add(new ValidationError("FollowerOf cannot refer to the same
activity to which it is attached", 204));
        return errors;
      }

      return errors;
    }
  }
}
```

FollowerOfAttachedPropertyValidator performs several validation checks to make certain that an appropriate value has been provided for the FollowerOf property. The Pick activity (the parent of the activity carrying the FollowerOf property being validated) is obtained using the Context property of ValidationManager. To get a better feel for writing validation logic, we suggest that you enhance the preceding code to include a validation check that is missing: A follower activity must follow a leader (and not another follower). It also may prove instructive for you to write a set of sample WF programs that exercise all of the validation checks for `Pick`. This is a great habit to develop as an activity writer; there is little use writing validation logic unless you have test cases to show that invalid WF programs are being correctly identified as such.

The code for the `Pick` activity is not quite complete; it requires standard cancellation logic, as discussed in Chapter 4.

Graph

As an example of another general-purpose composite activity, consider an activity called `Graph` (shown in Listing B.2) that represents a graph. The nodes of the graph are the `Graph` activity's child activities. The arcs of the graph (connections between nodes) are specified as metadata that is held by `Graph`. For simplicity's sake, we will limit ourselves here to acyclic graphs but there is no fundamental reason to disallow more complex graphs with cycles.

Listing B.2 Graph **Activity**

```
using System;
using System.Collections.Generic;
using System.ComponentModel;
using System.Workflow.ComponentModel;

namespace EssentialWF.Activities
{
  public class Graph : CompositeActivity
  {
    // All transitions must be true for a join
    // to take place
    private Dictionary<string, bool> transitionStatus;

    // If true, we have hit an exit activity and are
    // in the process of cancelling other activities
    private bool exiting;

    public Graph() : base()
    {
      base.SetReadOnlyPropertyValue(Graph.ArcsProperty,
        new List<Arc>());
    }
```

```csharp
public static readonly DependencyProperty
  ArcsProperty = DependencyProperty.Register(
    "Arcs",
    typeof(List<Arc>),
    typeof(Graph),
    new PropertyMetadata(DependencyPropertyOptions.Metadata |
      DependencyPropertyOptions.ReadOnly, new Attribute[]
        { new DesignerSerializationVisibilityAttribute(
          DesignerSerializationVisibility.Content) }
    )
  );

// Attached to exactly one child activity
public static readonly DependencyProperty IsEntryProperty =
  DependencyProperty.RegisterAttached(
    "IsEntry",
    typeof(bool),
    typeof(Graph),
    new PropertyMetadata(DependencyPropertyOptions.Metadata)
  );

public static object GetIsEntry(object dependencyObject)
{
  DependencyObject o = dependencyObject as DependencyObject;
  return o.GetValue(Graph.IsEntryProperty);
}

public static void SetIsEntry(object dependencyObject,
  object value)
{
  DependencyObject o = dependencyObject as DependencyObject;
  o.SetValue(Graph.IsEntryProperty, value);
}

// Attached to zero or more child activities
public static readonly DependencyProperty IsExitProperty =
  DependencyProperty.RegisterAttached(
    "IsExit",
    typeof(bool),
    typeof(Graph),
    new PropertyMetadata(DependencyPropertyOptions.Metadata)
  );

public static object GetIsExit(object dependencyObject)
{
  DependencyObject o = dependencyObject as DependencyObject;
  return o.GetValue(Graph.IsExitProperty);
}
```

```
public static void SetIsExit(object dependencyObject,
  object value)
{
  DependencyObject o = dependencyObject as DependencyObject;
  o.SetValue(Graph.IsExitProperty, value);
}

[DesignerSerializationVisibility(
  DesignerSerializationVisibility.Content)]
public List<Arc> Arcs
{
  get { return GetValue(ArcsProperty) as List<Arc>; }
}

protected override void Initialize(
  IServiceProvider provider)
{
  exiting = false;
  transitionStatus = new Dictionary<string, bool>();
  foreach (Arc arc in this.Arcs)
  {
    transitionStatus.Add(arc.name, false);
  }
  base.Initialize(provider);
}

protected override void Uninitialize(IServiceProvider provider)
{
  transitionStatus = null;
  base.Uninitialize(provider);
}

protected override ActivityExecutionStatus Execute(
  ActivityExecutionContext context)
{
  if (EnabledActivities.Count == 0)
    return ActivityExecutionStatus.Closed;

  foreach (Activity child in EnabledActivities)
  {
    // Graph validation logic ensures one entry activity
    bool entry = (bool)Graph.GetIsEntry(child);
    if (entry)
    {
      Run(context, child);
      break;
    }
  }
```

```
      return ActivityExecutionStatus.Executing;
  }

  private void Run(ActivityExecutionContext context,
    Activity child)
  {
    // we don't necessarily need to dynamically
    // create an AEC, but let's do it anyway
    // so we can more easily add looping later

    ActivityExecutionContextManager manager =
      context.ExecutionContextManager;
    ActivityExecutionContext c =
      manager.CreateExecutionContext(child);

    c.Activity.Closed += this.ContinueAt;
    c.ExecuteActivity(c.Activity);
  }

  void ContinueAt(object sender,
    ActivityExecutionStatusChangedEventArgs e)
  {
    e.Activity.Closed -= this.ContinueAt;
    ActivityExecutionContext context =
      sender as ActivityExecutionContext;

    // get the name before completing the AEC
    string completedChildName = e.Activity.Name;
    bool exitNow = (bool)Graph.GetIsExit(e.Activity);

    ActivityExecutionContextManager manager =
      context.ExecutionContextManager;
    ActivityExecutionContext c =
      manager.GetExecutionContext(e.Activity);
    manager.CompleteExecutionContext(c, false);

    if (exiting || exitNow)
    {
      // no executing child activities
      if (manager.ExecutionContexts.Count == 0)
        context.CloseActivity();

      else if (exitNow) // just completed an exit activity
      {
        exiting = true;
        foreach (ActivityExecutionContext ctx
          in manager.ExecutionContexts)
        {
```

```
        if (ctx.Activity.ExecutionStatus ==
          ActivityExecutionStatus.Executing)
        {
          ctx.CancelActivity(ctx.Activity);
        }
      }
    }
}
else
{
  // mark all outgoing transitions as true
  foreach (Arc arc in this.Arcs)
  {
    if (arc.FromActivity.Equals(completedChildName))
      this.transitionStatus[arc.name] = true;
  }

  foreach (Activity child in EnabledActivities)
  {
    bool entry = (bool)Graph.GetIsEntry(child);

    if (!entry)
    {
      // a child activity can run only
      // if all incoming transitions are true
      // and it is not the entry activity
      bool canrun = true;
      foreach (Arc arc in this.Arcs)
      {
        if (arc.ToActivity.Equals(child.Name))
          if (transitionStatus[arc.name] == false)
            canrun = false;
      }

      if (canrun)
      {
        // when we run a child activity,
        // mark its incoming transitions as false
        foreach (Arc arc in this.Arcs)
        {
          if (arc.ToActivity.Equals(child.Name))
            transitionStatus[arc.name] = false;
        }
        Run(context, child);
      }
    }
  }
}
```

```
    }

    // Cancellation logic
    ...
  }
}
```

One child activity of the `Graph` must be marked as the "entry" activity—the activity whose execution is the logical starting point for the set of child activities. Zero or more activities are marked as "exit" activities. If an "exit" activity completes successfully, all pending (still executing) activities elsewhere in the graph are canceled and the graph itself can report its own completion.

We can use the `Graph` activity to write WF programs that look like this (in XAML):

```xml
<Graph x:Name="graph1" xmlns="http://EssentialWF/Activities"
xmlns:x="http://schemas.microsoft.com/winfx/2006/xaml">
  <Graph.Arcs>
    <Arc FromActivity="A" ToActivity="B" />
    <Arc FromActivity="B" ToActivity="C" />
    <Arc FromActivity="B" ToActivity="D" />
    <Arc FromActivity="C" ToActivity="E" />
    <Arc FromActivity="D" ToActivity="E" />
    <Arc FromActivity="E" ToActivity="F" />
  </Graph.Arcs>
  <WriteLine x:Name="C" Text="c" />
  <WriteLine x:Name="A" Text="a" Graph.IsEntry="True" />
  <WriteLine x:Name="E" Text="e" />
  <WriteLine x:Name="D" Text="d" />
  <WriteLine x:Name="F" Text="f" Graph.IsExit="True" />
  <WriteLine x:Name="B" Text="b" />
</Graph>
```

The preceding WF program is a composition of activities that can be visualized as shown in Figure B.1.

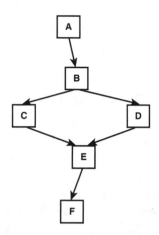

Figure B.1   A graph-based WF program

Each node in the graph is an activity. The activities in the example are all of type `WriteLine` but in fact there is no restriction at all on the type of child activity that is allowed within a `Graph`—these activities can be `Sequence`, `WriteLine`, `Interleave`, `Read`, or any activity that you choose, even another `Graph`.

The order in which the child activities of `Graph` execute is determined by the arcs that are captured as metadata associated with the `Graph`. In the preceding example, activity B acts like a split because the path of execution diverges at precisely that point in the program (activities C and D execute subsequently in an interleaved manner). Activity E acts like a join because two paths of execution are merged at precisely that point in the program (activity E does not execute until both C and D are complete).

The metadata of the `Graph` activity is just a set of arcs. The associated `Arc` type is a straightforward class with two dependency properties that hold the names of the activities connected by an arc:

```
using System;
using System.Workflow.ComponentModel;

namespace EssentialWF.Activities
{
  public class Arc : DependencyObject
  {
    internal string name;
```

```
public Arc() : base()
{
  name = Guid.NewGuid().ToString();
}

public Arc(string from, string to)
  : this()
{
  this.FromActivity = from;
  this.ToActivity = to;
}

public static readonly DependencyProperty
  FromActivityProperty = DependencyProperty.Register(
    "FromActivity",
    typeof(string),
    typeof(Arc),
    new PropertyMetadata(DependencyPropertyOptions.Metadata)
  );

public static readonly DependencyProperty
  ToActivityProperty = DependencyProperty.Register(
    "ToActivity",
    typeof(string),
    typeof(Arc),
    new PropertyMetadata(DependencyPropertyOptions.Metadata)
  );

public string FromActivity
{
  get { return GetValue(FromActivityProperty) as string; }
  set { SetValue(FromActivityProperty, value); }
}

public string ToActivity
{
  get { return GetValue(ToActivityProperty) as string; }
  set { SetValue(ToActivityProperty, value); }
}
  }
}
```

The code for the preceding Graph activity is not quite complete; it requires validation logic to ensure that the IsEntry and IsExit properties are used appropriately. It also requires standard cancellation logic, as discussed in Chapter 4.

The `Graph` activity can be enhanced to allow for the association of conditions with the split and join points in the graph, and also to allow loops.

Navigator

Graph notation is a great way of describing the nonlinear execution of statements within a program. But we do not need to limit ourselves to a single general-purpose `Graph` activity. For example, it is vital in some scenarios to use a graph-based composite activity that only allows a single child activity to execute at a time. The transitions between activities can be viewed as jumps (like `goto`) and can be used to model a wide range of dynamic control flow patterns such as nonlinear UI navigation among a set of UI elements. Consider the composite activity called `Navigator` that is shown in Listing B.3.

Listing B.3 `Navigator` Activity

```
using System;
using System.Collections.Generic;
using System.Collections.ObjectModel;
using System.ComponentModel;
using System.Workflow.ComponentModel;

namespace EssentialWF.Activities
{
  public class Navigator : CompositeActivity
  {
    public static readonly DependencyProperty
      StartWithProperty = DependencyProperty.Register(
        "StartWith",
        typeof(string),
        typeof(Navigator)
      );

    public string StartWith
    {
      get { return (string) GetValue(StartWithProperty); }
      set { SetValue(StartWithProperty, value); }
    }

    public static readonly DependencyProperty
      NavigateToProperty = DependencyProperty.RegisterAttached(
        "NavigateTo",
        typeof(string),
```

```
      typeof(Navigator)
  );

public static object GetNavigateTo(object dependencyObject)
{
  DependencyObject o = dependencyObject as DependencyObject;
  return o.GetValue(NavigateToProperty);
}

public static void SetNavigateTo(object dependencyObject,
  object value)
{
  DependencyObject o = dependencyObject as DependencyObject;
  o.SetValue(Navigator.NavigateToProperty, value);
}

public static readonly DependencyProperty
  NavigatingEvent = DependencyProperty.Register(
    "Navigating",
    typeof(EventHandler<NavigatorEventArgs>),
    typeof(Navigator)
  );

public event EventHandler<NavigatorEventArgs> Navigating
{
  add { base.AddHandler(NavigatingEvent, value); }
  remove { base.RemoveHandler(NavigatingEvent, value); }
}

protected override ActivityExecutionStatus Execute(
  ActivityExecutionContext context)
{
  if (this.TryNavigatingTo(context, this.StartWith))
    return ActivityExecutionStatus.Executing;

  return ActivityExecutionStatus.Closed;
}

private bool TryNavigatingTo(ActivityExecutionContext context,
  string nextActivityName)
{
  ActivityExecutionContextManager manager =
    context.ExecutionContextManager;

  //populate the history
  List<Activity> history = new List<Activity>();
  foreach (Guid ctxid in manager.PersistedExecutionContexts)
  {
```

```
    ActivityExecutionContext serializedContext =
      manager.GetPersistedExecutionContext(ctxid);
    history.Add(serializedContext.Activity);

    // GetPersistedExecutionContext above removed the context
    // so we need to explicitly add it back
    context.ExecutionContextManager.
      CompleteExecutionContext(serializedContext, true);
  }

  //raise the event
  NavigatorEventArgs args =
    new NavigatorEventArgs(history.AsReadOnly());
  RaiseGenericEvent(Navigator.NavigatingEvent, this, args);

  Activity nextActivity = null;
  if (args.NavigateTo != null)
    nextActivity = args.NavigateTo;
  else if (!string.IsNullOrEmpty(nextActivityName))
    nextActivity = this.GetActivityByName(nextActivityName);

  if (nextActivity != null)
  {
    ActivityExecutionContext innerContext =
      manager.CreateExecutionContext(nextActivity);
    innerContext.Activity.Closed += this.ContinueAt;
    innerContext.ExecuteActivity(innerContext.Activity);
    return true;
  }
  return false;
}

private void ContinueAt(Object sender,
  ActivityExecutionStatusChangedEventArgs e)
{
  ActivityExecutionContext context =
    sender as ActivityExecutionContext;
  ActivityExecutionContextManager manager =
    context.ExecutionContextManager;

  ActivityExecutionContext innerContext =
    manager.GetExecutionContext(e.Activity);

  //first, unsubscribe to the inner context's activity
  innerContext.Activity.Closed -= this.ContinueAt;

  //remove the inner context and serialize it
  manager.CompleteExecutionContext(innerContext, true);
```

```
      string nextActivityName = Navigator.GetNavigateTo(
        innerContext.Activity) as string;

      if (!this.TryNavigatingTo(context, nextActivityName))
        context.CloseActivity();
    }

    // Cancellation logic
    ...
  }

  public class NavigatorEventArgs : EventArgs
  {
    private ReadOnlyCollection<Activity> history = null;
    private Activity navigateTo = null;

    internal NavigatorEventArgs(ReadOnlyCollection<Activity> history)
    {
      this.history = history;
    }

    public Activity NavigateTo
    {
      get { return navigateTo; }
      set { navigateTo = value; }
    }

    public ReadOnlyCollection<Activity> History
    {
      get { return this.history; }
    }
  }
}
```

The `Navigator` activity has a set of child activities, but its execution logic will only allow a single child activity to execute at a time. Each child activity represents a named destination for navigation. `Navigator` maintains a history of all destinations previously visited (executed) and allows for revisiting of destinations. It is as if each child activity of the `Navigator` is a logical bookmark within the `Navigator`.

The `Navigator` activity applies an attached property named `NavigateTo` to each of its child activities. The value of the `NavigateTo` property can be the `Name` of any other child activity within the parent `Navigator`. You can think of the value of the `NavigateTo` property as the name of the next bookmark to jump to, or a label for a jmp instruction. A value of the empty string or `null` for the `NavigateTo` property is used to indicate the end of navigation and completes the execution of the `Navigator` activity. `Navigator` also has a `StartWith` property that names the child activity that will be the first to execute.

The following WF program puts our `Navigator` activity to use by capturing a simple, nonlinear control flow using `Navigator` and a set of `WriteLine` activities:

```
<Navigator x:Name="navigator1" StartWith="w3"
xmlns="http://EssentialWF/Activities"
xmlns:x="http://schemas.microsoft.com/winfx/2006/xaml">
  <WriteLine x:Name="w1" Text="One" Navigator.NavigateTo="w4"/>
  <WriteLine x:Name="w2" Text="Two" Navigator.NavigateTo=""/>
  <WriteLine x:Name="w3" Text="Three" Navigator.NavigateTo="w1"/>
  <WriteLine x:Name="w4" Text="Four" Navigator.NavigateTo="w2"/>
</Navigator>
```

Figure B.2 shows the preceding program visually.

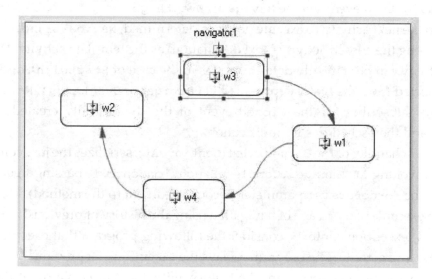

Figure B.2   A Navigator-based WF program

The output of this program is

```
Three
One
Four
Two
```

The preceding program defines the path of execution *statically* (at design-time) by specifying the value of the `NavigateTo` property of each child of the `Navigator`. In some cases this may be desirable; however, many scenarios demand a more flexible approach to deciding the next destination to navigate to. For this reason, we've chosen to *not* make `NavigateTo` a metadata property. Thus, the value of `NavigateTo` can be set dynamically during activity execution. And to accommodate this common pattern, the `Navigator` defines a `Navigating` event, which, when raised, is a convenient place for indicating the next activity that should execute.

The `Execute` method calls the method `TryNavigatingTo`, passing the value of the `StartWith` property. `TryNavigatingTo` returns `true` if it successfully schedules a child activity for execution. The implementation of `TryNavigatingTo` first raises the `Navigating` event, giving the user of the activity a chance to decide the next activity that should execute. `Navigator` reloads previously completed execution contexts and provides this history (of previously visited activities) to the subscriber of the `Navigating` event via the `NavigatorEventArgs`.

When the next activity to execute has been determined, `Navigator` creates a new AEC, passing the chosen activity (next destination) as the template activity. The template activity can be statically determined (as in the case of `StartWith`), or dynamically selected from the history (provided via `NavigatorEventArgs`). `Navigator`, of course, subscribes for the `Closed` event of the dynamically created activity instance and then schedules it for execution.

The event handler of the `Closed` event (`ContinueAt`), serializes the just-completed AEC by invoking `AECManager.CompleteExecutionContext`, passing `true` as the value for the `forcePersist` parameter (second argument to the method).

As an example of the usage of navigation using the history of previously executed (serialized) execution contexts, consider the following program that executes a single `WriteLine` activity. The program replays the execution of a previously executed `WriteLine` activity instance from the history, with a modified value of the `Text` property, five times:

```
<Navigator x:Name="navigator1" x:Class="NavigatingThePast"
StartWith="w1" Navigating="OnNavigating"
xmlns="http://EssentialWF/Activities"
xmlns:x="http://schemas.microsoft.com/winfx/2006/xaml">
  <WriteLine x:Name="w1" Text="1" />
  <x:Code>
```

```
<![CDATA[
    void OnNavigating(object sender, NavigatorEventArgs e)
    {
      if (e.History != null && e.History.Count > 0)
      {
        if (e.History.Count == 5)
          e.NavigateTo = null;

        else
        {
          // The last WriteLine in the history
          WriteLine w = (WriteLine)
            e.History[e.History.Count - 1];

          // Increment the Writeline's Text property by one
          w.Text = (Int32.Parse(w.Text) + 1).ToString();

          // This is now the new future, go there!
          e.NavigateTo = w;
        }
      }
    }
]]>
  </x:Code>
</Navigator>
```

The output of this program is

```
1
2
3
4
5
```

State Machine

Yet another graph-oriented style of programming allows WF programmers to explicitly describe programs as state machines. In each state, there is a set of possible inputs (stimuli) that will cause the program instance to move from one state to another. What we are exploring in this topic is how to allow the author of a program to *explicitly enumerate* all possible states for that program instead of using a structured style of programming in which the states are implicit.

The `StateMachine` activity is shown in Listing B.4. Each node in a state machine graph is just a label (not an activity, as in the case of the `Graph` activity). As with the `Graph` activity, transitions describe paths of execution from one state to another, but unlike `Graph`, a state machine always occupies exactly one state (node) at a time—there is no interleaving. Each transition is also associated with some form of input, which—when provided to the state machine—causes the state machine to move from one state to another.

Listing B.4 `StateMachine` Activity

```
using System;
using System.Collections.Generic;
using System.ComponentModel;
using System.Workflow.ComponentModel;
using System.Workflow.Runtime;

namespace EssentialWF.Activities
{
  public class Transition : DependencyObject
  {
    public Transition() : base() { }

    public static readonly DependencyProperty
      ToProperty = DependencyProperty.Register(
        "To",
        typeof(string),
        typeof(Transition),
        new PropertyMetadata(DependencyPropertyOptions.Metadata)
      );

    public static readonly DependencyProperty
      FromProperty = DependencyProperty.Register(
        "From",
        typeof(string),
        typeof(Transition),
        new PropertyMetadata(DependencyPropertyOptions.Metadata)
      );

    public static readonly DependencyProperty
      ActivityNameProperty = DependencyProperty.Register(
        "ActivityName",
        typeof(string),
        typeof(Transition),
        new PropertyMetadata(DependencyPropertyOptions.Metadata)
      );
```

```
    public static readonly DependencyProperty
      InputPropProperty = DependencyProperty.Register(
        "InputProp",
        typeof(string),
        typeof(Transition),
        new PropertyMetadata(DependencyPropertyOptions.Metadata)
      );

    public string To
    {
      get { return GetValue(ToProperty) as string; }
      set { SetValue(ToProperty, value); }
    }

    public string From
    {
      get { return GetValue(FromProperty) as string; }
      set { SetValue(FromProperty, value); }
    }

    public string ActivityName
    {
      get { return GetValue(ActivityNameProperty) as string; }
      set { SetValue(ActivityNameProperty, value); }
    }

    // Specifies the name of an activity property that
    // must be set prior to execution of the activity.
    // Alternatively, an activity type could be decorated
    // to indicate its input property.
    public string InputProp
    {
      get { return GetValue(InputPropProperty) as string; }
      set { SetValue(InputPropProperty, value); }
    }
}

public class StateMachineQuery { }

public class StateMachineAction
{
  public string ActivityName;
  public object Input;
}

public class StateMachine : CompositeActivity
{
  public StateMachine()
```

```csharp
    : base()
{
  base.SetReadOnlyPropertyValue(StatesProperty,
    new List<string>());

  base.SetReadOnlyPropertyValue(TransitionsProperty,
    new List<Transition>());
}

public static readonly DependencyProperty
  StatesProperty = DependencyProperty.Register(
    "States",
    typeof(List<string>),
    typeof(StateMachine),
    new PropertyMetadata(DependencyPropertyOptions.Metadata
      | DependencyPropertyOptions.ReadOnly,
      new Attribute[] {
        new DesignerSerializationVisibilityAttribute(
          DesignerSerializationVisibility.Content) }
    )
  );

public static readonly DependencyProperty
  TransitionsProperty = DependencyProperty.Register(
    "Transitions",
    typeof(List<Transition>),
    typeof(StateMachine),
    new PropertyMetadata(DependencyPropertyOptions.Metadata
      | DependencyPropertyOptions.ReadOnly,
      new Attribute[] {
        new DesignerSerializationVisibilityAttribute(
          DesignerSerializationVisibility.Content) }
    )
  );

[DesignerSerializationVisibility(
  DesignerSerializationVisibility.Content)]
public List<string> States
{
  get { return GetValue(StatesProperty) as List<string>; }
}

[DesignerSerializationVisibility(
  DesignerSerializationVisibility.Content)]
public List<Transition> Transitions
{
  get { return GetValue(TransitionsProperty)
    as List<Transition>; }
```

```
  }

  private string currentState;
  private Transition currentTransition;
  private List<string> history;

  protected override void Initialize(
    IServiceProvider provider)
  {
    this.currentState = "NONE";
    this.currentTransition = null;
    this.history = new List<string>();

    WorkflowQueuingService qService =
      provider.GetService(typeof(WorkflowQueuingService))
        as WorkflowQueuingService;
    if (!qService.Exists(this.Name))
      qService.CreateWorkflowQueue(this.Name, false);

    base.Initialize(provider);
  }

  protected override void Uninitialize(
    IServiceProvider provider)
  {
    this.currentState = "NONE";
    this.currentTransition = null;
    this.history = null;

    WorkflowQueuingService qService =
      provider.GetService(typeof(WorkflowQueuingService))
        as WorkflowQueuingService;
    if (qService.Exists(this.Name))
      qService.DeleteWorkflowQueue(this.Name);

    base.Uninitialize(provider);
  }

  protected override ActivityExecutionStatus Execute(
    ActivityExecutionContext context)
  {
    if (EnabledActivities.Count == 0)
      return ActivityExecutionStatus.Closed;

    this.currentState = "START";
    history.Add(currentState);

    WorkflowQueuingService qService =
```

```
      context.GetService<WorkflowQueuingService>();
   WorkflowQueue queue = qService.GetWorkflowQueue(this.Name);
   queue.QueueItemAvailable += this.ResumeAt;

   return ActivityExecutionStatus.Executing;
}

void ResumeAt(object sender, QueueEventArgs e)
{
   ActivityExecutionContext context =
      sender as ActivityExecutionContext;
   WorkflowQueuingService qService =
      context.GetService<WorkflowQueuingService>();
   WorkflowQueue queue = qService.GetWorkflowQueue(this.Name);

   object obj = queue.Dequeue();
   StateMachineAction action = obj as StateMachineAction;

   if (action != null)
   {
      if (currentTransition != null)
      {
         // state transition in progress
         Console.WriteLine("action rejected");
         return;
      }

      Transition proposed = null;
      foreach (Transition t in this.Transitions)
      {
         // Find the right transition
         if (t.ActivityName.Equals(action.ActivityName)
            && t.From.Equals(this.currentState))
         {
            proposed = t;
            break;
         }
      }

      if (proposed == null)
      {
         Console.WriteLine("action not valid: " + action.ActivityName);
         return;
      }

      foreach (Activity child in EnabledActivities)
      {
         if (child.Name.Equals(proposed.ActivityName))
```

```
                {
                  currentTransition = proposed;
                  Run(context, child, proposed.InputProp, action.Input);
                  return;
                }
              }
            }
          }
          else // query
          {
            StateMachineQuery query = obj as StateMachineQuery;
            if (query != null)
            {
              Console.WriteLine("Current State: " + this.currentState);
              Console.WriteLine("Current Transition: " + ((currentTransition == null)
  ? "-none-" : (currentTransition.ActivityName + "<" + currentTransition.From + ","
  + currentTransition.To + ">")));
              Console.Write("History: ");
              foreach (string s in this.history)
                Console.Write(s + (s.Equals("END") ? "" : "->"));
              Console.Write("\n");
              if (currentTransition == null)
              {
                Console.WriteLine("Possible Transitions:");
                foreach (Transition t in this.Transitions)
                {
                  if (t.From.Equals(this.currentState))
                    Console.WriteLine(" " + t.ActivityName + "<" + t.From + "," + t.To
  + ">" + " Input=" + t.InputProp);
                }
              }
            }

            else
            {
              Console.WriteLine("unrecognized input: " + obj.ToString());
            }
          }
        }

        private void Run(ActivityExecutionContext context,
          Activity child, string propName, object propValue)
        {
          ActivityExecutionContextManager manager =
            context.ExecutionContextManager;
          ActivityExecutionContext c =
            manager.CreateExecutionContext(child);

          // Use reflection to set the input property value
```

```
    object o = c.Activity;
    o.GetType().GetProperty(propName).GetSetMethod().
      Invoke(o, new object[] { propValue });

    c.Activity.Closed += ContinueAt;
    c.ExecuteActivity(c.Activity);
  }

  void ContinueAt(object sender,
    ActivityExecutionStatusChangedEventArgs e)
  {
    e.Activity.Closed -= this.ContinueAt;
    ActivityExecutionContext context =
      sender as ActivityExecutionContext;

    ActivityExecutionContextManager manager =
      context.ExecutionContextManager;
    ActivityExecutionContext c =
      manager.GetExecutionContext(e.Activity);
    manager.CompleteExecutionContext(c, false);

    currentState = this.currentTransition.To;
    history.Add(currentState);
    currentTransition = null;

    if (currentState.Equals("END"))
      context.CloseActivity();
  }

  // Cancellation logic
  ...
  }
}
```

In a state machine there are a few different places where child activities can be used: A specific activity may need to be executed whenever a particular state is entered; a specific activity may need to be executed whenever a particular state is exited; a specific activity may need to be executed whenever a particular transition is traversed. In the StateMachine activity shown in Listing B.4, we only associate activities with transitions, and not with entry into or exit from states, but this could easily be added.

The StateMachine activity creates a WF program queue, on which it receives inputs of two kinds. A StateMachineAction is used to effect a transition from one state to another; data is provided to the activity associated with a transition using a simple reflection-based design in which one property of the activity is designated as its input. A `StateMachineQuery` is used to obtain information about the current state of the state machine, the history of states traversed, and the possible next steps (allowed inputs).

Here is an example `StateMachine` program:

```
<StateMachine x:Name="m1" States="a, b, c, d" xmlns="http://EssentialWF/Activities
xmlns:x="http://schemas.microsoft.com/winfx/2006/xaml">
  <StateMachine.Transitions>
    <Transition From="START" To="a" InputProp="Text" ActivityName="w1" />
    <Transition From="START" To="c" InputProp="Text" ActivityName="w2" />
    <Transition From="a" To="a" InputProp="Text" ActivityName="w3" />
    <Transition From="a" To="b" InputProp="Text" ActivityName="w4" />
    <Transition From="b" To="c" InputProp="Text" ActivityName="w5" />
    <Transition From="c" To="b" InputProp="Text" ActivityName="w6" />
    <Transition From="c" To="d" InputProp="Text" ActivityName="w7" />
    <Transition From="d" To="START" InputProp="Text" ActivityName="w8" />
    <Transition From="d" To="END" InputProp="Text" ActivityName="w9" />
  </StateMachine.Transitions>
  <WriteLine Text="1" x:Name="w1" />
  <WriteLine Text="2" x:Name="w2" />
  <WriteLine Text="3" x:Name="w3" />
  <WriteLine Text="4" x:Name="w4" />
  <WriteLine Text="5" x:Name="w5" />
  <WriteLine Text="6" x:Name="w6" />
  <WriteLine Text="7" x:Name="w7" />
  <WriteLine Text="8" x:Name="w8" />
  <WriteLine Text="9" x:Name="w9" />
</StateMachine>
```

The preceding program can be visualized as shown in Figure B.3.

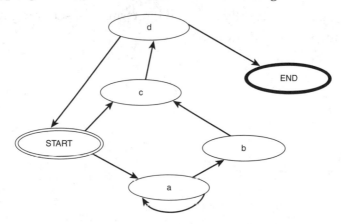

Figure B.3   A State Machine-based WF program

The output of the program will depend upon the series of `StateMachineAction` objects that are enqueued into the state machine's WF program queue. For example, we could traverse the states START, c, d, END. We could also traverse the states START, a, a, b, c, d, END. There are an unbounded number of outcomes for this state machine since there are loops in the possible execution paths.

In order to remain true to the state machine concept, in which the program is always in one state, the child activities of `StateMachine` should not create bookmarks. In this way, when input arrives, the `StateMachine` selects the appropriate transition (if any) and executes the child activity associated with that transition. The `StateMachine` can be said to traverse a transition (more or less) immediately if a *single* stimulus is always enough to move the state machine from one state to another. This, however, is not enforced in the preceding state machine implementation; it is possible to create transitions that do create bookmarks. For this reason, whenever a transition is in progress, any inputs of type `StateMachineAction` that are sent to the state machine are rejected.

For many if not most solutions, it makes sense to design programs not as explicit state machines but as structured programs that exploit (in their descriptions) the interleaving and control flow patterns that occur in the real-world process being modeled. Enumeration of all possible states is likely to be cumbersome. The `StateMachine` activity forces the WF program author to break down the logic of the program's control flow into uninterruptible segments. Generally speaking, this design approach does not scale well due to the explosion in the state space of even moderately sized programs, but can be useful in cases where the real-world process that is being modeled is naturally described in terms of a set of logical states. Consider the following structured program:

```
<Interleave>
  <Sequence>
    <Read x:Name="r1" />
    <Read x:Name="r2" />
  </Sequence>
  <Sequence>
    <Read x:Name="r3" />
    <Read x:Name="r4" />
  </Sequence>
  <Sequence>
    <Read x:Name="r5" />
    <Read x:Name="r6" />
```

```
    <Read x:Name="r7" />
    <Read x:Name="r8" />
  </Sequence>
</Interleave>
```

When an instance of the program above begins executing, it quickly becomes idle waiting for input directed at either r1, r3, or r5. This is one state (let's call it "135") for the program. If r3 completes its execution, the program moves to another state in which it can receive input for either r1, r4, or r5. This is state "145". But it also could have moved to state "235" or "136" if the bookmark for either r1 or r5 had been resumed instead. There are many possible paths of execution for this program (and a much larger number of paths for more complex programs that use interleaving), with a correspondingly large number of states needed to explicitly describe all possible paths.

The structured style of programming allows this logic to be expressed compactly. Of course, it is also possible to specify the logic of the preceding program using our Graph activity (or, for that matter, a PrioritizedInterleave). It is up to you to decide what style of programming suits the solution you are building, and whether custom composite activities (beyond even the ones shown in this appendix) are warranted.

Controller

Our final control flow pattern illustrates a situation in which external stimulus is the sole determinant of when and how often a child activity is executed. The Controller activity shown in Listing B.5 creates a WF program queue and listens for commands that tell it what child activities to execute. The Controller is completely passive and relies entirely on external code to drive the execution of its child activities.

Listing B.5 Controller Activity

```
using System;
using System.Workflow.ComponentModel;
using System.Workflow.Runtime;

namespace EssentialWF.Activities
{
  public class Controller : CompositeActivity
  {
    protected override void Initialize(
```

```
    IServiceProvider provider)
{
  WorkflowQueuingService qService = provider.GetService(
    typeof(WorkflowQueuingService))
      as WorkflowQueuingService;
  WorkflowQueue queue = qService.CreateWorkflowQueue(
    this.Name, false);
}

protected override void Uninitialize(
  IServiceProvider provider)
{
  WorkflowQueuingService qService = provider.GetService(
    typeof(WorkflowQueuingService))
      as WorkflowQueuingService;
  qService.DeleteWorkflowQueue(this.Name);
}

protected override ActivityExecutionStatus Execute(
  ActivityExecutionContext context)
{
  WorkflowQueuingService qService = context.GetService(
    typeof(WorkflowQueuingService))
      as WorkflowQueuingService;
  WorkflowQueue queue = qService.GetWorkflowQueue(this.Name);
  queue.QueueItemAvailable += this.ResumeAt;
  return ActivityExecutionStatus.Executing;
}

void ResumeAt(object sender, QueueEventArgs e)
{
  ActivityExecutionContext context =
    sender as ActivityExecutionContext;
  WorkflowQueuingService qService = context.GetService(
    typeof(WorkflowQueuingService))
      as WorkflowQueuingService;
  WorkflowQueue queue = qService.GetWorkflowQueue(this.Name);

  string s = (string)queue.Dequeue();

  if (s != null)
  {
    if (s.StartsWith("execute"))
    {
      // command will be something like 'execute w1'
      string[] tokens = s.Split(new char[] { ' ' });
      string name = tokens[1];
      Activity child = GetChildActivity(name);
```

```
      if (child != null)
      {
        ActivityExecutionContextManager manager =
          context.ExecutionContextManager;
        ActivityExecutionContext c =
          manager.CreateExecutionContext(child);
        c.Activity.Closed += this.ContinueAt;
        c.ExecuteActivity(c.Activity);
      }
    }
  }
}

void ContinueAt(object sender,
  ActivityExecutionStatusChangedEventArgs e)
{
  ActivityExecutionContext context =
    sender as ActivityExecutionContext;
  ActivityExecutionContextManager manager =
    context.ExecutionContextManager;
  ActivityExecutionContext c =
    manager.GetExecutionContext(e.Activity);
  manager.CompleteExecutionContext(c, false);
}

private Activity GetChildActivity(string name)
{
  foreach (Activity child in EnabledActivities)
  {
    if (child.Name.Equals(name))
      return child;
  }

  return null;
}

// Cancellation logic
...
  }
}
```

The `Controller` activity receives commands (as strings) from its WF program queue. When it receives a command, such as "`execute w1`", it will find the specified child activity ("`w1`" in this example) and schedule it for execution. It would be simple to extend this logic so that the `Controller` can also handle commands for canceling child activities and reporting its own completion.

For example, consider the following program:

```
<Controller x:Name="controller1"
xmlns="http://EssentialWF/Activities
xmlns:x="http://schemas.microsoft.com/winfx/2006/xaml">
  <WriteLine Text="1" x:Name="w1" />
  <WriteLine Text="2" x:Name="w2" />
  <WriteLine Text="3" x:Name="w3" />
</Controller>
```

The child activities can be executed in any order, according to the commands that are sent to the Controller via its WF program queue:

```
WorkflowInstance instance = runtime.CreateWorkflow(...);
string queueName = instance.GetWorkflowDefinition().Name;

...

instance.EnqueueItem(queueName, "execute w1", null, null);
instance.EnqueueItem(queueName, "execute w3", null, null);
instance.EnqueueItem(queueName, "execute w3", null, null);
instance.EnqueueItem(queueName, "execute w2", null, null);
```

The preceding external code will drive the WF program to produce the following output:

```
1
3
3
2
```

In this example, we are only using WriteLine activities, but the Controller supports child activities of any type. Child activities can execute in an interleaved manner (for example, if a second "execute" command arrives before the first child activity that is executed completes). In fact, the same child activity can be executed simultaneously (in a manner similar to that of InterleavedForEach).

The Controller activity also supports dynamic modifications, so it is easy to add child activities to a Controller within a running WF program instance. This makes it possible to write a WF program that is just an empty Controller activity. Child activities can be dynamically added to the Controller, and then scheduled for execution one or more times via the "execute" command, allowing the user to effectively write the program as it is running.

Where Are We?

The composite activities we developed in this appendix leverage the concepts explained in the main text of the book. Composite activities can be simple—such as a plain `Sequence`—but can also embody powerful control flow patterns that can be easily used in WF programs. As the developer of a WF program, you have many different ways of modeling a particular pattern, and you can decide what suits your solution best.

The composite activities we developed here are just the tip of the iceberg. There are as many control flow patterns as there are programs. You are not constrained by a fixed number of modeling constructs in WF, so you can craft custom composite activities that closely mirror control flow patterns of the real world.

Index

THIS BOOK IS SAFARI ENABLED

INCLUDES FREE 45-DAY ACCESS TO THE ONLINE EDITION

The Safari® Enabled icon on the cover of your favorite technology book means the book is available through Safari Bookshelf. When you buy this book, you get free access to the online edition for 45 days.

Safari Bookshelf is an electronic reference library that lets you easily search thousands of technical books, find code samples, download chapters, and access technical information whenever and wherever you need it.

TO GAIN 45-DAY SAFARI ENABLED ACCESS TO THIS BOOK:

- Go to **http://www.awprofessional.com/safarienabled**

- Complete the brief registration form

- Enter the coupon code found in the front of this book on the "Copyright" page

If you have difficulty registering on Safari Bookshelf or accessing the online edition, please e-mail customer-service@safaribooksonline.com.

Addison
Wesley

informIT

YOUR GUIDE TO IT REFERENCE

Articles

Keep your edge with thousands of free articles, in-depth features, interviews, and IT reference recommendations – all written by experts you know and trust.

Online Books

Answers in an instant from **InformIT Online Book's** 600+ fully searchable on line books. For a limited time, you can get your first 14 days **free**.

POWERED BY
Safari
TECH BOOKS ONLINE

Catalog

Review online sample chapters, author biographies and customer rankings and choose exactly the right book from a selection of over 5,000 titles.